Praise for *XQuery*

XQuery

XQuery

The XML Query Language

Michael Brundage

♦♦Addison-Wesley

Boston • San Francisco • New York • Toronto • Montreal
London • Munich • Paris • Madrid
Capetown • Sydney • Tokyo • Singapore • Mexico City

XQuery: The XML Query Language is an independent publication and is not affiliated with, nor has it been authorized, sponsored, or otherwise approved by Microsoft Corporation.

Many of the designations used by manufacturers and sellers to distinguish their products are claimed as trademarks. Where those designations appear in this book, and Addison-Wesley was aware of a trademark claim, the designations have been printed with initial capital letters or in all capitals.

The author and publisher have taken care in the preparation of this book, but make no expressed or implied warranty of any kind and assume no responsibility for errors or omissions. No liability is assumed for incidental or consequential damages in connection with or arising out of the use of the information or programs contained herein.

The publisher offers discounts on this book when ordered in quantity for bulk purchases and special sales. For more information, please contact:

U.S. Corporate and Government Sales
(800) 382-3419
corpsales@pearsontechgroup.com

For sales outside of the U.S., please contact:

International Sales
(317) 581-3793
international@pearsontechgroup.com

Visit Addison-Wesley on the Web: www.awprofessional.com

Library of Congress Cataloging-in-Publication Data
Brundage, Michael.
   The XML query language / Michael Brundage.
      p. cm.
   ISBN 0-321-16581-0 (alk. paper)
   1. Query languages (computer science) I. Title.

   QA76.7.B765 2004
   005.13'3—-dc22   2003022899

Copyright © 2004 by Pearson Education, Inc.

ISBN: 0-321-16581-0
Text printed on recycled paper
1 2 3 4 5 6 7 8 9 10—CRS—0807060504
First printing, January 2004

To my wife, Yvonne, and our son, Benjamin.

Contents

Part II Core Language Features

Part III Application

List of Figures

Foreword

It is with great pleasure that I present Michael Brundage's book about XQuery.

More than twenty years ago, several things happened in the still young field of computer science, which are all somehow related to the book you now keep in your hands: The relational model revolutionized the management of data and introduced the notion of declaratively querying data; the nested array theory influenced database researchers and APL language designers to develop declarative algebras to operate on hierarchical data such as nested relations; the notion of document markup was standardized as SGML and found wide deployment in the document management community; and computer language researchers developed the notion of functional languages and the theory of type systems.

Fast-forward to 1996: The database research community moved from object-model algebras that had their origin in the nested relational algebras to the field of semi-structure data management, which requires a data model that provides nesting of more complex and less regular structures. In the document management community, a couple of people, driven by the success of the SGML-based markup language HTML and the World-wide Web as well as by the complexity of SGML set out to produce an SGML-lite under the umbrella of the World-wide Web Consortium (W3C) that in 1997 came to be known as XML.

Luckily, the database researchers realized that XML provides the self-describing, hierarchical structure that is well-suited for managing semi-structure data, and some people in the document and database communities realized that the additional, more document-centric features of XML such as document order and mixed content actually seem to get us much closer to one of the holy grails of database and document management: a unifying model to describe structured, semi-structured data and document markup.

In 1998, the W3C organized a workshop to investigate whether there was a need for a query language on XML data. The response was overwhelmingly positive, and in late 1999 the XML Query working group was formed. Four years later, the working group is now finalizing the first version of the query language known as XQuery that combines important aspects of the last twenty-plus years of research in languages and data management such as declarativity, composability, functional semantics, and formal type systems.

When I first encountered XML in 1997, while working at Stanford University as a research associate on semi-structured data management and information integration, it quickly became clear to me that XML will play an important role in modeling markup and semi-structured data and serve as a lingua franca for information exchange. When the XQuery working group started, I joined the group as the primary representative for Microsoft Corporation and was lucky enough to be able to enlist Michael Brundage to build one of the first XQuery prototypes that helped us to understand and influence the design of the language.

This is not the only reason why Michael is highly qualified to write about XQuery. He is in the unique position of being an outsider with insider access and knowledge. This experience gives him a perspective on XQuery that should be very helpful for both the novice XQuery user, who wants to get to know the language, and the advanced XQuery user, who needs a comprehensive reference. He has written a book that is highly informative, logically organized, and goes beyond the pure reference characteristics of many programming and query language reference books. For instance, Michael identifies language properties and idioms that may surprise even advanced users of XQuery, and points out both the positive and negative aspects of a language which must satisfy a vast array of use cases, implementation environments, and interests.

With the publication of the W3C insider book *XQuery from the Experts: A Guide to the W3C XML Query Language*, Addison-Wesley is bringing you the ultimate collection of XQuery books that should be able to satisfy even the most inquisitive mind about XQuery.

Enjoy the book and keep it handy when you are in need of a dose of XQuery!

Michael Rys
Redmond, Washington
November 2003

Michael Rys is a program manager in Microsoft's SQL Server team responsible for XML technologies. He is representing Microsoft in the ANSI SQL and SQL/XML standardization efforts and in the XQuery working group and publishes regularly on all aspects of XML. His interests include declarative, set-oriented languages, data and document management and information integration.

Preface

XQuery is a deep and powerful new language, yet it's easy to pick up and start using productively right away. Accordingly, this book is designed as both an introduction for new XQuery users and a reference for experienced ones.

XQuery is the most complex XML standard to date, comprising well over a thousand pages of very dense and abstract implementation details. If you are creating an XQuery implementation yourself, you need to read them. Everyone else should read this book instead; it will save you a lot of time and confusion. This is the book I wanted when I first got started with XQuery, and am thrilled to have now.

I had the good fortune to become involved with the XQuery standard more than two years ago, before it even had the name. I implemented the first Microsoft XQuery prototype available at MSDN (but not later ones), prototypes of XQuery over SQL Server, and my own XQuery implementation for this book. I've also given several dozen presentations on XQuery, and wrote a chapter about it for a previous book. Currently, I'm responsible for the cross-language XML query representation and optimizer at Microsoft.

However, I've been primarily a user of XQuery rather than an implementer of it. All of this adds up to a unique perspective, which I've brought to bear in this book. I hope my experience with XQuery will benefit you greatly, whether you're using XQuery for the first time or the thousandth.

Who Should Read This Book?

This is a practical book, intended for every developer using XQuery regardless of your programming environment, whether you're a beginner or expert, or whether you're using XML for documents, Web services, databases, or other purposes.

You must be familiar already with the basics of XML 1.0. You need to understand concepts such as namespaces and qualified names, the different XML node kinds (element, attribute, and so on), and the difference between tags and elements. This book doesn't review XML or APIs for using it (like SAX and DOM).

However, you don't need to know XML Schema, XPath, XSLT, SQL, or any of the other technologies that are mentioned throughout this book. You can safely skip sections that compare XQuery to technologies you don't already know.

Organization

This book is organized into four major sections.

Part I introduces XQuery. Chapter 1 briefly touches on the reasons to use XQuery and then gives an overview of the entire language, pointing to later chapters for additional details. Chapters 2 to 4 cover the background material required throughout the rest of the book, starting with the XQuery Data Model and type system. You may want to skim over parts of these chapters and refer back to them later.

Part II drills into the details of XQuery expressions, from arithmetic to XML construction and everything in between.

Part III goes beyond the standards, exploring XQuery expressions whose behavior may surprise you and how to use XQuery to accomplish certain common tasks. Chapter 14 looks at features that might appear in future versions of XQuery.

Finally, Part IV is a comprehensive reference to the entire XQuery language, including appendices on the type system (Appendix A), core expressions (Appendix B), built-in functions (Appendix C), regular expressions (Appendix D), and grammar (Appendix E). These appendices are heavily cross-referenced among one another and the other chapters in the book for your convenience.

Resources

This book isn't tied to any particular implementation of XQuery, and I endeavored to test the examples on several different ones. At http://www.w3.org/XML/Query, the public Web site of the W3C XML Query Working Group, you'll find a list of many freely and commercially available XQuery implementations.

At this book's Web site, http://www.qbrundage.com/xquery, you will find updates and errata to the book as they become available. Additional resources can be found in the Bibliography at the end of this book.

I also encourage you to e-mail your questions and comments to me directly at xquery@comcast.net.

Although I am employed by Microsoft, this book is completely unrelated to Microsoft and its products. Except where noted previously, I played no role in any of Microsoft's XQuery implementations. Or, as the lawyers put it, this book is an independent publication and is not affiliated with, nor has it been authorized, sponsored, or otherwise approved by Microsoft Corporation.

Acknowledgments

I owe thanks for this book to a great many people, first and foremost the editors and staff at Addison-Wesley. I always wondered why authors gush about their help, and now I know. To Mary O'Brien, I offer my deepest gratitude, both for asking me at the JavaOne '02 conference to write this book, and also for all her support, encouragement, and advice during its development. Thanks also to Amy Fleischer, Rebecca Greenberg, Chanda Leary-Coutu, Heather Mullane, and Brenda Mulligan for the very hard work they put into making this book a success.

Many technical reviewers, co-workers, friends, and family provided useful feedback on various early drafts. You all helped make this book better than it would have been otherwise! Thanks to Brandon Berg, Mike J. Brown, Michael Champion, Daniel Dedu-Constantin, Damien Fisher, Ken Henderson, Tejal Joshi, Howard Katz, Ashok Malhotra, Eamon O'Tuathail, Dare Obasanjo, Carl Perry, Yvonne Quirmbach-Brundage, Lisa Rein, Ken Sall, and Naohiko Uramoto.

Thanks also to the entire W3C Query Working Group, who answered many questions and accepted at least some of my suggestions. Of these, thanks go especially to Michael Rys (who first introduced me to XQuery!), Don Chamberlain, Ashok Malhotra, and Michael Kay.

Finally, thanks to my wife, Yvonne, for all her patience, encouragement, love, and friendship during this book's development. I couldn't have done it without you!

PART I

Foundations

CHAPTER 1

A Tour of XQuery

1.1 Introduction

XQuery 1.0 is a concise but flexible query language for XML. XQuery is the product of many years of work by individuals and companies from around the world. Actively developed by the World Wide Web Consortium (W3C) XML Query and XSL Working Groups from the first W3C workshop on Query Languages in 1998 through today, XQuery contains ideas that are both decades old and brand-new.

XQuery is mainly intended for use with XML data, but is also finding uses as a language for data integration, even with data sources that may not be XML but can be viewed through an XML lens. Time will tell how successful XQuery will become, but the stage is set for it to become for XML what Structured Query Language (SQL) has become for relational data.

At the time of this writing, XQuery 1.0 is still in the draft stage, at Last Call. Consequently, some aspects of the language will change between now and the final Recommendation (when it becomes a standard). As much as possible, anticipated changes are noted throughout this book, and also at the book's Web site at `http://www.qbrundage.com/xquery`.

Also, as can be expected with a new language still under development, some parts of XQuery will strike you as a little rough or overly complex. In such cases (such as the data model and type system described in the next chapter), the design rationale is explained and numerous examples are provided to ease the learning process.

1.2 Getting Started

The many examples in this book are based on the current draft specifications. To run these examples, you need an XQuery implementation; several are listed on this book's Web site.

The XQuery standard gives implementations discretion in how they implement many of its features. Consequently, no two XQuery implementations are exactly the same. As much as possible, I have noted these potential differences throughout the book. However, I do not explain how to use any particular XQuery implementation in this book—please consult the implementation's documentation for instructions and differences between it and the official standard.

1.3 Notational Conventions

A few words about the notation used in this book: Important words and phrases are *italicized* when first introduced. Examples are always set off from the main text using a `fixed width font`, and sometimes appear on separate lines like Listing 1.1.

Listing 1.1 This is a sample listing

```
this is the example
```

In some cases, it helps to see not only the example but also what the expected result of executing it should be. A => symbol, as shown in Listing 1.2, separates examples from their results.

Listing 1.2 This is a sample listing with its evaluated result

```
example expression
=>
its result.

another example => another result
```

XML and XQuery are intricately tied to the Unicode character set (described in Chapter 8). To avoid confusion when describing some Unicode characters, I use the notation U+NNNN where NNNN is the corresponding hexadecimal number for that character (usually NNNN is a four-digit number). For example, U+003F is the question mark (?).

1.4 Why XQuery?

At some point, you should stop to wonder: Why use XQuery? Why not use some other XML query language, like XPath or XSLT? For that matter, why use a query language at all? Why not work with the XML data structures directly using an existing programming language and some XML API? These are important questions, so let's address them before diving into the technical features of the XQuery language.

1.4.1 Query Languages Versus Programming Languages

First, why use a new language that is specific to a particular domain (like querying XML) instead of an existing, general-purpose programming language? There are two main reasons: ease-of-use and performance.

When it comes to ease-of-use, existing programming languages have some obvious advantages: They usually offer expressive power, allowing complex ideas to be expressed in a few lines of code. They also leverage your existing knowledge, so you can be productive right away.

In contrast, domain-specific languages let you work with domain concepts (like XML) directly. For example, most general-purpose programming languages treat XML as any other API, instead of as a first-class part of the language. Instead of providing operators for constructing and navigating XML directly, you have to access it through an API layer. Just as text manipulation is easier in Perl than in, say, Fortran, so a single line of an XML query language like XSLT or XQuery can accomplish the equivalent of hundreds of lines of C, C#, Java, or some other general-purpose language.

As far as performance goes, there are three reasons that domain languages usually outperform general-purpose languages. One is that domain languages are usually optimized for tasks common to that domain. General-purpose programming languages have to perform well on a wide range of tasks, while XML query languages only have to perform well on a narrow set of common XML tasks. This focus may limit their applicability, but often yields superior performance.

Another is that the general-purpose language will use an API of some sort for working with that domain. The abstraction layer provided by that API almost always hides the internal data structures from software using the API. Information hiding is a great benefit to program design, but can introduce overhead and by definition prevents you from manipulating the underlying data directly. In contrast, a query language *is* the abstraction. When the query is executed, it has full access to all aspects of its own internal data structures.

However, the main reason XML query languages can outperform general-purpose programming languages is that they are less constrained. A programming language usually has to do exactly what you tell it to do, in the order you specified. Without extensive analysis, temporary intermediate results must be computed exactly as described. For example, using a C++ matrix library to multiply two matrices and then extract the value of a single entry usually computes the entire matrix product, even though only a single value was required.

In a query language, every temporary intermediate result is unimportant. As long as the query produces the correct, final "answer," how it computes that answer is irrelevant. Maybe it looks it up in a cache (because this query has been answered recently) or maybe it uses a new algorithm discovered yesterday. The program you write using the query language is unaffected; it automatically benefits from whatever new advances that take place in the underlying implementation.

This difference is often summarized by saying that query languages are *declarative* (stating what you want), while programming languages are *descriptive* (stating how you want it done). The difference is subtle, but significant.

Of course, these reasons are all generalizations, and therefore break down at a certain point. Sometimes general-purpose programming languages find ways to express the same features offered by domain languages, without complicating the language too much and without significant loss in performance. Sometimes domain languages are very poorly implemented, resulting in performance far worse than manually traversing the structures yourself.

However, the point is clear: Query languages enjoy certain advantages over traditional, general-purpose programming languages. These advantages are illustrated in the success of SQL for accessing relational data, and the successes of many other domain-specific "little languages," from regular expressions to shell scripts to graphics libraries.

1.4.2 XQuery Versus XPath, XSLT, and SQL

Returning to the original question, you may ask: Why XQuery instead of an existing query language like XPath or XSLT (or SQL)? (If you're not familiar with these languages, feel free to skip ahead to the next section.)

This question frames the choice incorrectly. XPath 1.0, XSLT 1.0, and SQL are great query languages, and XQuery does not replace them for every task. Each of these languages is useful in different situations.

XQuery is another tool in the XML developer's workshop, not the only tool. So the question becomes: *When* use XQuery instead of XPath or XSLT or SQL?

XPath 1.0 introduced a convenient syntax for addressing parts of an XML document. If you need to select a node out of an existing XML document or database, XPath is the perfect choice, and XQuery doesn't change that.

However, XPath 1.0 wasn't designed for any other purpose. XPath can't create new XML, it can't select only part of an XML node (say, just the tag omitting attributes and content), and—because of its conciseness—it can be hard to read and understand. XPath 1.0 also can't introduce variables or namespace bindings—although it does use them—and it has a very simple type system, essentially just `string`, `boolean`, `double`, and `nodeset` (a sequence of nodes in document order). If you need to work with date values, calculate the maximum of a set of numbers, or sort a list of strings, then XPath just can't do it.

XSLT 1.0 (which was developed at the same time as XPath) takes XML querying a step further, including XPath 1.0 as a subset to address parts of an XML document and then adding many other features. XSLT is fantastic for recursively processing an XML document or translating XML into HTML and text. XSLT can create new XML or (copy) part of existing nodes, and it can introduce variables and namespaces.

Some people say that XSLT 1.0 can't be optimized and isn't strongly-typed. However, both of these assertions are false: Every expression in XSLT has a compile-time type, and XSLT can certainly be optimized. XSLT 1.0 does have a small type system, and many implementations naively execute XSLT as written without any optimizations, so it's easy to see how these misconceptions came to exist.

However, XSLT 1.0 still has a few drawbacks, some of which could be easily corrected (and will be in the future XSLT 2.0 standard), and others that cannot be addressed without effectively creating a language like XQuery.

XSLT does not work with sequences of values (only sequences of nodes), but user-defined functions, joins, and other common operations can be awkward and difficult to write. A sorted outer join, grouping the result into pairs of adjacent nodes, can be expressed using XSLT, but most users won't ever figure out how to do it.

XML Schema 1.0 didn't exist when XSLT 1.0 was invented, so XSLT uses a different type system and has no operators for validation or other schema interactions.

XSLT 1.0 also uses an XML syntax, which is both a strength and a weakness. This is a strength because it goes "meta"—XSLT can process itself. However, XML is also very verbose compared to plain text, and authoring an XML document is overkill for simple processing tasks.

Finally, XSLT 1.0 encourages and often requires users to solve problems in unnatural ways. XSLT is inherently recursive, but most programmers today think procedurally; we think of calling functions directly ourselves, not having functions called for us in an event-driven fashion whenever a match occurs. Many people write large XSLT queries using only a single `<xsl:template>` rule, apparently unaware that XSLT's recursive matching capabilities would cut their query size in half and make it much easier to maintain.

XQuery takes a different approach from XSLT 1.0, with more functionality but similar results. XQuery is especially great at expressing joins and sorts. XQuery can manipulate sequences of values and nodes in arbitrary order, not just document order. XQuery takes a procedural approach to query processing, putting users in the driver's seat and making it easy to write user-defined functions, including recursive ones, but more difficult to perform pattern matching. Support for XML Schema 1.0 is built into XQuery, and XQuery was designed with optimization in mind.

XQuery also supports a really important feature that was purposely disabled in XSLT 1.0, something commonly known as *composition*. Composition allows users to construct temporary XML results in the middle of a query, and then navigate into that. This is such an important feature that many vendors added extension functions, such as `nodeset()` to XSLT 1.0, to support it anyway; XQuery makes it a first-class operation.

XSLT is still stronger than XQuery at certain tasks. XQuery is focused on generating XML instead of HTML and text, although it is capable of generating them. Compared to XSLT, XQuery's type system is much larger and more complex. And of course, XQuery is new, so XQuery implementations are less mature than XSLT ones.

SQL is a relational query language for databases, and several products and standards efforts extend it to handle XML. Although not designed to be an XML query language, SQL increasingly is finding use as one.

I mention SQL because XQuery has similarities to it in style and syntax, and both can be used to query databases. The biggest difference between

XQuery and SQL is that SQL focuses on unordered sets of "flat" rows, while XQuery focuses on ordered sequences of values and hierarchical nodes.

1.5 Documents and Databases

You may also question whether XQuery is right for your application. Whether you're working with documents or databases, you may wonder whether XQuery is designed primarily for the other.

Some years ago, there were documents, databases, and programs. Documents were units of semi-structured data (mostly unstructured text with some structural "markup" signifying logical parts of the document) usually stored as standalone files. Databases were self-contained storage systems with highly structured data organized into rigid tables with typed columns. Programs were source code stored in flat text files and parsed on demand to extract structure and meaning.

Each of these had its own community happily evolving independently of the others, with different tools and terminologies. The document community had word processors, document storage systems, scripting languages, and search engines; the database community had query builders, B-trees, indices, query languages, and query processors; the programming community had editors, source control systems, programming languages, and compilers.

And then XML happened.

In many ways, XML has brought these communities together. The increased contact has led many to realize that the challenges in their field are identical in essence to challenges in the other fields. However, each community has independently discovered very different ways of solving the same problem. For example, few database systems use just-in-time compilation and code generation techniques that are today common in compiler implementations; conversely, few programming languages use indices and cost-based optimizers that are common in databases.

Perhaps the most electrifying effects of XML have occurred between the database and document communities. The difficulties involved with storing and querying semi-structured documents have gained new prominence among database vendors; at the same time, the document community increasingly treats documents as "views" over structured data that can be queried and transformed into other representations.

XQuery was designed by people from all three communities to solve common document, database, and programming tasks. In places, XQuery has made compromises to one community or the other; for example, XQuery uses ordered sequences, regular expressions, recursion, and untyped data (document-centric features that are difficult for databases), but also supports joins and transformations, strongly-typed data, and allows expression evaluations to be reordered or skipped entirely through optimization (database-centric features that are difficult for document processors).

XQuery is a query language for both XML documents and databases. It makes no distinction between the two; to XQuery, it's all XML.

1.6 Typed and Untyped Data

XQuery can handle both ordinary XML and XML associated with an XML schema. These are colloquially known as *untyped* XML and *typed* XML, respectively.

If all your XML data is untyped, you may think that you don't need to understand XML Schema, and you're partially correct. However, you do need to understand the XQuery type system, which plays a major role.

XQuery uses XML Schema 1.0 as the basis for its type system. Consequently, these two standards share some terminology and definitions. XQuery also provides some operators such as `import schema` and `validate` to support working with XML schemas.

1.6.1 XML Schema Redux

If you are already familiar with XML Schema 1.0, then you have a head start on some of the more challenging aspects of XQuery, such as its type system.

Otherwise, this book will only teach you a subset required to use XQuery effectively. All you really need to know about XML Schema 1.0 for the purposes of XQuery is that it is an XML standard aimed at describing how to *validate* XML according to certain rules. For example, an attribute value might be required to be an integer, or an element might be required to contain certain subelements in a particular order. The set of validation rules that apply to a particular element or attribute constitute its *schema type*. The schema type is often given a qualified name so it can be referred to elsewhere.

When an XML document satisfies all of the schema rules associated with it, then it is *valid*; otherwise, it is *invalid*. XML used by XQuery is always well-formed, and every implementation supports untyped XML. Some implementations may also support XML data that is typed and valid, or even typed but invalid.

In XML Schema 1.0, some types are built in to the standard itself, and users can also define their own types. Types are either *primitive* (like float and string) or else *derived* from other types. (If you are already familiar with XML Schema, then you know it actually has several different kinds of derivation. The only one that is used in the XQuery type system is derivation by restriction. Throughout this book, "derived" means "derived by restriction.")

The XQuery type system consists of all of the built-in XML Schema types, plus seven XML node kinds, plus six more types that are new to XQuery. That's right; XQuery defines 59 built-in types (compared to 9 types in Java). Don't panic—you only need to understand a few of these types to use XQuery effectively.

1.6.2 The Types You Need

Every XQuery expression has a *static type* (compile-time) and a *dynamic type* (run-time). The dynamic type applies to the actual value that results when the expression is evaluated; the value is an *instance* of that dynamic type. The static type applies to the expression itself, and can be used to perform type checking during compilation. All XQuery implementations perform dynamic type checking, but only some perform static type checking.

Figure 1.1 depicts the XQuery types you need to know. Arrows show inheritance, and dotted lines indicate that some types in between have been omitted.

Every XQuery value is a *sequence* containing zero or more *items*. Each individual item in a sequence is a *singleton*, and is the same as a sequence of length one containing just that item. Consequently, sequences are never nested.

Every singleton item in XQuery has a type derived from item(). The item() type is similar to the object type in Java and C#, except that it is *abstract*: you can't create an instance of item(). (It's written with parentheses in part to avoid confusion with user-defined types with the same name and in part to be consistent with the XPath node tests.)

As shown in Figure 1.1, items are classified into two kinds: XML nodes and atomic values. Nodes derive from the type node(), and atomic values derive from xdt:anyAtomicType. Like item(), the node() and xdt:anyAtomicType types are abstract.

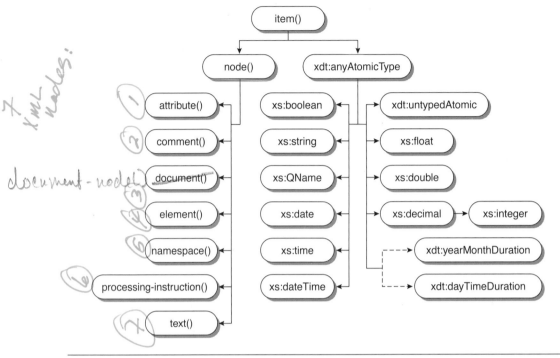

Figure 1.1 Part of the XQuery type system

You are probably already familiar with the seven XML node kinds depicted in Figure 1.1. XQuery provides several ways to create instances of XML nodes, which we'll explore later in this chapter and in Chapter 7.

Finally, there are 50 kinds of atomic types. Of these, you really only need to know fourteen—ten from XML Schema and four new ones (including the `xdt:anyAtomicType`) added by XQuery. The types you need to know are depicted in Figure 1.1. We explain them all in Chapter 2; some of their meanings are clear already from their names. Many examples of these types occur throughout the rest of the book.

All of the atomic type names are in one of two namespaces: The XML Schema type names are in the XML Schema namespace `http://www.w3.org/2001/XMLSchema`, which is bound to the prefix `xs`. The XQuery type names are in the XQuery type namespace `http://www.w3.org/2003/11/xpath-datatypes`, which is bound to the prefix `xdt`. These prefixes are built in to XQuery, and we'll use them throughout the book. (The namespaces are versioned to the current draft. The values given here correspond to the Last Call drafts available at the time of publication.)

Finally, it's worth mentioning that every user-defined type derives from one of the XML Schema built-in atomic types. The four XQuery atomic types, the seven node kinds, `item()`, and `node()` do not allow user derivation. In particular, it isn't possible to create your own node kind, although it is possible to create structural (complex) types using XML Schema and the `import schema` operator (see Chapter 9). Not all implementations support user-defined types and schema import.

1.6.3 The Types You Don't Need

While Figure 1.1 illustrates the types that you do need, Table 1.1 lists the XQuery types 36 from XML Schema that you don't need.

Many of these types exist in XQuery only because they existed in XML Schema, and are less "types" (in the traditional sense) than just validation rules. Each of these types does serve a purpose, but these purposes are often esoteric, like `xs:NOTATION`, or highly specialized, like `xs:language`, and so it's unlikely

Table 1.1 XML Schema types you don't need

xs:anySimpleType	xs:gYearMonth	xs:NMTOKENS
xs:anyType	xs:hexBinary	xs:nonNegativeInteger
xs:anyURI	xs:ID	xs:nonPositiveInteger
xs:base64Binary	xs:IDREF	xs:normalizedString
xs:byte	xs:IDREFS	xs:NOTATION
xs:duration	xs:int	xs:positiveInteger
xs:ENTITIES	xs:language	xs:short
xs:ENTITY	xs:long	xs:token
xs:gDay	xs:Name	xs:unsignedByte
xs:gMonth	xs:NCName	xs:unsignedInt
xs:gMonthDay	xs:negativeInteger	xs:unsignedLong
xs:gYear	xs:NMTOKEN	xs:unsignedShort

you'll ever need them (unless you already know what they do). For complete information about these lesser-used types, see appendix A.

1.7 A Sample Query

Figure 1.2 presents a prototypical XQuery for your reading pleasure. Each query consists of a *prolog* and/or a *body*. The prolog, if any, sets up the compile-time environment (schema and module imports, namespace declarations, user-defined functions, and so on). The body, if any, is evaluated to produce the value of the overall query.

The rest of this chapter highlights the various kinds of expressions that can occur in the prolog and body of an XQuery, and the remaining chapters drill into the details.

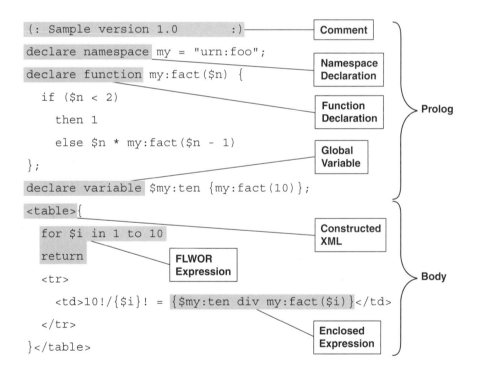

Figure 1.2 Anatomy of an XQuery

1.8 Processing Model

Every XQuery expression evaluates to a sequence (a single item is equivalent to a sequence of length one containing that item). Items in a sequence can be atomic values or nodes. Collectively, these make up the XQuery Data Model, described in Chapter 2.

XQuery is primarily designed as a strongly-typed language, meaning that every expression has a compile-time type, and must be combined with other expressions that have compatible types. When types are incompatible, the error can be detected and reported early (at compile-time). However, XQuery allows implementations to perform dynamic type checking instead, in which these errors are reported only during execution.

To understand the difference, consider the expression in Listing 1.3. If an implementation supports static typing, then this query will produce a compile-time error, because the `if` expression might evaluate to a string and strings cannot be added to integers. In implementations that use dynamic typing, the result depends on the value of the variable `$foo`. If it is true, then the query will succeed (because `if` evaluates to an integer); if it is false, then it will raise a dynamic type error.

Listing 1.3 Static typing versus dynamic typing

```
13 + if ($foo) then 30 else "0"
=>
43 or a type error, depending on the implementation and $foo
```

This book mostly describes the type rules in general, without respect to when they are applied. Consult your XQuery implementation's documentation to determine what kind of type checking it performs.

Next, let's turn our attention to the various kinds of XQuery expressions.

1.9 Comments and Whitespace

In XQuery, the whitespace characters are space (U+0020), tab (U+0009), carriage return (U+000D), and new line (U+000A). XQuery allows descriptive comments to appear anywhere that whitespace characters are allowed and ignored—which is almost everywhere. Their only purpose is to make code easier for humans to read.

XQuery comments begin with the two characters (: and end with the two characters :), as shown in Listing 1.4. Note that in places where whitespace characters are not ignored (such as string constants or direct XML constructors), comments are not ignored either but instead are treated as ordinary text.

Listing 1.4   Comments spice up any XQuery

```
(: You are here. :)
let $i := 42 (: This is also a comment. :)
return <x>(: This is not a comment. :)</x>
=>
<x>(: This is not a comment. :)</x>
```

1.10 Prolog

As mentioned earlier, every query begins with an optional section called the prolog. The prolog sets up the compile-time context for the rest of the query, including things like default namespaces, in-scope namespaces, user-defined functions, imported schema types, and even external variables and functions (if the implementation supports them). Chapter 5 explains all of these expressions. Each prolog statement must end with a semicolon (;).

For example, the query prolog in Listing 1.5 declares a namespace, and then the body of the query uses it.

Listing 1.5   Query prolog sets up static context

```
declare namespace x = "http://www.awprofessional.com/";
<x:foo/>
```

The query prolog also can be used to define global variables and to create user-defined functions for use in the rest of the query. The sample query shown previously in Figure 1.2 defines a recursive function, my:fact(), that computes the factorial of an integer, and then defines a global variable, $my:ten, that uses it.

Each function definition starts with the keywords declare function, followed by the name of the function, the names of its parameters (if any) and

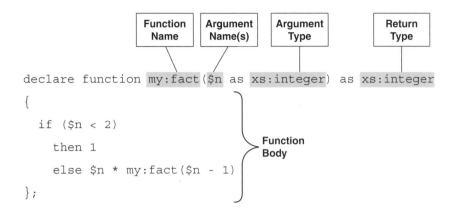

Figure 1.3 A prototypical user-defined function

optionally their types, optionally the return type of the function, and finally the body of the function (enclosed in curly braces). Figure 1.3 illustrates all of these parts, using the same example as in Figure 1.2 but with types added.

Queries may be divided into separate *modules*. Each module is a self-contained unit, analogous to a file containing code. Modules are most commonly used to define function libraries, which can then be shared by many queries using the `import module` statement in the prolog. Modules and user-defined functions are fully explained in Chapter 4. Note that not every implementation supports modules.

1.11 Constants

The constant value you will encounter most frequently is the *empty sequence*, written as left and right parentheses: `()`. Naturally enough, it denotes a sequence of length zero. XML constants are also very common, but are described later in Section 1.12. This section discusses constant atomic values such as booleans, strings, and integers.

1.11.1 Boolean Constants

Boolean constants are written as functions, `true()` and `false()`, mainly because that's how they were handled in XPath 1.0. These represent the two

boolean values true and false, respectively. The type of a boolean constant is
`xs:boolean`.

1.11.2 String Constants

String constants may be written using either single- or double-quotes, such as
`"hello"` and `'world'`. The choice makes no difference in meaning. In XQuery,
string values are always sequences of Unicode code points (see Chapter 8), and
may be the empty string. The type of a string constant is `xs:string`.

Escape the quote character by doubling it; for example, `''''` is a string
containing one apostrophe character. Also, string constants may contain the five
built-in XML entity references (`&amp;`, `&apos;`, `&gt;`, `&lt;`, and `&quot;`) or
XML character references (such as ` ` or `&#xB1;`), as shown in Listing 1.6.

Listing 1.6   String constants may contain entity and character references

```
"&lt; &amp; &gt; are special characters in XML"
=>
"< & > are special characters in XML"
```

1.11.3 Numeric Constants

There are three kinds of numeric constants: integers, floating-point numbers,
and fixed-point numbers.

Integer constants are written as a sequence of digits (0-9) with no decimal
point, for example `42`. The type of an integer constant is `xs:integer`. XQuery
defines unary - and + operators that can be used to negate the integer or
emphasize that it is positive, respectively. These operators can also be used with
the other number types below.

Decimal constants (that is, fixed-point numbers) are written using a
sequence of digits with a decimal point anywhere in the number, such as `42.` or
`4.2` or `.42`. The type of a decimal constant is `xs:decimal`. Decimal numbers
are commonly used to represent quantities with a fixed number of decimal
places, such as monetary values.

Double values (that is, double-precision floating-point numbers) are decimal or integer numbers with exponential notation after the number, such as
`42E0` or `4.2e+0` or `42E-2`. The type of a double constant is `xs:double`.

XML Schema defines the `xs:decimal` and `xs:integer` types to have arbitrary precision (allowing any number of digits), but XQuery allows implementations to use limited-precision types for efficiency in computations. Consequently, their behavior varies from one implementation to the next.

Some implementations provide arbitrary-precision integers and decimals. However, decimal is more commonly implemented using either 128 or 64 bits and integer is commonly implemented using 64 or 32 bits. The documentation for your XQuery implementation should clearly state what the implementation does.

1.11.4 Other Constants

Finally, a constant value of any type—the ones already described, the other built-in types, and user-defined types—can be constructed by writing the type name followed by a parenthesized string containing the value. For example, the expression `xs:float("1.25")` constructs an `xs:float` constant with the value 1.25 and `xs:ID("X1")` constructs an `xs:ID` constant with the value X1.

These expressions are known as *type constructors* because they construct a value of a given atomic type. The type constructors use the XML Schema validation rules for that type. For example, `xs:boolean("1")` and `xs:boolean("true")` result in the boolean constant true, exactly like the expression `true()`. However, `xs:boolean("wahr")` and `xs:boolean("vrai")` are errors, even on German and French systems, because `wahr` and `vrai` are not boolean representations accepted by XML Schema (and, therefore, are not accepted by XQuery either).

You can find the validation rules for every built-in atomic type in Appendix A.

1.12 XML

Although XQuery can be used to compute simple atomic values, more often it is used to produce XML output. This section briefly touches on the various ways to construct XML in a query (see Chapter 7 for more information).

All seven XML node-kinds are supported in XQuery. XML syntax can be used verbatim as XQuery expressions, as shown in Listing 1.7. These expressions are called *node constructors* because they construct XML nodes.

As you'll see in a moment, it's also possible to load XML from outside the query, or to compute parts of an XML structure using embedded XQuery expressions.

Listing 1.7 Constructing XML in XQuery is a snap

```
<hello world="this is" xmlns="http://www.awprofessional.com/">
  XQuery!!
  <!-- the last language you'll ever need -->
  <?or maybe not?>
  <![CDATA[Even CDATA sections are allowed]]>
</hello>
```

By leveraging the XML syntax with which you are already familiar, XQuery makes it simple to create XML values. However, the greatest flexibility comes in creating dynamic XML values that combine constant parts with parts that are computed by XQuery expressions.

To allow XQuery expressions to compute part or all of a node's content, XQuery reserves the two curly-brace characters ({}) in element and attribute constructors. The curly braces enclose an XQuery expression to be evaluated; the results of the XQuery are inserted into the XML structure at that point. Listing 1.8 demonstrates XQuery expressions in both attribute and element content.

Listing 1.8 XQuery expressions may be embedded in XML constructors

```
<x y="6*7 = {6*7}">
It is { true() or false() } that this is an example.
</x>
=>
<x y="6*7 = 42">It is true that this is an example.</x>
```

To use the curly braces as ordinary characters in an XML constant, they must be escaped by doubling them ({{ and }}) as shown in Listing 1.9 or by using character references. XQuery supports hexadecimal and decimal character references (such as), as well as the five built in named entity references (such as &) from XML.

Listing 1.9 Curly braces may be escaped by doubling them

```
<add>
  {{ 1 + 1  = { 1+1 }}}
</add>
=>
<add>{ 1 + 1 = 2 }</add>
```

Only some kinds of nodes can have computed content. XML comments and processing instructions are always constants in XQuery, and are written using the usual XML syntax `<!-- comment -->` and `<?processing instruction?>`, respectively. Curly braces in them are treated as ordinary characters instead of as expressions.

In addition to the usual XML syntax, XQuery provides an alternate keyword-style syntax for creating nodes. This alternate syntax allows not only the content but also the node name to be computed (for elements and attributes). Otherwise, computed constructors have the same effect as direct XML syntax; it's a matter of personal choice which you use.

Element nodes can be constructed using the usual XML syntax shown in Listing 1.7 or using an alternate syntax, shown in Listing 1.10, that allows their names and content to be computed by XQuery expressions.

Listing 1.10 Element nodes can be constructed using an alternate syntax

```
element { "any-name" } { "any content" }
=>
<any-name>any content</any-name>
```

Document nodes can be constructed only using this alternate syntax. Attribute and text nodes can be constructed using the alternate syntax, or can be constructed inside of XML elements as usual. Finally, namespace nodes are constructed only in element constants. All of these are shown in Listing 1.11.

Listing 1.11 Other computed constructors

```
document {
    element foo {
        attribute bar { 1 + 1 }
        text { "baz" }
        <x xmlns='urn:x'>Ordinary XML can be
        intermixed with the alternate syntax</x>
    }
}
=>
<foo bar="2">baz<x xmlns='urn:x'>Ordinary XML can be
      intermixed with the alternate syntax</x></foo>
```

An XQuery expression in a node constructor can result in the empty sequence, in which case it contributes nothing to the content, or it can result in a sequence containing more than one item. The rules in this case are somewhat complicated, but in general the values are separated by spaces. These effects are demonstrated in Listing 1.12.

Listing 1.12 Sequence content is flattened before inserting into XML

```
<x y="{ () }">{ (1, 2) }</x>
=>
<x y="">1 2</x>
```

Constructing XML turns out to be a very intricate process, in part because there are so many special cases in XML and XQuery, like how whitespace characters are handled and how XQuery values are represented as XML. For a complete explanation of all the rules, see Chapter 7.

1.13 Built-in Functions

Not counting the type constructors mentioned in Section 1.11.4, XQuery defines 110 built-in functions, counted by name. Both built-in and user-defined functions are invoked by writing the function name followed by zero or more argument values in parentheses, like `function(param1, param2)`. Function invocations are matched to function definitions by the function name and the number of arguments, which together are called the *function signature*.

For example, the number of items in a sequence can be counted using the `count()` function. A subsequence of several items can be selected using the `subsequence()` function. Sequences use 1-based indexing, so the first item in the sequence occurs at position 1. See Listing 1.13 for examples.

Listing 1.13 Some of the built-in sequence functions

```
count(("a", 2, "c"))                => 3
subsequence((-5,4,-3,2,-1), 3)      => (-3, 2, -1)
subsequence((-5,4,-3,2,-1), 2, 3)   => (4, -3, 2)
```

All of the built-in functions (except type constructors) belong to the namespace `http://www.w3.org/2003/11/xpath-functions`, which is bound to the prefix `fn`. This is also the default namespace for functions, which means that unqualified function names are matched against the built-in functions. For example, `true()` is the same as `fn:true()`, provided that you haven't changed the default function namespace or the namespace binding for `fn`. I generally omit the built-in prefix in this book.

Appendix C lists all of the built-in functions, sorted alphabetically for convenient reference, and you will encounter many of them throughout the following chapters.

1.14 Operators

Sequences of values are written with commas separating items in the sequence, as shown in Listing 1.14.

Listing 1.14 Comma creates a sequence of expressions

```
1, "fish"
```

Because the comma operator has the lowest precedence of all XQuery operators, sequences usually need to be enclosed in parentheses. In fact, parentheses can be used to group all kinds of expressions together, as shown in Listing 1.15.

Listing 1.15 Parentheses are used around sequences or to group expressions

```
()              => ()
(1, 2)          => (1, 2)
1 + 2 * 3       => 7
(1 + 2)*3       => 9
```

XQuery defines a rich assortment of other operators and expressions. In this chapter we scratch the surface of a few of them; for complete details, see Chapter 5 and Appendix B.

Some operators are unary prefix (such as - and +) or unary postfix (such as []), meaning they take a single operand and appear before or after it, respectively. Others are binary infix operators (such as `or` and +), meaning they appear between

their two operands. Some operators are written using punctuation symbols (like *
and /), while others are written using names (like `div` and `intersect`).

XQuery does not reserve keywords; instead, context is used to determine their meaning. Like XML, XQuery is a case-sensitive language. All XQuery keywords are lowercase.

1.14.1 Logic Operators

XQuery defines three logic operators: `and`, `or`, and `not()`. The `not()` operator is written as a function because that's how XPath 1.0 handled it; the other two are binary operators, as shown in Listing 1.16. Each of these operators performs the corresponding boolean calculation.

Listing 1.16 Boolean operators

```
true() and false()   => false()
true() or false()    => true()
not(false())         => true()
```

XQuery also provides an `if/then/else` operator to expression conditional statements. The `if` condition is always evaluated, and then only the corresponding branch (`then` if the condition is true, `else` if it is false) is evaluated and becomes the result of the entire expression, as shown in Listing 1.17.

Listing 1.17 Conditionals

```
if (true()) then "true" else "false"
=>
"true"
```

Conditionals may also be chained together one after another, as shown in Listing 1.18. The final else branch is always required.

Listing 1.18 A sequence of conditionals

```
if (expr < 0)
then "negative"
else if (expr > 0)
then "positive"
else "zero"
```

1.14.2 Arithmetic Operators

XQuery supports eight mathematical operators, corresponding to addition (+), subtraction (-), multiplication (*), division (div), integer division (idiv), modulo (mod), unary plus (+), and unary minus (-). Division is expressed using a keyword (div) instead of the usual slash operator, because slash is used for a different purpose (see Section 1.15). Listing 1.19 shows how these operators are used.

Listing 1.19 XQuery provides the usual arithmetic operators

```
1 + 2       => 3
3 - 4       => -1
1 * 2       => 2
1 div 2     => 5E-1
1 idiv 2    => 0
1 mod 2     => 1
+1.0        => 1.0
-1.0        => -1.0
2.0 * 3     => 6.0
2E1 div 4   => 5E0
```

In addition to these operators, XQuery also defines a few arithmetic functions, including round(), floor(), ceiling(), round-half-to-even(), abs(), sum(), min(), max(), and avg(). Listing 1.20 illustrates the use of some of these functions. Many XQuery implementations also provide additional mathematical capabilities through extension functions.

Listing 1.20 XQuery also defines several arithmetic functions

```
min((2, 1, 3, -100))        => -100
round(9 div 2)              => 5
round-half-to-even(9 div 2) => 4
```

Like XML construction, arithmetic has a lot of detailed rules, such as type promotion. For complete details, see Chapter 5 and Appendix B.

1.14.3 Text Operators

XQuery 1.0 doesn't define any text operators per se, although it does provide a large number of built-in functions for string manipulation, including regular expression matching and replacement.

Note that the plus operator (+) doesn't perform string concatenation. To combine strings, use either the `concat()` or the `string-join()` function.

Two of the most commonly used text functions are `substring()`, which can be used to extract zero or more characters from a given string value, and `string-length()`, which computes the length of a string. Like sequences, string positions are always 1.based, so the first character in the string occurs at position 1. Listing 1.21 demonstrates a few of the more common XQuery string functions.

Listing 1.21 Some of the built-in string functions

```
string-length("abcde")                  => 5
substring("abcde", 3)                    => "cde"
substring("abcde", 2, 3)                 => "bcd"
concat("ab", "cd", "", "e")              => "abcde"
string-join(("ab","cd","","e"), "")      => "abcde"
string-join(("ab","cd","","e"), "x")     => "abxcdxxe"
contains("abcde", "e")                   => true
replace("abcde", "a.*d", "x")            => "xe"
replace("abcde", "([ab][cd])+", "x")     => "axde"
normalize-space("  a  b cd  e  ")        => "a b cd e"
```

Two other very useful string functions are `string-to-codepoints()` and `codepoints-to-string()`. The first takes a string and returns the sequence of Unicode code points it contains. The second does the reverse; it takes a sequence of code points and returns the string containing those characters. Both are demonstrated in Listing 1.22.

Listing 1.22 Strings are sequences of Unicode code points

```
string-to-codepoints("Hello")      => (72,101,108,108,111)
codepoints-to-string((87,79,82,76,68)) => "WORLD"
```

Most string functions in XQuery accept an optional *collation* parameter. A collation describes how characters should be compared (in comparisons, sorts, and substring searches). For example, a case-insensitive collation would treat x and x as the same character; another common collation treats all punctuation characters as less than all letters.

In XQuery, collations are represented using URI strings. The only collation implementations are required to support is also the default collation, known as the Unicode code point collation. This collation corresponds to the URI http:// www.w3.org/2003/11/xpath-functions/collation/codepoint and it sorts characters according to their Unicode code points. Implementations are free to support any additional collations they wish; there is no standard for specifying collation names. See Chapter 8 for additional information and examples.

1.14.4 Comparison Operators

XQuery also supports many different comparison operators. The comparison operators are grouped into three categories: value, general, and node comparison operators.

Value comparison operators compare two singleton values and return true if the operands compare true (using the default collation for string comparisons), and false otherwise. The value comparison operators are all expressed using keywords: eq, ne, gt, ge, lt, and le. These have the expected meanings (for example, eq returns true if the values are equal, ne returns true if they are unequal, gt returns true if the first operand is greater than the second, etc.). Listing 1.23 illustrates some examples.

Listing 1.23 Value comparison operators work on singleton values

```
1 eq 1 => true
1 eq 2 => false
1 ne 2 => true
1 gt 2 => false
1 lt 2 => true
```

General comparison operators are similar to value comparisons, except that they operate on sequences. They return true if there exists an item in one sequence and in the second sequence such that the two compare true using the corresponding value comparison operator. The general comparison operators are represented using punctuation: =, !=, >, >=, < and <=.

As Listing 1.24 demonstrates, the general comparison operators sometimes produce surprising results. For example, (1, 2) = (2, 3) because there exists an item (2) in the first sequence and there exists an item (2 again) in the second sequence such that the two items are equal.

Listing 1.24 General comparison operators work on sequences

```
(1, 2, 3) = 4      => false
(1, 2, 3) = 3      => true
(1, 2) = (3, 4)    => false
(1, 2) != (3, 4)   => true
(1, 2) = (2, 3)    => true
(1, 2) != (2, 3)   => true
(1, 2) != (1, 2)   => true
```

Node Comparison Operators

Finally, there are three *node comparison* operators: <<, >>, and is. The node comparison operators depend on node identity and document order, which are explained in Chapter 2.

These operators work on sequences of nodes. Like the general comparisons, the node comparisons test whether there exists a node in the first sequence and there exists a node in the second sequence such that the comparison is true.

The is operator returns true if two nodes are the same node by identity. The << operator is pronounced "before" and tests whether a node occurs before another one in document order. Similarly, the >> operator is pronounced "after" and tests whether a node occurs after another one in document order. Listing 1.25 demonstrates the use of these three operators.

Listing 1.25 Node comparison operators work on sequences of nodes

```
<a/> is <b/>                    => false
<a/> isnot <a/>                 => true
doc("test.xml") is doc("test.xml") => true
x/.. << x                       => true
```

1.15 Paths

You have seen how to construct XML and how to operate on sequences of nodes and values, but of course the most important topic is the application of XQuery to existing (external) XML sources. This section explores the use of existing XML data. In the examples given in this section and the remainder of this chapter suppose team.xml is the XML document shown in Listing 1.26.

XQuery provides several functions to access existing XML data, including the `doc()` function. This function is similar to the `document()` function in XPath and XSLT: It takes a single argument, which is a string URI pointing to the XML source to be loaded, and returns the resulting document. For example, `doc("team.xml")` accesses the data source `team.xml`.

Given an XML document, the next step is to select some of the nodes it contains. Just as XSLT 1.0 used XPath 1.0 to select nodes, XQuery uses the XPath 2.0 path syntax. By conscious design, these paths are somewhat similar to file system paths, because both navigate a hierarchy of information.

Listing 1.26 The team.xml document

```
<?xml version='1.0'?>
<Team name="Project 42" xmlns:a="urn:annotations">
  <Employee id="E6" years="4.3">
    <Name>Chaz Hoover</Name>
    <Title>Architect</Title>
    <Expertise>Puzzles</Expertise>
    <Expertise>Games</Expertise>
    <Employee id="E2" years="6.1" a:assigned-to="Jade Studios">
      <Name>Carl Yates</Name>
      <Title>Dev Lead</Title>
      <Expertise>Video Games</Expertise>
      <Employee id="E4" years="1.2" a:assigned-to="PVR">
        <Name>Panda Serai</Name>
        <Title>Developer</Title>
        <Expertise>Hardware</Expertise>
        <Expertise>Entertainment</Expertise>
      </Employee>
      <Employee id="E5" years="0.6">
        <?Follow-up?>
        <Name>Jason Abedora</Name>
        <Title>Developer</Title>
        <Expertise>Puzzles</Expertise>
      </Employee>
    </Employee>
    <Employee id="E1" years="8.2">
      <!-- new hire 13 May -->
      <Name>Kandy Konrad</Name>
      <Title>QA Lead</Title>
```

```
        <Expertise>Movies</Expertise>
        <Expertise>Sports</Expertise>
        <Employee id="E0" years="8.5" a:status="on leave">
          <Name>Wanda Wilson</Name>
          <Title>QA Engineer</Title>
          <Expertise>Home Theater</Expertise>
          <Expertise>Board Games</Expertise>
          <Expertise>Puzzles</Expertise>
        </Employee>
      </Employee>
      <Employee id="E3" years="2.8">
        <Name>Jim Barry</Name>
        <Title>QA Engineer</Title>
        <Expertise>Video Games</Expertise>
      </Employee>
    </Employee>
  </Team>
```

For example, suppose you want to select the `Team` element at the top of the document. This can be done using the XQuery `doc("team.xml")/Team`. The slash operator iterates through every node in the expression on the left (the *context*), and for each such node performs the selection on the right (the *step*). In this case, the context is the root node of the document `team.xml`, and the step selects its `Team` element children. Any number of steps may be combined together in a path.

To select attribute nodes instead of elements, you can use the `@` symbol in front of the step name. For example, `doc("team.xml")/Team/@name` selects the attribute `name="Project 42"`.

Paths are easily one of the most important types of expressions in XQuery. Paths provide many other navigation operators for moving around the hierarchy, selecting different kinds of nodes, and filtering the nodes selected. Chapter 3 covers paths and navigation more generally.

1.16 Variables

Variables in XQuery are written using a dollar sign symbol in front of a name, like so: `$variable`. The variable name may consist of only a local-name like this one, or it may be a qualified name consisting of a prefix and local-name, like

`$prefix:local`. In this case, it behaves like any other XML qualified name. (The prefix must be bound to a namespace in scope, and it is the namespace value that matters, not the prefix.)

Several different expressions in XQuery can introduce new variables into scope. These are described in later in the book: function definitions (Chapter 4), global variable declarations (Chapter 5), FLWOR and quantification (Chapter 6), and `typeswitch` (Chapter 9). If there is already a variable in scope with that name, then the new definition temporarily overrides the old one.

It's worth observing that XQuery variables, despite being called "variable," are actually immutable. In fact, everything in XQuery is read-only; in XQuery 1.0, no expressions can change the values of variables or XML data. There are proposed extensions to XQuery (see Chapter 14) that would allow some values to be modified and may appear in future versions of the standard (and possibly the implementation you use today).

1.17 FLWOR

The central expression in XQuery is the so-called "flower expression," named after the first letters of its clauses—`for`, `let`, `where`, `order by`, `return`—FLWOR. FLWOR is an expression with many features, which are covered completely in Chapter 6.

The FLWOR expression is used for many different purposes in XQuery: to introduce variables, to iterate over sequences, to filter results, to sort sequences, and to join different data sources. The FLWOR expression in Listing 1.27 uses all five clauses to iterate over an existing document and return a result.

Listing 1.27 A typical FLWOR expression

```
for $i in doc("orders.xml")//Customer
let $name := concat($i/@FirstName, $i/@LastName)
where $i/@ZipCode = 91126
order by $i/@LastName
return
  <Customer Name="{$name}">
    { $i//Order }
  </Customer>
```

The `for` and `let` clauses may appear in any order relative to one another, and there may be any number of each, provided there is at least one `for` or `let` clause. Each `for` clause iterates through a sequence, binding a variable to each member of the sequence in turn. Each `let` clause assigns a variable to the value of an expression. Every variable introduced this way is in scope for the remainder of the FLWOR expression, including any `for/let` clauses that follow.

The optional `where` clause filters the possibilities, and the optional `order by` clause sorts the result into a particular order. Finally, the `return` clause constructs the result, which can be any expression at all.

A very simple FLWOR is shown in Listing 1.28. This example declares a variable (`$variable`) using a `let` clause, and then returns some expression (which might use that variable).

Listing 1.28 FLWOR can introduce variables into scope

```
let $variable := "any expression here"
return concat("xx", $variable, "xx")
=>
"xxany expression herexx"
```

A more complex example is shown in Listing 1.29. This FLWOR iterates through a sequence, and returns only those members that are greater than 3.

Listing 1.29 FLWOR is also useful for filtering sequences

```
for $i in (1, 2, 3, 4, 5)
where $i > 3
return $i
=>
(4, 5)
```

Often, simple FLWOR expressions can be expressed using paths instead. For example, Listing 1.29 could also be expressed as the path `(1,2,3,4,5)[. > 3]`. Path expressions are very concise, but can be difficult to comprehend.

FLWOR is especially useful when used together with paths. For example, consider the `team.xml` example in Listing 1.26. Suppose you want to list all employees alphabetically by last name. You can use a path to select the employee names, the `tokenize()` function to split the name into first and last parts, and then an `order by` clause to sort by the last name, as shown in Listing 1.30.

Listing 1.30 Sort employee names by last name

```
for $e in doc("team.xml")//Employee
let $name := $e/Name
order by tokenize($name)[2] (: Extract the last name :)
return $name
```

FLWOR is also commonly used to join a data source with itself or other data sources, as shown in Listing 1.31. For more examples, see Chapter 6.

Listing 1.31 Joining two documents together

```
for $i in doc("one.xml")//fish,
    $j in doc("two.xml")//fish
where $i/red = $j/blue
return <fishes> { $i, $j } </fishes>
```

multiple documents

1.18 Error Handling

XQuery distinguishes between *static errors* that may occur when compiling a query and *dynamic errors* that may occur when evaluating a query. Dynamic errors may be reported statically if they are detected during compilation (for example, `xs:decimal("X")` may result in either a dynamic or a static error, depending on the implementation).

Most XQuery expressions perform extensive type checking. For example, the addition `$a + $b` results in an error if either `$a` or `$b` is a sequence containing more than one item, or if the two values cannot be added together. For example, `"1" + 2` is an error. This is very different from XPath and XSLT 1.0, in which `"1" + 2` converted the string to a number, and then performed the addition without error.

XQuery also defines a built-in `error()` function that takes an optional argument (the error value) and raises a dynamic error. In addition, some implementations support the `trace()` function, which allows you to generate a message without terminating query execution. See Appendix C for examples.

Many other XQuery operations may cause dynamic errors, such as type conversion errors. As mentioned previously, often implementations are allowed to evaluate expressions in any order or to optimize out certain temporary expressions. Consequently, an implementation may optimize out some dynamic errors. For example, `error()` and `false()` might raise an error, or might return false. The only expressions that guarantee a particular order-of-evaluation are `if/then/else` and `typeswitch`.

1.19 Conclusion

Query languages are powerful tools for manipulating XML, and XQuery doesn't disappoint. With literally hundreds of operators and functions, it's a rich and feature-full language for constructing and navigating XML and typed values.

The core features of XQuery are its type system, XML constructors, navigation paths, and FLWOR ("flower") expressions, all of which are explained in later chapters. XQuery also provides many useful operators (Chapter 5) and even allows users to define their own functions (Chapter 4).

1.20 Further Reading

For more information on the development of the XQuery standard, look no further than *XQuery from the Experts: A Guide to the W3C XML Query Language* by Howard Katz. Essays from many of the committee members themselves explain some of the design decisions made along the way.

Many great books on XML are available; two of the better ones are *Essential XML: Beyond Markup* by Don Box, Aaron Skonnard, and John Lam, and *Learning XML* by Erik Ray and Christopher Maden. If you believe that you've already mastered these basics of XML, then I highly recommend taking your skills to the next level with *Effective XML: 50 Specific Ways to Improve Your XML* by Elliote Rusty Harold.

CHAPTER 2

Data Model and Type System

2.1 Introduction

Understanding the XQuery Data Model and type system is central to understanding all the rest of the XQuery language. The XQuery *Data Model* consists not only of the XML data over which a query operates, but also any other values that the query can produce (as either intermediate values or the final query result). The XQuery *type system* associates static types with every expression at compile time, and also dynamic types with every value in the data model. The data model and type system both involve a lot of details, but these details are fairly straightforward.

Almost every XML standard has introduced a data model slightly different from those of its predecessors, and XQuery is no different in this respect. This chapter first explores some previous data models and the reasons XQuery differs from them, and then focuses on the details of the XQuery Data Model itself.

The type system pervades all aspects of the XQuery Data Model and language. For better or worse, this type system is based on XML Schema 1.0, with some minor modifications (mostly to accommodate untyped XML data, unnamed nodes, and cardinalities). In this chapter I focus only on the parts of the XQuery type system that you need to know to effectively use XQuery.

Appendix A provides a reference for every type (even the ones you'll rarely need) and every aspect of the Data Model. Additional references on XML Schema 1.0 can be found in the "Further Reading" section at the end of this chapter.

2.2 An Overview of XML Data Models

What is XML? Is it an ordered sequence of characters or other lexical tokens? Is it a tree of nodes labeled with information? Is it a graph? Is it typed, and if so, what is its type system? Must the data model faithfully preserve all the lexical information present in the original XML document—including entity references, CDATA sections, and all space characters (even spaces between attributes), or can it treat some of this information as insignificant? And what exactly constitutes a "node," anyway?

An XML data model must answer these questions and many more; however, many of the possible answers conflict with one another. Effectively, each data model defines what information in an XML document "really matters" and what information is considered irrelevant for its purposes.

Over time, popular opinion as to what information is important and what can be ignored has shifted, reflecting a more general trend to view XML as data and not merely document markup. To better understand why there are so many XML data models, let's consider two simple examples.

2.2.1 Two Examples

Consider a block of text containing an entity or CDATA section in the middle of it, as shown in Listing 2.1. If the data model must preserve the entity or CDATA section with full fidelity, then the data model must maintain separate "nodes" or structures for each piece of information. In this example, one text node for the character sequence `Punctuation like` (including the trailing space), one entity node for the entity `&amp;`, another text node for the characters `and` (including the boundary space characters) a CDATA node for `<![CDATA[<]]>`, and finally a text node for the remaining characters `can be tricky in XML.` (including the leading space).

Listing 2.1 CDATA sections and entity references in the middle of text

```
<x>Punctuation like &amp; and <![CDATA[<]]> can be tricky in XML.</x>
```

However, you might instead prefer to work with this text directly as a single node containing the string value `Punctuation like & and < can be tricky in XML`. This approach resolves all entities and CDATA sections first, and then merges the result into a single text value.

The first approach loses no information, but requires a parser to perform more work—creating five nodes where one might suffice—and requires applications to handle text values that have been divided into separate chunks. The second approach is more efficiently represented and easier for most applications to consume, but loses some information about the original XML representation, whether characters were entitized, wrapped in CDATA blocks, or just appeared normally.

As a second example, suppose we are working with typed XML. The XML characters will be mapped to some other value space, like integers, so that we can work with them efficiently. This process drops leading zeros on numeric values, so it is certainly lossy. However, this approach is even lossier than we might first appreciate, as Listing 2.2 illustrates.

Listing 2.2 Comments and processing instructions may appear in a typed value

```
<x xsi:type="xs:integer">
   04<!-- comments are annoying -->2
</x>
```

XML allows comments and processing instructions to appear anywhere, even in the middle of a text value. In this example, preserving the comment would result in a sequence of three nodes: a text node with the value 04, a comment node, and another text node with the value 2. However, treating the XML as a typed value, as XML Schema does, would ignore the comment node and instead result in a single, typed value— the integer 42—losing the leading zero, whitespace characters, and the XML comment node.

Generally speaking, conflicts like these are what differentiate the different XML data models in use today. One data model chooses one solution, and another data model chooses a different (possibly incompatible) solution. In some cases, a data model may attempt to preserve both sets of information simultaneously, trading memory consumption for flexibility.

2.2.2 The Document Object Model (DOM)

Initially, most people viewed XML in the light of HTML, and believed the two should share a common API. This belief led to the creation of the Document Object Model (DOM) Levels 1 and 2. (Level 3 is under development at the time of this writing.) The DOM is especially popular as the component model in Web browsers. Although the DOM focuses on an API for working with XML data, this API implies an underlying data model.

In the DOM Data Model, all lexical information is preserved—entities and CDATA sections, for example, are kept as individual nodes in the DOM. It is tempting to think that the DOM is not typed, but actually the DOM does process the limited type information available in DTDs and applies some of this type information to its data model (for example, attributes may be ID-typed, which then confers special meaning to their parent elements).

For text processing, or manually navigating what is essentially an XML parse tree, the DOM is very useful. For query processing, the two most obvious drawbacks to the DOM are that it consumes a large amount of memory relative to the original text and that simple string comparisons must take into account the possibility of separate text nodes. Also, the DOM representation focuses more on the original lexical shape of the data than the underlying values it contains (storing, for example, the characters 042 instead of the integer 42). For these reasons and others, XML query languages have pretty much abandoned the DOM as an unworkable data model for XML query processing.

2.2.3 The XPath 1.0 Data Model

The XPath 1.0 Data Model picks up where the Document Object Model leaves off. The XPath Data Model is formally defined only for the XML data over which it operates; oddly, it doesn't consider the types of intermediate query expressions as part of its data model.

XPath has effectively five data types: boolean, double (called *number*), string, sequence of nodes (called *node-sets*), and external objects of unknown type. Host languages wrapped around XPath often add additional types, for example, XSLT has *result tree fragments*. Node-sets are always sorted in document order.

The XPath Data Model differs from the DOM in several respects. Character entities and CDATA sections are always expanded and merged with adjacent text nodes. XPath cannot determine whether text nodes contained entities or CDATA sections. Some DTD information (notably ID types using the id() function) can be queried and therefore must be processed and preserved, but other DTD information is also lost.

For query processing, the XPath 1.0 Data Model is not bad. Its main flaws are the omission of many other useful data types (such as integer or date), its inability to construct sequences of values, its inability to construct sequences of nodes sorted in arbitrary order, and its lack of support for XML Schema (which appeared later). The XPath Data Model is also specified too informally, something that the next data model discussed, the XML Infoset, addressed.

2.2.4 The XML Information Set (Infoset)

Around this time, the XML community realized that the informal treatment given to XML data models by previous standards efforts was insufficient. A more rigorous definition was required, one that could become the basis for future XML standards. This effort led to the creation of the XML Information Set, aka the Infoset.

The Infoset treats XML as a collection of *information items*. An Infoset always contains at least one information item—for the document node. Like the XPath data model, the Infoset is lossy with respect to the original XML syntax (if there was one; the Infoset is an abstraction that could be applied to other data sources, such as databases).

The Infoset doesn't preserve many kinds of syntactic information, including general parsed entities, CDATA sections, the difference between various end-of-line sequences, the difference between self-closed (`<x/>`) and empty (`<x></x>`) elements, the order in which attributes appear, and so on. It's clear that these decisions reflected the shift in thinking about what information was important and what wasn't.

From the point of view of XML query processing, the Infoset has one major characteristic, namely that it heralds the beginning of *virtual XML*, data that is viewed as though it were XML, without necessarily being XML.

The importance of this step is best explained by analogy. There was a time when mathematics concerned itself only with concepts having some physical meaning. Concepts like imaginary numbers and powers greater than three dimensions were initially resisted as too abstract, too disconnected from the real world. Similarly, before the Infoset, XML data models focused on the "physical" XML serialization format. The Infoset represents a major shift in thinking; for the first time, the XML data model is viewed as an abstraction that might be created from some entirely different data format.

2.2.5 The Post-Schema-Validation Infoset (PSVI)

The Infoset is still fundamentally untyped; it doesn't even require XML to be valid according to a DTD or schema. The XML Schema specification introduces validation information about an XML document, such as types, default values, whether content may be empty or not, relationships to other types, and so on. The Post-Schema-Validation Infoset (PSVI) is an Infoset that has been validated and augmented with additional information by the validation process.

The PSVI is almost ideal for XML query processing. It is abstract, relatively lightweight, and strongly-typed. However, it still suffers from a few drawbacks, probably the worst of which is that it represents only nodes and values inside of nodes—the data model always contains one node, which precludes possibilities like a "list of integers."

2.2.6 The XQuery Data Model

Ideally, XQuery would use one of the existing data models verbatim, such as the PSVI, without additions or caveats. Unfortunately, even the PSVI introduces a few difficulties for query languages, and these difficulties compelled XQuery to define its own data model that is almost, but not quite, the PSVI.

The greatest difficulty is that XQuery, like XPath, has intermediate expressions whose values are not XML and have no obvious XML analogue. For example, an XQuery expression can result in a list of integers and attributes, or a list of documents, neither of which is directly supported in the PSVI. Also, two of the requirements for XQuery are that it must be able to handle XML fragments (which are not directly supported by the Infoset either), and that it must support both typed and untyped XML data. Consequently, the XQuery Data Model covers more possibilities than either the Infoset or PSVI alone.

Finally, XQuery encountered difficulties when working with certain XML Schema types. For example, the duration types of XML Schema are not well suited to addition, comparisons, and other query operations. To compensate for these issues, XQuery has added a few types to the existing XML Schema type system.

2.3 Structure of the XQuery Data Model

Now that we've explored some of the XML data models that have been employed over the past years, let's focus on the details of the XQuery Data Model and type system. The justifications for all the previous data models should shed some light on the technical descriptions that follow. The XQuery Data Model is detailed but straightforward, given its design choices.

Note that the XQuery Data Model places no limitations on the number of nodes or the sizes of strings and names. However, some implementations may impose practical limits on the maximum size of a data model.

2.3.1 Items and Sequences

As mentioned in Chapter 1, every XQuery data model is an ordered *sequence* of zero or more *items*.

Items are always singletons. An item is equivalent to a sequence of length one containing that item, so, for example, (0) is equivalent to just 0. A sequence may be empty, but cannot contain other sequences (nested sequences are always flattened), so, for example, the sequence `(0, (), (1, 2))` is the same as `(0, 1, 2)`.

XQuery uses a *sequence type* expression to describe types. Except for the special sequence type `empty()` (which is the type of the empty sequence), sequence type consists of two parts: a *type name* and an optional *occurrence indicator*.

The type name can be any qualified name or one of several built-in type names, all of which are written like functions. The meaning of the type name is explained throughout the rest of this chapter. The occurrence indicator, if used, can be a plus sign (+), asterisk (*), or question mark (?), with the same meanings as in regular expressions: + denotes one or more (not empty), * means zero or more (any number), and ? means zero or one (not more). When the occurrence indicator is omitted, the sequence must contain exactly one item with the named type.

For example, `item()*` is the type of a sequence containing any number of items, while `item()` is the type of a sequence containing exactly one item. Several different types may be used to describe a particular value; for example, a sequence of integers (`xs:integer*`) is also a sequence of items (`item()*`). The type rules are fairly complex, so I'll wait until Section 2.6 to explain them.

Items are further classified into *atomic values* and *nodes*. Because the two item kinds are so different from one another, let's cover each one separately, starting with atomic values.

2.3.2 Atomic Values

Atomic values are so named to emphasize the fact that they are singletons with essentially no structure. XQuery defines 50 built-in atomic types, although as mentioned in Chapter 1, you really only need to know 14 of them. These types are described in Section 2.4, and all 50 are covered in Appendix A.

Every atomic value has an *atomic type* that derives from the special XQuery type `xdt:anyAtomicType`. As its name suggests, this type is used to represent any atomic type.

2.3.3 Nodes

Nodes are structures with many properties including kind, name, and type. There are seven node kinds in XQuery, the same as in XML. The `node()` type matches all node kinds, just like `xdt:anyAtomicType` matches any atomic value.

Unlike atomic values, each node has a unique identity that distinguishes it from every other node. Also, all nodes have an inherent ordering to them, known as *document order*, which actually applies even to nodes from different documents. These and other node properties are discussed in Section 2.5.

2.4 Atomic Types

Every built-in atomic type name belongs to one of two namespaces: the XML Schema namespace `http://www.w3.org/2001/XMLSchema`, which is bound to the prefix `xs`, or the XQuery type namespace `http://www.w3.org/2003/11/xpath-datatypes`, which is bound to the prefix `xdt`.

Atomic values can be obtained in several different ways. As shown in Chapter 1, some types can be constructed using literals, and almost all atomic types can be constructed using the type constructor syntax. Atomic values can also be extracted from typed XML data using the `data()` function (see Section 2.6.1). Type conversion operators such as `cast as` (see Chapter 9) can convert values of one atomic type to a different type. And finally, many other XQuery functions and operators result in atomic values. Of these, all but the last category can also result in a user-defined type (derived from one of the built-in types).

2.4.1 Untyped Data

XQuery uses a special type, `xdt:untypedAtomic`, for values from untyped XML data. This type derives from `xdt:anyAtomicType` and it behaves like a kind of weakly-typed string. In most cases it behaves exactly like `xs:string`, but some XQuery operators treat it differently in implicit type conversions. For example, `xs:string("1") + 1` is an error because the string and integer types are incompatible for addition, but `xdt:untypedAtomic("1") + 1` results in the double value `2E0`—first the untyped value is promoted to double, then the integer is also promoted to double, and then the two are added together.

In this way, the "untyped" type allows users to work with untyped data without needing to add lots of explicit casts to the query. In fact, for the most part untyped data causes expressions to have the same meaning they did in XPath 1.0 (in which strings were converted to `xs:double` by most expressions).

2.4.2 Boolean Types

Boolean values have the type `xs:boolean`, which derives from `xdt:anyAtomic-Type`. In XQuery, the two boolean constants true and false are written using the `true()` and `false()` functions, respectively. There are several other ways to create boolean values. One is to use the `xs:boolean()` type constructor, as mentioned in Chapter 1. Like all type constructors, this takes a single string argument and parses it into a boolean value. If the argument is "true" or "1," then it results in true; if it is "false" or "0," then it results in false, and anything else causes an error.

Another way is to use the `fn:boolean()` function, which takes any item sequence as its argument, and returns its Effective Boolean Value, as explained in Section 2.6.2. Many operators, such as `and` and `or`, convert their arguments to boolean using Effective Boolean Value.

Listing 2.3 illustrates these three ways to create boolean constants.

Listing 2.3 Different ways to construct boolean atomic values

```
false()              => false
boolean("false")     => true
boolean("")          => false
xs:boolean("false")  => false
xs:boolean("")       => error
```

2.4.3 Numeric Types

XQuery defines many numeric types, but you'll most frequently use the four types `xs:float`, `xs:double`, `xs:integer`, and `xs:decimal`, explained next.

2.4.3.1 Numerics Background

Numeric types in all languages have two main aspects: how they handle the decimal point (integral, fixed, or floating) and how they handle precision (limited, arbitrary).

Integral numbers have no decimal point. They represent only integer numbers within some range.

Fixed-point numbers have a fixed number of digits after the decimal point. When this number is zero, they are equivalent to integers, but when it is positive, they can represent fractional amounts. (Some implementations also allow this number to be negative, in which case the number is integral and that many digits in front of the decimal point are all zero.) Fixed-point numbers are commonly used in financial and scientific applications when greater control over rounding is required, or when fractional numbers need to be compared exactly.

Floating-point numbers may have a variable number of digits after the decimal point. Most numeric operations on them suffer from some amount of round-off error, but can be implemented more efficiently and in less space (trading accuracy for efficiency).

Limited-precision numbers can represent only a finite number of digits (the *precision*). For non-integer numbers, the number of digits after the decimal point is the *scale*. Limited-precision numbers occupy a fixed amount of space, and are commonly implemented in hardware. Limited-precision numbers are similar to fixed-width string buffers.

As the name suggests, arbitrary-precision numbers can represent any number of digits. Arbitrary-precision numbers are similar to resizable string arrays. They can grow as necessary to represent more digits. They are much more accurate than limited-precision numbers, but are rarely implemented in hardware. Consequently, they are often several hundred or thousand times slower than limited-precision numbers.

2.4.3.2 XQuery Numeric Types

XQuery defines sixteen numeric types, but you really need only four of them: `xs:integer`, `xs:decimal`, `xs:float`, and `xs:double`. These types correspond to integer, fixed-point, and single- and double-precision floating-point numbers, respectively. Most XQuery arithmetic expressions and functions promote their operands and arguments to one of these types (see Section 2.6.5).

The other 12 types all derive from `xs:integer` and represent special cases like `xs:unsignedByte` and `xs:positiveInteger`. Although a few implementations may optimize these types specially, they are available in XQuery primarily because they are part of XML Schema 1.0. XQuery has no complex number type.

In XQuery and XML Schema 1.0, the `xs:integer` and `xs:decimal` types are technically arbitrary-precision, but implementations are allowed to use limited-precision instead, so that arithmetic operations can be as efficient as possible. Because arbitrary-precision arithmetic is so much slower than limited-precision arithmetic commonly supported in hardware, most implementations do make this choice.

This implementation-defined behavior makes it impossible to port your XQuery applications from one implementation to another unless they make the same choice. Using limited precision to represent `xs:integer` or `xs:decimal` can also cause some confusion with derived types (like `xs:unsignedLong`, which occupies the range 0 to $2^{64}-1$) that may require more bits than the implementation used for the base type `xs:integer`. For this reason, I recommend avoiding the types derived from `xs:integer` unless your XQuery implementation uses arbitrary-precision arithmetic.

All numeric types support the type constructor syntax. If the string does not parse according to the rules for that type, or maps to a value out of range, then

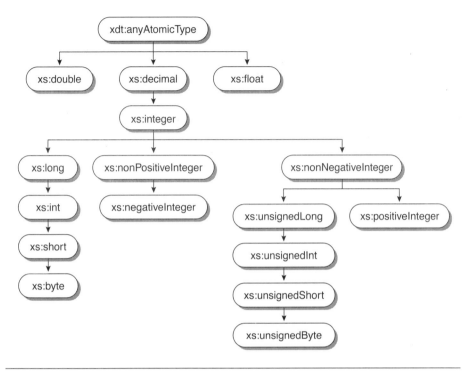

Figure 2.1 Number type hierarchy

an error is raised. For example, `xs:integer("010")` results in the integer 10, but `xs:positiveInteger("-2")` is an error.

The `xs:integer`, `xs:decimal`, and `xs:double` types can be constructed more simply using literal constants: Any sequence of digits without a decimal point is an integer literal. With a decimal point, the number is a decimal literal unless the number is followed by an exponent using scientific E-notation, in which case the number is a double literal. This means that in XQuery, `xs:decimal` is the default type for numbers containing decimal points (unlike other languages, in which float or double is the default). Listing 2.4 illustrates the difference.

Listing 2.4 Numeric literals

```
12345       (: xs:integer("12345")  :)
12.345      (: xs:decimal("12.345")  :)
12.345E0    (: xs:double("12.345")  :)
```

You should exercise some care when converting numeric types to and from string or other types, because the supported formats for numbers may not be what you expect (see Appendix A for exact definitions). In particular, XQuery uses a different conversion process from the one used by the `printf()` function in C.

Technically, the `xs:double`, `xs:float` and `xs:decimal` types are all unrelated to one another (`xs:integer` derives from `xs:decimal`). However, many XQuery operations do convert across these types. The general rule is that `xs:decimal` may be converted to `xs:float` or `xs:double`, and `xs:float` may be promoted to `xs:double`. See Section 2.6.5 for more information.

2.4.4 String Types

As with the numeric types, XQuery defines a large number of string types (13 in all—see Figure 2.2). However, you really only need the `xs:string` type, which represents any string value. String values can be constructed by single- or double-quoted strings and are also returned by most XQuery string functions. The `xs:string` type is used to represent a (possibly empty) sequence of Unicode code points (see Chapter 8).

The other string types all derive from `xs:string`. All of these types can be constructed using the type constructor syntax, such as `xs:ID("x")` or `xs:language("en-us")`, except for the three special types `xs:NMTOKENS`, `xs:IDREFS`, and `xs:ENTITIES` (greyed out in Figure 2.2). These three types are odd because in XML Schema they derive by list from `xs:string`, but XQuery already has types for lists of values. Consequently, XQuery uses the sequence type `xs:NMTOKEN*` instead of the schema type `xs:NMTOKENS`. However, these three types are still "built-in" to XQuery, for example, for use with `validate`. See Chapter 9 and Appendix A for more details.

XQuery places no limit on the maximum length of a string; however, most implementations impose practical limits of anywhere between 2^{16} bytes (64KB) and 2^{32} bytes (4GB). Note that implementations usually store strings internally in the UTF-16 encoding, so most characters occupy two bytes in memory and some require up to four. So-called surrogate pairs (two special characters in a row, used to represent code points that don't fit in two bytes) are treated as a single character by most string functions (e.g., string-length), so you won't ever notice the underlying implementation.

2.4.5 Calendar Types

XQuery defines five calendar types of interest: `xs:date`, `xs:time`, `xs:dateTime`, `xdt:dayTimeDuration`, `xdt:yearMonthDuration`. XQuery also defines

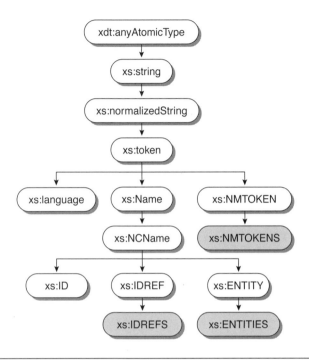

Figure 2.2 String type hierarchy

another type, xs:duration, and five Gregorian calendar types (with names like xs:gDay) that you are unlikely to use. For details on the xs:duration and Gregorian types, see Appendix A.

The xs:date, xs:time, and xs:dateTime types represent a single point in time. The xdt:dayTimeDuration and xdt:yearMonthDuration represent time spans. All of these types are constructed using the type constructor syntax and a string representation of the value.

Programming with calendar types is notoriously difficult for a variety of reasons. The types are complex and they must satisfy somewhat arbitrary conditions. Some applications must also account for irregularities in the value space, such as leap years to historical changes, and in some cases legislated requirements.

The XQuery syntax for dates and times is derived from the ISO 8601 standard. XQuery accepts values of the form ...YYYY-MM-DDThh:mm:ss.sssssss...Z where the letters Y, M, D, h, m, and s are replaced by digits for years, months, days, hours, minutes, and seconds, respectively. Hyphens are used to separate the date parts (years, months, days), colons are used to separate the time parts (hours,

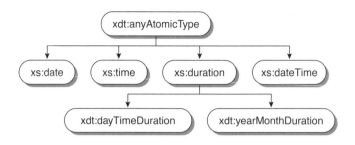

Figure 2.3 Calendar type hierarchy

minutes, seconds), and the letter T stands between the two. The seconds part can be fractional. The letter Z stands for an optional time zone designator. We explain each part next.

Also, XQuery defines functions for accessing each of these components, with names like `get-hours-from-dateTime()` and `get-year-from-date()`. See Appendix C for examples. These accessors may be simplified before XQuery is finalized.

Values of type `xs:date` have only the part before the T; `xs:time` values have only the part after the T; `xs:dateTime` values have both parts, including the T (see Listing 2.5).

Listing 2.5 Date and time values

```
xs:date("2004-02-08")                (: February 8, 2004 :)
xs:time("12:00:00")                  (: noon :)
xs:time("00:00:00")                  (: midnight :)
xs:datetime("2004-02-08T00:00:00")   (: midnight Feb 8, 2004 :)
```

The year must always contain at least four digits (which is also the maximum number of digits that implementations are required to support) and may be preceded by an optional + or - sign (+ is the default). Leading zeros must be used if the year would have fewer than four digits; otherwise, leading zeros are not allowed. The year 0000 is also not allowed, but otherwise every year between -9999 and 9999 inclusive is supported, and some implementations may support years beyond this range.

The month must be a value between 01 and 12 inclusive. The day must be a value between 01 and 31 inclusive, and must be valid for the given month. For example, 28 is the maximum day value allowed for month 2 (February) in non-leap years. Both day and month must have exactly two digits.

The hour must be a value between 00 and 23 inclusive; the minutes must be a value between 00 and 59 inclusive; and the seconds must be a value between 00 and 60 inclusive. All three parts must have exactly two digits, using leading zeros if necessary. The fractional seconds part is optional. Implementations are required to support a minimum of up to at least seven digits after the decimal point (100 nanosecond resolution), although this requirement may be relaxed to only six digits (to match ANSI/SQL). Seconds with values greater than 60 but less than 61 are allowed, but only for leap-seconds.

For types that have a time component—`xs:time` and `xs:dateTime`—the time zone component may be empty or may have a value in hours and minutes. When parsing string values, the time zone designator can be omitted or can be the character z; in both cases, it signifies Coordinated Universal Time (UTC). It can also specify a time offset in the form `+hh:mm` or `-hh:mm`, where the hours and minutes must both be two-digit numbers satisfying the same constraints as before. Listing 2.6 shows values with and without time zones.

Listing 2.6 Time zones may be used with types that have a time component

```
(: February 8, 2004, 3:41 pm, Pacific Standard Time :)
xs:dateTime("2004-02-08T15:41:00-08:00")

(: the same time in UTC :)
xs:dateTime("2004-02-08T23:41:00")
```

Note that this definition differs slightly from that of XML Schema 1.0: When no time zone is specified, the XQuery constructors normalize the values to the time zone z and have an empty sequence time zone part.

Durations define time and/or date spans. They are designed to be added to existing date/time values to produce new date/time values. For example, today plus a one-day duration is tomorrow.

The `xs:duration` type is part of the XML Schema 1.0 standard. The other two duration types were added by XQuery to make up for a deficiency in the `xs:duration` type, namely that it is not totally ordered for use in comparisons. Just as `xs:date` and `xs:time` can be viewed as subsets of `xs:dateTime`, so `xs:yearMonthDuration` and `xs:dayTimeDuration` can be viewed as subsets of `xs:duration`, containing only the year/month or only the day/time parts of the duration, respectively.

The format for a duration is PnYnMnDTnHnMnS. Every duration begins with the letter P (for "period" of time). The remaining parts are optional, although at least one part must be present. Each part consists of an arbitrary non-negative number (n) followed by a capital letter designating which part it represents:

year, month, day, hour, minute, or second, respectively. The entire duration may be negated by using a leading minus sign (leading plus is not allowed).

As before, the T separates the date and time parts of the duration. For durations, T is also used to disambiguate the M used for months from the M used for minutes. P1M designates one month, while PT1M designates one minute (and P1MT1M means one month and one minute). The T must be omitted in xdt:yearMonthDuration values, and also in xdt:dayTimeDuration values when there is no time component.

Unlike the numbers used in date/time values, the numbers in durations are not constrained to fit within any given range, and leading zeros are allowed. For all parts other than seconds, the number must be an integer; the seconds value can be any non-negative decimal number. Consequently, there are many different ways to represent the same duration, (e.g., P1Y is the same as P12M). Listing 2.7 shows two different durations.

Listing 2.7   Duration values

```
(: one year and ten months :)
xs:yearMonthDuration("P1Y10M")

(: two days and five minutes :)
xs:dayTimeDuration("P2DT5M")
```

2.4.6 Qualified Name Type

XQuery has one type for qualified names: xs:QName. This type is used to represent an XML name. Recall that XML names consist of two significant parts, the local name and namespace name. In some respects, xs:QName behaves like a structure containing this pair of values, and in other respects it behaves like an ordinary atomic value.

The xs:QName type is special in that it cannot be constructed using the type constructor syntax, but instead has its own special constructor function, expanded-QName(). This function takes two arguments, the namespace name and the local name, and constructs the corresponding xs:QName value. For example, expanded-QName("http://www.awprofessional.com/", "hello") constructs a QName with namespace part equal to http://www.awprofessional.com/ and local part equal to hello.

QName values can also be constructed using a prefix and local part by looking up the namespace in scope for that prefix. The function resolve-QName()

takes a qualified name string (with prefix) and an element to provide namespace scope, parses the string, looks up the namespace corresponding to that prefix, and returns the corresponding QName. If there isn't a prefix, then the default namespace is used. If there isn't a namespace in scope for a prefix, then an error is raised. For example, `resolve-QName("hello",  <x xmlns = "http://www.awprofesional.com/" />)` produces the same QName value as the previous example.

As with the calendar types, XQuery provides functions for accessing the individual parts of an `xs:QName` value: `get-local-name-from-QName()` and `get-namespace-from-QName()`. Each of these takes a QName value and returns an `xs:string` with the corresponding part of the QName value. These accessors are demonstrated in Listing 2.8.

Listing 2.8 QName accessors

```
get-local-name-from-QName(expanded-QName("", "x"))
=> "x"

get-namespace-uri-from-QName(expanded-QName("urn:foo", "x"))
=> "urn:foo"
```

2.4.7 Other Types

XQuery defines four other types not already mentioned in this chapter: `xs:anyURI`, `xs:NOTATION`, and the binary types `xs:base64Binary` and `xs:hexBinary`, all of which are from XML Schema 1.0. It is unlikely you will ever use these types, but if you do, see Appendix A for information.

XQuery also supports user-defined types (see Chapter 9). Any user-defined type can be named in an XQuery—for example, for use with the `validate` operator—but only types that *derive by restriction* can be constructed as values. Types that *derive by union* or *derive by list* such as `xs:IDREFS`, `xs:ENTITIES`, and `xs:NMTOKENS` cannot be constructed as values in a query.

2.5 Node Kinds

XQuery, like XPath, has seven node kinds. These have the type names `attribute()`, `comment()`, `document-node()`, `element()`, `namespace()`, `processing-instruction()`, and `text()`.

Table 2.1 Node properties

Property	Type	XQuery Accessor
attributes	attribute()*	attribute::*
base-uri	xs:anyURI?	fn:base-uri()
children	(element() | text() | comment() | processing-instruction())*	child::node()
identity	n/a	n/a
namespaces	namespace()*	fn:get-in-scope-prefixes()
nilled	xs:boolean?	n/a
node-kind	xs:string	fn:node-kind()
node-name	xs:QName?	fn:node-name()
order	n/a	n/a
parent	(element() | document-node())?	parent::node()
string-value	xs:string	fn:string()
type	xs:QName	n/a
typed-value	xs:anyAtomicType?	fn:data()
unique-id	xs:ID?	fn:unique-id()

Like atomic values, nodes can be obtained in a couple of different ways: by selecting them from existing XML documents (typed or untyped), or by using XQuery construction expressions (see Chapter 7) to create them in the query.

Nodes have several properties observable either directly or indirectly (see Table 2.1). Some properties apply only to certain kinds of nodes; in such cases, the value for other node kinds is the empty sequence. These properties are described in the following sections.

2.5.1 Kind, Identity, and Order

Nodes in the XQuery Data Model have three fundamental properties: node kind, node identity, and order. Every node has these properties.

The *node kind* of a node is its XML node kind (such as "element" or "comment"). XQuery has navigation operators that can select nodes by node kind (see Chapter 3) and type expressions such as `typeswitch` that can be used with them to compute the node kind as a string value (see Chapter 9).

Each node has a unique *node identity*. This identity is not a value, although XQuery provides comparison operators to determine whether two nodes have the same identity or not (see Chapter 5). Node identity should not be confused with similarly named but completely unrelated concepts such as the `xs:ID` type and the `unique-id` node property.

All nodes, even those from different documents, are ordered relative to each other. Like node identity, this ordering isn't directly observable as a value, although XQuery provides several operators that can be used to determine whether one node is ordered before or after another (again, see Chapter 5). This is an absolute ordering that doesn't depend on the current expression, and it shouldn't be confused with the relative position of a node in a sequence.

The node ordering is often called *document order*, because it corresponds to the order of appearance of these nodes in the XML serialization of a document—that is, a pre-order, left depth-first traversal of the tree. However, this nomenclature is misleading because even nodes from different documents are ordered relative to one another; in this case, the ordering can vary from one execution of a query to the next, although it is required to be stable during the execution of a single query.

2.5.2 Hierarchy

When we think of nodes, probably the first aspect that comes to mind is their hierarchical nature. In the XQuery Data Model, every node belongs to exactly one *tree*, and every tree has exactly one *root* node (trees are never empty). When the root node kind is document, the tree is called a *document*; otherwise, it is called a *fragment*. Some node properties relate to the structure of this tree; other properties (such as `unique-id`) may be scoped to a tree.

Navigation through this hierarchy is supported through a variety of operators (see Chapter 3), but in the XQuery Data Model it is quite simple: Every node has four properties related to hierarchy—parent, children, attributes, and namespaces.

The *parent* of a node is either the unique document or element node that contains it, or else the empty sequence (for the root node, which has no parent). The *children* of a node are the nodes it contains, and are always text, processing-instruction, comment, or element node kinds. The *attributes* and *namespaces* of a node are its sequences of attribute and namespace nodes, respectively, and may be empty. A node is the parent of its children, attributes, and namespaces.

Only the element and document node kinds may have children, and only the element node kind may have attributes and namespaces; for all other node kinds, these properties are always empty. The document node always has at least one child. The element node may have any number of children (including none), and also any number of attributes and any number of namespaces.

2.5.3 Node Name

Element and attribute nodes have a *node name* property that is the qualified name of the node; for all other node kinds this property is the empty sequence. The name property is accessible in an XQuery using the `node-name()` function, which takes a single node argument and returns the `xs:QName` value that is its name (or else the empty sequence, for node kinds that have no name). Remember that qualified names consist of the namespace and local parts only; the prefix matters only in the serialization format and isn't part of the data model.

For backwards compatibility with XPath 1.0, XQuery also supports three other functions for retrieving the name, or parts of the name, of a node: `name()`, `local-name()`, and `namespace-uri()`. All three functions take an optional node argument and return a string value. If no node is specified, then the current context item (see Chapter 3) is used as the argument.

The `local-name()` and `namespace-uri()` functions return the local and namespace parts of the node name, respectively. If the name doesn't have one of those parts, or if the node has no name, then the empty string is returned.

The `name()` function is somewhat unusual. It returns the unparsed name string, consisting of the prefix, if any, and the local part of the name. Implementations are allowed to preserve the original prefix used, or use any prefix in scope that is bound to the namespace of the node, or else generate a new prefix distinct from all prefixes in scope. If the node has no name, then `name()` returns the empty string.

Listing 2.9 shows the effect of these functions on an element node.

Listing 2.9 Accessing parts of the node name

```
node-name(<p:x xmlns="urn:foo"/>)
=>
xs:QName("urn:foo", "x")

local-name(<p:x xmlns="urn:foo"/>)
=>
"x"
```

```
namespace-uri(<p:x xmlns="urn:foo"/>)
=>
"urn:foo"


name(<p:x xmlns="urn:foo"/>)
=>
"p:x" (: some implementations do not preserve the prefix :)
```

2.5.4 Node Type and Values

Element and attribute nodes also have a *type* (for all other node kinds, the type property returns the empty sequence). Even if the XML data is untyped, the XQuery Data Model assigns a special type, `xdt:untypedAtomic`, to the node. Otherwise, the type of the node is its XML Schema type.

The XQuery Data Model treats each node type as a qualified name (`xs:QName`). Although this type name isn't directly accessible in an XML query, many operators, such as `typeswitch`, can use the type name of a node (see Chapter 9).

The *typed-value* and *string-value* of a node are used by many XQuery expressions, and consequently have functions dedicated to them: `fn:data()` and `fn:string()`, respectively. Both of these functions can be applied to a node, in which case they return its typed value or string value accordingly.

Actually, `fn:data()` takes any sequence of items and returns a sequence of atomic values. Items that are already atomic values are returned unchanged; items that are nodes are replaced by their typed values. For example, an element typed as `xs:integer` with the content `42` has as its `typed-value` the integer 42 (see Listing 2.10). Only simple-typed elements and attributes can have a typed value; for all other node kinds, and for complex-typed elements, the typed value is empty.

Listing 2.10 Accessing the typed value of a node

```
data(<y xsi:type="xs:integer">042</y>)
=>
42
```

The `string-value` of a node is always a single string, which is the string representation of the node. This string may differ from the original representation of the node. For example, the `string-value` of a node with complex content is the concatenation of the string values of all its descendants (see Listing 2.11).

Listing 2.11 Accessing the string value of a node

```
string(<y>a<x>b</x><x>c</x>d</y>)
=>
"abcd"
```

Additionally, the XQuery Data Model keeps track of whether an element is *nilled*. Nillable elements are typed elements that allow their content to be empty. For example, an integer normally must contain some digits; a nillable integer allows no digits to occur (in which case the typed value is the empty sequence). The `nilled` property is true for an element node if it is nillable and its typed-value is empty; otherwise, `nilled` is false. This property is not directly accessible in an XQuery, although there are several expressions that can indirectly test whether an element is nil, such as the path `self::*[@xsi:nil="true"]` or the type test `instance of element(*, * nilled)`. See Chapter 9 for additional information about nil elements.

2.5.5 Other Node Properties

Document, element, and processing-instruction nodes also have a *base-uri* property, which can be accessed using the `base-uri()` function. This function takes a single node argument and returns an `xs:anyURI` value or the empty sequence. For other node kinds, `base-uri()` returns the base-uri of the parent node, or the empty sequence if there is none.

Some elements may have an attribute that is typed as `xs:ID` (using a schema or DTD). There can be only one such attribute on an element. Every ID within a tree must be unique, and satisfy the lexical constraints of the `xs:ID` type (see Appendix A). The unique ID of an element can be retrieved using the `unique-id()` function.

2.6 Common Type Conversions

Now that you understand the core features of the XQuery Data Model and type system, you're ready to learn about three related operations that are applied by many XQuery expressions: atomization, Effective Boolean Value, and sequence type matching.

2.6.1 Atomization

Atomization is the process of turning a sequence of items into a sequence of atomic values. Atomization is applied by many expressions that work only on atomic values (for example, arithmetic operators).

Atomization takes a sequence of items and returns atomic values in it unchanged, but replaces nodes by their typed values. The typed value of a single node can itself be a sequence of atomic values; for example, a node typed as xs:IDREFS by an XML Schema atomizes to a sequence of xs:IDREF values.

An expression can be atomized explicitly by applying the data() function as shown in Listing 2.12; however, many operators also atomize their operands implicitly (see Chapter 5).

Listing 2.12 Atomization

```
data((1, 2, <x>3 4</x>) (: assume x has type xs:integer* :)
=>
(1, 2, 3, 4)
```

2.6.2 Effective Boolean Value

The *Effective Boolean Value* (EBV) is the process of converting a sequence of items into a logical value (true or false). The EBV can be computed explicitly by applying the boolean() function, and many operators, such as and and or, apply EBV implicitly to their operands (see Chapter 5).

The EBV of a sequence is false if the sequence is empty, true if the sequence contains more than one item, and otherwise depends on the single item. The EBV of a singleton boolean value is that value unchanged. The EBV of a string is false if the string is empty, and true otherwise. The EBV of a number is false if the number is zero or NaN, and true otherwise. For all other types (including nodes), the EBV is true. In other words, EBV essentially tests for existence, non-zero and non-NaN numbers, and non-empty strings.

Don't confuse EBV with a cast to xs:boolean type, which follows a different set of rules (see Chapter 9).

2.6.3 Sequence Type Matching

Section 2.3.1 introduced the sequence type syntax, which can be used to express the type of an expression. For example, `xs:integer*` means a sequence of zero or more integers, and `(element() | document-node())?` means zero or one document or element nodes.

Because XQuery is strongly-typed, meaning that every expression has a type and that types of values used together must be "compatible"— an integer cannot be added to a string, for example. As mentioned in Chapter 1, some implementations perform type checking statically, while others perform only dynamic type checking. Also, many XQuery operators (see Chapter 9) perform various kinds of type checking. The process of determining whether one type matches another is called *sequence type matching*.

Sequence type matching is a complex process, but central to the design of the XQuery language. Although this is explained completely here, you can safely skim the explanation below for now and return to it as necessary.

2.6.3.1 Type Matching Algorithm

If two sequence types are exactly equal, then of course they match. More commonly you find yourself wondering, for example, whether an `xs:integer` expression can be used in place of an `xs:decimal` one (or vice versa), or whether a sequence of elements can be used for a sequence of nodes (or vice versa).

The only expression that matches the `empty()` type is the empty sequence. Otherwise, the expression must match both the occurrence indicator and item type parts of the sequence type.

If there isn't an occurrence indicator, then the expression matches only if it is a singleton. If the occurrence indicator is +, then the expression matches only if it is non-empty. If the occurrence indicator is ?, then the expression matches only if it is empty or a singleton. Every expression matches the * occurrence indicator.

Independently, each item in a non-empty sequence must match the item type. The item type `item()` matches any item. An atomic type name matches that type and any type derived (by restriction) from that type. For example, the `xs:decimal` type matches an expression with type `xs:integer` (because `xs:integer` derives from `xs:decimal`); however, the `xs:integer` type does not match an expression with type `xs:decimal`.

The `node()` item type matches any node. The other node kind item types, such as `comment()` or `text()`, match only those node kinds. The `element()`, `document-node()`, `processing-instruction()`, and `attribute()` item kinds may take an optional argument. Without an argument, these match any node of that kind.

When the `processing-instruction()` type is used with an optional string argument, it matches only processing-instruction nodes whose name (aka `PITarget`) is that value. For example, `processing-instruction("X")` matches `<?X?>` but not `<?Y?>`, while `processing-instruction()` matches both.

When the `document-node()` type is used with an optional element test argument, it matches document nodes containing a single element matching that element test. For example, `document-node(element(X))` matches any document node containing a single element named X, while `document-node()` matches any document node at all.

Element and attribute sequence types are much more complicated. When used without arguments, or when used with wildcard arguments, they match any element or attribute at all. For example, `element()`, `element(*)`, and `element(*,*)` match all elements. Otherwise, these tests can specify a name and or a type, in which case they match only nodes with that name or type (or derived from that type by restriction). For example, `attribute(@foo)` matches attributes named `foo`, while `attribute(@foo, xs:integer)` matches any attribute named `foo` whose type is `xs:integer` (or a type derived from `xs:integer`). See Appendix A for additional examples.

2.6.4 Subtype Substitution

Most XQuery expressions, especially those that work with numbers, allow *subtype substitution*. Subtype substitution takes place whenever an expression requires some type T but will accept a value whose type is a subtype of T. For example, a function declared as taking an argument of type `xs:decimal` will accept a value of type `xs:integer` passed to it, because `xs:integer` is a subtype of `xs:decimal`. Subtype substitution does not change the value.

Subtype substitution is similar to subclassing in object-oriented languages. In such languages, a variable of type T may be assigned to an object that is a subclass of T. The type of the variable is still T, even though the type of its value is a subclass of T.

2.6.5 Numeric Type Promotion

Many XQuery numeric expressions, especially arithmetic operators and function invocations, apply numeric *type promotion*. Type promotion is a common feature of most languages, although in XQuery it behaves a little differently than usual.

The type `xs:float` can be promoted to `xs:double`. This type promotion may cause loss of precision but doesn't otherwise change the value.

The type `xs:decimal` can be promoted to both of the types `xs:float` and `xs:double`. The result is the floating-point value of that type that is closest to the original decimal value. This promotion can cause loss of precision and may alter the value significantly when the decimal value is much larger than the largest possible, or smaller than the smallest, floating-point value of that type.

The second of these allows `xs:integer`—and other subtypes of `xs:decimal`—to be promoted to `xs:float` or `xs:double`, first by performing subtype substitution treating the `xs:integer` (or other subtype) as an `xs:decimal` value, and then applying the type promotion rule for `xs:decimal`.

2.7 Conclusion

In this chapter, we explored the XQuery Data Mode and type system. Every XQuery Data Model consists of a sequence of items. Items are nodes or atomic values.

There are seven kinds of nodes. Every node belongs to exactly one tree; every tree is a document or fragment (depending on whether the root node is a document node or not). Nodes have various properties, some of which are directly obtainable in a query, such as name and kind, and others that cannot be retrieved as values but do affect many query operations, such as identity and document order.

Atomic values are instances of atomic types (built-in or user-defined). They can be created within a query itself, or retrieved from typed XML nodes. Early XML query languages such as XSLT had too few types, a problem XQuery deftly avoids with its 50 atomic types. Of these, you'll certainly use at least eight: `xs:boolean`, `xs:string`, `xs:integer`, `xs:decimal`, `xs:double`, `xdt:anyAtomicType`, `xdt:untypedAtomic` and `xs:QName` and possibly another six: `xs:float`, `xs:date`, `xs:time`, `xs:dateTime`, `xdt:yearMonthDuration`, and `xdt:dayTimeDuration`. If you ever need any of the rest, Appendix A awaits you.

XQuery provides a convenient atomic value constructor syntax, `typename ("value")`, that can be used to construct any atomic type, even user-defined ones, except for those types, like `xs:IDREFS`, that are derived by list or union. XQuery also provides a convenient node constructor syntax, already mentioned in Chapter 1 and described in greater detail in Chapter 7.

Many XQuery operations implicitly promote or convert their arguments. Two common cases are atomization and Effective Boolean Value, which result in a sequence of atomic values or a boolean value, respectively.

And finally, XQuery uses a sequence type syntax to describe types of expressions. A process known as sequence type matching is applied to determine when an expression with one type may be used in a context expecting a different type.

2.8 Further Reading

An understanding of XML Schema is not necessary to use XQuery, but will certainly be helpful in understanding some of the deeper complexities of the XQuery type system. The book *Definitive XML Schema* by Priscilla Walmsley is a great practical introduction to XML Schema.

W3C references for the many other data models briefly mentioned in this chapter can be found in the Bibliography. A deep look at the design influences and rationale of XQuery and its data model and type system can be found in Chapter 1 of the book *XQuery from the Experts: A Guide to the W3C XML Query Language* by Howard Katz. The book *Data on the Web: From Relations to Semistructured Data and XML* by Serge Abiteboul, Dan Suciu, and Peter Buneman explores some of the connections between the document and database models, from a more academic perspective.

CHAPTER 3

Navigation

3.1 Introduction

Once you've constructed or loaded XML in a query, you need a way to *navigate* over that hierarchical data. In many ways, construction and navigation are the primary operations in any XML query language. XQuery provides a litany of navigation expressions, and this chapter explores them all. Readers who are already familiar with XPath 1.0 may safely skim this chapter. XQuery has some differences from XPath 1.0, but they are minor.

Navigation involves starting from one part of an XML data model and moving to another part of the data model. Navigation can involve local steps, for example, moving from a node to one of its neighbors, or global steps, such as moving from a node to a completely different part of the data model, or even another document.

 If you're familiar with relational databases, it may help to reflect that navigating is to XML nodes what cursoring is to relational rowsets. Like using regular expressions to parse strings, using navigation in a query is generally more efficient in space and time than manually traversing an XML structure.

3.2 Paths

Navigation involves starting from one part of an XML document and moving to another part of the document (or a different document). XQuery performs navigation using *paths*. Paths were invented in 1970 for use with the PDP-11 file system. The path concept has been so generally useful that it has found broad application in a variety of systems, including XML query processing.

In XQuery, every path consists of a sequence of *steps* which, conceptually at least, are executed in order from left to right. A step consists of three parts, illustrated in Figure 3.1:

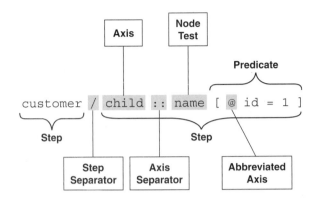

Figure 3.1 Anatomy of a path

- A direction of travel, called the *axis*
- A description of the nodes to select upon arrival, called the *node test*
- Zero or more filters to further narrow that selection (each filter is called a *predicate*)

By allowing some of these parts to be abbreviated or omitted entirely, XQuery keeps paths very concise. Each of these parts is described next, and then Section 3.5 has many examples demonstrating how to use paths to accomplish common tasks.

Each step affects the *evaluation context* for the next step. This context and how it changes with each step are described in Section 3.4, but for now it's enough to know that there is a *current context item* that affects—and is affected by—each step in the path. Except for predicates, navigation steps can be applied only when the current context item is a node (in which case it is often called the *current context node*).

3.2.1 Beginnings

Every path starts somewhere. For the purpose of XQuery navigation, there are effectively three places from which a path can begin:

- The current context node
- The root of the tree in which the current context node resides
- Any other node set, such as a variable or an XML constructor

With each successive step, the path may move to other nodes or alter the context.

The root of the tree in which the current context node resides is selected by a lone forward slash (/) or equivalently using the built-in `root()` function. Paths beginning from the root are *absolute*. In contrast, paths starting from the current context node are *relative*. Paths may also start from certain other expressions, such as variables, function calls, or parenthesized expressions (XQuery does not give a name to such paths).

From these humble beginnings, paths may navigate anywhere in the document, or even to other documents, step by step. Listing 3.1 shows a few paths. In a path, individual steps are almost always separated by one forward slash (/). (The exception, two forward slashes (//), is described in Section 3.2.4.)

Listing 3.1 Absolute, relative, and other paths

```
/AbsolutePath/First/Second
RelativePath[. = "fun"]
$other//x
id("other")[@y > 1]/z
```

Paths with more than one step always result in a (possibly empty) sequence of nodes, sorted in document order. To sort nodes in some other order, you must use a FLWOR expression (see Chapter 6).

3.2.2 Axes

Each step consists of three parts: the axis (optional), the node test, and zero or more predicates. XPath defines a total of thirteen axes, and all but the `namespace` axis appear in XQuery. Of these, the four simplest and most commonly used ones are `child`, `attribute`, `parent`, and `self` (see Table 3.1). The other axes are explained in Section 3.2.4.

Table 3.1 The four basic axes and their abbreviations

Axis name	Abbreviation	Equivalent examples	
attribute	@	x/attribute::y	x/@y
child		x/child::y	x/y
parent	..	x/parent::node()	x/..
self	.	x/self::node()	x/.

The child axis is so common that it is the default axis if no axis name is specified explicitly. The other three common axes all have shorthand abbreviations for convenience. XPath gets much of its succinctness from these shorthand forms. When the non-abbreviated name is used, it is followed by two colons (`::`) to distinguish axis names from XML qualified names (which contain at most one colon).

These four axes behave exactly as their names suggest:

- The `child` axis navigates into the children of the current context node.
- The `attribute` axis navigates into the attributes of the current context node.
- The `self` axis essentially goes nowhere (navigating into the current context node itself).
- The `parent` axis navigates to the parent of the current context node.

For example, x, which is short for `child::x`, selects the child elements named x from the current context node, while x/y, which is short for `child::x/child::y`, first selects the child elements named x from the current context node just like the previous example, and then from those selects the child elements named y.

3.2.3 Node Tests

Following the axis is the second part of the step, the *node test*. Node tests come in three varieties: names (qualified or unqualified), node kinds, and wildcards.

3.2.3.1 Name Tests

By far the most common node test is the *name test*. A name test selects only those nodes with the same name. Names in XQuery, as in XML, are case-sensitive. For example, the absolute path /x/y/@z starts at the root of the current document, navigates to the top-level elements named x, navigates to their child elements named y, and finally navigates to their attribute nodes named z. If you were to execute this XQuery over the XML document in Listing 3.2, it would select the two attributes named z and no other nodes.

Name tests can also select names that are in an XML namespace. However, this process is fairly complicated, so this description is deferred until Section 3.6.1.

Listing 3.2 A sample XML document

```
<x thisAttribute="isNotSelected">
  <y z="1"/>
  <y z="2" thisAttribute="alsoIsNotSelected" </y>
</x>
```

3.2.3.2 Node Kind Tests

Name tests are not the only node tests available in navigation steps. In fact, some kinds of XML nodes (for example, text, comment, and document nodes) have no names at all. To select nodes by kind, XQuery uses the same *node kind tests* used by sequence type matching (described in Chapter 2). Listing 3.3 shows two node kind tests.

Listing 3.3 Examples of node kind tests

```
x/comment()              (: select all comment children of x :)
x/attribute()            (: select all attributes of x :)
attribute(@*, xs:integer) (: select all integer attributes :)
attribute(y)             (: select all attributes named y :)
attribute(y, xs:integer) (: select integer attributes named y :)
```

Recall from Chapter 2 that the `node()` node test matches any kind of node, including the document node. The `text()` and `comment()` node kind tests match text nodes and comment nodes, respectively. The `processing-instruction()` node test accepts an optional name argument. When no name is specified, it matches all processing instruction nodes; otherwise, it matches only those with the same name.

The `document-node()` test matches the invisible document node that occurs at the root of any tree loaded from an XML document using `doc()` (or constructed using the document constructor—see Chapter 7). It accepts an optional argument specifying an element node kind test, in which case it matches the document node only if its element content matches that element test.

And finally, the `element()` and `attribute()` node kind tests accept optional name and type arguments. Without these extra arguments, they match all elements and attributes, respectively; with these arguments, they match only elements or attributes that have the specified name and/or type. The name or type can also be *, in which case it matches all names or all types, respectively. The name specified in an `attribute()` test must start with an `@` symbol to emphasize that it matches attributes.

3.2.3.3 Wildcards

Sometimes you want to select all nodes whose name is in a particular namespace, or conversely all nodes with the same local name regardless of the namespace. There are two equivalent ways to accomplish this goal. One is to use predicates; in fact, as you will see later, predicates can be used to perform all kinds of tests.

A more succinct way is to use the third kind of node test, the *wildcard*. Wildcard node tests combine aspects of both name and node kind tests; the names matched depend on the wildcard, and the node kind matched depends on the axis. The attribute axis by default selects attribute nodes; all other XQuery axes select elements by default. The default node kind is called the *principal node kind* for the axis.

XQuery supports three wildcard node tests. Two of these come from XPath 1.0: the star (`*`), which matches any name at all, and a qualified star (`prefix:*`) that matches all names in the namespace to which the prefix is bound. XQuery adds a third wildcard node test, `*:local-name`, which matches all names with the given local name and any namespace.

The only difference between the star wildcard `*` and the `node()` node kind test is that `node()` matches every kind of node with any name, while `*` matches only nodes of the principal node kind (with any name).

3.2.4 Other Axes

XQuery supports two more axes from XPath 1.0, called `descendant` and `descendant-or-self`. The `descendant` axis matches all descendants of the current context node. (It is the closure of the child axis under fixed-point recursion.) The `descendant-or-self` axis includes the current context node as well, and so is equivalent to the union of the descendant and self axes.

The `descendant-or-self` axis is so commonly used that it has its own abbreviation, `//`. Some caution should be observed when using it; it's easy to make mistakes when using predicates with `//` (see Chapter 11 for examples).

Additionally, implementations are allowed but not required to support the other six axes from XPath: `ancestor`, `ancestor-or-self`, `following`, `following-sibling`, `preceding`, and `preceding-sibling`. The first two of these are the inverses of `descendant` and `descendant-or-self` axes. They select all the ancestors of the current node (`ancestor-or-self` includes the node itself).

The `following` and `preceding` axes select all the nodes in the same document as the current context node that occur before and after it, respectively. There's really no reason to use them in XQuery, because the `>>` and `<<` node comparison operators allow you to write the same meaning more compactly (see Chapter 5).

Finally, the `following-sibling` and `preceding-sibling` axes restrict their selections to the siblings of the current context node (that is, those nodes having the same parent as it).

3.2.5 Predicates

The third and final part of each navigation step consists of zero or more *predicates*. Like the node test, each predicate acts as a filter on the selected nodes, eliminating some from consideration and keeping the rest. For each node selected by the current step, the current context item is set to that node and then the predicate condition is evaluated with that context.

Any XQuery expression may be used inside a predicate; the meaning of the predicate depends on the type of the expression it contains. There are two cases: numeric and boolean predicates.

3.2.5.1 Numeric Predicates

Numeric predicates select nodes by their position in the current context. For example, `/x/y[1]` selects the first `y` child element of each `x` element. As this example demonstrates, predicates bind tightly to the current step. To apply a predicate to the entire results of a path, you must use parentheses. For example, `(/x/y)[1]` selects the first `y` element out of all the nodes selected by `/x/y`.

Because paths can start with other kinds of expressions, such as parenthesized expressions, predicates can be applied to more than just sequences of nodes. For example, the expression `("a", "b", "c")[2]` selects the second item in the sequence, the string `"b"`.

Numeric predicates, like the ones in Listing 3.4, filter by position. In general, when a predicate evaluates to a number N, it's as if the predicate were actually the boolean-valued predicate `position()=N`. For example, the path `/x[1]` is equivalent to the path `/x[position() = 1]`. This expansion applies not only to numeric constants, but also to any numeric-typed expression. For example, the path `/x[@y + 1]` is equivalent to the path `/x[position() = @y + 1]`.

Listing 3.4 Numeric predicates filter by position

```
(//Customer)[2]
Fruit[@index + 1]
```

The position is 1-based (the first item in the sequence is at position 1). When the predicate evaluates to a non-integral value, a value less than 1, or a value greater than the length of the sequence, then the predicate will be false for all items in the sequence and the result will be the empty sequence. In other words, it isn't an error to select an index that is out of bounds for the sequence.

3.2.5.2 Boolean Predicates

All other kinds of predicate expressions, such as the ones in Listing 3.5, filter a sequence so that only those items for which the predicate evaluates to true are kept. The predicate is converted to a boolean value by computing the Effective Boolean Value of the expression.

Listing 3.5 All other predicates filter as boolean conditions

```
/x[@a=1 and @b=1]
/x[@a=1]/y[@b < 2]
```

As described in Section 2.6.2, the Effective Boolean Value acts as an existence test on sequences. Consequently, when the predicate is itself a path, the predicate evaluates to true if and only if the node(s) selected by that path exist. For example, `x[y]` matches all `x` elements that have a `y` child element, and `x[not(@y)]` matches all `x` elements that don't have a `y` attribute.

3.2.5.3 Successive and Nested Predicates

Several predicates can be applied to a step, with the effect that each predicate is evaluated with respect to the nodes remaining after the previous predicate.

The order of evaluation of the predicates is always left to right, which matters only when computing positional predicates. For example, the path x[1][@y=2] selects the first x element (if there is one), and then only if that element has a y attribute whose value is 2; while the path x[@y=2][1] selects all x elements that have a y attribute whose value is 2, and then from that set selects the first one. Over the XML <x y="3"/><x y="2"/> the first path selects nothing (because the first x element has y="3"), while the second path selects the second element.

Predicates can also be nested. For example, the path x[y[@z=1] = 2] selects all x elements where there exists a y element with a z attribute equal to 1 and the value of the y element itself equals 2.

3.3 Navigation Functions

All of the navigation we've considered so far amounts to local steps: from the current context, navigate to some nearby nodes. However, XQuery also defines functions that can navigate more globally to other parts of a document or different documents. These functions are summarized in Table 3.2, and fully documented in Appendix C.

Of these, the doc() function is the only one you are likely to commonly use. It takes a single string argument, which is treated as the URI location of an XML document. It then loads that document and returns the correspon-

Table 3.2 Navigation functions

Function	Meaning	XPath 1.0?
collection()	A named sequence	No
doc()	Navigate to the root of the named XML document	No
id()	Navigate to the (unique) element with this ID	Yes
idref()	Navigate to the elements that refer to this one	No
root()	Navigate to the root of the current document	No

ding XQuery Data Model instance. Certain aspects of this process, such as security permissions and schema validation, vary from one implementation to the next.

If the document cannot be found or is not well-formed, some implementations will raise an error, although they are also allowed to just return the empty sequence. (This is mainly to allow certain XQuery optimizations; for example, `doc("x")[false()]` could be optimized into the empty sequence without attempting to load the document.)

The other functions are much less commonly used, so we defer their description to Appendix C.

3.4 Navigation Context

Every XQuery expression is evaluated within a *context*, and several of the context effects have a bearing on navigation. The context can vary during the evaluation of a path, and some context information can be accessed using functions or other expressions. XPath 1.0 defines six expression context information items, and XQuery adds nine more, all listed in Table 3.3.

Expression context is divided into *static context*, which is available during the compilation of the query, and *evaluation context*, which is available while the expression is being evaluated dynamically. Some context information is global to an entire query, while other context information is local and may vary during compilation or evaluation.

3.4.1 Input Sequence

One value in the evaluation context is the *input sequence*. This sequence can be accessed using the `input()` function, and doesn't change during the execution of a query. This value defines the initial context sequence (for example, used by relative paths at the top of the query) and may be empty.

3.4.2 Focus

Part of the XQuery evaluation context is called the *focus*. Predicates and navigation steps change the focus. This focus consists of three items: the *context item*, the *context position*, and the *context size*.

Table 3.3 XQuery expression context

Context item	Accessed with	Static or dynamic	XPath 1.0?
in-scope namespaces	`get--in-scope-prefixes()`	static	Yes
default element namespace	N/A	static	No
default function namespace	N/A	static	No
in-scope schema definitions	N/A	static	No
in-scope functions	N/A	static	Yes
in-scope collations	N/A	static	No
default collation	`default-collation()`	static	No
base-uri	`base-uri()`	static	No
in-scope variables	`$variable`	both	Yes
context item	`.`	dynamic	Yes
context position	`position()`	dynamic	Yes
context size	`last()`	dynamic	Yes

current date and time	`current-date()`
	`current-time()`
	`current-dateTime()`
		dynamic	No

implicit timezone	`implicit-timezone()`	dynamic	No
input sequence	N/A	dynamic	No

When evaluating a path, the focus changes with each step and predicate. For example, when evaluating the path `x[@y=1]/z`, the step `x` selects a sequence of nodes, which defines the focus for the predicate. The context size is the number of nodes selected by `x`, and then for each node in that sequence, the predicate is evaluated. The node becomes the current context item, and the context position is its position within that sequence. If the predicate evaluates to true, then the node is kept in the result, otherwise it is omitted. The result of this step becomes the focus for the next step z.

The current context item can be accessed using the dot (.) expression, and in fact x[@y=1] is short for x[./@y = 1]. Every relative path in a predicate begins at the current context item.

The current context position can be accessed using the function position(). For example, when evaluating the path x[position() > 3], the predicate eliminates the first three items in the sequence selected by x.

Finally, the context size can be accessed using the function last(). For example, the path x[last()] selects the last child element named x. The efficiency of the last() function depends on the implementation. In cases where you are streaming through an XML input, last() always requires at least a little buffering to evaluate, and can require a lot of buffering. For example, x[count(y) < last()] must first count the number of x child elements, and then iterate through each of them testing the condition. (Implementations that preload the XML into memory or a database are less affected by this consideration, because they may already have the sequence length available.)

3.4.3 Variable Declarations

XQuery can also declare and use *variables*. Certain expressions, such as FLWOR and typeswitch, introduce new variables into scope. Some implementations also allow externally defined variables to be passed to an XQuery. You'll see examples of both of these later.

There are two aspects to variable context. In the static context are all the *variable declarations*, that is, the names and static types of the variables that are available to the XQuery expression. The evaluation context also contains this information, along with the variable values (and their dynamic types), called the *variable bindings*.

Variables are accessed by name using an expression such as $variable. Attempting to use a variable that isn't in the static context (that is, not in scope) causes a compile-time error.

3.4.4 Namespace Declarations

The static context also includes *namespace declarations*, which may be defined in the query prolog or in element constructors. The namespace declarations are just a set of prefix and namespace pairs that allow prefixes to be used to stand in for the namespace names. XQuery allows for two different kinds of default namespaces, one for resolving element and type names, and the other for resolving function names (see Chapter 5 for additional details about the query prolog).

3.4.5 Function Declarations

The static context also includes all functions available to the query. These include the built-in XQuery functions, as well as user-defined functions (see Chapter 4) and possibly other extension functions provided by the implementation (see Chapter 14).

XSLT 1.0 provides a `function-available()` function for determining whether a function is in the static context, but XQuery doesn't have an equivalent.

3.4.6 Collations

Collations are used for string comparisons and sorting; the default collation and possibly other in-scope collations are part of the static context. See Chapter 8 for details.

3.5 Navigation Examples

To illustrate the navigation concepts introduced in this chapter, let's consider a variety of different navigation tasks over the sample XML document, `team.xml`, from Chapter 1. For convenience, it's repeated in Listing 3.6.

This document contains employee information from a fictitious organization. The data consists primarily of `Employee` elements, in which parent/child relationships in the XML correspond to manager/employee relationships in the organization. Just to spice things up a bit, the document also contains a few comments and processing instructions.

Listing 3.6 The team.xml document

```
<?xml version='1.0'?>
<Team name="Project 42" xmlns:a="urn:annotations">
  <Employee id="E6" years="4.3"> ◖
    <Name>Chaz Hoover</Name>
```

```
  <Title>Architect</Title>
  <Expertise>Puzzles</Expertise>
  <Expertise>Games</Expertise>
<Employee id="E2" years="6.1" a:assigned-to="Jade Studios">
  <Name>Carl Yates</Name>
  <Title>Dev Lead</Title>
  <Expertise>Video Games</Expertise>
  <Employee id="E4" years="1.2" a:assigned-to="PVR">
    <Name>Panda Serai</Name>
    <Title>Developer</Title>
    <Expertise>Hardware</Expertise>
    <Expertise>Entertainment</Expertise>
  </Employee>
  <Employee id="E5" years="0.6">
    <?Follow-up?>
    <Name>Jason Abedora</Name>
    <Title>Developer</Title>
    <Expertise>Puzzles</Expertise>
  </Employee>
</Employee>
<Employee id="E1" years="8.2">
  <!-- new hire 13 May -->
  <Name>Kandy Konrad</Name>
  <Title>QA Lead</Title>
  <Expertise>Movies</Expertise>
  <Expertise>Sports</Expertise>
  <Employee id="E0" years="8.5" a:status="on leave">
    <Name>Wanda Wilson</Name>
    <Title>QA Engineer</Title>
    <Expertise>Home Theater</Expertise>
    <Expertise>Board Games</Expertise>
    <Expertise>Puzzles</Expertise>
  </Employee>
</Employee>
<Employee id="E3" years="2.8">
  <Name>Jim Barry</Name>
  <Title>QA Engineer</Title>
  <Expertise>Video Games</Expertise>
</Employee>
</Employee>
</Team>
```

Each `Employee` has an `id` attribute that we will assume has been typed as `xs:ID` with a DTD or XML Schema so that it can be looked up by the `id()` lookup function. And finally, the `team.xml` document contains some "annotations" in another namespace (`"urn:annotations"`). These attributes describe additional information about the employees and are used here to demonstrate navigation using qualified names and the other wildcard node tests.

For the first example, the `team.xml` document is loaded using the `doc()` function. For the remaining examples, we will assume that this document is already the input sequence, so that all paths are resolved relative to it without loading it explicitly.

As our first task, consider finding the names of all employees. Because `Employee` elements occur at many different levels in the XML, use the descendant navigation shortcut `//` to match every `Employee` element descendant of the root document node. Finally, select their child elements named `Name`. The result is a list of the names of all employees in the document (returned in document order), as shown in Listing 3.7.

Listing 3.7 Find the names of all employees

```
doc("team.xml")//Employee/Name
=>
<Name>Chaz Hoover</Name>
<Name>Carl Yates</Name>
<Name>Panda Serai</Name>
<Name>Jason Abedora</Name>
<Name>Kandy Konrad</Name>
<Name>Wanda Wilson</Name>
<Name>Jim Barry</Name>
```

Suppose instead we want to select only some of the employees, subject to some condition as in Listing 3.8.

Listing 3.8 Name all employees who have been at the company less than two years

```
//Employee[@years < 2]/Name
=>
<Name>Panda Serai</Name>
<Name>Jason Abedora</Name>
```

This path is the same as the previous one, except that a predicate has been added to the `Employee` step. We want to filter the `Employee` elements so that we select only those whose `years` attribute has a value less than 2. So we use the attribute axis `@` and the less-than comparison operator `<` to compare the years attribute against 2. Then from these filtered employees, their names are selected as in the previous example.

We can also search for attributes in another namespace. For example, we could search for all employees currently assigned, as shown in Listing 3.9.

Listing 3.9 Find all employees currently assigned

```
declare namespace ann = "urn:annotations";
//Employee[@ann:assigned]/Name
=>
<Name>Carl Yates</Name>
<Name>Panda Serai</Name>
```

In this query, we have used the query prolog to declare a namespace prefix, and then used this prefix in the attribute name test `@ann:assigned` to match attributes with the local name equal to `assigned` and namespace equal to `urn:annotations`. Note that the prefix used in the query can be (and in this case is) different from the one used in the original document.

By putting the attribute test in the predicate with no comparison, we test for its existence. The predicate is converted using the Effective Boolean Value rule, which tests whether the sequence is non-empty. Consequently, this XPath finds all employees with an assignment, regardless of what that assignment actually is. Similarly, we could find all employees who lack an assignment by applying the `not()` function, as shown in Listing 3.10.

Listing 3.10 Find all unassigned employees

```
declare namespace ann = "urn:annotations";
//Employee[not(@ann:assigned)]/Name
=>
<Name>Chaz Hoover</Name>
<Name>Jason Abedora</Name>
<Name>Kandy Konrad</Name>
<Name>Wanda Wilson</Name>
<Name>Jim Barry</Name>
```

The query to find all employees with an expertise in puzzles is superficially similar to the previous query. The previous query needed to compare attribute values; this query (see Listing 3.11) needs to compare child element values.

Listing 3.11 Find all employees skilled in puzzles

```
//Employee[Expertise = "Puzzles"]/Name
=>
<Name>Chaz Hoover</Name>
<Name>Jason Abedora</Name>
<Name>Wanda Wilson</Name>
```

This case is made somewhat more difficult by the fact that employees may have more than one expertise. Consequently, we must test whether there exists any child expertise element with the desired value. Fortunately, the general comparison operators like < and = are defined so that they already do this existence test implicitly (see Chapter 5). Thus, the predicate `Expertise = "Puzzles"` tests whether there exists a child element named `Expertise` whose string value is `"Puzzles"`.

Navigation can also be used to compute other values. For example, Listing 3.12 counts the number of employees in one division.

Listing 3.12 Count the number of people in Chaz Hoover's organization

```
count(//Employee[Name="Chaz Hoover"]/descendant-or-self::Employee)
=>
7
```

The `count()` function computes the number of items in a sequence (see Chapter 5). First we must locate the employee named Chaz Hoover, which can be done using a query like the ones used previously. But then we must count all the employees contained in the sub-tree rooted at Chaz Hoover—in other words, all the descendant `Employee` elements. By using the `descendant-or-self` axis, we have included Chaz Hoover himself in this count. We could exclude him by instead using the `descendant` axis as in the path `count(//Employee[Name="Chaz Hoover"]/descendant::Employee)`.

Instead of counting the entire organization, we could instead count only those employee elements directly under Chaz Hoover, as shown in Listing 3.13.

Listing 3.13 Count the number of Chaz Hoover's direct reports

```
count(//Employee[Name="Chaz Hoover"]/Employee)
=>
3
```

Instead of performing a descendant query with `//`, we have used ordinary child navigation `/` to select only those employees who report directly to Chaz Hoover. This task could also be accomplished in another way, using the parent axis, as shown in Listing 3.14.

Listing 3.14 Use the parent axis to count Chaz Hoover's employees

```
count(//Employee[../Name="Chaz Hoover"])
=>
3
```

Here we first find every `Employee` in the document. Then, we check to see if the parent element has the name Chaz Hoover. We use the `..` abbreviation to navigate to the parent, and then compare its child `Name` element. This query is usually much slower than the previous one, although some implementations can optimize it so that both perform identically.

We can also find other kinds of elements in the tree. For example, we could extract all comment and processing-instruction nodes by using node kind tests, as illustrated in Listing 3.15.

Listing 3.15 Find all comments and processing instructions

```
//comment() | //processing-instruction()
=>
<?Follow up?>
<!-- new hire 13 May -->
```

In this query, we used the union operator `|` to combine the results of both paths. We could have also written `//(comment() | processing-instruction())` to achieve the same effect. (See Chapter 5 for more information about the union operator.)

Notice that the XML declaration `<?xml version='1.0'?>` at the top of the document did not match. Although it looks like a processing instruction, XML doesn't treat it as part of the data model, so XQuery doesn't either. Finally, Listing 3.16 demonstrates looking up elements by their IDs.

Listing 3.16 Find all employees with the same job function as employee E0

```
//Employee[Title = id("E0")/Title]/Name
=>
<Name>Wanda Wilson</Name>
<Name>Jim Barry</Name>
```

Because we wish to find all employee names satisfying some condition, we know that the path will consist of `//Employee/Name` and use a predicate to limit which employees are matched. This predicate should select all employees with the same title as that of employee `E0`. Employee `E0` can be found using the `id()` navigation function: `id("E0")`. Then all that remains is to compare the current employee's title against that of `E0`.

Notice that instead of using `id()`, we could use an absolute path inside the predicate to search from the root of the document to find the employee with id `E0`: `//Employee[Title = //Employee[@id="E0"]/Title]/Name`. This path has the advantage that it doesn't require a DTD or schema to type the `id` attribute. However, it is more complex to write and usually will perform worse than the `id` lookup (which most implementations optimize into an index or table lookup). This path essentially performs a join of the document with itself. Joins like this are often expressed using FLWOR expressions (described in Chapter 6).

3.6 Navigation Complexities

This section discusses the last remaining navigation topics. All of these were either too esoteric or too complex to merit including in the previous sections.

3.6.1 Namespaces

XPath 1.0 doesn't have a way to introduce namespace declarations and doesn't use the prefixes of the data it is navigating. Consequently, any namespace prefixes used in an XPath expression must be defined outside of it. In XQuery, namespaces can be declared in the query prolog (covered in Chapter 5), or using namespace declarations in XML elements (Chapter 7).

Table 3.4 Qualified names versus expanded names

	Prefix	Local	Namespace	Example
Qualified name	Yes	Yes	No	`foo:bar`
Expanded name	No	Yes	Yes	`{urn:baz}bar`

Recall that a *qualified name* consists of two parts, the *prefix* and the *local name*, separated by a colon (`:`). The prefix is bound to a namespace, but is otherwise unimportant for the purposes of navigation. Instead, it is better to think in terms of expanded names. An *expanded name* is the namespace and local name parts of a name (ignoring the prefix). Table 3.4 summarizes the differences between the two.

The second example in Table 3.4 is fabricated; XML and XQuery don't have a syntax for expanded names. Instead, they always associate the namespace with a prefix, and then use a qualified name.

In prose descriptions, expanded names are often written with the namespace part in curly braces (`{}`), like this: `{namespace}local-name`. When there isn't a namespace (because the name was unqualified or had an empty namespace), then the expanded name is written as just `{}local-name`. Again, this syntax isn't used in XML or XQuery, just in descriptions of how they work.

Listing 3.17 XML with namespaces

```
<root xmlns:x="uri1">
  <x:one fish="red"/>
  <two x:fish="blue" xmlns="uri2"/>
</root>
```

For example, in the XML shown in Listing 3.17, there are three elements with qualified names: `root`, `x:one`, and `two`. The expanded names of these elements are `{}root`, `{uri1}one`, and `{uri2}two`, respectively. There are two attributes with qualified names: `fish` and `x:fish`. The first of these has the expanded name `{}fish`, the second has the expanded name `{uri1}fish`.

Expanded names are more verbose than qualified names, which explains why qualified names are used instead. However, most operations—including validation and navigation—operate only on the namespace and local name parts of XML names, usually completely ignoring the prefixes that were used in the original XML serialization.

Suppose doc("sample.xml") accesses the XML shown in Listing 3.18.

Listing 3.18 sample.xml

```
<this xmlns="urn:default" xmlns:ns1="urn:one">
  <is a="complex">
    <ns1:example ns2:attr="42" xmlns:ns2="urn:two"/>
  </is>
</this>
```

Then you could navigate into it using the XQuery shown in Listing 3.19.

Listing 3.19 Path using namespaces

```
declare namespace x = "urn:default";
declare namespace y = "urn:one";
declare namespace z = "urn:two";
doc("sample.xml")/x:this/x:is/y:example/@z:attr
```

The query prolog introduces three namespace declarations, binding the prefixes x, y, and z to the namespaces urn:default, urn:namespace1, and urn:namespace2, respectively. The path then uses these namespaces to perform its qualified name tests: x:this, x:is, y:example, and z:attr. Again, notice that the prefixes in the document and the prefixes in the XQuery are completely unrelated to one another; all that matters are the local name and namespace parts of the names.

XQuery provides two functions that can access the namespaces in scope on a node. The get-in-scope-prefixes() function takes one argument, an element node, and returns a list of strings (in any order) that are the namespace prefixes in scope for that element. An empty string is listed for the default namespace declaration, if any.

The get-namespace-uri-for-prefix() function can look up the namespace value for a prefix. It takes two arguments, an element node and a string prefix, and returns the string that is the namespace bound to that prefix (use the empty string to look up the default namespace declaration). If there is no namespace bound to that prefix, then this function returns the empty sequence. Both effects are demonstrated by the examples in Listing 3.20.

Listing 3.20 Querying the namespaces in scope

```
declare namespace x = "urn:default";
get-in-scope-prefixes(doc("sample.xml")/x:this)
=>
("ns1", "")

declare namespace x = "urn:default";
get-namespace-uri-for-prefix(doc("sample.xml")/x:this, "ns1")
=>
"urn:one"
```

3.6.2 Node Identity

Navigation has some interesting interactions with node identity. When navigating over constructed XML, it's important to realize that the construction process copies nodes used as content, thereby "losing" their node identity.

For example, in the expression `<x>{doc("y.xml")//y}</x>`, the nodes selected by the path are copied into the x element. If you then navigate into that constructed XML, you get different nodes (by identity) than the originals, as demonstrated by Listing 3.21. (See Chapter 7 for more information).

Listing 3.21 Navigating over constructed XML

```
(<x>{doc("y.xml")//y}</x>)//y is doc("y.xml")//y   => false
```

The `doc()` function is special in that whenever the same string value is passed to it, the same node (by identity) is returned. This special behavior prevents you from writing a user-defined function that fully emulates `doc()` using construction, because every time your function is invoked it constructs a new node instance. The difference is demonstrated in Listing 3.22.

Listing 3.22 The `doc()` function can't be completely simulated by your own

```
declare namespace my = "http://www.awprofessional.com";
declare function my:doc($dummy as xs:string) as node() {
  document {
    element root { () }
  }
```

```
};

doc("a.xml") is doc("a.xml")        => true (if a.xml exists)
my:doc("a.xml") is my:doc("a.xml") => false
```

3.6.3 Other Context Information

In addition to the context items listed in Section 3.4, XQuery provides several other less commonly used values in the expression context.

The *base uri* property is part of the static context and is used by the `doc()` function when resolving relative URIs. This property can also be accessed using the `base-uri()` function.

The current *XML space* policy is part of the static context and can be changed by the query prolog. It determines how space characters are handled in XML constructors (see Chapter 7).

The static context may also provide schema definitions from imported schemas and a default validation mode and/or validation context. These determine what user-defined type names are available for use in type tests and other type operators. See Chapter 9 for examples.

Finally, the *current date/time* and the *implicit timezone* properties are part of the evaluation context. Despite their names, these don't really provide the current time, but just some point in time determined by the implementation. The value doesn't change during the execution of a query. These values can be accessed using the `current-date()`, `current-time()`, `current-dateTime()`, and `implicit-timezone()` functions (see Appendix C).

3.7 Conclusion

In this chapter, we investigated one of the primary features of XQuery, navigation. We delved into the syntax and meaning of path expressions, and how the evaluation context affects (and is affected by) their evaluation.

The chapter discussed the six required XQuery axes (`attribute`, `child`, `descendant`, `descendant-or-self`, `parent`, and `self`) and the six optional ones (`ancestor`, `ancestor-or-self`, `preceding`, `preceding-sibling`, `following`, and `following-sibling`). In addition, it described the name tests, node kind tests, and wildcards that can be used with axes to select nodes by name, kind, and type.

Predicates can be used to filter an expression by other criteria, including position. Also, XQuery provides several navigation functions, including the important `doc()` function, which loads external XML data.

We also explored how to solve a variety of real-world tasks using path navigation. Because paths are so important to XQuery, many additional examples appear throughout this book, especially in Chapters 10 and 11.

3.8 Further Reading

For more information about XPath 1.0, see the W3C Recommendation at `http://www.w3.org/TR/xpath`. The book *Essential XML Quick Reference: A Programmer's Reference to XML, XPath, XSLT, XML Schema, SOAP, and More* by Aaron Skonnard and Martin Gudgin is also a good XPath reference.

A brief history of Unix, including the advent of paths, appears in the article "The Evolution of the Unix Time-sharing System" by Dennis Ritchie. This article has been published in several computer science publications, and is also available online at `http://cm.bell-labs.com/cm/cs/who/dmr/hist.html`.

CHAPTER 4

Functions and Modules

4.1 Introduction

In any programming language, functions are one of the most powerful tools available to a developer. XQuery provides both a large built-in function library and the ability to create your own functions. XQuery also allows implementations to interoperate with externally defined functions from other languages.

Every XQuery function has a qualified name, zero or more typed arguments, and a return type. Together, these constitute a function's *signature*. User-defined functions also have a function body (an XQuery expression that defines the function's behavior).

This chapter finishes laying the foundation of XQuery by describing how to invoke built-in and external functions and how to create and invoke user-defined functions.

4.2 Built-in Function Library

XQuery 1.0 defines over one hundred built-in functions, all summarized in Appendix C. Some of these functions come from XPath 1.0, but most are new to XQuery. They range in functionality from the simple `string-length()` to complex regular expression handlers like `matches()`.

Every built-in function resides in the namespace `http://www.w3.org/2003/11/xpath-functions`, which is bound to the predefined namespace prefix `fn`. Because this is also the default function namespace in XQuery, this prefix is generally omitted from built-in function names. For example, the built-in `count()` function takes one sequence argument and computes its length. Its signature is `fn:count($seq as item()*) as xs:integer`. This means that its name is `fn:count`, it takes one argument, `$seq`, which is a sequence of zero or more items, and it returns an `xs:integer`.

Some built-in functions are *overloaded*, meaning that there are several functions with the same name but different arguments and/or return types. One built-in function, `concat()`, is special in that it takes any number of arguments. In contrast, user-defined functions are never overloaded, and always take a fixed number of arguments.

For example, the built-in function `starts-with()` comes in two forms:

```
fn:starts-with($str as xs:string?, $sub as xs:string?)
                as xs:boolean?
```

and

```
fn:starts-with($str as xs:string?, $sub as xs:string?,
            $collation as xs:string) as xs:boolean?
```

The first form takes two arguments, both of which are sequences containing zero or one `xs:string` values. It returns a sequence containing zero or one `xs:boolean` values. The second, overloaded form takes a third argument, `$collation`, which must be a singleton `xs:string` value.

Colloquially, we would say that the `starts-with()` function takes two arguments and an optional third argument, although in reality these are separate overloaded functions.

4.3 Function Invocation

Functions are invoked by name, passing a comma-separated list of parameter values, one value for each argument required by the function. For example, the `starts-with()` function can be invoked as shown in Listing 4.1

Listing 4.1 Passing more than one argument

```
starts-with("abracadabra", "abra") => true
```

This parameter list isn't itself a sequence because XQuery doesn't allow nested sequences, and the individual parameters can themselves be sequences. For example, the `count()` function can be invoked as shown in Listing 4.2. This invocation passes a sequence of values as the single argument to `count()`.

Listing 4.2 Passing a sequence of values as a single argument

```
count((1, 4, 9)) => 3
```

The empty sequence can also be passed to functions that accept it. For example, `count(())` returns the integer 0, and `starts-with((), ())` returns the empty sequence.

If the name used in the function invocation is not prefixed, then the default function namespace is used. This is usually the built-in function namespace; however, you can choose a different default namespace by using the `default function namespace` declaration in the query prolog, as shown in Listing 4.3. The built-in function namespace is still available through the prefix `fn`.

Listing 4.3 Changing the default function namespace

```
declare default function namespace "urn:my-functions";
count((1, 2, 3))      (:invokes your count function :)
fn:count((1, 2, 3))  (: invokes the built-in count function :)
```

XQuery 1.0 always determines the function to be invoked by comparing names and number of arguments (the *arity*). If there isn't a function with that name and arity, then an error is raised.

To evaluate a function invocation, XQuery first evaluates each of the parameter expressions passed to the function, in any order. If an implementation can determine that a parameter isn't used, then it's allowed to not evaluate it (for optimization purposes).

A complication arises when the types of the parameters passed to the function differ from the types of arguments it expects. For example, what should XQuery do with `starts-with(123, 1)`, or, for that matter, `starts-with(xs:token ("xyz"), "x")`? To resolve this conundrum, XQuery implicitly applies *function conversion rules* (described next) to each of the parameters.

4.4 Function Conversion Rules

When the expected type of an argument is an atomic type (or sequence of atomic types), then the corresponding parameter passed to the function is first atomized, producing a sequence of zero or more atomic values. Each `xdt:untypedAtomic` value in this sequence is cast to the expected atomic type. Each numeric value that can be promoted to the expected type is promoted. This atomized/promoted/cast value becomes the parameter value passed to the function.

Then, whether the expected type of the argument is atomic or not, the parameter value is matched against the expected argument type using sequence type matching. If the types match—which includes the possibility of subtype substitution—then the function invocation succeeds with these values; otherwise, a type error is raised. (The atomization, numeric type promotion, subtype substitution, and sequence type matching rules are all defined in Chapter 2.)

The function conversion rules may seem complex, but in practice functions mostly do what you expect. Returning to the examples of the previous section, `starts-with(123, 1)` invokes a function that expects two atomic arguments. So, using the rules above, first each argument is atomized (both are already atomic values), and type promotion doesn't apply (because the expected arguments are non-numeric). Sequence type matching then fails because the parameters have type `xs:integer`, but `starts-with()` expects `xs:string?`, and these types don't match.

In contrast, `starts-with(xs:token("xyz"), "x")` succeeds because sequence type matching accepts the first argument (`xs:token` is a subtype of `xs:string`) and also the second argument (`xs:string` matches the expected type `xs:string?`).

4.5 User-Defined Functions

Although XQuery's built-in function library is vast, you will quickly find yourself wanting to write your own XQuery functions. Many of the examples in this book involve user-defined functions.

User-defined functions (aka UDFs) are declared after the query prolog but before the main part of the query, using the `declare function` expression. This expression takes the function signature, followed by an expression enclosed in curly braces (`{}`) that defines the body of the function, and ends with a semicolon. If the declared function name doesn't use a prefix, then it doesn't have a namespace (not even the default function namespace).

If the return type of the function isn't specified, then it defaults to `item()*` (the most generic type possible). Similarly, if any of the parameter types are omitted, then they also default to `item()*`. The parameters must have distinct names, and are in scope for the entire function body. The type of the function body expression must match, according to sequence type matching, the declared return type for the function.

For example, Listing 4.4 shows a trivial user-defined function that takes no parameters and returns the empty sequence. The return type of the function is declared to be `empty()`.

Listing 4.4 A very simple user-defined function

```
declare function empty-sequence() as empty() {
  ()
};
```

Listing 4.5 illustrates a more interesting user-defined function. This function computes the absolute value of an integer passed to it. It takes one integer argument (`$i`), and returns an integer that is the absolute value of the argument.

Listing 4.5 A slightly more interesting user-defined function

```
declare function abs($i as xs:integer) as xs:integer {
  if ($i < 0) then -$i else $i
};
```

As another example, consider the `distance()` function in Listing 4.6, which takes a three-dimensional point (expressed as x, y, and z coordinates) and returns the square of its distance from the origin.

Listing 4.6 A function with three parameters

```
declare function distance($x as xs:double,
                          $y as xs:double,
                          $z as xs:double) as xs:double {
  $x*$x + $y*$y + $z*$z
};
```

User-defined functions are one of the few places in XQuery where some of the many derived types, such as `xs:positiveInteger`, can be useful. Derived types can be used to constrain the arguments passed to a function, without having to write any code to enforce the constraint yourself. For example, the `abs()` function in Listing 4.5 could return an `xs:nonNegativeInteger`, as shown in Listing 4.7.

Listing 4.7 Derived types can be useful to constrain functions

```
declare function abs($i as xs:integer) as xs:nonNegativeInteger {
  (if ($i < 0) then -$i else $i) cast as xs:nonNegativeInteger
};
```

In this way, derived types act as a kind of assertion mechanism, verifying that the arguments passed to the function and the value it returns satisfy all appropriate constraints. However, unlike asserts—which are commonly used only during design time—type conversions affect the meaning and performance of a query, so use them wisely.

4.6 Recursion

XQuery also allows user-defined functions to invoke themselves (*recursion*). Recursion is commonly used when processing XML, due to its tree-like nature. For example, the function in Listing 4.8 recursively computes all the ancestors of a node.

Listing 4.8 Recursively computing the ancestors of a node

```
declare function ancestors-or-self($n as node()?) {
  if (empty($n))
  then ()
  else (ancestors-or-self($n/..), $n)
};
```

Recursive functions are especially useful in XQuery because XQuery cannot change the value of an assigned variable, so certain iterative approaches cannot be implemented easily or efficiently.

For example, consider writing your own `pow()` function, which computes an integer raised to some power. In some programming languages you might write a loop that iteratively accumulates the result. In XQuery, this computation is most easily expressed using recursion, as in Listing 4.9.

Listing 4.9 Recursively computing integer powers

```
declare function pow($b as xs:integer, $exp as $xs:integer)
                                              as xs:integer {
  if ($exp > 0)
  then $b * pow($b, $exp - 1)
  else 1
};

pow(2, 3)   => 8
pow(2, 16)  => 65536
```

Both of these examples used a conditional if/then/else to guard against infinite recursion. For additional examples of recursion, such as a `deep-copy()` function, see Chapter 10.

4.7 External Functions

Some implementations support externally defined functions (and parameters). The mechanism by which this is done varies from one implementation to the next. XQuery itself provides only the syntax to use when declaring these externals, shown in Listing 4.10. Essentially, they are like ordinary user-defined functions except that the `external` keyword is used instead of a function body.

Listing 4.10 Some implementations support external functions and variables

```
declare function foo($param as xs:integer) as xs:string external;
declare variable $var as xs:decimal external;
```

4.8 Modules

XQuery allows queries to be organized into modules. Most XQuery programs consist of a single module, the *main module*, but larger programs may have additional *library modules*.

A library module must contain a `module` declaration in its query prolog, and no query body (only user-defined functions and global variables). The module declaration associates a target namespace with the module, which is used to identify the module again later for import.

The target namespace also becomes the default function namespace for the module (unless you specify a different default using the `default function namespace` declaration in the prolog). The name of every function and global variable in the module must have the same namespace as the target namespace, as shown in Listing 4.11.

Listing 4.11 A sample library module

```
module namespace my = "urn:my-functions";
declare function my:one() { 1 };
declare function my:two() { 2 };
```

Any module may import library modules using the `import module` statement in the query prolog. For example, Listing 4.12 imports all of the user-defined functions and global variables that were defined in the library module that is Listing 4.11.

Listing 4.12 Using the library module defined in Listing 4.11

```
import module namesepace my = "urn:my-functions";

my:one() + my:two()
```

Modules are especially convenient when writing lots of user-defined functions. You can group related functions into one namespace, and put them into their own module, to be reused over and over again by other queries you write. However, support for modules varies from one implementation to another; implementations aren't required to support them at all. For more information about the `module` declaration and `import module` statements, see the Query Prolog section at the end of Chapter 5.

4.9 Conclusion

Each user-defined function has a qualified name, a return type, and zero or more typed parameters. When invoking a function, both its parameter values and its return value are implicitly converted, if necessary, using the function conversion rules.

XQuery provides a large built-in function library and also empowers you to write your own functions. User-defined functions cannot overload each other or existing built-in functions. XQuery also allows implementations to provide access to externally defined functions, which are declared in the query with XQuery types.

PART II

Core Language Features

CHAPTER 5

Basic Expressions

5.1 Introduction

XQuery is a large language, with many different kinds of expressions. Some of these expressions are so basic that they will appear in almost every query you will write.

This chapter focuses on the most fundamental XQuery operators and functions, beginning with comparisons and sequence manipulation, proceeding to arithmetic, logic, and finally touching on the details of the query prolog not already described in previous chapters.

Even if the XML data you are working with is untyped, the XQuery expressions you write are typed. To illustrate the interactions of types and expressions, we'll use the typed XML fragment shown in Listing 5.1 as the input sequence in the examples throughout this chapter.

Each element in this fragment has the atomic type indicated; the `<untyped>` element has type `xdt:untypedAtomic`. Note that there are two string-typed elements, for contrast.

Listing 5.1 The types.xml document

```
<root>
  <integer xsi:type="xs:integer">12</integer>
  <decimal xsi:type="xs:decimal">3.45</decimal>
  <float   xsi:type="xs:float"  >67.8</float>
  <double  xsi:type="xs:double" >0.9</double>
  <string  xsi:type="xs:string" >12</string>
  <string  xsi:type="xs:string" >x</string>
  <untyped>012</untyped>
</root>
```

5.2 Comparisons

Comparisons appear in almost every XQuery expression, whether testing for equality, determining the larger of two values, filtering a sequence, or joining two data sources (to name just a few uses of comparisons).

XPath 1.0 defined six comparison operators: >, <, >=, <=, =, and !=, known in XQuery as *general comparisons*. XQuery keeps these (with some modifications) and adds nine new comparison operators: the six *value comparisons* gt, lt, ge, le, eq, and ne; the *node comparison* is; and the two *order comparisons* << ("before") and >> ("after").

XQuery also defines two built-in comparison functions, listed in Table 5.1 and described briefly later in this section (see Appendix C for more information).

The reason there are so many different comparison operators is the same reason there are so many different XML data models. Some people want lexical equality (in which two values are equal if and only if their string representations are identical), while others want value equality (in which the lexical representation is disregarded, and only the underlying typed value matters). Some people want to compare nodes based on their content, others on their node identity, while others still want complete structural comparisons (aka *deep equality*). XQuery handles all of these cases.

5.2.1 Value Comparisons

The six value comparisons are binary operators that test whether the left operand is equal to (eq), not equal to (ne), greater than (gt), greater than or equal to (ge), less than (lt), or less than or equal to (le) the right operand. These operators first apply some implicit type conversions to their operands, and then return a single xs:boolean value corresponding to whether the comparison is true or false. Listing 5.2 demonstrates all of them.

Table 5.1 XQuery built-in comparison functions

Function	Meaning
compare	Compare two atomic values
deep-equal	Compare two entire sequences, using deep equality on nodes

Listing 5.2 The six value comparison operators

```
2 le 1  => false
2 lt 1  => false
2 ge 1  => true
2 gt 1  => true
2 ne 1  => true
2 eq 1  => false
```

First, both operands are atomized (as described in Chapter 2), turning them into sequences of atomic values (if they weren't already). If after atomization either operand isn't a single value, then an error is raised. Consequently, both of the expressions in Listing 5.3 result in errors.

Listing 5.3 Value comparisons operate only on singletons

```
() eq 0       => error
(0, 1) eq 0   => error
```

Numeric type promotion and subtype substitution are applied (also described in Chapter 2), meaning that numeric types are promoted to a common type, and when one operand is a subtype of the other, it is promoted to that type. To support lexical comparisons, untyped operands (that is, operands typed as xdt:untypedAtomic) are cast to xs:string and thus compared using their string values. If after all this the values have different types, then an error is raised. Otherwise, they are compared using the rules for that type, resulting in either true or false.

The examples in Listing 5.4 illustrate value comparisons on simple atomic constants. The ones in Listing 5.5 use the XML fragment introduced at the beginning of this chapter to select typed nodes and compare them.

Listing 5.4 The effects of type conversions on value comparisons

```
2 gt 1           => true  (: compared as xs:integer :)
2 gt 1.0         => true  (: compared as xs:decimal :)
2 eq 1E0         => true  (: compared as xs:double :)
2 eq "1"         => error (: incompatible types :)
```

Listing 5.5 Value comparisons used on nodes

```
string eq integer    => error (: two string values :)
untyped eq integer   => true  (: compared as xs:double :)
string[1] eq untyped => false (: compared as xs:string :)
string[1] eq integer => error (: incompatible types :)
```

Every type supports comparison using eq and ne. However, only the following totally ordered types (and subtypes of them) support the other value comparison operators: xs:boolean, xs:string, xs:date, xs:time, xs:dateTime, xdt:year-MonthDuration, and xdt:dayTimeDuration, and the numeric types (xs:integer, xs:decimal, xs:float, and xs:double). All other types result in an error when used with gt, ge, lt, or le. Listing 5.6 demonstrates a few value comparisons.

Listing 5.6 Value comparisons work on almost all types

```
"a" eq "b"       => false  (: depends on default collation :)
0E0 eq -0E0      => true
true() gt false() => true
```

String values are compared using the default collation. Usually this is the Unicode code point collation, meaning two strings compare as equal if and only if they contain exactly the same sequence of Unicode code points. However, most implementations support other collations (see Section 5.6). String comparison is the same as the one performed by the built-in compare() function (see Appendix A).

Values of type xs:boolean are ordered so that true compares greater than false. Binary values (xs:hexBinary and xs:base64Binary) and values of type xs:anyURI and xs:NOTATION compare as equal if they have the same length and code points, irrespective of collation.

Finally, two xs:QName values are compared by comparing their local name and namespace parts separately (using code points). The values are equal if their local names are equal and both lack namespaces, or if their local names are equal and their namespaces are equal.

5.2.2 General Comparisons

Value comparisons are fine when you have two singleton values to compare, but what about comparing sequences of values? The answer depends on the kind of comparison you want to perform.

The general comparison operators support the most common case, existential sequence comparisons. That is, each general comparison operator tests whether there exists an item in the left operand sequence and independently there exists an item in the right operand sequence such that the two items compare true. (Chapter 6 shows how to perform other kind of sequence comparisons, such as memberwise.) Listing 5.7 shows all of the general comparison operators in use.

Listing 5.7 The six general comparison operators

```
2 <= 1  => false
2 < 1   => false
2 >= 1  => true
2 > 1   => true
2 != 1  => true
2 = 1   => false
```

Like the value comparison operators, the general comparisons first atomize both operands. However, the general comparison operators work on sequences with any number of members, apply slightly different type conversions, and differ in their handling of the `xdt:untypedAtomic` type. For example, none of the comparisons in Listing 5.8 result in errors, in contrast to the analogous expressions using value comparisons.

Listing 5.8 General comparisons work on sequences

```
0 = 0      => true
() = 0     => false
(0, 1) = 0 => true
```

Finally, the items are compared using the corresponding value comparison operator (differing only in how they handle untyped data, explained next). The six general comparison operators `=`, `!=`, `<`, `<=`, `>`, and `>=` correspond to the six value comparison operators `eq`, `ne`, `lt`, `le`, `gt`, and `ge`. These operators apply numeric type promotion and subtype substitution as described in the previous section, and then compare the two values. The overall general comparison is true if the value comparison is true for any pair of items, otherwise it's false.

During this pairwise comparison, if either item being compared is untyped, then a special conversion takes place: If both operands are untyped (that is, typed as `xdt:untypedAtomic`), then both are cast to `xs:string`. If one is untyped and the other is numeric, then both are cast to `xs:double`. Otherwise, if one is untyped, then it is cast to the type of the other operand. In contrast, the value comparison operators by themselves always convert untyped values to `xs:string`. Listing 5.9 illustrates some of these differences, using the XML document in Listing 5.1 as the input sequence.

Listing 5.9 The effects of type conversions on general comparisons

```
2 > 1                => true  (: compared as xs:integer :)
2 > 1.0              => true  (: compared as xs:decimal :)
2 > 1E0              => true  (: compared as xs:double :)
2 > "1"              => error (: incompatible types :)
string = integer     => error (: incompatible types :)
untyped = integer    => true  (: compared as xs:double :)
string = untyped     => false (: compared as xs:string :)
```

By now, you may have realized two unusual characteristics of the general comparison operators. One is that they don't test whether two sequences are exactly identical. The expression (1, 2) = (1, 3) results in true because there exists a member in the left sequence (1) and a member in the right sequence (1) such that they are equal, even though the sequences themselves are different. The expression (1, 2) != (1, 2) also results in true, because there exists a member in the left sequence (1) and a member in the right sequence (2) that are unequal, even though the sequences as a whole are the same. Listing 5.10 demonstrates this effect, and its interaction with `not()`.

Listing 5.10 General comparisons test existence, with surprising results

```
(1, 2) = (2, 3)          => true
(1, 2) = (1, 2)          => true
(1, 2) != (1, 2)         => true
not((1,2) = (1,2))       => false
```

The `deep-equal()` function (described in Section 5.2.4) and the iteration operators of Chapter 6 provide other ways to compare sequences, instead of testing existence.

Another unusual characteristic is that the general comparison operators are nondeterministic when errors are involved. For example, (1, "2") = 1 might raise a type error (because comparing `xs:string` with `xs:integer` isn't allowed), or it might return true (because 1 equals 1). The answer depends on the order in which the implementation iterates through the sequences, which may vary from one implementation to the next, and may vary even within a single implementation during the execution of a query. For more surprises, see Chapter 11.

5.2.3 Node Comparisons

Nodes can be compared in even more ways than values. Because the value and general comparison operators atomize their operands, they compare the atomic values of nodes. However, you may also want to compare nodes by their identity, by their order within a document, or by their names and structure instead of just simple values (so-called "deep equality"). For these purposes, XQuery provides the node comparison operator `is`, the order comparison operators `<<` ("before") and `>>` ("after"), and a built-in function, `deep-equal()`, respectively.

Both the node and order comparisons require that their operands be either single nodes or the empty sequence, otherwise an error is raised. If either operand is the empty sequence, then the comparison returns the empty sequence. Otherwise, it returns the boolean result of the comparison (true or false)

The node comparison operator `is` returns true if the two nodes are the same node (by identity), otherwise it returns false. Its interactions with constructed nodes, variables, and the `doc()` function (recall it always returns the same node for the same string) are shown in Listing 5.11.

Listing 5.11 The node comparison operator `is`

```
<x/> is <x/>                      => false

let $a := <x/> return $a is $a    => true

doc("team.xml") is doc("team.xml") => true
```

The order comparison operator `<<` returns true if the left node appears before the right node in document order, otherwise it returns false. The `>>` operator returns the opposite—true if the left node appears after the right node in document order. Remember, nodes from different documents have an implementation-dependent ordering (although that ordering doesn't change during the execution of a query). Listing 5.12 demonstrates the before and after operators.

Listing 5.12 The two order comparison operators

```
let $a := <x><y/></x> return $a << $a/y   => true
let $a := <x><y/></x> return $a >> $a/y   => false
```

Node identity and order comparisons are most commonly used when navigating an existing XML document. For example, you may want to test whether two paths select the same node, or whether the node selected by one path appears before the node selected by another path.

When using paths with these operators, keep in mind that both operands need to select at most one node. If a path may select multiple nodes, use one of the operators from Chapter 6 to iterate through the sequence and compare each member individually, as shown in Listing 5.13.

Listing 5.13 Node comparisons are most commonly used with navigation

```
for $oldtimer in doc("team.xml")//Employee[@years > 7]
for $lead in doc("team.xml")//Employee[contains(@title, "Lead")]
where $oldtimer is $lead
return $oldtimer
```

5.2.4 Sequence and Tree Comparisons

Although the general comparisons can compare members of sequences (using existence) and the node and order comparisons can compare nodes (using identity), sometimes you want to compare an entire sequence or an entire XML tree at once. The `deep-equal()` built-in function performs both of these tasks (see Listing 5.14).

Listing 5.14 The `deep-equal()` function compares entire sequences and trees

```
(1, 2) = (2, 3)              => true
deep-equal((1, 2), (2, 3)) => false
deep-equal((1, 2), (1, 2)) => true
<x/> is <x/>                => false
deep-equal(<x/>, <x/>)     => true
deep-equal(<a><b c="1"/></a>, <a><b c="2"/></a>) => false
deep-equal(<a><b c="1"/></a>, <a><b c="1"/></a>) => true
```

It takes two sequences as arguments, and an optional third argument specifying the collation to use when comparing string values (the default collation is used otherwise). It then tests whether the two sequences are exactly equal. Nodes are compared as entire trees, not merely by identity or value.

It compares node kinds, names, and contents of the entire subtree defined by each node, ignoring all processing-instruction and comment nodes. (Attributes are treated as unordered, but otherwise ordering matters.) The schema types of nodes aren't compared, nor are certain other node properties such as base URI, so `deep-equal()` doesn't perform an exact comparison of the two data models.

5.3 Sequences

Now that we've explored the ways to compare values, nodes, and sequences, let's examine the other operators XQuery provides, starting with the sequence operators. XQuery provides several operators that are specifically dedicated to constructing, combining, and otherwise manipulating sequences.

Recall also that in XQuery, sequences contain only atomic values and nodes, and are never nested. Sequences are ordered using 1-based indices (so the first member appears at position 1). The empty sequence is denoted using empty parentheses `()`.

Unlike XPath 1.0, XQuery sequences may contain duplicate nodes (by identity). For example, the expression `let $a := <a/> return ($a, $a)` constructs a sequence containing the same element twice. This is different from the expression `(<a/>, <a/>)`, which constructs a sequence containing two different elements—both of which happen to have the same name and content.

XQuery defines five main operators for working with sequences: concatenation (the comma operator `,`), union (the `union` keyword or the vertical bar `|`), intersection (`intersect`), difference (`except`), and range (`to`).

XQuery also defines a plethora of built-in functions dedicated to sequence manipulation, as shown in Table 5.2. Most of these are highlighted in this section, all of them are completely covered in Appendix C.

5.3.1 Constructing Sequences

XQuery uses the comma operator to concatenate sequences together. For example, given the two sequences `(1, 2)` and `(1, 3)`, their concatenation `((1, 2), (1, 3))` is the (flattened) sequence `(1, 2, 1, 3)`.

Table 5.2 XQuery built-in sequence functions

Function	Meaning
count	The length of the sequence
distinct-values	Remove all duplicate values
empty	True if the sequence is empty
exists	True if the sequence is non-empty
index-of	Find an item in the sequence
insert-before	Insert items into a sequence
remove	Remove items from a sequence
reverse	Reverse a function
subsequence	Select a subsequence
unordered	Hint that ordering is unimportant

As this example shows, concatenation doesn't remove duplicates (by value or node identity). Duplicate values can be removed by applying the distinct-values() function. For example, distinct-values(((1, 2), (1, 3))) results in the sequence (1, 2, 3) or (2, 1, 3) (the order in which duplicates are removed is implementation-dependent). Distinct values are often useful when grouping; see Chapter 6 for examples.

Duplicate nodes (by node identity) can be removed by using the union operator to combine the lists. For example, let $a := <a/> return ($a, $a) results in a sequence containing the same node twice, but let $a := <a/> return $a union $a results in a sequence containing only one node. Like distinct-values(), the order in which duplicate nodes are removed is implementation-dependent. Because paths already eliminate duplicates and sort node sequences by document order, the same effect can be achieved using a path. For example, let $a := <a/> return ($a, $a)/. removes the duplicate node by application of the navigation step /..

When combining paths in a union, it is common to use the abbreviation | (vertical bar) instead of the keyword union. For example, doc("team.xml")// Employee/(Name | Title) selects all Name and Title child elements (in document order) from each Employee element.

Not only can XQuery combine sequences using set union and set concatenation, but it can also subtract them using set intersection (`intersect`) and set difference (`except`). Both of these operators accept only node sequences; an error is raised if either operand contains an atomic value.

The `intersect` operator computes all the nodes that appear in both of its arguments. (Duplicate nodes are removed from the result, if necessary.) For example, `doc("team.xml")//Employee/.. intersect doc("team.xml")/Team` finds the parent nodes of all `Employee` elements and intersects this set with the root `Team` element. The result is the root `Team` element (because it's the only node in both sets). It's somewhat uncommon to use intersect and except with paths; this example could have been expressed more efficiently as a predicate— `doc("team.xml")/Team[Employee]`— but on occasion these set operators can be useful.

The `except` operator computes the asymmetric difference of two sets. That is, the expression `A except B` results in all nodes that are in `A` but not in `B` (with duplicates removed). The symmetric difference—the nodes that are in one of `A` or `B` but not both—can be calculated either by taking the union of the two asymmetric differences or else computing the difference of their union with their intersection (see Listing 5.15).

Listing 5.15 Two ways to compute the symmetric difference

```
(A except B) union (B except A)
(A union B) except (A intersect B)
```

Finally, XQuery provides an operator, `to`, that constructs a sequence of consecutive integers. It takes two integer operands and computes the sequence of all the integers between them (inclusive). When the first operand is greater than the second, the empty sequence is returned; when the two operands are equal, the sequence consists of that one integer. The `to` operator is demonstrated in Listing 5.16.

Listing 5.16 The range operator is a great way to construct integer sequences

```
1 to 4    =>    (1, 2, 3, 4)
4 to 1    =>    ()
4 to 4    =>    (4)
```

Ranges are most useful when iterating, because implementations can optimize the expression to avoid buffering the entire sequence in memory.

The `to` operator ordinarily constructs sequences of consecutive integers, but it's easily adapted to use other increments. For example, the predicate `[. mod 2]` can be applied to keep all the odd numbers and `[. mod 2 = 0]` keeps all the even numbers, as shown in Listing 5.17.

Listing 5.17 Ranges can be used to construct other kinds of integer sequences

```
(0 to 10)[. mod 2]      => (1, 3, 5, 7, 9)
(0 to 10)[. mod 2 = 0]  => (0, 2, 4, 6, 8)
```

5.3.2 Processing Sequences

As the previous section shows, predicates are a natural way to select members from a sequence by position. For example, `$seq[1]` selects the first item in the sequence, while `$seq[last()]` selects the last item in the sequence. If the index is out of bounds then the empty sequence is returned (not an error).

The `reverse()` function reverses the order of items in a sequence. A range of values can be selected either using comparisons in the predicate, or using the `subsequence()` function. For example, `$seq[1 <= position() and position() <= 3]` selects the first three items of the sequence; so does `subsequence($seq, 1, 3)`. Listing 5.18 demonstrates the use of `subsequence()`, `reverse()`, and numeric predicates to filter sequences.

Listing 5.18 Selecting items from a sequence

```
("a", "b", "c")[1]                 => "a"
("a", "b", "c")[last()]            => "c"
("a", "b", "c")[-1]                => ()
reverse(("a", "b", "c"))           => ("c", "b", "a")
subsequence(("a", "b", "c"), 2)    => ("b", "c")
subsequence(("a", "b", "c"), 1, 2) => ("a", "b")
```

The built-in functions `empty()` and `exists()` can be used to test whether a sequence is empty or not, respectively. More generally, the `count()` function computes the length of a sequence, as shown in Listing 5.19.

Listing 5.19 Computing or testing the sequence length

```
count(("a", "b", "c"))  => 3
count(())               => 0
empty(())               => true
empty((1, 2))           => false
exists(())              => false
exists((1, 2))          => true
```

XQuery also provides functions for searching a sequence for an item (`index-of()`), constructing a new sequence from an existing one with an item inserted into it (`insert-before()`), and constructing a new sequence from an existing one by removing an item from it (`remove()`).

The `index-of()` function takes two arguments: the sequence and the item to search for (by value). Optionally, a third collation argument may be specified for string searches. It returns a list of all integer positions at which the item occurs, in order from least to greatest (empty if the item doesn't occur in the sequence).

Note that the `index-of()` function can be very inefficient on large sequences because it doesn't stop searching at the first occurrence. Some implementations may optimize `index-of($seq, $value)[1]` (the first index) and `index-of($seq, $value)[last()]` (the last index).

The `insert-before()` function takes three arguments: the original sequence, the insertion position, and a sequence of zero or items to be inserted. It performs the requested insertion (inserting before the insertion point). Similarly, the `remove()` function takes two arguments—the sequence and a position to exclude. It returns the sequence consisting of all items except the one at that position. Note that neither of these functions alters the original sequence. These three functions are demonstrated in Listing 5.20.

Listing 5.20 Searching, inserting into, and removing from sequences

```
index-of((4, 5, 6, 4), 5)          => 2
index-of((4, 5, 6, 4), 7)          => ()
index-of((4, 5, 6, 4), 4)          => (1, 4)
insert-before((1, 2, 3, 4), 2, (5, 6)) => (1, 5, 6, 2, 3, 4)
insert-before((1, 2, 3, 4),-2, (5, 6)) => (5, 6, 1, 2, 3, 4)
insert-before((1, 2, 3, 4), 4, (5, 6)) => (1, 2, 3, 5, 6, 4)
insert-before((1, 2, 3, 4), 5, (5, 6)) => (1, 2, 3, 4, 5, 6)
remove((4, 5, 6, 4), 2)            => (4, 6, 4)
remove((4, 5, 6, 4), 4)            => (4, 5, 6)
```

The `index-of()` function can be paired with the `position()` function to remove all occurrences of a particular value from a sequence, as shown in Listing 5.21.

Listing 5.21 Removing by value instead of by index

```
declare function remove-value($seq, $val as xdt:untypedAtomic) {
  $seq[position() != index-of($seq, $val)]
};

remove-value((4, 5, 6, 4), 4)    =>  (5, 6)
```

Finally, XQuery provides the `unordered()` function as an optimization hint. This function just tells an implementation that the sequence order is unimportant; for example, paths normally always sort by document order, but perhaps you don't need this. The effects are implementation-dependent.

5.4 Arithmetic

XQuery isn't a language designed for heavy-duty mathematics, but it does support eight of the most common arithmetic expressions: addition (`+`), subtraction (`-`), multiplication (`*`), floating-point division (`div`), integer division (`idiv`), modulus (`mod`), unary plus (`+`), and unary minus (`-`). In addition, XQuery provides nine built-in arithmetic functions, listed in Table 5.3. XQuery doesn't define more complex arithmetic operations such as trigonometry or logarithms, although these may be available in some XQuery implementations through extension functions.

The syntax used for the arithmetic operators can be tricky. Except for addition, all of them can be used in other contexts with different meanings unrelated to arithmetic: The division and modulo operators (`div`, `idiv`, `mod`) are valid names, and can be used in paths (no keywords are reserved). For example, the query `div idiv mod` selects the elements named `div` and `mod`, and then computes their integer division. Confusing!

The punctuation symbols are also a common source of confusion: The hyphen is a valid name character and must be separated by names with a space or else it will be parsed as part of the name. The plus symbol is used in some type expressions, and the multiplication operator is used in both type expres-

Table 5.3 XQuery built-in arithmetic functions

Function	Meaning
floor	Round down (to negative infinity)
ceiling	Round up (to positive infinity)
abs	Compute the absolute value
min	Compute the minimum value
max	Compute the maximum value
avg	Compute the average value
sum	Compute the sum
round	Round to the closest integer, ties rounded up
round-half-to-even	Round to the closest integer, ties to nearest even number

Table 5.4 Beware of the XQuery punctuation rules

Example	Meaning
a-1	The name a-1
a - 1	a minus 1
a/b	The path a/b
a div b	a divided by b
a * b	a multiplied by b
div/* cast as div*	Child elements of div cast to the type div*

sions and as a path wildcard. The examples in Table 5.4 illustrate their meanings in different contexts.

Except for idiv and unary plus, all of these operators were available in XPath 1.0, but behave somewhat differently in XQuery. In XPath 1.0, all arithmetic operations were carried out in double-precision floating-point arithmetic. In XQuery, the arithmetic rules reflect the many more numeric types that are available.

Like the comparison operators, the arithmetic operators first atomize both operands. If either operand is the empty sequence, then the expression results in the empty sequence (not an error). If either operand isn't a singleton, then an error is raised.

Otherwise, numeric type promotion is applied (as described in Chapter 2), and the two numbers are added (see Listing 5.22). The only other type that is allowed is untyped data (`xdt:untypedAtomic`). Operands that are untyped are promoted to `xs:double` for all operators except `idiv`, which promotes untyped values to `xs:integer`.

Listing 5.22 Arithmetic operators atomize and perform numeric promotion

```
1 + 2              => 3
1 + 2.0            => 3.0
1 + 2E0            => 3E0
untyped - 2        => 1E1
string - 2         => error (: incompatible types :)
() * 0             => ()
() + (2, 0)        => ()
(1, 1) + (2, 0)    => error (: non-singleton operands :)
```

The behavior of the addition, subtraction, multiplication, and division operators should be mostly what you would expect. Except for the division of integers, which results in a decimal value, all of these result in a value with the same type as the operands after numeric type promotion has been applied.

The integer division operator `idiv` requires that both of its operands be integers, otherwise an error is raised. It then carries out truncating integer division (so `5 idiv 3` equals 1). The `mod` operator computes the modulus (the value that is left over from division). Neither of these operators is commonly used.

See Appendix B for rigorous definitions of all the arithmetic operators. Listing 5.23 provides examples of `*`, `div`, `idiv`, and `mod`.

Listing 5.23 Multiplication, division, and modulus operators

```
1 * 2          => 2
1.0 * 2.0      => 2.0
1E0 * 2E0      => 2.0E0
float * float  => xs:float("4596.84")
3 div 1        => 3.0
1.0 div 2      => 0.5
1E0 div 2      => 5E-1
```

```
1.0 div 0      => error (: divide-by-0 error :)
1E0 div 0      => INF   (: double, float support division by 0 :)
3 mod 2        => 1
3 mod 1.5      => 0.0
3 mod 1.2      => 0.6
3 mod 2.2      => 3.0
3E0 mod 2      => 1E0
7 idiv 2       => 3
7 mod 2        => 1
7 div 2        => 3.5
7 idiv 2.0     => error (: idiv works only on integers :)
```

Arithmetic operators can overflow or underflow. For decimal values, implementations are required to report overflow and to return 0.0 on underflow. For all other types, implementations are allowed to choose between raising an error and allowing the overflow or underflow to occur (with various results—see Appendix B for details).

Note also that floating-point arithmetic is performed according to the IEEE 754 specification, including the special values positive and negative zero (0.0 and -0.0), positive and negative infinity (INF and -INF), and a (non-signaling) not-a-number value (NaN). Consequently, dividing an xs:double or xs:float value by zero isn't an error. Listing 5.24 shows some of these interactions.

Listing 5.24 Special floating-point values

```
1E0 div 0          =>  INF
-1E0 div 0         => -INF
0E0 div 0          =>  NaN
0 div 0            =>  error (: integer division by zero :)
1 div (-1E0 div 0) => -0.0
```

Generally speaking, fixed-point arithmetic should perform exact arithmetic without loss of precision. In practice, xs:decimal is usually implemented with limited precision. Because fixed-point arithmetic isn't commonly supported in hardware, most XQuery implementations are forced to emulate it in software. Consequently, fixed-point arithmetic often suffers from relatively poor performance and inconsistent behavior across implementations when compared to floating-point arithmetic. You should use decimal arithmetic only when your applications require it.

Finally, XQuery provides a few arithmetic functions for computing aggregate statistics over sequences of numbers and rounding.

The max(), min(), sum(), and avg() functions compute the maximum, minimum, sum, and average of a sequence of numbers, respectively. The max() and min() functions actually work on values of any type; they accept an optional second argument specifying the collation to use when comparing string values. They can even be used on sequences containing different types of numbers (for example, max((1, 1.5))), but the details are somewhat complicated (see Appendix C).

Listing 5.25 Aggregation functions

```
max((1, 2, 3))        => 3
min((1, 2, 3))        => 1
avg((1, 2, 3))        => 2.0
sum((1, 2, 3))        => 6
sum(("a", "b", "c")) => error (: not numbers :)
```

There are seven rounding modes in popular use today, and XQuery provides functions for four of them (Chapter 10 shows how to implement the other three). All four take any number, and return a number of the same type. The floor() function takes a number and returns the greatest integer less than it (rounding down toward negative infinity). The ceiling() function returns the least integer greater than its argument (rounding up toward positive infinity). The round() and round-half-to-even() functions round to the closest integer, but differ in how they handle ties (such as 0.5). The round() function always rounds ties up, while the round-half-to-even() function rounds ties to the nearest even number. The round-half-to-even() function also accepts an optional second argument, which specifies the precision at which to do the rounding (see Appendix C). Listing 5.26 illustrates the rounding functions.

Listing 5.26 Rounding functions

```
floor(2.2) => 2.0
floor(2.5) => 2.0
floor(2.6) => 2.0
round(2.2) => 2.0
round(2.5) => 3.0
round(2.6) => 3.0
round-half-to-even(2.2) => 2.0
```

```
round-half-to-even(2.5) => 2.0
round-half-to-even(2.6) => 3.0
ceiling(2.2) => 3.0
ceiling(2.5) => 3.0
ceiling(2.6) => 3.0
```

XQuery doesn't provide any other arithmetic functions, although it's possible to construct your own (and implementations may also provide some). For example, Listing 5.27 defines an exponentiation function that raises its first argument to the power of its second argument.

Listing 5.27 An exponentiation function

```
declare function pow($b as xs:integer,
                     $exp as xs:integer) as xs:integer {
  if ($exp < 1)
    then 1
  else
    $b * pow($b, $exp - 1)
};


pow(2, 10) => 1024
pow(2, 20) => 1048576
```

5.5 Logic

Like most languages, XQuery can express all the familiar concepts from boolean logic, including the two boolean constants (true, false), the boolean operators (and, or, not), and conditionals (if/then/else). (In fact, XQuery supports the full predicate calculus: conjunction, disjunction, conditions, and existential and universal quantification.)

The and and or operators are written as keywords, but for compatibility with XPath 1.0, the not() operator is written as a function. All three implicitly coerce their operands to the xs:boolean type by applying the Effective Boolean Value (defined in Chapter 2), as if by a call to the boolean() function. These operators are demonstrated in Listing 5.28.

Listing 5.28 Logical operators apply the Effective Boolean Value

```
true() or false()     => true
1 or 0                => true
true() and false()    => false
1 and 0               => false
"1" and "0"           => true  (: boolean("0") = true :)
not(true())           => false
not(())               => true
```

The effects of EBV can be surprising; for example, `not("false")` results in false—because EBV looks at the string length, not its content, so `"false"` is converted to true, and then negated by `not()`—while `not(xs:boolean("false"))` results in true.

XQuery allows the `and` and `or` operators to short-circuit (on both sides), meaning that implementations are allowed to evaluate either operand first, and then if its value determines the result of the entire expression, the other operand doesn't need to be evaluated at all. For example, `false()` and `error()` can result in false or raise an error; so can `error()` and `false()`. Consequently, these operators have implementation-defined behavior in the face of errors.

In contrast, the `if/then/else` conditional statement always evaluates the `if` condition, and then if the condition is true it evaluates the `then` branch, otherwise it evaluates the `else` branch. The `else` branch isn't optional, although you can often return the empty sequence to achieve the same effect. Like the other boolean operators, the condition is converted to `xs:boolean` by applying the Effective Boolean Value.

As shown in Listing 5.29, any number of conditionals may be chained together, like so: `if ... then ... else if ... then ... else if ... then ... else ...`, in which the conditions are tested one after another until either one of them is found to be true, in which case that branch is taken, or else the `else` branch is evaluated. Exactly one branch is evaluated. The branches of a conditional need not have the same types.

Listing 5.29 Conditional statements

```
if (exists(x/y/z)) then "yes" else "no"
if ($x = 'a') then 1 else if ($x = 'b') then 2 else 0
```

5.6 Query Prolog

Every XQuery module contains an optional *query prolog*. The query prolog may first declare a version, followed by certain declarations and imports in any order. After these come the user-defined functions, if any. Together, these set up the initial static context for the query. Every declaration and function definition must be followed by a semicolon (see Table 5.5).

Chapter 4 described modules and user-defined functions. In this section, we focus on the other items that make up the query prolog.

5.6.1 Version Declaration

Optionally, a query may declare the XQuery version to which it has been authored; at this time, the only supported version is `"1.0"`. This feature exists in anticipation of future XQuery versions (see Chapter 14), but for now it always takes the form shown in Listing 5.30.

Listing 5.30 XQuery version

```
xquery version "1.0";
```

5.6.2 XML Space Declaration

The *XML space declaration* affects how whitespace in the query affects element construction (see Listing 5.31). The whitespace policy can also be changed later in the query by element constructors. See Chapter 7 for details.

Listing 5.31 XML space declaration

```
declare xmlspace preserve;
```

The XML space declaration can have one of two values, `strip` or `preserve`, written as keywords, not strings. The default is `strip`. More than one XML space declaration in the prolog results in an error.

5.6.3 Base URI Declaration

The *base URI declaration*, shown in Listing 5.32, changes the base-uri. The `base-uri` is mainly used by the `doc()` function to resolve relative URIs.

Table 5.5 Declarations that may appear in a query prolog

Declaration	Meaning
`xquery version "1.0";`	Specify the XQuery version
`declare xmlspace mode;`	Set the default xmlspace policy
`declare default collation "uri";`	Set the default collation
`declare base-uri "uri";`	Declare the base-uri
`declare namespace prefix = "uri";`	Declare a namespace prefix
`declare default element namespace "uri";`	Set the default element namespace
`declare default function namespace "uri";`	Set the default function namespace
`declare variable $name { expr };` `declare variable $name as type { expr };`	Define a global variable
`declare variable $name external;` `declare variable $name as type external;`	Declare an external global variable
`module prefix = "uri";`	Declare this to be a library module and bind the namespace prefix

`import module "uri";`
`import module "uri" at "hint";`
`import module namespace prefix = "uri";`
`import module namespace prefix =`
`"uri" at "hint";`
	Import a library module into this one and optionally declare a namespace prefix

`import schema "uri";`
`import schema "uri" at "hint";`
`import schema namespace prefix "uri";`
`import schema namespace prefix "uri"`
`at "hint";`
`import schema default element`
`namespace "uri";`
`import schema default element`
`namespace "uri"`
`at "hint";`
	Import schema types and optionally declare a namespace prefix

`declare validation mode;`	Set the default validation mode

Listing 5.32 Base URI declaration

```
declare base-uri "http://www.awprofessional.com/";
```

5.6.4 Default Collation Declaration

The *default collation declaration* affects text processing, including string comparisons and sorting. The only collation that implementations are required to support is `http://www.w3.org/2003/11/xpath-functions/collation/codepoint`, which is also the default when no default collation declaration is used.

The default collation declaration takes a constant string value, which must be supported by the implementation. Listing 5.33 shows a hypothetical collation. More than one collation declaration results in an error.

Listing 5.33 Default collation declaration

```
declare default collation
        "http://www.awprofessional.com/xquerycollations/en-us";
```

The default collation cannot be changed by any other expression, although most functions that are affected by collation accept an optional argument that explicitly specifies the collation to use. See Chapter 8 for an explanation of collations.

5.6.5 Namespace Declarations

The XQuery prolog may contain any number of *namespace declarations*. These introduce a prefix/namespace binding into scope for all the rest of the XQuery. As with collation declarations, each namespace value must be a constant string value. The namespace must not be the empty string, and the prefix must not begin with the characters "xml" (having any case, such as "XmL"). Listing 5.34 provides two examples.

Listing 5.34 Namespace declarations

```
declare namespace foo = "urn:bar";
declare namespace awl = "http://www.awprofessional.com/";
```

Multiple declarations for the same prefix in the query prolog raise an error, although namespace declarations in an XML element constructor may override them without error (see Chapter 7).

Table 5.6 Built-in namespaces

Prefix	Namespace
fn	http://www.w3.org/2003/11/xpath-functions
xdt	http://www.w3.org/2003/11/xpath-datatypes
xml	http://www.w3.org/XML/1998/namespace
xs	http://www.w3.org/2001/XMLSchema
xsi	http://www.w3.org/2001/XMLSchema-instance

The five namespace declarations listed in Table 5.6 are built in, and correspond to the XQuery Function, XQuery Data Types, XML, XML Schema, and XML Schema Instance namespaces, respectively. Whenever these prefixes occur in this book, they are bound to their default namespace values. You may override these namespace prefixes in the prolog if you wish, although this isn't recommended (unless you're purposely trying to intercept all XQuery built-in functions and/or data types).

It is also possible to declare two namespaces to be used by default in unprefixed names. The *default element namespace* affects unprefixed element names in navigation and construction; the *default function namespace* affects unprefixed function names in function invocations (excluding the function name used in the `declare function`). Both are shown in Listing 5.35. An error results when there is more than one default element namespace or more than one default function namespace declaration in the query prolog.

Listing 5.35 Default namespace declarations

```
declare default element namespace "http://your.org/";
declare default function namespace "http://your.org/";
```

If a default element namespace isn't declared in the prolog, then all unprefixed element names belong to no namespace. Otherwise, they belong to the declared default element namespace. Unprefixed function names used in function invocations use the default function namespace. If one isn't provided by the user, then it defaults to the built-in namespace, http://www.w3.org/2003/11/xpath-functions (which is also bound to the prefix fn).

5.6.6 Global Variable Declarations

The prolog may declare global variables and external parameters (if the implementation supports externals). Global variables have a value computed in the query itself; external parameters are declared in the query, but their values are completely unknown until runtime.

Both are declared using `declare variable`, followed by a variable name, optionally the static type of the variable, and then either the variable value enclosed in curly braces, or else the `external` keyword indicating that it is an external parameter, and finally the trailing semicolon. The examples in Listing 5.36 demonstrate the various kinds of variable declarations.

Listing 5.36 Global variable declarations

```
declare variable $zero { 0 };
declare variable $decimalZero as xs:decimal { 0.0 };
declare variable $inf as xs:double { 1E0 div $zero };
declare variable $userName as xs:string external;
declare variable $userDoc { doc(concat($userName, ".xml")) };
```

The variable value must match the declared type. If no type is specified, then the type is either the static type of the value expression, or else `xs:anyType` if the variable is external.

Variable values may refer to other variables defined before them; they may also refer to functions imported from other modules (provided the import module statement occurs before the variable) or built-in functions. There is no way to assign a default value to external parameters (as in XSLT); if an external parameter value isn't supplied when executing the query, or if its value doesn't match the variable type, then an error is raised.

5.6.7 Module Imports and Declaration

As explained in Chapter 4, XQuery queries are organized into modules. A library module contains a *module declaration* and no query body; a main module doesn't contain a module declaration but may contain a query body. The module declaration appears in the query prolog, and consists of the keyword `module` followed by a string literal that is the target namespace for this module, as shown in Listing 5.37.

Modules are imported by target namespace into other modules (library or main) using an `import module` statement in the query prolog. This imports all the global variables and user-defined functions from that module into the current one. All types used in the function signatures and global variable types must be defined in the current module, or else an error is raised.

Listing 5.37 Library modules contain a module declaration but no query body

```
module "urn:my-library";
declare variable $version { "1.0" };
declare function description() { "This is a library module" };
```

Listing 5.38 Modules can be imported into other modules

```
import module namespace my = "urn:my-library";
if ($my:version = "1.0") then my:description()
else error("Library version mismatch")
```

The `import module` may optionally assign a prefix to the module namespace as in Listing 5.38, and may optionally suggest a module location to the implementation. See Appendix B for details.

5.6.8 Schema Imports and Validation Declaration

Finally, the query prolog may also import XML schema definitions into an XQuery, so that the types defined in the schemas are available to the query, and may also define a default validation mode.

The `import schema` statement is similar to the `import module` statement. It specifies the namespace that is imported, optionally declares a prefix for that namespace, and optionally suggests a location hint to the implementation. In addition, the `import  schema` statement may assign the namespace to the default element or default function namespace. The example in Listing 5.39 imports a schema, and then declares a variable using one of the types from that schema.

Listing 5.39 Schema types can be imported

```
import schema namespace my = "urn:my-types" at "mytypes.xsd"
declare variable $my:zipcode { "98052" cast as my:zip }
```

The query prolog may also override the default validation mode (which is `lax`) using the validation declaration shown in Listing 5.40. This declaration takes one of the keywords `lax`, `skip`, or `strict`, and sets that to be the default validation mode for the validate operator and element constructors. The validation mode can also be changed in the query during validation; see Chapter 9 for details.

Listing 5.40 Sample validation mode declaration

```
declare validation strict;
```

5.7 Conclusion

XQuery, like all good query languages, is filled with a rich variety of expressions. These form the basic vocabulary out of which you can write many XQuery programs.

In this chapter, we first explored the operators that can compare items by value, node identity, and document order. We also examined the `deep-equal()` function, which compares sequences exactly (using deep structural equality on nodes). Next, we reviewed the functions and operators that are dedicated to sequence manipulation, including constructing and filtering sequences, as well as computing aggregate values such as the maximum or length of a sequence.

We also investigated the XQuery arithmetic functions and operators, which build on the numeric type support and type promotions described in Chapter 2. XQuery provides basic facilities for simple arithmetic calculations and functions for four rounding modes. Higher-order arithmetic operations such as exponentiation, logarithms, trigonometry, factorials, random numbers, or bitwise manipulation are not built in, although some implementations may provide them as extension functions.

From there, we progressed to the XQuery facilities for expressing logical conditions. XQuery supports two-valued Boolean logic, with its two constants (`true()`, `false()`) and the usual Boolean operators (`and`, `or`, `not()`). XQuery also supports conditional expressions using the `if`/`then`/`else` keywords, as well as other more complex operators, such as existential and universal quantification (which are described in the next chapter). And finally, we ended this chapter with an examination of the query prolog, which controls the context in which XQuery expressions are compiled and evaluated.

5.8 Further Reading

For more information about floating-point numbers, I highly recommend the article "What Every Computer Scientist Should Know About Floating Point Arithmetic" by David Goldberg in *ACM Computing Surveys*, 1991, which is also available online from `http://citeseer.nj.nec.com/goldberg91what.html`. IBM maintains a fantastic archive of information about decimal arithmetic online at `http://www2.hursley.ibm.com/decimal/decimal.html`, which also contains pointers to information about floating-point arithmetic and rounding modes.

For a dense but practical book on logic from the software engineering point of view, look no further than the book *Logic in Computer Science: Modelling and reasoning about systems* by Michael Huth and Mark Ryan, and its Web site, `http://www.cs.bham.ac.uk/research/lics`. If you're a professional software developer, this is probably the last logic book you will ever need.

CHAPTER 6

Iteration

6.1 Introduction

Most programming languages adopt one of two styles of expressions: iteration or application. *Iterative expressions* explicitly loop through sequences one member at a time. *Applicative expressions* apply operations to entire sequences at once (implicitly iterating through the sequence and applying the operation to each member).

As we saw in Chapter 3, navigation paths have an applicative style—each step implicitly iterates over the nodes selected by the previous step. However, the rest of XQuery has adopted an iterative style of programming. This chapter explores the XQuery expressions that perform iteration.

The FLWOR (pronounced "flower") expression is the most powerful of these, capable of introducing variables, filtering sequences, sorting and grouping, iterating over sequences to produce some result, and joining different data sources, all at once.

XQuery also provides iteration expressions for existential (some) and universal (every) quantification, which test whether a condition holds for any or every member of a sequence, respectively.

6.2 FLWOR

As its name suggests, FLWOR consists of five major clauses: for, let, where, order by, and return. Every FLWOR begins with one or more for and/or let clauses (in any order), followed by an optional where clause, an optional order by clause, and finally one return clause. The five clauses are demonstrated by the example in Listing 6.1.

Listing 6.1 FLWOR consists of five clauses

```
for $i at $pos in doc("puzzles.xml")//puzzle
let $j := doc("games.xml")//game
where $i/@name = $j/@name
order by @price descending
return $i
```

Before I explain how FLWOR works, let's first compare FLWOR to equivalent expressions in the popular SQL and XSLT languages. The XQuery FLWOR expression is very similar to SQL SELECT statements and XSLT <xsl:for-each/> loops. If you are already familiar SQL or XSLT, then you may find it helpful to think of FLWOR in terms of the equivalent expressions from these languages. If you're not already familiar with SQL or XSLT, you may want to skip ahead to Section 6.2.3.

6.2.1 Compared to SQL

The similarities between SQL and XQuery are striking. Both XQuery and SQL have a where clause, which filters the overall expression according to a boolean condition. Both XQuery and SQL have an order by clause, which sorts the selection according to some criteria. Both languages also can declare variables and assign them to values. Listing 6.2 shows a SQL query similar to FLWOR.

Listing 6.2 SQL queries also contain five clauses

```
DECLARE @Variable1, @Variable2, ...
SELECT Column1, Column2, ...
FROM Table1, Table2, ...
WHERE ...
ORDER BY ...
```

Where the languages differ—aside from the fact that SQL is generally case-insensitive while XQuery is case-sensitive—are the ways in which they iterate over data and construct results.

In SQL, all sequences are flat. Consequently, a simple FROM clause naming tables (or views, or subqueries) suffices to describe the data sources, and a simple SELECT clause suffices to list the values to be selected from these sources. SQL is nonpositional, so you can be vague about the order of iteration over these data sources.

In XQuery, the sequences may be flat or they may be hierarchical, and they are almost always ordered. Consequently, the `for` clause may simply name collections like in SQL), or it may describe paths or other more complex expressions that navigate these collections, and the order in which the iteration is performed is significant. Similarly, the `return` clause doesn't simply return values from these data sources, but may construct entirely new shapes (which are also ordered).

The similarities between SQL and XQuery aren't accidental. SQL has been a highly successful language for data processing, and its features have evolved to fulfill common needs. XQuery has these same needs and more, and therefore provides functionality that includes and surpasses that of SQL.

6.2.2 Compared to XSLT

The correspondence between XSLT and XQuery may be less obvious, but they are actually more closely related than SQL and XQuery, because both XSLT and XQuery both work with hierarchical, ordered data sources. In fact, many people have questioned the need for XQuery at all, when XSLT 1.0 can express so many of the same concepts.

The selection criteria of the `<xsl:for-each>` loop is similar to the `for` clause of FLWOR. The main difference is that a single FLWOR expression may have any number of `for` clauses, but you have to nest `<xsl:for-each>` loops to achieve the same effect. Variable assignment in XSLT is performed using `<xsl:variable>` and is similar to the XQuery `let` clause.

The `where` clause of XQuery can be achieved in XSLT using either `<xsl:if>` or else predicates on the select expression. The `order by` clause of XQuery loosely corresponds to the `<xsl:sort>` expression of XSLT, and the `return` clause in a FLWOR expression corresponds to the body of the `<xsl:for-each>` loop. Listing 6.3 shows an XSLT expression similar to the XQuery FLWOR expression.

Listing 6.3 XSLT `for-each` loops are similar to FLWOR

```
<xsl:for-each select="$sequence">
    <xsl:variable name="i" value="./@attr"/>
    <xsl:sort />
    <return/>result here</return>
</xsl:for-each>
```

The most obvious difference between XSLT and XQuery is that XSLT is expressed using XML while XQuery is not. Other less obvious but even more significant differences are that XQuery allows sequences of atomic values, has a richer type system, and allows composition (iterating over the results of other expressions). It is also somewhat easier to join two data sources in XQuery than in XSLT, or to express certain kinds of grouping operations.

As with SQL, the similarities between XSLT and XQuery aren't accidental. Both languages must navigate and construct XML, and must handle all of its nuances. In many ways, XQuery is a refinement of the ideas that preceded it.

6.2.3 Introducing Variables

The FLWOR expression is one of several XQuery expressions that introduces variable assignments. FLWOR actually introduces three kinds of variable bindings.

One kind of variable assignment in FLWOR occurs with the `let` clause. In fact, the simplest possible FLWOR expression consists of a single `let` clause followed by a `return` clause (see Listing 6.4).

Listing 6.4 The simplest FLWOR expression consists of let and return

```
let $variable := "value"
return $variable
```

The `let` keyword is followed by a variable (`$name`), optionally the variable's type, the assignment operator (`:=`), and any XQuery expression at all (even another FLWOR).

The effect is to introduce the variable named by the `let` clause into scope and assign it to the given expression (the *binding*). As shown in Listing 6.5, each variable is in scope for all the rest of the FLWOR expression—that is, the `where`, `order by`, and `return` clauses, and any other variables introduced after it. (However, a variable cannot refer to itself in its own binding.)

Listing 6.5 Variables are in scope for all the rest of the FLWOR

```
let $x := 1
let $y := $x
where $x > 0 or $y < 0
order by $x, $y
return ($x, $y)
```

Variables cannot be reassigned once declared, and cannot be redeclared in the same scope.

The other two kinds of variable assignment in FLWOR are iteration and position; both are introduced using the `for` clause.

The `for` clause takes a variable, an optional type declaration, optionally the `at` keyword followed by a position variable, the `in` keyword (instead of assignment), and finally the XQuery expression to iterate through. Listing 6.6 demonstrates all of these parts.

The effect is that the variable, and the optional position variable if used, are both in scope for the remainder of the FLWOR expression. These variables change in value during the execution of the FLWOR statement; the variable is assigned to each item in the sequence in turn, and the position variable is assigned to the current position within this sequence.

Listing 6.6 The `for` clause iterates through a sequence (optionally with position)

```
for $item at $pos in $sequence
return  <x index="{$pos}">{ $item }</x>
```

Each FLWOR expression may contain any number of variable bindings, in any order, as long as there is at least one `let` or `for` clause. XQuery also allows you to introduce several variables in a single clause, by separating each variable introduction with commas. Listing 6.7 demonstrates both variable styles.

Listing 6.7 FLWOR expressions may introduce many variables

```
for $i in doc("one.xml")//foo, $j in $i//foo
let $k := $i//bar, $m := $j//bar
for $n in doc("two.xml")//foo
where count($k) > count($n//bar)
  and count($n//bar) > count($m)
return $n
```

The order in which these variables and clauses appear in the FLWOR expression is significant, as explained next.

6.2.4 Tuples

The *tuple space* is essential to understanding how FLWOR works. A tuple space is like a matrix: Each row is a *tuple*, and each row in the tuple space has the same number of columns as all the others. Tuples are similar to ordinary sequences, except that they may themselves contain sequences (i.e., tuples are nested).

Tuples and tuple spaces aren't formally part of the XQuery Data Model, but the FLWOR operator is defined (and best explained) in terms of them. During evaluation, each FLWOR expression corresponds to one tuple space.

Every variable introduced by `for` and `let` clauses generates another column in the tuple space. When visualizing tuple spaces, I also like to add columns for each of the `where` and `return` clauses, as well as each expression in the `order by` clause. For example, the FLWOR expression in Listing 6.8 corresponds to a tuple space with six columns: one each for the `$i`, `$pos`, and `$j` variables introduced by `for` and `let`, one for the `where` clause, one for the `order by` expression, and one for the `return` clause.

Listing 6.8 A sample FLWOR

```
for $i at $pos in reverse (1 to 10)
let $j := $i * $i
where $j <= 50
order by $i
return ($pos, $i)
```

Determining the number of rows in the tuple space is somewhat more complicated. If there are only `let` clauses (no `for` clause), then there is one row in the tuple space. Otherwise, count the lengths of the sequences over which each `for` variable iterates, and multiply them together to get the number of rows.

In the example given in Listing 6.8, there are ten rows in the corresponding tuple space, because there is one `for` variable and it iterates over a sequence of length 10. The tuple space for this FLWOR expression is shown in Table 6.1. Notice that the last column contains a nested sequence.

Only rows for which the `where` clause is true are kept in the final result. So in this example, the first three rows will be omitted.

Next, the rows are sorted according to the order by clause. By default, the `order by` clause sorts in ascending order (you'll see other kinds of sorting in Section 6.6). In this example, sorting by the `order by` column reverses the order of the rows.

Finally, after filtering by the `where` clause and sorting by the `order by` clause, the `return` clauses are concatenated together in order (from top to bottom) into one flat sequence. Listing 6.9 shows the result of executing this FLWOR expression.

Table 6.1 The tuple space corresponding to Listing 6.8

$i	$pos	$j	where	order by	return
10	1	100	false	10	(1, 10)
9	2	81	false	9	(2, 9)
8	3	64	false	8	(3, 8)
7	4	49	true	7	(4, 7)
6	5	36	true	6	(5, 6)
5	6	25	true	5	(6, 5)
4	7	16	true	4	(7, 4)
3	8	9	true	3	(8, 3)
2	9	4	true	2	(9, 2)
1	10	1	true	1	(10, 1)

Listing 6.9 The result of executing the FLWOR expression in Listing 6.8

```
(10, 1, 9, 2, 8, 3, 7, 4, 6, 5, 5, 6, 4, 7)
```

Visualizing tuple spaces becomes slightly more difficult when there are multiple `for` variables. Each subsequent `for` variable splits the existing rows. Consider, for example, Listing 6.10. This query constructs a tuple space with four columns and eight rows (the length of the first sequence times the length of the second sequence).

Listing 6.10 A FLWOR expression that joins two sequences

```
for $x at $p in ("a", "b")
for $y in (1, 2, 3, 4)
where $p * $y > 5
return ($x, $y)
```

Looking just at the first variable, we would get two rows. Now split each of those rows into four rows (one row for each item in the second sequence), to get the total of eight rows shown in Table 6.2. Only the last two rows satisfy the `where` clause, so the final result is the sequence `("b", 3, "b", 4)`.

When the `return` clause or one of the variable bindings is itself a FLWOR expression, then the tuple spaces are nested. For example, the query in Listing 6.11 produces the nested tuple space shown in Table 6.3, because the first `return` clause itself returns a FLWOR.

Table 6.2 The tuple space corresponding to Listing 6.10

$x	$p	$y	where	return
"a"	1	1	false	("a", 1)
"a"	1	2	false	("a", 2)
"a"	1	3	false	("a", 3)
"a"	1	4	false	("a", 4)
"b"	2	1	false	("b", 1)
"b"	2	2	false	("b", 2)
"b"	2	3	true	("b", 3)
"b"	2	4	true	("b", 4)

Table 6.3 The tuple space corresponding to Listing 6.11

$i	return	
7	**$j**	**return**
	1	8
	2	9
	3	10
9	**$j**	**return**
	1	10
	2	11
	3	12

As in the non-nested case, the return clauses are concatenated together in order (after filtering and sorting). The result of executing this query is the sequence (8, 9, 10, 10, 11, 12).

Listing 6.11 A nested FLWOR expression

```
for $i in (7, 9)
return
  for $j in 1 to 3
  return $i + $j
```

6.3 Quantification

Before learning how to accomplish practical tasks such as joins and grouping using FLWOR, let's first discuss two related operators, some and every. These operators are like "mini-FLWORs" containing only for and where clauses, except that instead of for, these use the keywords some and every, and instead of returning a sequence of values, they return a single boolean value.

Both operators are followed by a variable name, the keyword in, the sequence to iterate over, the keyword satisfies, and finally the condition to be tested for each member of the sequence. The condition is implicitly converted to boolean using Effective Boolean Value. Both operators are illustrated in Listing 6.12.

Listing 6.12 The some and every operators

```
some $emp in doc("team.xml")//Employee satisfies $emp/@years > 5
every $emp in doc("temp.xml")//Employee satisfies $emp/@years > 5
```

Like the for clause in FLWOR, variables introduced this way are in scope for the rest of the expression (in this case, the condition), and additional variables may be introduced by separating them with commas as in Listing 6.13.

Listing 6.13 Quantification may introduce several variables at once

```
some $i in (1, 2), $j in (1, 3) satisfies $i = $j
```

The some operator implements what is known as *existential quantification*. This is just a fancy term meaning that it tests whether there exists a combination of variable bindings such that the condition is true. Similarly, the every operator implements universal quantification. It tests whether every combination of variable bindings satisfies the condition.

For example, the query in Listing 6.13 returns true, because there exists an assignment to $i (1) and an assignment to $j (1), such that the two are equal. However, the same query using every instead of some would return false, because then there exists an assignment to $i (1) and an assignment to $j (3) such that the condition doesn't hold.

These operators are entirely redundant with FLWOR, but they may allow you to express some queries using a more natural syntax (especially every, which is somewhat awkward when written as FLWOR). These equivalences are depicted in Listing 6.14.

Listing 6.14 The some and every operators are equivalent to FLWOR

```
some variables satisfies condition
<=>
exists(for variables where condition return 1)

every variables satisfies condition
<=>
empty(for variables where not(condition) return 1)
```

6.4 Joins

The primary use of the FLWOR expression is to *join* one or more sequences together (or with themselves) to produce some result. The result may be drawn from the members of the sequences, like database joins, or constructed new in the query.

Joins express relationships between sequences. When two unrelated, independent sequences are combined, then we get a *cross-product*, the simplest kind of join. The XQuery in Listing 6.15 creates a cross-product of two sequences.

Listing 6.15 The cross-product of two sequences

```
for $i in (1, 2, 3)
for $j in (3, 4, 5)
return ($i, $j)
=>
(1, 3, 1, 4, 1, 5, 2, 3, 2, 4, 2, 5, 3, 3, 3, 4, 3, 5)
```

Cartesian join

More commonly, however, the join eliminates some items in the cross-product from consideration. For example, you might select only those members from both sets that are equal, like in Listing 6.16. This is called an *inner join*, because it includes only values that are in both sequences. (This particular example is also an *equi-join*, because it uses the equality operator. Most implementations specially optimize equi-joins.)

Listing 6.16 An inner join of two sequences

```
for $i in (1, 2, 3)
for $j in (3, 4, 5)
where $i = $j
return ($i, $j)
=>
(3, 3)
```

A more realistic example would join two XML documents. So let's recall the team.xml document from Chapter 1 (Listing 1.26), and consider a second XML source, projects.xml, listed in Listing 6.17.

Listing 6.17 The projects.xml document

```
<?xml version='1.0'?>
<Projects>
  <Project id="X1" owner="E2">
    <Name>Enter the Tuple Space</Name>
    <Category>Video Games</Category>
  </Project>
  <Project id="X2" owner="E1">
```

```
    <Name>Cryptic Code</Name>
    <Category>Puzzles</Category>
  </Project>
  <Project id="X3" owner="E5">
    <Name>XQuery Bandit</Name>
    <Category>Video Games</Category>
  </Project>
  <Project id="X4" owner="E3">
    <Name>Micropoly</Name>
    <Category>Board Games</Category>
  </Project>
</Projects>
```

A simple inner join between these documents is demonstrated in Listing 6.18. This query iterates through the `Project` elements from `projects.xml` and the `Employee` elements from `team.xml` and finds all pairs such that the project's owner attribute is equal to the employee's id attribute. This kind of join result is called a *one-to-one join*, because each item in the first sequence has (at most) one corresponding item in the second sequence.

To enhance readability, I've reformatted the result in this example and all the others in this chapter with extra whitespace (by using new lines and sometimes indentation).

Listing 6.18 A one-to-one join between the projects.xml and team.xml documents

```
for $proj in doc("projects.xml")/Projects/Project
for $emp in doc("team.xml")//Employee
where $proj/@owner = $emp/@id
return $proj/Name, $emp/Name
=>
<Name>Enter the Tuple Space</Name>
<Name>Carl Yates</Name>
<Name>Cryptic Code</Name>
<Name>Kandy Konrad</Name>
<Name>XQuery Bandit</Name>
<Name>Jason Abedora</Name>
<Name>Micropoly</Name>
<Name>Jim Barry</Name>
```

There are several interesting directions to go from here, such as changing the join condition or the result format. Let's consider changing the result first, and then explore other kinds of join conditions.

In this example, the output is somewhat confusing because the natural pairing of employees and projects has been lost when the tuple space result was flattened (remember, sequences in XQuery aren't nested). To achieve a hierarchical result, we need to use XML. In Listing 6.19, we wrap each pair with a new `Assignment` element. The curly braces inside the element cause its contents to be evaluated as XQuery expressions. (See Chapter 7 for details about XML construction.)

Again, whitespace has been inserted to make the results easier to read.

Listing 6.19 The same join as Listing 6.18, but using XML to group results

```
for $proj in doc("projects.xml")/Projects/Project
for $emp in doc("team.xml")//Employee
where $proj/@owner = $emp/@id
return <Assignment>{ $proj/Name, $emp/Name }</Assignment>
=>
<Assignment>
  <Name>Enter the Tuple Space</Name>
  <Name>Carl Yates</Name>
</Assignment>
<Assignment>
  <Name>Cryptic Code</Name>
  <Name>Kandy Konrad</Name>
</Assignment>
<Assignment>
  <Name>XQuery Bandit</Name>
  <Name>Jason Abedora</Name>
</Assignment>
<Assignment>
  <Name>Micropoly</Name>
  <Name>Jim Barry</Name>
</Assignment>
```

Another confusing aspect about the result is that there are two `Name` elements with different meanings. Conflicting node names (and just a general desire to change names) are common when joining XML data sources together. Listing 6.20 uses the XML constructor syntax to create attributes instead of copying the elements from the original document. (See Chapter 7 for more examples of XML constructors.)

Listing 6.20 The same join as Listings 6.18 and 6.19, but reshaping the results

```
for $proj in doc("projects.xml")/Projects/Project
for $emp in doc("team.xml")//Employee
where $proj/@owner = $emp/@id
return
<Assignment proj="{$proj/Name}" emp="{$emp/Name}" />
=>
<Assignment proj="Enter the Tuple Space" emp="Carl Yates" />
<Assignment proj="Cryptic Code"          emp="Kandy Konrad" />
<Assignment proj="XQuery Bandit"         emp="Jason Abedora" />
<Assignment proj="Micropoly"             emp="Jim Barry" />
```

Other kinds of joins are possible. For example, Listing 6.21 shows a *many-to-many join*, so named because many items from the first sequence may correspond to many items from the second sequence.

Listing 6.21 A many-to-many join between team.xml and projects.xml

```
for $proj in doc("projects.xml")/Projects/Project
for $emp in doc("team.xml")//Employee
where $proj/Category = $emp/Expertise
return
<Assignment proj="{$proj/Name}" emp="{$emp/Name}" />
=>
<Assignment proj="Enter the Tuple Space" emp="Carl Yates" />
<Assignment proj="Enter the Tuple Space" emp="Jim Barry" />
<Assignment proj="Cryptic Code"          emp="Chaz Hoover" />
<Assignment proj="Cryptic Code"          emp="Jason Abedora" />
<Assignment proj="Cryptic Code"          emp="Wanda Wilson" />
<Assignment proj="XQuery Bandit"         emp="Carl Yates" />
<Assignment proj="XQuery Bandit"         emp="Jim Barry" />
<Assignment proj="Micropoly"             emp="Wanda Wilson" />
```

Many-to-many joins are problematic in XML, in part because node values are duplicated. In small examples like these, this duplication may not seem like much of a problem, but in large examples it can significantly affect the size of the result. It can also create problems with node identity, because now the "same" node is copied multiple times to the output.

One way to partially address this problem is to change the join into an *outer join*. A *left outer join* includes members from the outer (left) sequence, even when there isn't a member of the inner (right) sequence satisfying the join condition. Similarly, a *right outer join* keeps items from the inner sequence even when there isn't a corresponding member of the outer sequence. A *full outer join* keeps items from both sequences.

This technique is illustrated in Listing 6.22, using an outer FLWOR statement to iterate over the first sequence and create one element for each project. An inner FLWOR performs the join, returning zero or more employee names. Separating the join into two FLWOR statements, with the outer one always returning something, is what makes this an outer join.

Listing 6.22 An outer join between the team.xml and projects.xml documents

```
for $proj in doc("projects.xml")/Projects/Project
return
<Assignment proj="{$proj/Name}">{
  for $emp in doc("team.xml")//Employee
  where $emp/Expertise = $proj/Category
  return $emp/Name
}</Assignment>
=>
<Assignment proj="Enter the Tuple Space">
  <Name>Carl Yates</Name>
  <Name>Jim Barry</Name>
</Assignment>
<Assignment proj="Cryptic Code">
  <Name>Chaz Hoover</Name>
  <Name>Jason Abedora</Name>
  <Name>Wanda Wilson</Name>
</Assignment>
<Assignment proj="XQuery Bandit">
  <Name>Carl Yates</Name>
  <Name>Jim Barry</Name>
</Assignment>
<Assignment proj="Micropoly">
  <Name>Wanda Wilson</Name>
</Assignment>
```

Although the outer join no longer duplicates project names, it still duplicates employee names. In other words, it is a *one-to-many* join.

The traditional "fix" for representing one-to-many and many-to-many relationships in XML is to select each element exactly once, and to use `xs:ID`/`xs:IDREF` values in the XML output to express the relationship. This technique requires that the elements being referred to have unique `xs:ID` values.

Listing 6.23 demonstrates a FLWOR query that generates a list of employee IDs for each project. This data can then be used with navigation functions like `id()` to find the corresponding `Employee` elements, instead of duplicating them in the result. This technique has the drawback that two joins will be performed: one to produce the result, and another to consume it. However, typically implementation optimizes ID lookup so that it's faster than arbitrary joins.

Listing 6.23 Use `xs:ID` relationships instead of duplicating elements

```
for $proj in doc("projects.xml")/Projects/Project
return
<Assignment proj="{$proj/Name}" emps="{
    for $emp in doc('team.xml')//Employee
    where $emp/Expertise = $proj/Category
    return $emp/@id
  }"/>
=>
<Assignment proj="Enter the Tuple Space" emps="E2 E3" />
<Assignment proj="Cryptic Code"          emps="E6 E5 E3" />
<Assignment proj="XQuery Bandit"         emps="E2 E3" />
<Assignment proj="Micropoly"            emps="E0" />
```

Not all joins are equi-joins. The query in Listing 6.24 finds all projects for which the owner doesn't have expertise in that project category. (Chapter 11 explains why this query uses `not(=)` instead of `!=`.)

Listing 6.24 Not all joins are equi-joins

```
for $proj in doc("projects.xml")/Projects/Project
for $emp in doc("team.xml")//Employee
```

```
where $proj/@owner = $emp/@id
  and not($proj/Category = $emp/Expertise)
return <Mismatch>{$emp/Name, $proj/Name}</Mismatch>
=>
<Mismatch>
  <Name>Kandy Konrad</Name>
  <Name>Cryptic Code</Name>
</Mismatch>
<Mismatch>
  <Name>Jason Abedora</Name>
  <Name>XQuery Bandit</Name>
</Mismatch>
<Mismatch>
  <Name>Jim Barry</Name>
  <Name>Micropoly</Name>
</Mismatch>
```

Another kind of join is the *self-join*, which joins a sequence with itself. Self-joins are very common when working with recursive data, such as in the `team.xml` document. In fact, we've already seen one example in Chapter 3 already, copied here as Listing 6.25.

Listing 6.25 A self-join using path navigation

```
doc("team.xml")//Employee[Title =
                doc("team.xml")//Employee[@id="E0"]/Title]/Name
```

The meaning of this path may be more easily discerned when it's written as a FLWOR expression, like in Listing 6.26. Both queries do the same work, but the second query using FLWOR makes the join more explicit.

Listing 6.26 The same self-join as Listing 6.25 using FLWOR instead

```
let $emp := doc("team.xml")//Employee
for $i in $emp, $j in $emp
where $i/Title = $j/Title and $j/@id = "E0"
return $i/Name
```

6.5 Comparing Sequences

There are many different ways to compare two sequences: member-wise, existentially, and universally to name just three. This section shows how to perform these different kinds of sequence comparisons. Effectively, each kind of sequence comparison is just another kind of join.

6.5.1 Existential Comparison

In Chapter 5 you learned that the general comparison operators compare sequences existentially. They test whether there exists a member in each sequence such that the comparison is true. For example, to test whether there exists a member of one sequence that is greater than a member of a second sequence, you can write `$seq1 > $seq2`.

However, the general comparison operators can only perform simple comparisons, and not more complex conditions. Fortunately, XQuery provides many other ways to express existential comparison.

One is to use the `some` operator. For example, the previous comparison could also have been expressed as `some $a in $seq1, $b in $seq2 satisfies $a > $b`. However, `some` is more flexible because it allows you to express other kinds of conditions. For example, suppose that instead of merely comparing one member against another, you want to test whether it's greater by a certain amount (say, 3). Then you could use the query `some $a in $seq1, $b in $seq2 satisfies $a > $b + 3`.

Path expressions are a simpler but somewhat less expressive way to perform existential comparisons, applying a predicate condition to each node in a step. For example, you could write `exists($seq1[. > $seq2])`. Like `some`, paths can express more complex conditions. For instance, you could express the same comparison using `some` using the path `exists($seq1[ . - 3 > $seq2])`. Paths are very concise, but can be harder to read and can have unintended consequences. For example, the expression `exists($seq1[ . > $seq2 + 3])` results in an error because addition cannot be applied to a sequence of more than one item.

The most general-purpose way to perform an existential comparison is using FLWOR expressions. For example, you could write `for $a in $seq1, $b in $seq2 where $a > $seq2 return $a`. This not only compares the two sequences, but also returns all the members of the first sequence that satisfied the condition. To test that at least one such member exists, just wrap the FLWOR expression with the `exists()` function. Listing 6.27 compares these three styles side-by-side.

Listing 6.27 Three ways to existentially compare two sequences

```
some $a in $seq1, $b in $seq2 satisfies $a > $b
$a[. > $seq2]
exists(for $a in $seq1, $b in $seq2 where $a > $b return $a)
```

6.5.2 Memberwise Comparison

The `deep-equal()` function compares sequences memberwise. It tests whether the two sequences have the same length, and if so, whether each pair of corresponding members compares true. However, this function always performs deep equality. XQuery doesn't have a built-in function that performs memberwise comparison by node identity, or that performs any other kind of memberwise action.

For instance, suppose that you want to take two sequences of numbers and add or compare them memberwise. The easiest way to express memberwise operations in XQuery is to use a join on position. The idea is to keep track of which position you are at as you iterate through the first sequence, so that you can pick out the member of the second sequence that is at the same location.

For example, the function in Listing 6.28 is similar to `deep-equal()`, except that it compares nodes by identity instead of using deep equality.

Listing 6.28 `deep-equal()`, without the deep

```
declare function shallow-equal($seq1 as node()*,
                               $seq2 as node()*) as xs:boolean {
  if (count($seq1) != count($seq2))
  then false()
  else
    empty(
      for $i at $p1 in $seq1
      for $j at $p2 in $seq2
      where $p1 = $p2 and $i is not $j
      return 1
    )
};
```

For another example, the query in Listing 6.29 returns true if every member of the first sequence is greater than the corresponding member of the second sequence.

Listing 6.29 Compare two sequences memberwise

```
count($seq1) = count($seq2)
and empty(
  for $i at $p1 in $seq1
  for $j at $p2 in $seq2
  where $p1 = $p2 and not($i > $j)
  return 1
)
```

These examples could also be expressed using predicates to apply an implicit join. For example, Listing 6.30 is another way to achieve the same effect as in Listing 6.29.

Listing 6.30 An equivalent way to compare two sequences memberwise

```
count($seq1) = count($seq2)
and empty(
  for $i at $p in $seq1
  where not($i > $seq2[$p])
  return 1
)
```

You may notice the similarity between this query and the every operator. Unfortunately, every doesn't provide a way to introduce position variables, but you can compensate for this by using the to operator to range up to the length of the sequence, as in Listing 6.31.

Listing 6.31 Yet another way to produce the same effect

```
count($seq1) = count($seq2)
and
every $p in 1 to count($seq1) satisfies $seq1[$p] > $seq2[$p]
```

Another consideration when writing these comparisons is the decision as to how to handle exceptional conditions: If one sequence is longer than the other, do you want to return false, raise an error, or ignore the extra members?

Because `$seq[$pos]` returns the empty sequence when `$pos` goes beyond the end of the sequence, you could omit the `count()` comparison to ignore additional members when the sequences don't have the same length, as in Listing 6.32. Alternatively, you can use a conditional and the `error()` function to raise an error when the sequences differ in length.

Listing 6.32 Ignore leftover members

```
empty(for $i at $p in $seq1 where not($i > $seq2[$p]) return 1)
```

6.5.3 Universal Comparison

Another way to compare sequences is to require that a condition be true for every member of the sequence. Section 6.3 already showed how to perform universal quantification using the `every` operator (or an equivalent FLWOR). Like existential quantification, universal quantification can be expressed in several forms, some of which are shown in Listing 6.33.

Listing 6.33 Universal quantification, like existential, has many forms

```
every $a in $seq1, $b in $seq2 satisfies $a gt $b

empty( for $a in $seq1
       where not($a > $seq2)
       return $a )

empty($seq1[not(. > $seq2)])
```

Another option is what might be called universal memberwise comparison: Require every member to compare true against its corresponding member in the other sequence. As before, you have to decide how to handle the case that the sequences differ in length. The example in Listing 6.34 returns false if the two sequences differ in length. It uses the fact that every pair of members satisfies a condition if no pair of them fails it.

Listing 6.34 Universal memberwise comparison

```
count($seq1) = count($seq2)
and empty( for $i at $pos in $seq1
           where not($i > $seq2[$pos])
           return $i )+
```

6.6 Sorting

FLWOR expressions have a natural ordering, which is determined by the bindings of the `for` variables (the row order of the tuple space). However, the `order by` clause may be used to apply some other ordering. The `order by` clause takes a list of expressions, called *sort keys*.

The `order by` clause sorts the tuple space according to each of the sort keys in order. It's important to understand that it's the rows of the tuple space that are sorted, not the final (flattened) result. The sort keys don't have to be returned in the result. Listing 6.35 demonstrates a simple sort.

Listing 6.35 The `order by` clause sorts the result (after the `where` clause)

```
for $i in (4, 2, 3, 1)
order by $i
return $i
=>
(1, 2, 3, 4)
```

Each sort key is first evaluated and atomized; if the result isn't empty or a singleton, then an error is raised. Untyped values are cast to `xs:string`. A sort key must evaluate to the same type for every tuple in the tuple space, and the type must be totally ordered (i.e., support the `gt` operator). Sorting depends on the `gt` value comparison operator, which depends on the collation when comparing `xs:string` values. The example in Listing 6.36 may produce a different result from the one given here, depending on the default collation.

Listing 6.36 Sorting by string values depends on the default collation

```
for $i in doc("team.xml")//Employee
where exists($i//Employee)
order by $i/@id descending
return $i/Name
=>
<Name>Chaz Hoover</Name>
<Name>Carl Yates</Name>
<Name>Kandy Konrad</Name>
```

When the first sort key evaluated for two tuples results in a tie, then subsequent sort keys are used to break the tie. If all the keys tie, then the order of the tied tuples is implementation-defined unless the `stable` keyword is used in front of the `order by` keyword. In that case, the tied tuples retain their original ordering relative to each other. In Listing 6.37, the first two results tied, so their original relative order is preserved.

Listing 6.37 Stable sorting preserves the original order of ties

```
for $i in (<a b="z">2</a>, <a b="x">1</a>, <a b="y">1</a>)
stable order by $i
return $i
=>
<a b="x">1</a>
<a b="y">1</a>
<a b="z">2</a>
```

Each sort key expression may be followed by modifiers that control how that key affects the sort order. The most common modifiers are ascending and descending (ascending is the default) with the obvious effect. The other modifiers, `empty least` and `empty greatest`, control how the empty sequence and NaN sort relative to all other values.

When `empty least` is specified, then the empty sequence sorts less than all other non-empty values, and NaN sorts less than all other non-empty and non-NaN values. When `empty greatest` is specified, then the empty sequence sorts greater than all other non-empty values, and NaN sorts greater than all other

Table 6.4 The ordered tuple space corresponding to Listing 6.38

$i	$key	return
2E0	()	2E0
1E0	()	1E0
NaN	NaN	NaN
3E0	3E0	3E0

non-empty and non-NaN values. Listing 6.38 demonstrates the interaction between empty least and these special values.

Listing 6.38 Empty least and greatest affect how NaN and () sort

```
for $i in (1E0, 2E0, 3E0, 0E0 div 0)
let $key := if ($i < 2.5) then $i else ()
order by $key empty least, $i descending
return $i
=>
(2E0, 1E0, NaN, 3E0)
```

These modifiers are demonstrated by Listing 6.38, which generates the ordered tuple space illustrated in Table 6.4. Because the first sort key has empty least, the two empty sequences sort least, followed by NaN, followed by 3E0. Then the second key is used to break the tie between the first two values. Because it has descending, 2E0 sorts before 1E0, producing the final result shown.

When sorting by string values, it's important to pay attention to Unicode normalization and collation. For example, you may want letters to sort in a case-insensitive way, or you may want alternate spellings of the same phonetic symbol to sort the same way. The former is controlled by collation, while the latter is controlled by Unicode normalization. Support for both of these depends partly on the implementation (see Chapter 8 for details). You can also apply string functions such as lower-case() in the sort key, although this will generally perform less well than using collation.

6.7 Grouping

When joining two sequences together, sometimes you also want to sort the result by something that depends on the result. For example, you might want to group cities by region with regions sorted by the sum of their city populations, or list team leads by the number of people or the average years of experience accumulated on their team.

Queries like these follow a *grouping* pattern, and some languages (such as SQL) have dedicated operators to support them. Other languages, such as XSLT and XQuery, express group queries just like any other query, and then implementations vary in how well they recognize the grouping patterns and execute them.

For example, consider listing team leads in decreasing order by the number of direct reports they have. The query in Listing 6.39 performs this grouping.

Listing 6.39 A simple grouping query that sorts team leads by team size

```
for $i in doc("team.xml")//Employee
let $reports := count($i/Employee)
where $reports > 0
order by $reports descending
return <Employee name="{$i/Name}" reports="{$reports}"/>
=>
<Employee name="Chaz Hoover" reports="2"/>
<Employee name="Carl Yates" reports="2"/>
<Employee name="Kandy Konrad" reports="1"/>
```

In this query, we first iterate over all `Employee` elements in the `team.xml` document. Then, for each employee, we calculate the number of direct reports (that is, the number of `Employee` element children). We filter the result with a `where` clause to eliminate employees who have no direct reports. The `order by` clause reverse sorts by the number of direct reports, and finally the `return` clause constructs a meaningful result.

Instead, we could reverse sort the list by the average number of years on each team. This is a somewhat more complicated query, in part because we must iterate over all the `Employee` descendants and calculate their average years of experience. Because the `avg()` function takes only sequences of atomic values, when we pass it the sequence of year attributes, it first applies the function conversion rules (Chapter 2), which atomizes this list of nodes and produces a sequence of values.

We use the `descendant-or-self` axis directly instead of the abbreviation `//`, so that we include the lead's years of experience in the average. The `round-half-to-even()` function is used to round the result to two decimal places.

Listing 6.40 Team leads reverse sorted by average years of experience on their team

```
for $i in doc("team.xml")//Employee
let $years := avg($i/descendant-or-self::Employee/@years)
where exists($i/Employee)
order by $years descending
return <Employee name="{$i/Name}"
                  years="{round-half-to-even($years, 2)}"/>
=>
<Employee name="Chaz Hoover" years="4.82"/>
<Employee name="Carl Yates" years="2.63"/>
<Employee name="Kandy Konrad" years="8.35"/>
```

Conceptually, this query produces the nested tuple space depicted in Table 6.5. In the interest of space, this table shows only the employee ID values instead of the entire `Employee` nodes. The `$years` column requires an implicit join between each `Employee` and its descendants, and then computes the average, which is listed in the `order by` column. In practice, some implementations may optimize queries like these to compute the aggregate on the fly.

It's important to note also that the `order by` and `return` clauses aren't evaluated when the `where` clause is false (avoiding, for example, potential error cases).

You might also like to generate a nice XHTML table containing the results, with two employees per line. In this case, you want to group the results by position but after they have been sorted as above. This can be accomplished by applying another FLWOR query to the original one, like in Listing 6.41.

Listing 6.41 Generating a table of the results, grouped into pairs

```
<table>
  <tr>
    <th>Employee</th><th>years</th>
    <th>Employee</th><th>years</th>
  </tr>
{
  let $emps :=
    (for $i in doc("team.xml")//Employee
```

Table 6.5 The tuple space corresponding to Listing 6.40

$i/@id	$years	where	order by	return
E6	@years 4.3 6.1 1.2 0.6 8.2 8.5	true	4.8166666	`<Employee name="Chaz Hoover" years="4.82"/>`
E2	@years 6.1 1.2 0.6	true	2.6333333	`<Employee name="Carl Yates" years="2.63"/>`
E4	@years 1.2	false		
E5	@years 0.6	false		
E1	@years 8.2 8.5	true	8.35	`<Employee name="Kandy Konrad" years="8.35"/>`
E0	@years 8.2	false		
E3	@years 8.5	false		

```
    let $years := avg($i/descendant-or-self::Employee/@years)
    where exists($i/Employee)
    order by $years descending
    return <Employee name="{$i/Name}"
                     years="{round-half-to-even($years, 2)}"/>
  for $e at $pos in $emps
  let $next := $emps[$pos + 1]
  where $pos mod 2 = 0
  return
  <tr>
    <td>{string($e/@Name)}</td><td>{string($e/@years)}</td>
    <td>{string($next/@Name)}</td><td>{string($next/@years)}</td>
  </tr>
}</table>
```

6.8 Conclusion

The XQuery FLWOR expression introduces variables using `let`, iterates over sequences using `for`, filters and joins sequences using `where`, sorts the remaining items using `order by`, and constructs a result using `return`. FLWOR is the central expression of most queries, and the most powerful.

The `some` and `every` expressions are simplified FLWOR statements that test whether some or every member of a sequence (or sequences) satisfy some condition. They can be convenient when trying to write easy-to-read queries.

6.9 Further Reading

Every XQuery developer should own a copy of *An Introduction to Database Systems* by C. J. Date, currently in its 8th edition. Although focused on the relational data model, this classic contains much useful information on joins, grouping, and data in general.

The FLWOR expression comes directly from Quilt, which was a precursor to XQuery. For a historical perspective on Quilt, check out the Web site at `http://www.almaden.ibm.com/cs/people/chamberlin/quilt.html`.

CHAPTER 7

Constructing XML

7.1 Introduction

In Chapter 3, you learned how to access XML that exists outside the query and navigate over it. In this chapter, you will learn how to construct XML directly in a query. Constructing XML is useful for several purposes, including creating a new result shape (*transformation*), representing temporary intermediate data structures (*composition*), and organizing data into conceptual groups (*views*).

XQuery has expressions for constructing all seven of the well-known XML node kinds: element, attribute, text, document, comment, processing-instruction, and namespace. For all of these node kinds, XQuery supports two different construction expressions: one with a syntax similar to XML, and an alternate XQuery syntax primarily used for nodes whose names or contents are computed from XQuery expressions.

XML construction is a fairly complex process. Handling whitespace characters, namespace nodes, sequences of atomic values, and types are some of its trickier aspects.

Constructed XML elements and attributes are validated against the in-scope schema types (see Section 7.10). Use type operators such as `validate` to apply different or more specific types to constructed XML nodes (see Chapter 9).

7.2 Element Nodes

XQuery provides two different ways to construct elements: the *direct constructor* and the *computed constructor*. The direct constructor is essentially the XML syntax slightly modified to support embedded XQuery expressions. The element name is constant, but its content can be totally or partially computed by XQuery expressions. The computed constructor is specific to XQuery and is most commonly used when the element name is computed by some other XQuery expression (although it can also be used when the name is constant).

153

7.2.1 Direct Element Constructor

The XML syntax for constructing elements should be familiar to you already, and XQuery uses it directly. For example, the XQuery `<x/>` in Listing 7.1 constructs a sequence containing one element named x, while the XQuery `<x><y/></x>` constructs an element named x that contains another element named y.

Listing 7.1 Direct element construction

```
<x/>
<x></x>
<x><y/></x>
```

The characters in between the start and end tags of the element are its content. When an element is constructed using a self-closing tag (`<x/>`) or with separate start and end tags with no characters in between (`<x></x>`), its content is empty. The syntax choice makes no difference.

Just like in XML, element nodes may contain any other kind of node except document. The other node kinds are explained later in this chapter. Character references, character entity references, and CDATA sections are also allowed, but become ordinary text; that is, the XQuery Data Model doesn't "remember" that they were CDATA or references.

When any part of an element's content is enclosed by curly braces (`{}`), the enclosed expression is evaluated as an XQuery. All other content is treated as ordinary character data. To use a curly brace character as an ordinary character, it must be escaped by doubling it or by using a character entity reference.

For example, the XQuery element constructed by `<x>a{1+1}</x>` contains the text value a2. The character a is kept unchanged, but the curly-brace enclosed expression 1+1 is treated as an XQuery expression, evaluated, and produces the result 2. To output the expression literally, without computing it, double-up its curly braces like this: `<x>a{{1+1}}</x>`. This XQuery results in an x element whose text content consists of the six characters a{1+1}.

The exact rules for element content are quite a bit more involved than this; see Section 7.11 for complete details.

7.2.2 Computed Element Constructor

XQuery supports a second syntax for constructing elements consisting of the `element` keyword followed by two expressions: the name and the content. The name can be either an ordinary name constant or an XQuery expression enclosed in braces. Listing 7.2 shows both of these possibilities. The content is always an enclosed expression.

Listing 7.2 Computed element construction

```
element x { 1 + 1 }
element { concat("x", ":y") } { 1 + 1 }
```

For example, the XQuery expression `element x { 1 + 1 }` is equivalent to the XQuery `<x>{1 + 1}</x>`. It computes an element with the name `x`, and whose content is evaluated from the XQuery expression `1 + 1`. More commonly, however, this syntax is used when the name isn't constant. For example, the XQuery expression `element { concat("a", 1 + 1) } { "x" }` computes both the element name (in this case, `a2`) and the content.

The name expression is converted to a qualified name as follows: If the name expression results in an `xs:QName` value, then that value is used directly. If the name results in an `xs:string` value, then that string is parsed as a `QName` using the in-scope namespaces. No other type of value is allowed as the name expression.

Again, the rules for evaluating element content are involved; see Section 7.11.

7.3 Attribute Nodes

XQuery also supports two styles of attribute construction: direct attribute constructors, and computed constructors similar to the computed constructors for elements.

7.3.1 Direct Attribute Constructors

The usual XML syntax for attributes (attributes in an element's start tag between the element name and the tag end character >) constructs attributes directly. Attribute values may appear inside single or double quotes; the quote character must be escaped (using an entity or by doubling it) when used in the content.

As with element content, an attribute value may contain character data, including character entities, and enclosed expressions are evaluated as XQuery expressions. Curly braces must be doubled to be used as character content. Listing 7.3 shows two examples of direct attribute constructors.

Listing 7.3 Direct attribute construction

```
<x a="value1" b='value2' />
<y a="{1+2}" b="{{1+2}}"/>
```

Like elements, attribute content requires some special rules to handle whitespace and sequences of values. See section 7.11 for details.

7.3.2 Computed Attribute Constructors

XQuery provides an alternate syntax for attributes, similar to that for elements, using the `attribute` keyword. For example, `attribute name { "value" }` constructs an attribute with the given name and value. Listing 7.4 shows a computed attribute constructor on its own and another in an XML element as part of its computed content.

Listing 7.4 Computed attribute construction

```
attribute { xs:QName("a") } {1+2}
<x>{ attribute a {1+2} } </x>
```

As with elements, the main reason to use the computed attribute constructor is that the name can be computed from an enclosed XQuery expression. However, another reason to use the alternate syntax is to construct an attribute node without a parent element. For example, you might write a function that computes an "attribute group" and uses it over and over again in other elements, as shown in Listing 7.5. Of course, this means that attributes don't always have a parent node, which can cause some difficulties when serializing out the data model (see Chapter 13).

Listing 7.5 Computed attribute constructor can create "floating" attributes

```
declare function my-attrs() as attribute()* {
  (attribute one { "1" },
   attribute two { "2" },
   attribute three { "3" })
};
```

```
<x>
  <y>{ my-attrs() }</y>
  <z>{ my-attrs() }</z>
</x>
=>
<x>
  <y one="1" two="2" three="3"/>
  <z one="1" two="2" three="3"/>
</x>
```

7.4 Text Nodes

Text nodes can actually be created in three ways:

- Using element content (explained in section 7.11)
- Using the computed text constructor syntax text { *content* }, where *content* is any sequence of XQuery expressions
- Using the CDATA syntax (described at the end of this section)

In the computed text constructor case, the content sequence is first atomized; if the atomized sequence is empty, then no text node is constructed. Otherwise, the atomic values are converted to xs:string and joined together with a space character between each pair—exactly like a call to the built-in string-join() function—and the resulting string value is the value of the text node.

Because text nodes are already nameless, the main reason to use this alternate syntax is to create "floating" text nodes without parent elements. The computed text constructor can also be useful when you need fine-grained control over whitespace handling in element content (see Section 7.11).

Sometimes, mainly in elements, the text value contains a lot of special characters that would require escaping or entitization if you wrote them normally. Instead of escaping or entitizing every such character, you can use a CDATA constructor. (In XQuery, CDATA constructors can be used anywhere, not just in elements.)

The CDATA constructor has the form <![CDATA[chars]]> where chars is a sequence of zero or more characters, excluding the sequence]]> (in other words, exactly like it works in XML). The CDATA constructor creates a text node whose value is that string of characters.

A common misconception is that the CDATA constructor allows you to represent other characters, such as control characters, that aren't legal in XML, but in fact it doesn't allow this—it just gives you a way to avoid writing lots of character entities. (However, not all XQuery implementations enforce the XML rules; check the documentation accompanying your implementation.)

7.5 Document Nodes

XQuery provides a computed document constructor, `document { content }`, which constructs a document node with the given content. This constructor creates a new document node, copying all the content and stripping it of useful type information.

If the content sequence contains document or attribute nodes, an error is raised. Sequences of one or more consecutive atomic values are replaced by text nodes containing those atomic values converted to `xs:string` and joined together with spaces in between, like a call to the `string-join()` function. All other items in the content sequence are deep-copied—losing their node identity—and given new types: elements are typed as `xs:anyType`, attributes as `xs:anySimpleType`.

The new document node isn't validated against a schema, nor are XML well-formedness rules checked. If its content is empty, then an empty document node is constructed.

The main reason to use the document constructor, aside from the effects just mentioned, is to simulate a document loaded by the built-in `doc()` function. For example, let's suppose you wish to write a function that will return a computed document instead of one loaded from XML. Your first attempt would probably look like Listing 7.6, and it would be wrong.

Listing 7.6 Incorrect implementation of a pseudo-document function

```
declare function pseudo-doc() {
  <x>
    <y/>
  </x>
};
```

The problem with this implementation becomes clear when you consider a path like `pseudo-doc()/x`. This path returns the empty sequence, instead of matching the x element as you might expect. The first step constructs the x element, and then the second step selects its child elements named x—but there aren't any.

We can solve this problem by using the `document` constructor, as in Listing 7.7.

Listing 7.7 Correct implementation of a pseudo-document function

```
declare function pseudo-doc() as document-node() {
  document {
    <x>
      <y/>
    </x>
  }
};
```

With this correct definition, the first step of the path `pseudo-doc()/x` selects the document node, and the second step finds its child element named x, as expected.

7.6 Comment Nodes

XQuery supports the XML syntax for comment nodes, so you can write `<!--content-->` to create an XML comment node, where `content` is any sequence of characters not containing the terminator sequence `-->`.

XQuery also provides a computed comment constructor, with the comment keyword followed by an expression enclosed in curly braces. The expression is evaluated, atomized, and the resulting values converted to string and concatenated with space characters in between to produce the comment content. XML comment nodes shouldn't be confused with XQuery comments, which don't have any effects on a query. Listing 7.8 shows both comment constructor styles.

Listing 7.8 Direct and computed comment construction

```
<!-- this is a comment -->
comment { "this is a comment" }
```

7.7 Processing Instruction Nodes

Processing instruction nodes are constructed using the usual XML syntax: `<?name content?>`, where `name` is any valid, unprefixed XML name, and `content` is any sequence of characters not containing the terminator sequence `?>`. They can also be constructed using the `processing-instruction` keyword followed by an enclosed name expression and an enclosed content expression. In both cases, the name part is optional. Listing 7.9 demonstrates both styles of construction.

Listing 7.9 Processing instruction constructors

```
<?hello world?>
processing-instruction { "hello" } { "world" }
```

Although the XML declaration `<?xml version="1.0"?>` that may appear at the top of an XML file looks like a processing instruction, it isn't. It cannot be selected or constructed by XQuery.

7.8 Namespace Nodes

XML namespaces can be bewildering. On the one hand, they are data similar to ordinary attributes; on the other hand, they are meta-data that affects how other XML names are interpreted. On the one hand, they are nodes with unique identities; on the other hand, they are copied by some data models into each node in their scope.

One of the biggest debates while designing XQuery was what to do with an expression like `<foo xmlns="urn:bar"/>`. How should the *namespace declaration attribute* (`xmlns="urn:bar"`) affect the element? What about computed constructors, such as `<foo>{ attribute xmlns {"urn:bar"} }</foo>` or even `<foo xmlns="{concat('urn:', 'bar')}"/>`? Should these even be allowed?

Because namespace declaration attributes are so nuanced, in XQuery it's generally best to forgo them entirely and put all namespace declarations in the query prolog. However, XQuery also accepts and uses namespace declaration attributes when they appear in direct element constructors. In Listing 7.10, the first element uses the namespace declaration in the prolog, while the second element uses a namespace declaration attribute to accomplish the same effect.

Listing 7.10 Two different ways to declare a namespace

```
declare namespace foo="urn:one";
<foo:x/>
<bar:y xmlns:baz="urn:two"/>
```

Despite its name, the namespace declaration attribute doesn't cause an attribute to be constructed; instead, it constructs a namespace node and puts the namespace prefix (or default element namespace) into scope for that element and all of its content. The namespace declaration attribute cannot be computed; its content must be a literal string.

XQuery also supports a computed namespace constructor, demonstrated in Listing 7.11, in which the prefix is still constant but the namespace value can be computed by an arbitrary XQuery expression. The namespace value is processed the same as the content expressions in the computed comment and processing instruction constructors described previously.

Listing 7.11 Computed namespace constructor

```
<foo:x>{ namespace foo { "bar" } }</x>
=>
<foo:x xmlns:foo="bar"/>
```

As in XML, the namespace prefixes `xml` and `xmlns` are special and cannot be overridden. However, any of the other XQuery built-in namespace prefixes, such as `xs` and `fn`, can be overridden using a namespace declaration attribute (just as they can be overridden using namespace declarations in the prolog).

7.9 Composition

Navigation over constructed nodes is called *composition*.

In XSLT 1.0, constructed elements create *result tree fragments* and composition is specifically disallowed. In contrast, XQuery encourages composition; constructed nodes aren't any different than nodes loaded from a document, and can be manipulated or navigated in the same way (see Listing 7.12). Most implementations eliminate unnecessary temporary nodes (although some things can prevent this optimization; see Chapter 13).

Listing 7.12 XQuery supports composition of construction and navigation

```
(<x><y><z/></y></x>)//z
=>
<z/>
```

Because XQuery doesn't have structural types other than XML and flat sequences, composition enables you to construct your own hierarchical data structures, usually without significant loss in efficiency.

As a simple example, consider creating a point element that has x, y, and z attributes (corresponding to those coordinates). You could then write functions that use these point elements, and extract the coordinate values using attribute navigation, as shown in Listing 7.13. (If you're familiar with XML Schema and your XQuery implementation supports schema import, then you should consider creating complex types to associate with your data structures.)

Listing 7.13 Composition facilitates custom XML "data structures"

```
declare function make-origin() as element(point) {
  <point x="0" y="0" z="0"/>
};

declare function length-squared($p as element(point)) as xs:double {
  $p/@x * $p/@x + $p/@y * $p/@y + $p/@z * $p/@z
};

declare function scale($p as element(point),
                       $scale as xs:double) as element(point) {
  <point x="{$p/@x * $scale}" y="{$p/@y * $scale}"
                             z="{$p/@z * $scale)" />
};

make-origin()
=>
<point x="0" y="0" z="0" />

scale(<point x="1" y="2" z="3"/>, 2)
=>
<point x="2" y="4" z="6" />

length-squared(make-origin())              => 0E0
length-squared(<point x="1" y="2" z="3"/>) => 1.4E1
```

7.10 Validation

If you don't use complex types from XML Schema, or if your implementation doesn't support `import schema`, then you can skip this section.

Every constructed element is implicitly validated against the current validation context, exactly like the `validate` expression (see Chapter 9). If the validation mode is `skip`, then no validation is actually performed; instead, the element is typed as `xs:anyType`, and its attributes are typed as `xdt:untypedAtomic`.

Validation is a complex process that not only augments the data model with type information for this element and its attributes, but may also add attributes (with default values) to the element.

When the element name is a constant qualified name, whether used in a direct element constructor or a computed one, it is added to the validation context; otherwise, the validation context is reset to `global`, regardless of whatever the initial or default validation context was. The new validation context is used for nested expressions.

7.11 Element and Attribute Content

The complete rules for handling element and attribute content are somewhat more complex than you might expect, mainly due to three complications: special characters, such as < or {; whitespace characters, which have special meaning in both XQuery and XML; and embedded XQuery expressions.

7.11.1 Character Escapes

In addition to the doubled-up curly brace escapes, XQuery supports three kinds of character references: hexadecimal, decimal, and named entities.

As in XML, entity references all begin with an ampersand (&) and end with a semicolon (;). XQuery has five named entities corresponding to the five special characters: less-than (<), greater-than (>), ampersand (&), quote ("), and apostrophe ('). These characters and their named entity references are listed in Table 7.1.

Numeric entities can be written in either decimal or hexadecimal format. Decimal numeric entities are written `&#N;` where N is any decimal number. Hexadecimal numeric entities are written `&#xN;` where N is any hexadecimal number. Hexadecimal characters may be uppercase or lowercase, but the x that

Table 7.1 The five named character entities supported by XQuery

Named escape	Numerical escape (decimal)	Numerical escape (hexadecimal)	Result
&lt;	&#60;	&#x3C;	<
&gt;	&#62;	&#x3E;	>
&amp;	&#38;	&#x26;	&
&quot;	&#34;	&#x22;	"
&apos;	&#39;	&#x27;	'

precedes the value must be lowercase. In both cases, the number denotes a Unicode character code point (see Chapter 8) and must be a valid XML character. For example, the character reference &#0; isn't valid because character 0 (NULL) isn't a valid XML character.

As mentioned in Section 7.4, CDATA sections can be useful when text contains many characters that would require escapes, as demonstrated by Listing 7.14.

Listing 7.14 CDATA sections eliminate the need for entity escapes

```
<x><![CDATA[Special characters such as <, >, and & do not need to be
escaped in a CDATA section]]></x>

<x><![CDATA[However, the CDATA section cannot contain its terminator
sequence, ], ], >.  This character sequence can be split across two CDATA
sections, like this: ]]]]><![CDATA[>]]></x>
```

7.11.2 Whitespace

Recall that XML whitespace consists of sequences of any of the four characters space (U+0020), tab (U+0009), line-feed (U+000A), and carriage return (U+000D). One of the more useful character escapes is the non-breaking space character U+00A0 ( ), which is *not* treated as whitespace by XML or XQuery, but is often treated as an ordinary space character by other applications (such as Web browsers).

As in HTML, whitespace in XML is mostly insignificant; applications that depend on whitespace being preserved exactly as written are in for a difficult time. That said, XQuery has very well-defined rules for how and when white-space characters are *preserved*, *stripped*, or *normalized*.

Whitespace preservation keeps the whitespace characters exactly as written. Whitespace stripping removes boundary whitespace (explained momentarily). Whitespace normalization replaces consecutive whitespace characters with a single space character. (A variant known as new-line normalization replaces any end-of-line character sequence with a single line-feed character.)

Boundary whitespace is whitespace that occurs by itself in between XML constructors and/or enclosed XQuery expressions, excluding whitespace constructed using character entity references. For example, boundary whitespace occurs between the `y` and `z` elements in the expression `<x><y/> <z/></x>`, and between these elements and the enclosed XQuery expression in `<x><y/> {1+1}  <z/></x>`. However, in the expression `<x>y  z</x>` there isn't any boundary whitespace, nor is there any in the expressions `<x>  y  z  </x>` or `<x><y/>&#x20;<z/></x>`.

Boundary whitespace is preserved or stripped depending on the current *XML space policy*. This policy can be set in the query prolog using the XML space declaration, as shown in Listings 7.15 and 7.16. The default is `strip`.

Listing 7.15 Preserve boundary whitespace

```
declare xmlspace preserve;
<x><y/> {1+1} <z/> a b </x>
=>
<x><y/> 2  <z/> a b </x>
```

Listing 7.16 Strip boundary whitespace

```
declare xmlspace strip;
<x><y/> {1+1} <z/> a b </x>
=>
<x><y/>2<z/> a b </x>
```

Computed whitespace isn't boundary whitespace either; for example, the expression `<x>{" "}</x>` always results in `<x> </x>`, regardless of the XML space policy.

In addition to all these rules, users may explicitly normalize whitespace or trim whitespace off the ends of string values using built-in text processing functions such as `normalize-space()` (see Chapter 8). Additionally, whitespace characters in attribute constructors are normalized (exactly like in XML).

Note that validation effectively removes whitespace (as well as other content); for example, if a schema has provided an element declaration for the name x with type `xs:integer`, then `<x> 1<!--2-->3 </x>` removes the whitespace characters (and the comment) and creates an element named x containing the integer 13.

7.11.3 Content Sequence

Finally, it remains to be explained how the content sequence of elements and attributes is computed, given that the content can contain both character data and embedded XQuery expressions that evaluate to nodes, atomic values, and sequences of these. The attribute content sequence is the simpler of the two, so let's consider that first.

7.11.3.1 Attribute Content

First, entity and character references are resolved into the corresponding strings. Each block of character data is treated as an atomic value of type `xs:string` containing those characters. Whitespace normalization is applied to this character data.

Next, each enclosed expression is evaluated and atomized. If the result is the empty sequence, then the empty string is used. Otherwise, each atomic value is converted to `xs:string` and joined together with space characters in between (exactly like the `string-join()` function). Either way, the result is a string value. The example in Listing 7.17 demonstrates these rules.

Listing 7.17 Examples of the attribute content rules

```
<x a="12&apos;" b="{1,2}" c="12{3, 4}56" d="1{2+3}4"/>
=>
<x a="12'" b="1 2" c="123 456" d="154"/>
```

Finally, the sequence of strings is concatenated together without spaces to produce the final attribute value. The type of the attribute is initially `xdt:untypedAtomic`, although validation, which happens implicitly for element constructors, may assign a type to the attribute.

7.11.3.2 Element Content

The rules for evaluating element content are detailed but straightforward. They consist primarily of three main steps, described next with examples.

First, any entity and character references are resolved into their corresponding strings. Boundary whitespace is stripped, and the remaining character sequences are converted to text nodes containing those characters (one text node for each consecutive block of text).

Second, any nested constructors are evaluated, resulting in new nodes.

Third, any enclosed XQuery expressions are evaluated. Each one results in a sequence of items. If an item is a node, then it is deep-copied (destroying its identity and replacing all element types with `xs:anyType` and attribute types with `xs:anySimpleType`). Each sequence of consecutive atomic values are converted to string just like in the attribute case (converted to string and joined together with space characters in between), and a text node containing that string value is constructed in their place. The examples in Listing 7.18 illustrate these rules.

Listing 7.18 Examples of the element content rules

```
<a><b>12</b><c>{1,2}</c><d>12{3, 4}56</d><e>1{2+3}4</e></a>
=>
<a><b>12</b><c>1 2</c><d>123 456</d><e>154</e></a>

<x>{ attribute y { 1 }, element z { "a", "b" }, text { " c " }</x>
=>
<x y="1"><z>a b</z> c </x>
```

At this point, the content sequence has been normalized to consist entirely of nodes. Several error cases are checked next; if any of the following conditions occurs, then an error is raised:

- Any node is a document node
- An attribute node occurs after a non-attribute node
- Two or more attributes have the same name
- A namespace node occurs after a non-namespace node

Listing 7.19 demonstrates two of these error cases. Note that these rules are different from XSLT 1.0, which, for example, allows implementation to use the last attribute given when names collide.

Listing 7.19 Some XML rules are applied to element construction

```
<x a="1" a="2"/> => error("Duplicate attribute a")

<x>y{ attribute z { 1 }}</x>
=> error("Attribute after text content")
```

Otherwise, adjacent text nodes are concatenated (without spaces between) and replaced by single text nodes, and the final sequence becomes the content of the element. If the sequence is empty, then the element is constructed but empty.

7.12 Conclusion

This chapter shows the myriad ways an XQuery can create new XML nodes.

For elements and attributes, XQuery supports two methods of construction: one direct constructor syntax that is essentially XML—extended to allow enclosed XQuery expressions, and one computed constructor syntax that is uniquely XQuery (typically used to construct nodes whose names are computed). Constructed elements are implicitly validated.

For comment and processing instruction nodes, XQuery uses the direct XML syntax without modification. For document nodes, XQuery supports only a computed constructor syntax. Namespace nodes are created implicitly, based on the in-scope namespaces.

Text nodes are created implicitly in element content, may be created explicitly using a computed constructor syntax, and may be created using CDATA section constructors (exactly as in XML).

7.13 Further Reading

For more information about the XQuery Data Model, see Chapter 2 of this book. You may also be interested in the official standards, such as the XQuery Data Model specification at `http://www.w3.org/TR/query-datamodel/`, the XML specification at `http://www.w3.org/TR/1998/REC-xml-19980210`, and Namespaces in XML at `http://www.w3.org/TR/1999/REC-xml-names-19990114/`.

CHAPTER 8

Text Processing

8.1 Introduction

You may recall a time when the string was seemingly a very simple data type. Computing the length of a string or converting it to lowercase or uppercase was a trivial exercise. (However, your trivial solution almost certainly worked for only one particular language or locale.)

Well, no more. Unicode is considerably more complex than the strings of yore. With characters that occupy one or many bytes, simple operations like computing the string length are no longer so simple. There are special cases like the famous "Turkish I" in which the ordinary letter I (U+0049) in the Turkish language turns into a lowercase special dotless ı (U+0131) instead of the usual dotted i (U+0069). Changing the case of a string can actually change its length; for example, the German *eszett* ß (U+00DF) turns into the uppercase letter S repeated (U+0053 U+0053).

This chapter explains enough of the W3C Character Model and the functions XQuery provides for working with it so that you can effectively and productively work with XML text. XQuery 1.0 doesn't define operators for performing full-text search; however, this functionality is being considered for a future version of the standard (see Chapter 14 for details).

8.2 The XML Character Model

8.2.1 Background

The W3C Character Model is based on the Universal Character Set (UCS), commonly called Unicode. Unicode 4.0 is the most recent version at the time of this writing, although most implementations do not yet support the latest version. Unicode 4.0 defines some 96,382 characters. Of these, 70,027 (more than 70%) are Chinese-Japanese-Korean (CJK) characters. Because these numbers exceed 2^{16}, some characters' representations require more than two bytes.

Characters are complicated not because there are so many of them, but because they have so many different aspects—speech (aural rendering), writing (visual rendering), computer representation (storage), computer input method (key/pen strokes), collation rules (sorting), case rules, and so on—and every culture has defined different rules for these aspects. For example, in one language a character may represent several spoken syllables, while in another several characters may represent a single syllable. Similarly, several characters may be combined into a single visual glyph, or several glyphs may be required to represent a single character.

Unicode defines a unified framework for working with characters by carefully delineating among these different aspects. XML and XQuery are most affected by four character aspects: storage, computation (including computing length or changing case), encoding for transmission, and collation. This section focuses on the first two of these; for more information about encoding and collation, see Sections 8.3 and 8.4, respectively.

8.2.2 Code Points

Every possible character from the Universal Character Set is assigned a nonnegative integer called the *code point*. As mentioned in Chapter 1, each code point is denoted with the string "U+" in front of the hexadecimal value of the code point. For example, U+0032 represents code point with hex number 32 (50 decimal). Code points can range in value from U+0000 to U+10FFFF inclusive (that is, 0 to $16^5 + 16^4 - 1 = 111411$ decimal), although not every code point has been assigned to a character.

XQuery strings are sequences of Unicode code points, and XQuery provides functions—string-to-codepoints() and codepoints-to-string()—for converting between the string representation and a sequence of integer code points. Listing 8.1 shows these functions in action.

Listing 8.1 Strings are sequences of Unicode code points

```
string-to-codepoints("Hello") => (72, 101, 108, 108, 111)
codepoints-to-string((87, 111, 114, 108, 100)) => "World"
```

Internally, implementations are free to store these string values any way they wish. However, most implementations typically use UTF-16, a variable length encoding in which most characters are represented using two bytes, and occasionally four bytes are required. For more information on encodings, see Section 8.3.

XQuery and XML place no inherent limits on the maximum length of a string value or text node content, although most implementations will limit these to some reasonable value such as one kilobyte, one megabyte, one gigabyte, two gigabytes, and so on.

8.2.3 Normalization

Unfortunately, code points aren't the end of the story, because some characters have more than one code point representation. For example, the small accented letter á may be represented as either U+00E1 (a code point dedicated to this character) or the sequence U+0061 U+0301 (the code point for an ordinary a, followed by the code point for a combining accent). The first representation is a *precomposed form*, and the second is a *decomposed form*. The special character U+0301 is an example of a *combining character*.

Defining consistent string operations, such as comparisons or sorting, when some characters have multiple equivalent yet different representations, is impossible. To solve this conundrum, the W3C Character Model defines a process called *normalization*. Normalization involves choosing one representation to be the canonical form, and then changing all equivalent representations into this canonical form. It depends on the application which form is the most appropriate choice.

Unicode defines four different normalization forms, but the W3C Character Model allows only one of them: the one that chooses the simplest precomposed form, known as normalization form C (NFC).

For example, in the W3C Character Model, the accented a (á) is always normalized to U+00E1. XQuery uses this normalization form, but also provides access to the other Unicode normalization forms through the normalize-unicode() function. This function takes the string value to be normalized, and a second argument that names the normalization form. (See Appendix C for the other normalization forms.) In general, you should apply Unicode normalization whenever sorting or comparing text values; otherwise, you may treat two equivalent forms of the same value as different values (as in Listing 8.2).

Listing 8.2 Normalization is required for most purposes, including sorting

```
codepoints-to-string(225) = codepoints-to-string((97, 769))
=> false

codepoints-to-string(225) =
   normalize-unicode(codepoints-to-string((97, 769)), "NFC")
=> true
```

XML introduces an additional complication, which is that whitespace characters (the four values U+0009, U+000A, U+000D, and U+0020) are often considered equivalent and unimportant. For example, XML has a rule known as *attribute value normalization*, in which whitespace characters are normalized to U+0020 and leading and trailing whitespace characters are removed. XQuery provides a function, normalize-space(), that can perform this normalization.

8.3 Character Encodings

Character encodings must be one of most often asked about and least well-understood aspects of XML. As you've seen, XQuery strings are defined in terms of code points. However, implementations have several different options for storing these code points in memory and for serializing them as XML data.

A *character encoding* tells how to interpret a sequence of bytes as a sequence of code points. Character encodings can be *fixed-width*, in which every character takes up the same number of bytes, or *variable-width*, in which some characters are stored more compactly than others. Fixed-width encodings are somewhat easier to work with (e.g., computing the length of a string is easy), but can be very inefficient for representing string data when the required character set covers only a fraction of the encoding space. Variable-width encodings allow for smaller representations of the most commonly used code points, but are more complex to work with (e.g., computing the length of a string is difficult) and, depending on the data, can be less efficient than fixed-width encodings.

The UTF-8 character encoding is the default encoding used by XML, and is commonly used for text files and URI strings. UTF-16 is commonly used to store

Unicode strings in memory, and is the default encoding used by some standards, such as XSLT 1.0. Both of these are variable-width encodings; they use less space for characters with lower-numbered code points, and more space for those with higher numbers. If you have a choice, you should really use one of these.

Other popular encodings include the fixed-width encodings ASCII (7-bit or 8-bit), EBCDIC (8-bit), ISO 8859-1 (8-bit), Windows-1252 (8-bit), UCS-2 (16-bit), UCS-4 (32-bit), UTF-32 (32-bit), and Shift_JIS. A complete list of hundreds of encodings is maintained by the Internet Assigned Names Authority (IANA) at `http://www.iana.org/assignments/character-sets`. In general, you should avoid these other encodings.

One challenge of working with character encodings is that many have been designed to be partially or wholly compatible with others. This design conveniently allows the use of one encoding where another was expected, but can also lead to situations in which a system appears to be working correctly until "unusual" characters are input. For example, UTF-8 is completely a superset of ASCII; therefore, ASCII-encoded data can be given to a UTF-8 processor but not the other way around. If an ASCII processor is fed UTF-8 data, it may still function correctly until a character outside the range of ASCII is encountered (and possibly even then, depending on how those non-ASCII characters are handled). Always thoroughly test your code.

Another challenge is that diagnostic tools may fail to display the character data as they should, either because they are themselves not prepared to handle the encoding, or because the font used lacks appropriate symbols (glyphs) for those characters.

This can lead to false negatives, in which the system appears to be broken because a font doesn't display a character correctly, even though the data is present and valid. For example, many fonts use square boxes to display special characters. The data may be present and valid but drawn on-screen as a box. Or the box may be an indication that something is wrong. You really have to inspect the underlying bytes to find out.

It can also lead to false positives, in which the system appears to be working because the data is rendered by a diagnostic tool, when in fact the data is not correctly encoded. For example, there are special characters such as … (U+2026) and » (U+00BB) that can appear to be made up of the separate individual characters . (U+002E) and > (U+003E), respectively. In some fonts, one may be indistinguishable from the other.

Or to take an even more common example, the so-called "smart" curly quote and apostrophe symbols " (U+201C), " (U+201D), ' (U+2018), and ' (U+2019) aren't allowed in XML and XQuery except in strings or text content; only the ordinary, straight quote symbols " (U+0022) and ' (U+0027) are treated as quote symbols (for delimiting strings and attribute values). Using the incorrect form can lead to bewildering error messages.

8.4 Collations

Given these complexities, comparing and sorting strings becomes a real challenge. Collations provide a way to customize sort and comparison behavior. A collation is just a name that describes a way of handling text data.

The default collation used by XQuery, and in fact the only collation that implementations are required to support, is the *Unicode code point collation*. In this collation, characters are ordered according to their underlying code point values. Two characters are equal if and only if they are the same code point.

However, this collation isn't always the one you want. For example, this collation sorts uppercase letters lower than lowercase letters—but maybe you want the two to be equal. Also, this collation intermixes letters and punctuation symbols, but perhaps you want all punctuation characters to be sorted first.

You may override the default collation by specifying an alternative in the query prolog, using the `declare default collation` declaration shown in Listing 8.3. More than one default collation declaration results in an error.

Listing 8.3 Overriding the default collation in the query prolog

```
declare default collation http://anyuri.org/;
```

Notice that the collation is named by a string literal containing a URI. The URI for the Unicode code point collation is `http://www.w3.org/2003/11/xpath-functions/collation/codepoint`. Implementations are free to support any additional collations they wish; there isn't a standard for specifying collation names.

In Java, collations are typically defined using the class `java.text.RuleBasedCollation`. The collation can be defined by a locale (such as `"en_US"` for the American English dialect or `"fr_FR"` for French) or by constructing a string that describes how individual characters compare to one another, such as `"< a,A < b,B < c,C"`. The locale names in this implementation use an underscore to separate the language and region codes.

In .NET, collations are typically defined using the class `System.Global-ization.CultureInfo`. The locale names conform to RFC 3066 and use a hyphen separator as in `"en-US"` or `"fr-FR"`.

Because XQuery requires the collation to be a URI value, implementations may map these locale names to URI values, for example, `"en_US"` might be implemented using `"http://www.awprofessional.com/collations/en-US"`.

Another popular collation is the Unicode Collation Algorithm, not to be confused with the code point collation defined by XQuery. Implementations aren't required to support the Unicode Collation Algorithm.

8.5 Text Operators

In XQuery, the plus operator (+) is used only for arithmetic and doesn't concatenate strings. To concatenate strings, use the `fn:string-join()` or `fn:con-cat()` functions described in the next section.

XQuery defines all the general comparison operators (=, !=, <, >, and <=, >=) and value comparison operators (eq, ne, lt, gt, le, and ge) to work on string values. The equality and inequality operators test whether two strings are equal or unequal. The other operators test whether one string comes before or after another. All of these comparisons are performed using the default collation.

8.6 Text Functions

XQuery includes all of XPath 1.0 string functions, and many more besides. These functions are summarized in Table 8.1, and explained completely in Appendix C.

8.7 Conclusion

Strings in XQuery are represented using either single or double straight quotation marks, but not the special curly quote characters. Every XQuery string is a sequence of Unicode code points. XQuery doesn't have a character type, although you can work with the underlying Unicode code point values as inte-

Table 8.1 XQuery text-processing functions

Function	Meaning	Uses collation
codepoints-to-string	Convert a sequence of integer code points into a string	No
compare	Compare two strings	Yes
concat	Concatenate two or more strings	No
contains	True if one string contains another as a substring	Yes
ends-with	True if one string ends with another	Yes
escape-uri	Apply URI percent-escaping	No
lower-case	Convert a string to lowercase	No
matches	Perform regular-expression matching	No
normalize-space	Apply XML whitespace normalization	No
normalize-unicode	Apply Unicode normalization	No
replace	Perform string replacement	No
starts-with	True if one string starts with another	Yes
string-join	Concatenate strings with a delimiter	No
string-length	Compute the length of a string (in characters)	No
string-to-codepoints	Convert a string into a sequence of integer code points	No
substring	Compute a substring of a string	No
substring-after	Compute the substring occurring after another	Yes
substring-before	Compute the substring occurring before another	Yes
tokenize	Split a string at delimiters	No
translate	Perform character replacement	No
upper-case	Convert a string to uppercase	No

gers. XQuery also defines a rich set of functions for manipulating strings, from the usual string length and other accessors to the more powerful regular expressions and Unicode and whitespace normalization functions. Many of these functions accept an optional collation argument; using the default collation as another collation is not specified.

8.8 Further Reading

The Unicode Consortium at `http://www.unicode.org/` is an excellent source of information about Unicode, character sets, and character encodings. This information is available in book form as *The Unicode Standard, Version 4.0.*

The *W3C Character Model* is defined at `http://www.w3.org/TR/charmod/` and points to most of the relevant Unicode standards, including the *Unicode Collation Algorithm* (Unicode Technical Report #10, available at `http://www.unicode.org/unicode/reports/tr10/`) and the *Unicode Case Mappings* (now part of the Unicode 4.0.0 standard at `http://www.unicode.org/versions/Unicode4.0.0/`).

RFC 3066 (*Tags for the Identification of Languages*, available at `http://www.ietf.org/rfc/rfc3066.txt`) lists language codes commonly used in collation names. A convenient table can be found at `http://msdn.microsoft.com/library/default.asp?url=/library/en-us/cpref/html/frlrfSystemGlobalizationCultureInfoClassTopic.asp`. The site at `http://www.cs.tut.fi/~jkorpela/chars/` contains comprehensive tables and tutorials on character encodings.

For an excellent practical overview of regular expressions, Jeffrey Friedl's book *Mastering Regular Expressions* can't be beat.

CHAPTER 9

Type Operators

9.1 Introduction

As described in Chapters 1 and 2, every XQuery expression has a static (compile-time) type, even if the value is "untyped" (the type `xdt:untypedAtomic`). During evaluation, these expressions result in values, and the values have dynamic types (consistent with the static types of the expressions that produced them).

All XQuery implementations perform dynamic type checking, and some perform static type checking. Consequently, there are times when you need to change the type of an expression or value.

This chapter focuses on the many functions and operators XQuery provides for working with types. These operators break down into roughly four categories:

- Operators that cast values of one atomic type into values of another atomic type
- A typeswitch operator that can take different actions based on the dynamic type of an expression
- Operators that perform schema validation
- Operators that import schemas and work with XML data according to its schema types

Some XQuery implementations differ in their handling of types from the description given here. As mentioned previously, some XQuery implementations don't perform static type checking. Some may not support importing schemas or user-defined types. Check the documentation accompanying your implementation to find out what limitations it has.

9.2 Cast and Castable

As mentioned in Chapter 2, any value can be converted to a value of a different type using the type constructor syntax `typename(value)`, where `typename` is the name of the target type. This syntax is equivalent to writing `value cast as typename`. Stylistically, the constructor syntax typically is used only for constant values, such as `xs:date("2004-07-11")` and the `cast as` operator is used for non-constant values, such as `$dateTimeVariable cast as xs:date`. However, the two are completely interchangeable.

Casting a value to another type can cause an error if the value is incompatible with that type. Before I explain how these type conversions work, it's worth pointing out that XQuery provides an operator, `castable as`, to test whether a conversion would succeed without actually performing it. Listing 9.1 shows how it is used.

Listing 9.1 The operators `cast as` and `castable as`

```
"2" cast as xs:integer     => 2
"2" castable as xs:integer => true
"X" cast as xs:integer     => error (: not a valid integer :)
"X" castable as xs:integer => false
```

It's also worth observing that "cast" in XQuery really means "conversion." Unlike some languages, in which the word "cast" is often used to mean moving up or down the type hierarchy without changing the value, the XQuery cast often changes the underlying value (in addition to the type). XQuery has a separate operator, `treat as`, that moves up or down the type hierarchy without changing the value (see Section 9.4 for details).

Both `cast as` and `castable as` first atomize their operand. If the result has more than one atomic value, then `cast` raises an error while `castable as` returns false. If the result is an empty sequence, then the conversion succeeds only if the target type has the optional occurrence indicator (`?`), and the result is the empty sequence. When successful, `cast` converts the value to the target type, while `castable as` returns true. Listing 9.2 demonstrates the effects of these rules.

Otherwise, if the result has only a single atomic value, it is converted to the target type, using the rules described in the next section.

Listing 9.2 The target type allows a sequence of zero or one atomic values

```
(1, 2) cast as xs:integer?      => error
(1, 2) castable as xs:integer?  => false
1 cast as xs:integer?           => 1
1 cast as xs:integer            => 1
() cast as xs:integer?          => ()
() cast as xs:integer           => error
() castable as xs:integer       => false
```

9.3 Type Conversion Rules

Any system of type conversions must trade flexibility for simplicity. Simplify the rules by eliminating most possibilities, and they become too inflexible for practical use. Extend the rules to cover every possible situation, and they become complex and potentially very inefficient.

The three main challenges facing the XQuery type conversion rules are information loss, conflicting string representations, and internationalization/localization issues.

Type conversions often suffer from information loss. Starting with a value, converting it to a different type, and then converting it back into its original type may result in a very different value from the original. This loss of information typically occurs for one of two reasons: Either the intermediate type cannot represent as many values as the original type, or else the conversion algorithm itself is lossy (perhaps because some information is considered insignificant).

An example of the former is the conversion of an integer into boolean and back into integer. Because the boolean type has only two values, at most two integer values can round-trip through this conversion; all the others must lose information.

An example of the latter is the conversion from string into integer—leading zeros are discarded by the integer type, so the values `"1"`, `"01"`, and `"001"` are all converted into the same integer value (`1`). When converting from integer back into string, which string format should be used? XQuery chooses one string format for each type, called the *canonical representation*. This rule is simple, but at a cost to flexibility.

Conflicting string representations occur when different languages (human or computer) have different ideas about what they should be. For example, in XPath 1.0 the canonical representation of infinity is `"Infinity"`, while in XML Schema 1.0 the canonical representation is `"INF"`. XQuery chose to go with the XML Schema representation instead of XPath 1.0. As another example, the canonical representation of the boolean value true (in XPath, XML Schema, and XQuery) is "true." However, all of these representations are English-language specific.

Keep these compromises in mind when reading the XQuery type conversion rules in the following sections.

9.3.1 Converting Up and Down the Type Hierarchy

Ordinarily, converting to a supertype is unnecessary (thanks to subtype substitution). Often `treat as` (see Section 9.4) is more appropriate than converting to a subtype. In any case, it's possible to apply `cast as` to an expression and convert it to a subtype or a supertype. What should happen in these cases?

When converting to a supertype, only the type changes—the value remains the same. When converting to a subtype, except for converting `xs:decimal` to `xs:integer`, the value must satisfy all the schema constraints of the target type. Conceptually, this is done by first converting the value to string (using its canonical representation), and then converting that string value to the target type. For example, when converting from `xs:integer` to `xs:negativeInteger`, conceptually the integer is first converted to string, and then that value is parsed as a negative integer.

The main reason for this indirect description is to ensure that the value satisfies all the lexical constraints of the target schema type, as well as any value constraints. These constraints are described for all of the built-in derived types in Appendix A.

Converting from `xs:decimal` to its subtype `xs:integer` is the one exception to this rule. This conversion actually truncates any decimal digits of the `xs:decimal` value, keeping only the integer part.

9.3.2 Converting Across the Type Hierarchy

Most type conversions involve converting from one type to an unrelated type. This conversion is defined by first turning it into a conversion between built-in primitive atomic types, and then enumerating all of those possible conversions.

XQuery effectively splits the type conversion into three conceptual parts: First, if the operand type derives from a primitive type or `xs:integer`, then the

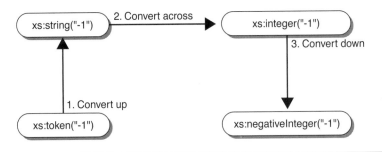

Figure 9.1 Evaluating `xs:token("-1")` cast as `xs:negativeInteger`

operand is converted to that primitive type or `xs:integer` (in other words, convert up). Second, that value is converted to the primitive type (or `xs:integer`) supertype of the target type (in other words, convert across). Finally, the converted value is converted to the target type (convert down). This process is illustrated in Figure 9.1, converting `xs:token` (which derives from `xs:string`) to `xs:negativeInteger` (which derives from `xs:integer`).

9.3.2.1 Conversion to/from String

For the purposes of type conversions across the hierarchy, XQuery treats the three types `xs:string`, `xdt:untypedAtomic`, and `xs:anySimpleType` essentially the same way. (The only difference among them is that `xs:anySimpleType` can be used to describe types such as `xs:IDREFS` that derive by list, and such types cannot be converted to `xdt:untypedAtomic`.)

Except for `xs:NOTATION`, every type can be converted to one of these types without error. Consequently, string conversions aren't mentioned again in this chapter.

When converting a value from one of these types to some other type, the string value is parsed according to the rules for the target type. When converting a value of some other type to one of these types, the value is converted to string using its canonical representation. The canonical representations for all types are listed in Appendix A, as are charts that summarize the type conversions explained here.

9.3.2.2 Conversion to/from Numeric Types and Boolean

Any of the numeric types (`xs:integer`, `xs:decimal`, `xs:float`, and `xs:double`) and `xs:boolean` may be converted to and from one another. When converting a number to `xs:boolean`, the result is true if the number is not NaN and non-zero.

When converting a boolean to a number type, true converts to 1 and false converts to 0 (in that type). Listing 9.3 illustrates some of these conversions.

Listing 9.3 The boolean true corresponds to non-zero, non-NaN numbers

```
true() cast as xs:integer  => 1
true() cast as xs:decimal  => 1.0
true() cast as xs:double   => 1E0
false() cast as xs:integer => 0
0 cast as xs:boolean       => false
0.0 cast as xs:boolean     => false
0E0 cast as xs:boolean     => false
2.5 cast as xs:boolean     => true
```

When converting between number types, the value is widened or shortened (using truncation if necessary) to the target type. As one example, the integer 1 converts to the decimal 1.0 and the double 1E0. As another example, the decimal 1.5 converts to the integer 1 (truncating the decimal digits).

When the value cannot be represented, for example, xs:double("INF") cast as xs:decimal , then an error is raised. When the value would underflow or overflow for example, xs:double("1E200") cast as xs:float, then the result is zero or infinity (or negative infinity), respectively.

9.3.2.3 Conversion to/from Calendar Types

There are three "families" of calendar types: ordinary date/time types (xs:date, xs:time, and xs:dateTime), duration types (xs:duration, xdt:dayTimeDuration, and xdt:yearMonthDuration), and Gregorian types (xs:gYear, xs:gMonth, xs:gDay, xs:gYearMonth, and xs:gMonthDay). Let's consider each family separately.

When converting from xs:date or xs:time to xs:dateTime, the original value (including its time zone, if any) is kept, and the other half of the xs:dateTime value is filled with a dummy value. For no good reason, the dummy value chosen is different for each type: When converting from xs:date to xs:dateTime, the time part is all zero. When converting from xs:time to xs:dateTime, the date part is the value of current-date().

In the other direction, converting from xs:dateTime to xs:date or xs:time, only the corresponding parts are kept (including the time zone). The xs:date type cannot be converted to the xs:time type (and vice versa).

Listing 9.4 Converting among the date/time types

```
xs:date("2004-07-11") cast as xs:dateTime
=> xs:dateTime("2004-07-11T00:00:00")

xs:time("15:14:15.9") cast as xs:dateTime
=> xs:dateTime("todayT00:00:00")
where today is replaced with the value from current-date()

xs:dateTime("2004-07-11T15:14:15.9") cast as xs:date
=> xs:date("2004-07-11")

xs:dateTime("2004-07-11T15:14:15.9") cast as xs:date
=> xs:time("15:14:15.9")
```

The `xs:date` and `xs:dateTime` types can also be converted into any of the Gregorian types (but not vice versa). Perhaps surprisingly, the Gregorian types cannot be converted to one another; for example, attempting to convert `xs:gYear` to `xs:gYearMonth` raises an error. When converting from `xs:date` or `xs:dateTime` to one of the Gregorian types, only the corresponding parts of the date are kept. A few examples are provided in Listing 9.5.

Listing 9.5 Converting from `xs:date` or `xs:dateTime` to Gregorian types

```
xs:date("2004-07-11") cast as xs:gYear
=> xs:gYear("2004--")

xs:date("2004-07-11") cast as xs:gMonthDay
=> xs:gMonthDay("-07-11")

xs:dateTime("2004-07-11T15:14:15.9") cast as xs:gDay
=> xs:gDay("--11")
```

Finally, the duration types can be converted to one another, except that `xdt:yearMonthDuration` cannot be converted to or from `xdt:dayMonthDuration`. Because these two types inherit from `xdt:duration`, most of the conversions don't change the underlying value. The only interesting cases occur when converting from `xs:duration` to one of its sub-types, and then only the corresponding parts of the duration are kept.

Listing 9.6 Converting among the duration types

```
xs:duration("P2Y3MT5.6S") cast as xs:dayTimeDuration
=> xs:dayTimeDuration("PT5.6S")

xs:duration("P2Y3MT5.6S") cast as xs:yearMonthDuration
=> xs:yearMonthDuration("P2Y3M")
```

9.3.2.4 Conversion to/from Binary Types

The binary types `xs:hexBinary` and `xs:base64Binary` can be converted to `xs:boolean`, but only when they contain a single byte whose value is 0 or 1 (which then convert to false and true, respectively). All other cases are errors.

9.4 `treat as`

The `treat as` operator performs *down-casting* at compile-time—it doesn't change the dynamic type (or value) of an expression. You need it only in implementations that perform static type checking. An *up-casting* operator is unnecessary in XQuery because, as explained in Chapter 2, subtype substitution allows any expression to be used where a supertype of it is expected.

Because `treat as` is a down-cast, the target type must derive from the original type. If at run-time the actual value is incompatible with the target type, the result is an error. Otherwise, the value (and its run-time type) is unchanged. The examples in Listing 9.7 demonstrate the difference between `treat as` and `cast as`.

Listing 9.7 Treat down-casts at compile-time; cast converts at run-time

```
3.0 treat as xs:integer => 3.0 (: still a decimal :)
3.5 treat as xs:integer => run-time error
                           (: 3.5 is not an integer :)
"3" treat as xs:integer => compile-time error
                           (: integer does not derive from string :)

3.0 cast as xs:integer => 3
3.5 cast as xs:integer => 3 (: truncation :)
"3" cast as xs:integer => 3
```

Unlike `cast as`, whose target type must name a sequence containing at most one atomic type, `treat as` accepts any sequence type, including user-defined complex types (see Section 9.6) and node tests with names.

This second capability has wider utility than just type conversions. For example, let's suppose you have a function that accepts any element, but at some point you want to return an error if the element name isn't the one you expect. You could write the expression shown in Listing 9.8.

Listing 9.8 One way to check an element name and error if they don't match

```
if(node-name($theElement) != "foo") then error() else $theElement
```

Or, instead, you could use `treat as` shown in Listing 9.9 to accomplish the same task.

Listing 9.9 Another way to do the same thing as Listing 9.8, but using `treat as`

```
$theElement treat as element(foo)
```

9.5 `instance of` **and** `typeswitch`

The `typeswitch` operator is similar to a series of `if`/`then`/`else` conditions using `instance of`. The `typeswitch` contains one or more `case` clauses and exactly one `default` clause. It takes an arbitrary expression (in parentheses like an `if` condition), checks its run-time type, and selects the first matching `case` (or the `default` if there is no match). The partial query in Listing 9.10 demonstrates the use of `typeswitch`.

Listing 9.10 `typeswitch` branches on the run-time type of an expression

```
declare variable $var external;
(: ... :)
typeswitch ($var) {
  case xs:integer return "xs:integer"
  case xs:double  return "xs:double"
  case xs:string  return "xs:string"
  case xs:date    return "xs:date"
```

```
(: ... :)
default        return "unknown"
}
```

Each case clause may optionally declare a variable. The variable is in scope for the rest of that clause, typed according to that clause, and bound to the expression value. The same variable name can be used in multiple clauses, as in Listing 9.11.

Listing 9.11 Simulating the predicate operator

```
declare function apply-predicate($context, $condition) {
  typeswitch ($condition) {
    (: numeric predicates filter by position :)
    case $pos as xs:integer return item-at($context, $pos)
    case $pos as xs:float   return item-at($context, $pos)
    case $pos as xs:double  return item-at($context, $pos)
    case $pos as xs:decimal return item-at($context, $pos)

    (: all others are converted to boolean using EBV
       and then return the expression or the empty sequence :)
    default return if (boolean($condition)) then $context else ()
  }
};
```

The order of the clauses matters, because only the first matching one is taken. Consequently, you generally want to list all subtype clauses first, and then clauses for their supertypes later.

9.6 User-Defined Types

This section assumes that you are already familiar with the XML Schema 1.0 standard, and that your XQuery implementation supports schema imports. If not, feel free to skip ahead to Section 9.7 (Conclusion).

User-defined types can be specified in an XML Schema and then imported for use in a query. Various properties of these types, such as nil and default values, affect the behavior of the query. Also, XQuery provides operators for accessing the typed content of XML data that has an associated schema, or for validating XML according to a schema.

9.6.1 Schema Imports

The only way to import user-defined types into an XQuery is to use one or more `import schema` instructions in the query prolog. Each schema import names a schema target namespace, optionally binds a prefix to that namespace (or sets it to be the default element namespace), and optionally provides a location hint.

Importing a schema imports all of its top-level (global) types into scope. (Local types can be accessed using a validation context path, described later.) If two type names conflict, then an error is raised; in particular, you cannot override the built-in types. Listing 9.12 demonstrates the use of `import schema`.

Listing 9.12 User-defined types are available through schema import

```
import schema "urn:foo";
import schema namespace b = "urn:bar";
import schema default element namespace "urn:baz" at "baz.xsd";
<x b:y="1"/> (: constructs an element {urn:baz}x with an attribute
               {urn:bar}y. Both must be valid according to the
               schema definitions of those types :)
```

XQuery allows implementations to not support `import schema` because of its complexity. Check the documentation accompanying your XQuery implementation to determine its level of support for XML Schema.

9.6.2 Typed Content

As you learned in Chapter 7, constructed elements are validated according to the type names in scope. Consequently, in an expression like Listing 9.12, the global schema types are automatically applied to any constructed elements.

In that example, suppose that the attribute `b:y` is typed as `xs:integer` in its corresponding schema. Then we can extract that typed, integer value using the `data()` function. In fact, `data()` just applies atomization to the node, and atomization (explained in Chapter 2) retrieves its typed value. As you've seen throughout the book, many other XQuery expressions implicitly atomize nodes as well. Listing 9.13 demonstrates the use of `data()`.

Listing 9.13 The `data()` function atomizes nodes into their typed content

```
data(<x xsi:type="xs:decimal">12.34</x>) => 12.34
```

Implementations may also apply schema types to XML documents accessed through the `doc()` function, the `collection()` function, and/or the `input()` sequence. How this is done varies from one implementation to the next, but has the effect of making those typed values available to the `data()` function just like constructed XML.

Even if you have untyped XML, you can apply the `validate` operator (described next) to apply schema type information to it. In this way, you can turn untyped data into typed data, or even change the type of data from one schema to another.

As mentioned previously, `element()` and `attribute()` node kind tests accept up to two arguments, the second of which can be a type name (or `*` to mean any type). This can be used to match nodes according to their type. For example, `element(*, xs:integer)` selects all elements with any name and type `xs:integer`. See Chapter 3 for additional information about the node kind tests.

9.6.3 Validation

XQuery has one operator, `validate`, that performs schema validation. It behaves like an expensive cast in which you don't specify the destination type. Instead, the data is validated against the in-scope schema types (by name) and the corresponding type information applied to it and all the nodes it contains.

The `validate` operator takes three expressions: a *validation mode*, a *validation context*, and a curly-brace-enclosed expression to be validated. The mode and context are optional, and default to their values in the current static context. The enclosed expression must evaluate to a single node. It validates the enclosed expression according to the given mode, context, and in-scope schema types, returning the (now typed) node. For example, the expression in Listing 9.14 constructs an element and then validates it against the current validation context.

Listing 9.14 Use `validate` to apply in-scope schema types to a node

```
validate { <x/> }
```

The `validate` operator can in some cases alter the value and structure of the underlying XML data (for example, the application of default values where previously attributes were nonexistent), and always assigns type information to each XML element and attribute node.

There are three validation modes—`lax`, `skip`, and `strict`—with the same meanings as in XML Schema 1.0. The default mode is `lax`, but can be changed either in the query prolog using a `validation` declaration, or in a `validate` expression. The effects of all three modes are shown in Listing 9.15.

Listing 9.15 Validation mode affects how validation is performed

```
(: suppose there is a type name for x with xs:integer,
   and no type name for y :)

validate strict { <x><y/></x> }
=> error (no type for y)

validate lax { <x><y/></x> }
=> <x xsi:type="xs:integer"><y xsi:type="anyType"/></x>

validate skip { <x><y/><x/> }
=> <x xsi:type="xs:anyType"><y xsi:type="anyType"/></x>
```

The `strict` validation mode requires that every element present has a corresponding in-scope type and validates without error. The `skip` validation mode doesn't validate at all; instead, every element is typed as `xs:anyType` and every attribute is typed as `xdt:untypedAtomic` (exactly like the `document` constructor). The `lax` validation mode mixes the two by applying `strict` validation to all elements with in-scope types, and `skip` validation to the rest.

There are also three kinds of validation contexts: `global`, `type(name)`, or a path. The validation context is changed only by `validate` and element constructors. Its default value is `global`. All three validation contexts are shown in Listing 9.16.

Listing 9.16 Validation context describes where to find the type name

```
validate global {<x/>}     (: look for x at the top level :)
validate type("y") {<x/>} (: look for x in top-level type y :)
validate y/z {<x/>}        (: look for x in type z in type y :)
```

Global validation validates the expression according to the top-level element names declared in the in-scope schemas. Validation contexts that use `type()` applied to some name select the type of that name from the in-scope schemas and validate the expression in the context of that type. Validation contexts can also use paths (starting from `type()` or some type name) to drill down into locally defined element types that aren't globally visible. The paths used are very simple, consisting only of `/` and element type names.

9.7 Conclusion

The XQuery type system permeates every other aspect of the language. You can do a lot in XQuery without ever using type operators, but when you need one, you really need it. XQuery fills these needs with conversion operators (`cast as` and `castable as`) and a static cast operator (`treat as`), operators that inspect the run-time type of a value (`instance of` and `typeswitch`), and an operator that interacts with XML Schema (`validate`).

Additional type-related examples and some "surprises" can be found in Chapters 10 and 11, respectively. Appendix A covers every built-in type, and also contains several handy charts and diagrams. (I've taped a copy of the type hierarchy diagram to my monitor, and if you're going to work with XQuery a lot, I encourage you to do the same.)

9.8 Further Reading

An explanation of XML Schema 1.0 is well outside the scope of this book, but fortunately there are many other books already available on it. One of the best is Priscilla Walmsley's *Definitive XML Schema*.

PART III

Application

CHAPTER 10

Practical Examples

10.1 Introduction

In the past four years I've answered a lot of questions about XPath and XQuery, and it seems that few of them (questions or answers) were written down anywhere. Well, that's easily fixed.

In this chapter, I've collected some opinionated (but practical) advice about using XQuery. I've also listed solutions to various frequently asked questions about XQuery. It's worth noting that in some cases problems that are very difficult or inefficient to solve in XQuery have easy or more efficient solutions using another programming language or vendor extensions. Use what works.

But first, a few words about XQuery style.

10.2 Style

Queries, like most programs, are really written for people to read. Consequently, it's worth spending some time pondering how to craft your XQuery programs so that they are easier for others (and yourself!) to read.

10.2.1 Case

XML and XQuery are case-sensitive languages, so case matters. All XQuery keywords are lowercase.

It's common practice in XML and XQuery to also use lowercase for prefixes and variable names ($i instead of $I). It's also common to use single-letter variable names when the variable is unimportant (especially with for, some, every, and typeswitch), and descriptive variable names everywhere else (especially let, declare variable, and declare function).

Type and attribute names, and occasionally variable names, are traditionally written using *camel case* (with the first word lowercased and subsequent words title-cased, like dateTime), although there are exceptions to this rule (such as `anyURI` and `QName`), and some people prefer hyphenated lowercase words (like `local-name`). The W3C standards have set a bad example here; you should choose one style and apply it consistently.

Element names are commonly written either *Pascal-cased* with no separators between words (like `ElementType`) or else camel-cased (like `complexContent`).

XQuery function names are commonly written using hyphenated lowercase (such as `substring-after()`), except when they include a name that uses a different case convention (such as `current-dateTime()`). Listing 10.1 illustrates some of these common conventions.

Listing 10.1 Common case conventions for XQuery names

```
prefix:local
$variable
<ElementsUsePascalCase attributesUseCamelCase=""/>
myFunction() or my-function()
```

I find punctuation characters (other than underscore) confusing in XML node and type names and recommend against their use. In a query, `customer.id` looks like an object reference, and `total-recall` looks like subtraction, but each is actually a single XML name.

10.2.2 Spaces

Do you enjoy living and working under cramped conditions? Personally, I'm a little claustrophobic, and so is your code. Don't be stingy when it comes to whitespace; use it wisely to visually offset independent expressions in your queries.

Some XQuery expressions depend on sufficient space. For example, a hyphen is a valid XML name character, so `foo-bar` is an element name, not `foo` minus `bar`. You have to write `foo - bar` to perform subtraction. It's best to form the habit of always separating operands and operators by a single whitespace character, even when it's not strictly necessary (see Listing 10.2).

Listing 10.2 Whitespace loves you—why not love it back?

```
1 + 2 * (x - 3) div 4

(: isn't that easier to read than: :)
1+2*(x-3)div4
(: which is incorrect anyway, because x-3 and div4 are names :)
```

There isn't any difference between <x></x> and <x/>, so you might as well write the latter (it's more concise, and the less code you have to wade through the better). Some people also like to separate the element name and the closing tag with a space, like <x />.

It's common practice to write elements containing only attributes and text on a single line, but to write elements containing comments, processing instructions, or other elements on multiple lines, as shown in Listing 10.3. Use two or more whitespace characters (or one tab) as indentation, when this can be done without interfering with the expression. (Chapter 7 explains the interactions between XML construction and whitespace handling.)

Listing 10.3 Write simple elements on one line and complex elements on multiple lines

```
<Simple attributes="only">or text</Simple>
<Complex>
  <!-- content -->
  <or/>
  mixed content
</Complex>
```

Similarly, FLWOR expressions are commonly written with each clause on its own separate line, although XQuery doesn't require this. Sometimes if the FLWOR expression is short enough, it's reasonable to write it inline. Some people also like to align the first characters of the expressions that follow each keyword in the FLWOR (this is a popular convention in the SQL language). You may find you prefer to align the first characters of each line, or both. Listing 10.4 demonstrates these line and indentation conventions.

Listing 10.4 Put each FLWOR clause on a separate line unless the FLWOR is short

```
    for $i in doc("example.xml")
    let $j := count(for $k in $i//* return $k/x)
  where $i/@a > 10
     or $i/@b < 10
order by $j
  return $i

for      $i in doc("example.xml")
where    $i/@a > 10
order by $i/@b
return   $i
```

10.2.3 Braces

Developers are notoriously picky about where they put their braces. Leave your clothes and half-eaten food all over the room, but never misplace a brace! I'd be crazy to tell you where to put your braces. However, I will point out that brace placement matters in XQuery, due to the interaction between boundary whitespace characters and XML constructors (see Chapter 7 for details).

Whether you prefer to open and close your braces at the same indented level like Listing 10.5, or whether you prefer to open and close them on the same lines as in Listing 10.6, try to be consistent.

Listing 10.5 Everyone uses braces on new lines at the same level

```
declare function foo()
{
  bar()
};

<Fired>
{
  for $i in doc("team.xml")//Employee
  where $i/@years < 20
  return $i
}
</Fired>
```

Listing 10.6 Except those who use braces on the same lines at different levels

```
declare function foo() {
  bar()
};

<Fired>{
  for $i in doc("team.xml")//Employee
  where $i/@years < 20
  return $i
}</Fired>
```

Too many developers shy away from using parentheses (possibly as a knee-jerk reaction to LISP). Although too many parentheses can obscure a query, most queries suffer from the opposite problem. Parentheses rarely hurt readability, and always clarify your intentions.

One place you should always use parentheses is to wrap FLWOR expressions when either the FLWOR is followed by a comma or the return clause returns a list. Consider, for example, the XQuery `for $i in (1,2) return 3, 4`. This expression results in `(3, 3, 4)`, because FLWOR binds more tightly than the comma operator; consequently, it's parsed as `(for $i in (1,2) return 3),4`.

No matter what you expected it to return, someone else expected the other result. Always use parentheses in this case to make clear whether you meant `(for $i in (1,2) return 3),4` or whether you actually meant `for $i in (1,2) return (3,4)`.

10.2.4 Slice

Treat XQuery like you would any programming language. For something really short, simple, or ad hoc, write a single query, but for anything long, complex, or planned, use functions and modules to structure the program.

Except for `typeswitch` and XML construction, individual XQuery functions should rarely be more than ten lines long. By its very nature, `typeswitch` tends to contain many different case statements. XML construction is verbose, and that's just the way it is. It can make sense to modularize the XML into separate functions (especially for things like recursive processing or reusable blocks of XML), but don't overdo it.

10.2.5 Concise

Brevity is a virtue. Don't obfuscate your queries, but do spend some time improving their clarity and conciseness. For example, don't write silly queries like the one in Listing 10.7 when a simple path will do.

Listing 10.7 FLWOR is overkill for this query

```
for $i in doc("team.xml")//Employee
where $i/@years > 1
return $i

(: why not just use
  doc("team.xml")//Employee[@years > 1]
instead? :)
```

Anyone can write a ten-page query; it's honestly not impressive. However, few people can write a clear, one-page query that does the same work. Simplicity requires (and deserves) time and practice.

10.3 Idioms

Over time, certain patterns have shown up again and again in XPath and XQuery. I call these idioms, because unless I "knew" them, I'd probably never have figured them out from the basic rules. If you want to become a native XQuery speaker, master its idioms.

10.3.1 Text Idioms

Most XML applications need to manipulate text. Here are solutions to a few of the more common string tasks.

10.3.1.1 Reverse a String

The dreaded interview question: reverse a string (or a linked-list, or a palindrome, or...).

XQuery doesn't provide any built-in function for reversing a string, but using a combination of FLWOR and the built-in `string-to-codepoints()` and `codepoints-to-string()` functions, as shown in Listing 10.8, you can write your own. This function converts the string into a list of characters, reverses that list, and then converts the (now reversed) list back into a string.

Listing 10.8 Reverse a string

```
declare function reverse-string($str as xs:string?) as xs:string? {
  codepoints-to-string(
    reverse(string-to-codepoints($str))
  )
};
```

Reversing a palindrome is left as an exercise to the reader. Another way to reverse a list (without the `reverse()` function) is shown in Listing 10.9.

Listing 10.9 Reverse a list

```
declare function reverse-list($list) {
  for $i at $p in $list
  order by $p descending
  return $i
};
```

10.3.1.2 Comma-Separated Values

You'd think XML might have killed the comma-separated values (CSV) format, but apparently not (after all, even XQuery uses it in places, such as function arguments and sequences).

If you ever need to take a list of values and construct a comma-separated (or space-separated, or other-separated) string containing them, look no further than the built-in `string-join()` function (see Listing 10.10).

Listing 10.10 Use `string-join()` to combine sequences of values

```
string-join((1, 2, 3), ", ")
=>
"1, 2, 3"
```

10.3.1.3 Lower-, Upper-, and Title-Case

Perhaps the most frequently asked question about XPath 1.0 is how to compare two strings or navigate in a case-insensitive fashion. Related questions are how to completely uppercase, lowercase, or title-case a string, or how to navigate XML ignoring case. Some of these problems persist even in XQuery. Navigating case-insensitively in XQuery is solved in Section 10.3.2.2.

XQuery has partially solved these problems by providing `lower-case()` and `upper-case()` functions (see Listing 10.11). XPath 1.0 has only the `translate()` function (which is also available in XQuery, although `replace()` is better). Neither has a `title-case()` function.

Listing 10.11 Lowercase is easy in XQuery

```
lower-case($theString)
```

The only robust solution for the remaining missing functionality such as title-case is to use vendor extensions (or in XSLT, script) to implement the missing functionality. Chapter 8 shows that functions like `title-case()` (and in XPath/XSLT 1.0, `lower-case()`) are very complex to implement from first principles.

For all you XPath 1.0 and XSLT 1.0 users out there, the `translate()` function can sort of convert a string to lowercase (or uppercase), but suffers from the limitation that you must explicitly list the characters you wish to convert—so unless you specify the entire Unicode table as arguments, your application will not be properly internationalized. See Listing 10.12 for an example. Use script (shown in Listing 10.13) or other vendor extensions for robust programs, and `translate()` for cases in which the possible input strings are restricted.

Listing 10.12 Almost, but not quite, lowercase in XPath 1.0

```
translate($theString,
  'ABCDEFGHIJKLMNOPQRSTUVWXYZ',
  'abcdefghijklmnopqrstuvwxyz')
```

In XQuery, you should generally avoid the `translate()` function, because its other string functions are much more powerful.

Listing 10.13 Lowercase in XSLT 1.0 using embedded script

```
<xsl:stylesheet version="1.0"
    xmlns:xsl="http://www.w3.org/1999/XSL/Transform"
    xmlns:my="urn:foo">
<xsl:template match="*[my:toLower(local-name()) = 'ABC'">
  <!-- this template matches elements with names
       abc, Abc, aBc, AbC, ... -->
</xsl:template>
<ms:script xmlns:ms="urn:schemas-microsoft-com:xslt"
         language="JavaScript" implements-prefix="my">
  function toLower(s) {
    return s.ToLower();
  }
</ms:script>
</xsl:stylesheet>
```

10.3.1.4 Test for ASCII Characters

The regular expression language used by XQuery (see Appendix D) provides many cool features. One of them is the ability to match characters based on their Unicode code point range. This feature can be used to test whether a string consists entirely of 7-bit or 8-bit ASCII characters (or conversely, whether it includes non-ASCII characters), which can be useful when writing certain kinds of applications. Listing 10.14 demonstrates this use.

Listing 10.14 Regular expressions can test character classes using \p

```
declare function is-seven-bit-ascii($str as xs:string) as xs:boolean {
  matches($str, "\p{IsBasicLatin}*")
};

declare function is-eight-bit-ascii($str as xs:string) as:xs:boolean {
  matches($str, "\p{IsLatin-1Supplement}*")
};
```

10.3.2 Navigation Idioms

XQuery provides such a rich set of navigation operators that you might think every possible task is easily and obviously solved using them. If only it were so! Almost every day someone asks me a navigation question. The phrase "How do I select all nodes that …?" is hallmark sign of a navigation problem in need of a solution.

10.3.2.1 Select Elements and Attributes Simultaneously

Sometimes you need to process data that is somewhat irregular in shape. For example, you may need to select all child elements and attributes of the current node with some name. Fortunately, this is easy to do in XQuery, using the union operator as shown in Listing 10.15.

Listing 10.15 Select elements and attributes named y from the element $x

```
$x/(@y | y)
```

In XPath 1.0, the union operator wasn't allowed in a step, so you had to break this into separate paths: (`$x/@y | $x/y`).

10.3.2.2 Navigate Case-Insensitively

Although XML is case-sensitive, sometimes you need to ignore case when navigating (usually because you're trying to work around XML instead of with it, but that's another story).

Because XQuery provides `lower-case()` and `upper-case()`, navigating in a case-insensitive way is easily done using predicates, as shown in Listing 10.16. This example matches all elements named `foo` or `FOO` or `Foo` or `fOo` or any other case variant of `foo`.

Listing 10.16 Navigating case-insensitively

```
*[lower-case(local-name(.)) = "foo"]
```

10.3.2.3 Select Nodes by Type

XPath 1.0 is blissfully schema-unaware. One feature people most hoped XQuery and XPath 2.0 would provide is the ability to select nodes by their schema type.

This functionality is available in several forms, including `instance of` and `typeswitch`. However, the simplest solution is to just use the `element()` and `attribute()` node kind tests.

For example, to select all elements that are integers (or derived from `xs:integer`), you can use the `element()` node kind test and pass it the type name, as shown in Listing 10.17.

Listing 10.17 Select all integer element children of the current context node

```
element(*, xs:integer)
```

Similarly, to match all attribute nodes that have type integer, you would use `attribute(*, xs:integer)`.

When you want to match a couple of different types at the same time, `instance of` in a predicate sometimes is more convenient. For example, Listing 10.18 selects all elements of type `xs:float` or `xs:double` (or any subtype of these). Instead, you could use a union of two `element()` node kind tests, as shown in Listing 10.19. For more than a few types at once, `instance of` and unions quickly grow tiresome, and `typeswitch` becomes a better choice.

Listing 10.18 Select nodes by type in XQuery

```
*[(. instance of xs:float) or (. instance of xs:double)]
```

Listing 10.19 Another way to do the same thing

```
element(*, xs:float) | element(*, xs:double)
```

10.3.2.4 Test Whether Two Nodes Are in the Same Tree

As you saw in Chapter 5, XQuery provides convenient node comparison operators to test whether two expressions evaluate to the same node, or whether one node comes before another in document order. However, XQuery doesn't have an operator that tests whether two nodes belong to the same document or fragment.

There are several possible ways to solve this, but the simplest one is to compare their root nodes (because every node belongs to a tree and every tree has a unique root, which must then be the same if and only if the nodes are in the same tree). Listing 10.20 demonstrates this technique.

Listing 10.20 Test whether two nodes $n1 and $n2 are in the same tree

```
root($n1) is root($n2)
```

10.3.2.5 Select All Leaf Elements

Leaf elements are those elements that don't have any children. So the path in Listing 10.21 selects all leaf elements under the current context node (in both XPath 1.0 and XQuery).

Listing 10.21 Select all leaf elements under the current context node in XPath and XQuery

```
.//*[not(node())]
```

Replace the predicate with `not(*)` to allow leaves to contain text, comments, or processing instructions (but not elements).

10.3.2.6 Select All Ancestors

XPath provides convenient axes (`ancestor` and `ancestor-or-self`) for selecting the ancestors of a node, and most XQuery implementations support these axes. For those that don't, it's straightforward to construct a recursive XQuery function that returns a list of all the ancestors of a node in document order. Listing 10.22 provides such a function.

Listing 10.22 Select ancestors in XQuery implementations without `ancestor::node()`

```
declare function ancestors($n as node()?) as node()* {
  if (empty($n)) then ()
  else (ancestors($n/..), $n/..)
};
```

10.3.2.7 Select the First Common Ancestor

Another common task in tree-walking is to calculate the first node that is in the ancestor list of two existing nodes (aka, the *first common ancestor*). XPath doesn't provide a function to calculate this directly, but it can be achieved with a nasty predicate that computes the intersection of the two ancestor lists and selects the last ancestor in document order (which is the first one in reverse-document order). Listing 10.23 shows how difficult this is with XPath 1.0.

Listing 10.23 Select the first common ancestor of two nodes $n1 and $n2 in XPath 1.0

```
$n1/ancestor-or-self::node()
  [count(. | $n2/ancestor-or-self::node()) =
   count($n2/ancestor-or-self::node())] [1]
```

XQuery supports set intersection directly, so we no longer need the nasty predicate. If the implementation supports ancestor axes, then we can use them; otherwise, we can use the previous solution to select the ancestors. Listing 10.24 shows how much easier this is with XQuery.

Listing 10.24 Select the first common ancestor in XQuery

```
declare function fca($n1 as node()?, $n2 as node() {
  (ancestors($n1) intersect ancestors($n2))[last()]
};
```

10.3.2.8 Select All Siblings

One common operation on trees is to select all the immediate siblings of a given node. Oddly, XPath and XQuery have no axis for doing this; however, it can easily be achieved using the `preceding-sibling` and `following-sibling` axes. The path in Listing 10.25 selects all siblings of the current context node.

Listing 10.25 Select all siblings in XPath 1.0

```
preceding-sibling::node() | following-sibling::node()
```

Unfortunately, not every XQuery implementation supports these axes. Also, this union can be expensive to compute. Another solution is to use the parent axis. Because only one node can exist at the root of a document or fragment, a node with no parent has no siblings either. Just be sure to exclude the node itself, so that you select only its siblings. Listing 10.26 demonstrates this technique.

Listing 10.26 Select all siblings in XQuery

```
../node() except .
```

Sometimes you also want to select the node itself along with all its siblings ("sibling-or-self"). Here you have to be careful that you don't lose the node if it has no parent. One way is to combine the node with the children of its parent using the union operator as shown in Listing 10.27.

Listing 10.27 Select sibling-or-self in XQuery (or XPath 1.0)

```
. | ../node()
```

10.3.2.9 Calculate the Maximum Depth

Sometimes you need to calculate the maximum depth (or some other cost) over a subtree rooted at a particular node. In XQuery 1.0, this problem is greatly simplified through the use of `max()` and the ability to construct sequences of numbers, as shown in Listing 10.28.

Listing 10.28 Calculate the maximum depth of a subtree in XQuery

```
declare function max-depth($root as node()?) as xs:integer {
  max(
    (: for each leaf element :)
    for $i in $root/descendant-or-self::*[not(*)]
    (: count its depth :)
    return count($i/ancestor::*)
  )
};
```

In contrast, XPath and XSLT 1.0 have no max() function.

So that you can appreciate how much simpler XQuery makes this problem, two XSLT 1.0 solutions are shown in Listings 10.29 and 10.30. The first solution is done using "pure" XSLT, by selecting all nodes such that there is no other node with more ancestors. The second uses embedded script to call out to a JScript max() function and doesn't work in every XSLT implementation.

Listing 10.29 Calculate the maximum depth in XPath 1.0/XSLT 1.0

```
<xsl:template name="max-depth">
  <xsl:variable name="all" select=".//*[not(*)]"/>
  <xsl:variable name="initial-depth" select="count(ancestor::node())"/>
  <xsl:for-each select="$all">
    <xsl:variable name="depth" select="count(ancestor::node())"/>
    <xsl:variable name="first-node"
                  select="$all[count(ancestor::node()) = $depth][1]"/>
    <xsl:variable name="is-deepest"
                  select="not($all[count(ancestor::node()) > $depth])"/>
    <xsl:if test="$is-deepest and
                  generate-id(current()) = generate-id($first-node)">
      <!-- Print the value only once by stopping at the first node
           that is the deepest (in case of ties) -->
      <xsl:value-of select="$depth - $initial-depth"/>
    </xsl:if>
  </xsl:for-each>
</xsl:template>
```

Listing 10.30 Calculate the maximum depth in XSLT using JScript

```
<ms:script language="JScript" implements-prefix="my"
          xmlns:ms="urn:schemas-microsoft-com:xslt">
function maxDepth(node) {
  var leaves = node.selectNodes('.//*[not(*)]');
  var d = 0;
  for (var i=0; i &lt; leaves.length; i++) {
    d = max(d, leaves.item(i).selectNodes('ancestor::node()').length;
  }
  return d;
}
</ms:script>
```

10.3.3 Sequence Idioms

Because every XQuery expression evaluates to a sequence, sequence manipulations are almost as common as text and navigation. This section considers some of the more common tasks involving sequence operations.

10.3.3.1 Union, Intersection, and Difference

XPath 1.0 provides a set union operator, the vertical bar (|), to compute the union of two sets (which returns all nodes from both sets combined, with duplicates nodes removed). However, XPath 1.0 doesn't provide a way to compute the intersection (all nodes that are simultaneously in both sets), the difference (all nodes that are in one set and not in the other), or the symmetric difference (all nodes that are in exactly one of the two sets).

XQuery completely solves this for node sequences by providing `intersect` and `except` operators that compute the intersection and difference, respectively. The `except` operator is asymmetric; to compute the symmetric difference (all nodes that are in either sequence but not both), use one of the two expressions shown in Listing 10.31.

Listing 10.31 Two equivalent ways to compute the symmetric difference in XQuery

```
declare function symmetric-difference($set1 as node()*,
                                      $set2 as node()*) as node()* {
  ($set1 except $set2) union ($set2 except $set1)
```

```
};

declare function symmetric-difference2($set1 as node()*,
                                        $set2 as node()*) as node()* {
  ($set1 union $set2) except ($set1 intersect $set2)
};
```

For XPath 1.0 users, one workaround (which also works in XQuery 1.0) makes clever use of the `count()` function, shown in Listings 10.32, 10.33, and 10.34.

Listing 10.32 Computing the intersection of `$set1` with `$set2` in XPath 1.0

```
$set1[count(. | $set2) = count($set2)]
```

Listing 10.33 Compute the difference of `$set1` with `$set2` in XPath 1.0

```
$set1[count(. | $set2) != count($set2)]
```

Listing 10.34 Compute the symmetric difference of `$set1` with `$set2` in XPath 1.0

```
$set1[count(. | $set2) != count($set2)] |
$set2[count(. | $set1) != count($set1)]
```

All of these work only on sequences of nodes. What if you want to compute the union, intersection, or difference of two sequences of values (using equality in place of node identity)?

To compute the union of two sequences of values (removing duplicates), the expression `distinct-values(($seq1, $seq2))` works well. Intersection and difference are more complicated; we could use the same `count()` technique as before, but a better approach is to use FLWOR to join the two sequences and apply `distinct-values()` to the result to remove duplicates, as shown in Listings 10.35 and 10.36.

Listing 10.35 Intersection of sets of values

```
declare function value-intersect($seq1, $seq2) as xdt:untypedAtomic* {
  distinct-values(
    for $i in $seq1
    where some $j in $seq2 satisfies $i eq $j
```

```
      return $i
   )
};
```

Listing 10.36 Asymmetric difference of sets of values

```
declare function value-except($seq1, $seq2) as xdt:untypedAtomic* {
   distinct-values(
      for $i in $seq1
      where every $j in $seq2 satisfies $i ne $j
      return $i
   )
};
```

10.3.3.2 Select Every Other Member

When looping through a sequence, sometimes you want to increment by a fixed number other than 1. For example, you may want to select every second member, or every third. FLWOR always iterates through a sequence one by one.

Using a combination of FLWOR and range (`to`), the query in Listing 10.37 loops through all the nth members of a sequence (starting with the first, then (n+1), then (2n+1, etc.). When $n is 2, this selects every other member of the sequence.

Listing 10.37 Iterate through every nth member of a sequence $seq

```
for $i in (1 to count($seq))[. mod $n = 1]
let $nth-member := $seq[$i]
return $nth-member (: or whatever you want to do :)
```

This is also sometimes done by iterating through the entire sequence, and filtering out all but the nth members, as shown in Listing 10.38.

Listing 10.38 Another way to do it

```
for $i at $pos in $seq
let $nth-member := $seq[$i]
where $pos mod $n = 1
return $nth-member (: or whatever you want to do :)
```

10.3.3.3 Permutations

Another common sequence operation involves rearranging the members of a sequence, also known as *permutations*. Permutations of a sequence containing any kinds of items are commonly identified with permutations of the integers ranging from 1 to the length of the sequence. For example, you can use the sequence (3, 2, 1) to identify the permutation that returns the third, second, and first members (in that order) of a sequence.

Given a sequence to be permuted, and a permutation of the integers, the function in Listing 10.39 computes that permutation.

Listing 10.39 Compute the permutation of a sequence

```
declare function permute($seq, $perm as xs:integer*) {
  for $i in $perm
  return $seq[$i]
};
```

10.3.4 Type Idioms

Some of the most important new idioms in XQuery are those that work with types. Sometimes the type conversions are a little tricky, and other times XQuery has no built-in function to work with the typed value.

10.3.4.1 Binary Data

XQuery doesn't provide built-in functions for working with binary values, but XQuery is expressive enough that we can write our own. In practice, implementations may provide extension functions that are more efficient than the ones here.

A sequence of bytes can be encoded in base64 by grouping the data into 3-byte blocks, splitting each block into four 6-bit numbers, and then using table lookup to map those 6-bit values to their corresponding base64 characters. The = symbol is used for "missing" trailing characters. In this way, base64 causes a 4:3 expansion ratio over the original data size.

The built-in `codepoints-to-string()` function converts the sequence of character values into a string, which can then be cast into the `xs:base64Binary` data type. This conversion is implemented in Listing 10.40.

Listing 10.40 Encoding a sequence of bytes into base64-encoded binary data

```
declare function base64-encode($b as xs:integer*) as xs:base64Binary {
  codepoints-to-string(
    let $len := length($b)
    let $table := ( 65 to  90,  (: A-Z :)
                    97 to 122,  (: a-z :)
                    48 to  57,  (: 0-9 :)
                    43, 47 )    (: + / :)
    for $byte0 at $p in $b
    where $p mod 3 = 0
    return
      let $byte1 as xs:integer? := $b[$p + 1]
      let $byte2 as xs:integer? := $b[$p + 2]

      (: Convert the three bytes into four characters :)
      let $c0 := $table[$byte idiv 4]
      let $c1 := $table[sum(($byte0 mod 4)*64, $byte1 idiv 16)]
      let $c2 := if (empty($byte1)) then 61 (: pad with = :)
                 else $table[sum(($byte1 mod 16)*16, $byte2 idiv 64)]
      let $c3 := if (empty($byte2)) then 61 (: pad with = :)
                 else $table[$byte2 mod 64]
      return ($c0, $c1, $c2, $c3)
  )
  cast as xs:base64Binary
};
```

From an XQuery point of view, the most interesting aspect of this function is how it converts the bytes of the original sequence into characters in the destination sequence. This could be done in many different ways; I've elected to extract the bytes (if they exist) using positional predicates. I've typed them as xs:integer? in this example to emphasize the fact that they may be empty.

At the end of the sequence, these bytes may be empty, in which case we want to pad the final result with one or two = characters and treat the missing bytes as if they were zero. Because the + operator returns the empty sequence when either of its operands are empty, we must use the sum() function instead of just writing ($byte0 mod4)*64 + $byte1 idiv 16. There are many other ways to handle this, such as using if/then/else.

Decoding base64 data works similarly but in reverse; the string value is extracted and converted to a sequence of character values, which are then mapped into 6-bit values and combined four at a time into three bytes of binary data.

In the implementation shown in Listing 10.41, trailing = symbols and invalid characters are mapped into the empty sequence, and I use the + operator to exploit this (dropping the last two bytes when padded). I've elected to append trailing = symbols so that the string length is always divisible by 4. A more efficient implementation would handle the last octet separately from the rest.

Listing 10.41 Decoding base64-encoded binary data into a sequence of bytes

```
declare function base64-decode($b as xs:base64Binary?) as xs:integer* {
  let $str := string-to-codepoints($b cast as xs:string)
  let $c := ($str, subsequence((61, 61, 61), 1, length($str) mod 4))
  return
    let $table := ( 65 to  90,   (: A-Z :)
                    97 to 122,   (: a-z :)
                    48 to  57,   (: 0-9 :)
                    43, 47 )     (: + / :)
    for $ch at $p in $c
    where $p mod 4 = 0
    return
      let $c0 := index-of($table, $ch)
      let $c1 := index-of($table, $c[$p + 1])
      let $c2 := index-of($table, $c[$p + 2])
      let $c3 := index-of($table, $c[$p + 3])

      (: Convert the four characters into three bytes :)
      let $byte0 := sum($c0 * 4, $c1 idiv 16)
      let $byte1 := ($c1 mod 16)*16 + ($c2 idiv 4)
      let $byte2 := ($c2 mod 4)*64 + $c3
      return ($byte0, $byte1, $byte2)
};
```

It's much easier (but less space-efficient, with a 2:1 expansion ratio) to work with binary data as xs:hexBinary. In this case, you need only extract pairs of characters at a time, and map them into hexadecimal values (or vice versa). Listing 10.42 illustrates both.

Listing 10.42 Encoding and decoding hexBinary data

```
declare function hex-encode($seq as xs:integer*) as xs:hexBinary {
  codepoints-to-string(
    let $table := (48 to 57, 65 to 70)   (: 0-9, A-F :)
    for $b in $seq
    return ($table[$b idiv 16], $table[$b mod 16])
  )
  cast as xs:hexBinary
};

declare function hex-decode($bin as xs:hexBinary) as xs:integer* {
  let $chars := string-to-codepoints($bin cast as xs:string)
  for $c0 at $p in $chars
  where $p mod 2 = 0
  return
    let $c1 := $chars[$p + 1]
    let $byte0 := if ($c0 < 65) then ($c0 - 48) else ($c0 - 55)
    let $byte1 := if ($c1 < 65) then ($c1 - 48) else ($c1 - 55)
    return $byte0 * 16 + $byte1
};
```

10.3.5 Logic Idioms

XQuery is a very logical language, but it doesn't provide an XOR operator or direct support for three-valued logic. The following sections address both of these issues.

10.3.5.1 Boolean XOR

It may seem strange to use the = and != operators on boolean expressions, instead of using and and or operators. The usual reason is to achieve a kind of "XOR" effect.

If $a and $b are boolean expressions, then $a = $b is almost the same as the lengthier expression ($a and $b) or (not($a) and not($b)) which in some languages is written $a xor $b. You may recall from Chapter 5 that they differ in how they handle the empty sequence; $a = $b returns the empty sequence if either $a or $b is empty, while the boolean expression returns false() if only one is empty, and true() if both are empty. Listing 10.43 uses the boolean definition to write an `xor()` function, but the equality operator could be used instead, depending on how you want to handle the empty sequence.

Listing 10.43 Computing "exclusive or" (XOR)

```
declare function xor($a, $b) {
  ($a and $b) or (not($a) and not($b))
};
```

10.3.5.2 Three-Valued Logic

XQuery has two-valued logic, but you can simulate three-valued logic using the empty sequence as the third value (sometimes called "maybe," "unknown," or "null"). Functions that perform three-valued boolean operations are shown in Listing 10.44.

Listing 10.44 Simulating three-valued logic in XQuery

```
declare function and3($lhs as xs:boolean?,
                      $rhs as xs:boolean?) as xs:boolean? {
  if ($lhs = false() or $rhs = false()) then false()
  else if (empty($lhs) or empty($rhs)) then ()
  else true()
};

declare function or3($lhs as xs:boolean?,
                     $rhs as xs:boolean?) as xs:boolean? {
  if ($lhs = true() or $rhs = true()) then true()
  else if (empty($lhs) or empty($rhs)) then ()
  else false()
};

declare function xor3($lhs as xs:boolean?,
                      $rhs as xs:boolean?) as xs:boolean? {
  $lhs = $rhs
};

declare function not3($arg as xs:boolean?) as xs:boolean? {
  if (empty($arg)) then () else not($arg)
};
```

```
declare function if3($cond as xs:boolean?,
                     $lhs, $mid, $rhs) as xs:boolean? {
  if(empty($cond)) then $mid
  else if ($cond)  then $lhs
  else $rhs
};
```

Interestingly enough, so many XQuery operators return the empty sequence when an operand is empty that these operators already appear to be "three-valued." For example, `$a + $b` is `()` if either `$a` or `$b` is empty, as is `$a = $b`.

This behavior is similar to what you would find in languages that support three-valued logic, such as SQL, and causes some unexpected results. For example, `$a = false()` differs from `not($a)` in how it handles the case that `$a` is the empty sequence. When `$a` is empty, the expression `$a = false()` results in the empty sequence, but `not($a)` results in true.

10.3.6 Arithmetic Idioms

XQuery isn't strongly oriented toward mathematical applications (lacking both trigonometric functions and control over floating-point arithmetic, and allowing implementations to vary in their arithmetic support), but when you need to do the math, these examples will come in handy.

10.3.6.1 *IsNaN*

XQuery doesn't provide a function to test whether a number is `NaN`, and you cannot merely write `$x = NaN`—this will always be false, even when `$x` is `NaN`, because `NaN` compares false to every other value (including itself). However, it's possible to exploit this property of `NaN` to write your own `isNaN()` function, as in Listing 10.45. This strange-looking little function tests whether a value doesn't equal itself. The only value that doesn't equal itself is `NaN`.

Listing 10.45 Testing whether a value is `NaN`

```
declare function isNaN($x as xdt:anyAtomicType) as xs:boolean {
  $x ne $x
};
```

10.3.6.2 Median

XQuery provides functions for computing the sum and average of a sequence, but not the median. The function in Listing 10.46 does the job by first sorting the sequence by value, and then choosing the middle value (or the average of the two middle values, when there is a tie).

Listing 10.46   Calculating the median of a sequence

```
declare function median($seq) as xdt:anyAtomicType? {
  let $sorted := (for $i in $seq order by $i return $i)
  let $half := count($sorted) div 2
  return avg(($sorted[floor($half)], $sorted[ceiling($half)]))
};
```

10.3.6.3 Rounding Modes

Rounding modes are subtle and deserve more attention in your applications than they probably receive. In many industries, the particular choice of rounding mode is actually legislated (for example, when converting between American dollars and European euros).

Although it may seem that there are as many different ways to round as there are stars in the sky, seven rounding modes are in widespread use today (and another two less common modes). These rounding modes all have descriptive names according to how they round non-integral numbers and how they handle the ties (when ties can occur).

Round-up always rounds non-integral numbers up to the next higher integer (that is, in the direction of positive infinity along the number line). *Round-down* always rounds down to the next lower integer (toward negative infinity). *Round-to-zero* rounds in the direction of zero; it's the same as round-down for positive numbers and the same as round-up for negative numbers. *Round-away-from-zero* has these switched.

Round-to-nearest takes a different approach; instead of always rounding in an absolute direction, it rounds locally to the nearest available integer. However, in this rounding mode a tie is possible, since a number can be exactly midway between two integers. So this case is divided into several variations that differ in how they handle the tie case.

Three of the more popular variations are round-half-up, round-half-down, and round-half-even (also known as *banker's rounding*). *Round-half-up* always rounds the tie up (toward positive infinity). *Round-half-down* always rounds the tie down (toward negative infinity). *Round-half-even* always rounds toward the even integer. (Two less common variations are *round-half-to-zero* and *round-half-away-from-zero*, with the obvious definitions.)

Of these seven rounding modes, XQuery supports only four natively: round-up (`ceiling()`), round-down (`floor()`), round-half-up (`round()`), and round-half-even (`round-half-to-even()`). However, the remaining modes can be implemented using these, as shown in Listing 10.47. Some XQuery implementations may provide these rounding modes as more efficient extension functions.

Listing 10.47 Nine rounding modes for mortal men, one language to rule them all

```
declare function round-up($x as xdt:anyAtomicType) {
  ceiling($x)
};

declare function round-down($x as xdt:anyAtomicType) {
  floor($x)
};

declare function round-to-zero($x as xdt:anyAtomicType) {
  if ($x > 0) then floor($x) else ceiling($x)
};

declare function round-away-from-zero($x as xdt:anyAtomicType) {
  if ($x < 0) then floor($x) else ceiling($x)
};

declare function round-half-up($x as xdt:anyAtomicType) {
  round($x)
};

declare function round-half-down($x as xdt:anyAtomicType) {
  -round(-$x)
};

declare function round-half-even($x as xdt:anyAtomicType) {
  round-half-to-even($x)
};

declare function round-half-to-zero($x as xdt:anyAtomicType) {
```

```
    if ($x > 0) then -round(-$x) else round($x)
};

declare function round-half-away-from-zero($x as xdt:anyAtomicType) {
    if ($x < 0) then -round(-$x) else round($x)
};
```

10.3.6.4 Random Number Generation

Computing random numbers requires changeable, persistent state: at a minimum, the last number generated; for higher-quality random number generators (RNGs), an entire table of values must be maintained.

At first glance, this might appear impossible to accomplish in a "functional" language like XQuery, but it can be done by passing the state around as an argument, and returning it along with the random number value.

As a first attempt at constructing an RNG, consider the function in Listing 10.48. This function implements a simple *linear congruential generator* (LCG) using modulo arithmetic. Because each random number acts as the seed for the next one, the random value itself is the state.

Listing 10.48 A simple linear congruential random number generator

```
declare function rand-lcg($seed as xs:integer) as xs:integer {
    (: The Marsaglia "super-duper" LCG :)
    (69069*$seed + 1) mod 4294967296
};
```

Another kind of RNG is the *multiple recursive generator* (MRG). This generator keeps the previous N values as state. In Listing 10.49, N is two. This implementation returns not only the new random value, but also the previous value. The entire result must be used as state to the next invocation, but only the first value in the sequence is the random number to be used.

Listing 10.49 A simple multiple recursive random number generator

```
declare function rand-mrg($seed as xs:integer*) as xs:integer* {
    if (count($seed) != 2) then error("Bad seed")
```

```
    else
      (: One of the L'Ecuyer MRGs :)
      let $r := (46325 * $seed[1] + 1084587 * $seed[2]) mod 4294967295
      return ($r, $seed[1])
};
```

10.3.6.5 Factorial

In XQuery, the factorial is most easily computed using recursion as in Listing 10.50.

Listing 10.50 Computing $n factorial for any positive integer $n

```
declare function factorial($n as xs:integer) as xs:integer {
  if ($n > 1) then $n * factorial($n - 1) else 1
};
```

10.3.6.6 Square Root

Because XQuery has no built-in square-root function, the best we can do is to use an approximation algorithm (or rely on an external function). This example uses the Newton-Raphson method to approximate sqrt($x). Other approximation techniques may yield better results. The work is divided between the two functions shown in Listing 10.51, one to start the iteration and the other to recursively refine the approximation.

Listing 10.51 Approximating square root

```
declare function sqrt($x as xs:double) as xs:double {
  (: Guess an initial value, and iterate 20 times :)
  step(20, $x * 5E-1)
};

declare function step($n as xs:integer, $x as xs:double) as xs:double {
  let $next := $x * (1.5E0 - $x * $x * $x * 5E-1)
  return if ($n <= 0) then $next else step ($n - 1, $next)
};
```

10.3.6.7 Complex Numbers

XQuery doesn't support complex numbers directly, but they can be represented as pairs of numbers (say xs:double). For example, the functions in Listing 10.52 perform "complex arithmetic" using this representation.

Complex numbers could also be represented using an element type. On implementations that support static typing, this approach allows you to create a custom element type to represent complex numbers, making your code easier to read and helping to catch compile-time errors. However, it also uses XML nodes, which are generally heavier-weight than simple lists of numbers.

Listing 10.52 Complex arithmetic can be simulated using pairs of numbers

```
declare function complex-to-string($complex as xs:double*) {
  if (count($complex) != 2) then error("Invalid complex number")
  else concat(string($complex[1]), " + ", string($complex[2]), "i")
};

declare function real($complex as xs:double*) as xs:double {
  if (count($complex) != 2) then error("Invalid complex number")
  else $complex[1] treat as xs:double
};

declare function imag($complex as xs:double*) as xs:double {
  if (count($complex) != 2) then error("Invalid complex number")
  else $complex[2] treat as xs:double
};

(: depends on sqrt() example in Listing 10.51)
declare function magnitude($complex as xs:double*) as xs:double {
  if (count($complex) != 2) then error("Invalid complex number")
  else sqrt($complex[1]*$complex[1] + $complex[2]*$complex[2])
};

declare function add-complex($lhs as xs:double*,
                             $rhs as xs:double*) as xs:double* {
  if (count($lhs) != 2 or count($rhs) != 2) then error("Invalid")
  else ($lhs[1] + $rhs[1], $lhs[2] + $rhs[2])
};

declare function multiply-complex($lhs as xs:double*,
```

```
                                $rhs as xs:double*) as xs:double* {
  if (count($lhs) != 2 or count($rhs) != 2) then error("Invalid")
  else ($lhs[1] * $rhs[1] - $lhs[2] * $rhs[2],
        $lhs[1] * $rhs[2] + $lhs[2] * $rhs[1])
};


  (: etc. :)
```

10.3.6.8 Linear Algebra

The arithmetic operators in XQuery all work on individual values. Sometimes, however, it would be nice to add two sequences together at once, or to perform other vector and matrix manipulations. Vectors can be represented directly in XQuery as sequences of values. Matrices can be too, but require an additional row or column count value to be entirely self-contained.

Listing 10.53 provides some of the more common vector operations. The last two depend on the sqrt() function from Listing 10.51.

Listing 10.53 Vector operations

```
declare function vector-add($lhs, $rhs) {
  if (count($lhs) != count($rhs)) then error("Vector length mismatch")
  else
    for $i at $p in $lhs
    return $i + $rhs[$p]
};


declare function vector-subtract($lhs, $rhs) {
  if (count($lhs) != count($rhs)) then error("Vector length mismatch")
  else
    for $i at $p in $lhs
    return $i - $rhs[$p]
};


declare function vector-negate($arg) {
  for $i in $lhs
  return -$i
};
```

```
declare function original($len as xs:integer) {
  for $i in (1 to $len)
  return 0
};

declare function vector-dot($lhs, $rhs) {
  if (count($lhs) != count($rhs)) then error("Vector length mismatch")
  else
    sum(
      for $i at $p in $lhs
      return $i * $rhs[$p]
    )
};

(: requires the sqrt() function from Listing 10.51 :)
declare function vector-length($arg) {
  sqrt(vector-dot($arg, $arg))
};

declare function vector-distance($lhs, $rhs) {
  vector-length(vector-subtract($lhs, $rhs))
};
```

10.4 Conclusion

In this chapter, we've explored how to solve common, practical tasks using XQuery. I also highly recommend the next chapter, which explores some less practical, but very surprising facts about XQuery.

The XQuery rich navigation and aggregation operators make most navigation tasks possible. The only difficulties are in figuring out how to represent them (paths can be tricky) and in handling border cases, such as nodes that lack parents or children.

Sequences are also straightforward to work with, and are readily used to represent state and certain kinds of data structures (like complex numbers and vectors). Types are another matter; XQuery doesn't define any built-in functions for working with the binary data stored in `xs:base64Binary` and `xs:hexBinary` types, so I've provided some here.

10.5 Further Reading

The XQuery built-in support for sophisticated math is somewhat lacking, but easily made up for with user-defined functions. Simple techniques for arithmetic approximation and random-number generation are part of most undergraduate computer science courses and are available in many references. At `http://random.mat.sbg.ac.at/~charly/server/server.html` you'll find a comprehensive comparison of many different random number generators, including the two used in this chapter. A practical online resource for randomness (and hashing) in general is `http://burtleburtle.net/bob/index.html`.

And finally, check out the extension functions provided by your implementation. Extension functions provide an efficient, if not very portable, way to enrich your XQuery experience. See also Chapter 14 for a quick look at some of the existing XQuery implementations.

CHAPTER 11

Surprises

11.1 Introduction

I once e-mailed an "XPath Quiz" containing six multiple-choice questions about XPath 1.0 to the XML development team at Microsoft. Of those who replied, not one person answered all six questions correctly (although a few got five right). Evidently, XPath is a subtle language filled with hidden complexities, even for the experts who have implemented it! Or as I sometimes exaggerate, "XPath is all special cases."
As an even larger and more complex language containing most of XPath 2.0 as a subset, XQuery multiplies the surprises. Understanding some of these hidden complexities will illuminate the inner workings of these languages and assist you in mastering their nuances (not to mention any pop quizzes).

This chapter considers many borderline or otherwise odd cases that illustrate what may be surprising behavior in XQuery. Unlike the previous chapter, most of the examples here are unlikely to arise as-is in practice, although you are very likely to encounter the underlying concepts in one situation or another.

11.2 Confusion over Meaning

To be useful, a language must be concise. One way to achieve brevity is to not say everything you mean, instead relying on context or other implicit meaning to convey your intent. However, hidden meaning is a double-edged sword, as the examples in this section demonstrate.

11.2.1 Numbers Like 3.14 Are Decimal, Not Double

One of the most common errors new XQuery users make is that they assume number constants with a decimal point in them, such as 3.14, are doubles (double-precision floating-point numbers). However, in XQuery these numbers are decimals. Decimal arithmetic is generally implemented in software instead of hardware, and as demonstrated by Listing 11.1 behaves very differently from double arithmetic (see also Chapter 2).

Listing 11.1 Decimals versus doubles

```
3.14   div 0 => error (division by zero)
3.14E0 div 0 => INF   (positive infinity)
```

11.2.2 Predicates Index Sequences, Not Strings

Another common error occurs when a user writes an XQuery like `"xyz"[2]` and expects it to return `"y"`.

The fact is that predicates index sequences, not strings. The expression `"xyz"` is a sequence of length 1 containing that string value. Consequently, `"xyz"[2]` attempts to select the second member of that sequence, and finding none, returns the empty sequence. Use the `substring()` function to index into a string (see also Chapters 3 and 8). Listing11.2 shows both sequence and string indexing.

Listing 11.2 Predicates index sequences, not strings

```
("x", "y", "z")[2]    => "y" (: second item :)
"xyz"[2]              => ()  (: second item :)
substring("xyz", 2, 1) => "y" (: second character :)
```

11.2.3 `not(=)` Is Not `!=`

The not-equals operator (`!=`) has a different meaning from `not()` applied to the equals operator (`=`). In contrast, `ne` has the same meaning as `not()` applied to `eq`.

The reason for these differences is *implicit existential quantification*. The `=` and `!=` operators implicitly check for existence, but `eq` and `ne` do not. When `not()` is applied to the outside of the equality operator, it negates the existence test as well as the equality test. When `!=` is used, only the equality test is negated; the existence test is not. This difference is illustrated in Listing 11.3 (see also Chapter 5).

The first query in Listing 11.3 selects all elements named x where there exists an attribute named y whose value is equal to 1. The second query negates this condition, matching the exact opposite—it selects all elements x where there doesn't exist an attribute y whose value is equal to 1. This includes elements where there doesn't exist a y attribute at all, and also those where one exists but it isn't equal to 1.

The third query, using != , is slightly different. It selects all elements x where there exists an attribute y whose value isn't equal to 1. In other words, it requires the attribute to exist. Consequently, not(=) matches <x/> but != does not.

Listing 11.3 not(=) versus !=

```
x[@y = 1]       (: matches <x y="1"/> but not <x/> or <x y="2"/>  :)
x[not(@y=1)]    (: matches <x y="2"/> and <x/> but not <x y="1"/> :)
x[@y != 1]      (: matches <x y="2"/> but not <x/> or <x y="1"/>  :)
```

11.2.4 Arithmetic Isn't Associative

In school, you may have learned that the two equations (a + b) + c and a + (b + c) give the same answer because arithmetic is associative. This simple truism leads to others, such as that a + b = c is equivalent to a = c - b.

In XQuery, most operators have implicit effects such as type conversions, atomization, and quantification that cause this basic math rule to no longer hold true (see Chapter 5). For example, consider the two queries in Listing 11.4.

Listing 11.4 Two queries that seem to be equivalent but are not

```
/x[1 + 2 = y]
/x[    2 = y - 1]
```

To understand why these two queries are different, consider their effects over the XML document shown in Listing 11.5.

Listing 11.5 An XML instance on which they differ

```
<x>
  <y>2</y>
  <y>3</y>
</x>
```

The first query selects x when there exists a y child element equal to 1+2 (in other words, 3). There exists such a y (the second child of x), so the predicate is true and this path selects x.

In contrast, the second query selects x when 2 is equal to y - 1. The path y selects both y child elements, and then the subtraction operator implicitly atomizes them and checks that the result is a single value. In this case, the result would be two values, and so this query raises an error. (In XPath 1.0, instead of causing an error this query performs the subtraction on the first y element only, and then the predicate evaluates to false and the final result is the empty sequence. The result is still different from the first query.)

11.2.5 Predicates + Abbreviated Axes = Confusion

Take care when mixing predicates with abbreviated axes. For example, consider the XPath //*[1]. At first glance, intuition might suggest that this query selects the first element in the entire document; however, your intuition is incorrect. Consider the expansion of the // abbreviation shown in Listing 11.6.

Listing 11.6 Expanding //

```
/descendant-or-self::node()/child::*[1]
```

This XPath starts at the root document node, then selects all the descendant nodes of it including itself (in other words, every node in the document), and then *for each of these nodes*, selects the first child element. (The "for each" and child axis are implicit in the original path.)

Consequently, the XPath //*[1] actually selects the first child element of every node in the document. The superficially similar query (//*)[1] selects the first element in the entire document, because now the position test applies to the entire set of nodes selected by //* (see also Chapter 3).

To see the difference in action, consider the document <x><y/></x>. The path //*[1] selects both elements x and y, while (//*)[1] selects only x.

11.2.6 Node Sequences Are Different from Node Siblings

Constructed nodes in an ordinary sequence aren't related to each other, but nodes in element or document content are related. Consider the XQuery in Listing 11.7 and try to predict the outcome.

Listing 11.7 A sequence of two unrelated nodes, and a sequence of two node siblings

```
let $y := <y/>
let $x := <x/>
let $unrelated := ($x, $y)
let $related := (<z>{ $unrelated }</z>)/*
return $unrelated[1] << $unrelated[2],
       $related[1]   << $related[2]
```

At first glance, both the `$unrelated` and the `$related` variables seem to have the same value: a sequence of two elements, the first named x and the second named y. However, in the `$related` variable these two nodes are siblings of one another, while in the other they are not. Consequently, navigation and document order behave differently for these two variables.

Because the relative order of two unrelated nodes is implementation-dependent, the comparison `$unrelated[1] << $unrelated[2]` can return either false or true. In contrast, the comparison `$related[1] << $related[2]` is always true.

11.2.7 No Sub-Tree Pruning

Selecting an element means selecting not just the tag that starts the element, but also all of its content (attributes, children, etc.). In some query languages (but not XQuery), there exists a feature known as *sub-tree pruning*, which allows you to select a node and only part of its content.

For example, consider the XML shown in Listing 11.8. Suppose you want to select the customer from Washington, but only with those orders that happened on a particular date—that is, prune the `Order` elements inside the `Customer` element, to produce the result shown in Listing 11.9.

Listing 11.8 `Customer` elements containing `Order` elements

```
<Customer state="WA">
  <Order date="2004-05-13"/>
  <Order date="2004-05-30"/>
  <Order date="2003-07-11"/>
</Customer>
<Customer state="CA">
```

```
   <Order date="2004-12-31"/>
   <Order date="2003-10-31"/>
</Customer>
```

Listing 11.9 The first `Customer` element with its sub-tree pruned

```
<Customer state="WA">
  <Order date="2004-05-13"/>
</Customer>
```

The path `Customer[@state="WA"]/Order[@date="2004-05-13"]` doesn't do what you want. It selects the first `Order` element under the first `Customer` element, but not the `Customer` element itself. The path `Customer[@state="WA"]` `[Order[@date="2004-05-13"]]` also doesn't do what you want—it selects the entire `Customer` element (and all of its `Order` element children).

The closest that XQuery can come to sub-tree pruning (which ordinarily preserves the identity of the original nodes) is to construct a copy of the desired portions of the tree. One way to do this is to select the inner results and wrap them with construction, as shown in Listing 11.10. Technically this is new construction, not pruning, but if it gets the job done that's good enough.

Listing 11.10 One way to "prune" in XQuery

```
for $i in Customer[@state='WA']
return <Customer>
        { $i/@* } (: copy all attributes :)
        { $i/Order[@date = "2004-05-13"] } (: copy only some Orders :)
       </Customer>
```

In XSLT 1.0, this would typically be done using `<xsl:copy-of/>`, which allows you to copy a node and insert your own content into the copy. XQuery doesn't have an equivalent; you must copy each portion manually.

11.2.8 Type Conversions

Sometimes the type conversions in XQuery just don't do quite what you expect. As an example, consider trying to convert strings like `"2.8"` or `"2.0"` into `xs:integer`. You probably expect the first case to raise an error, and the second case to succeed and produce the integer 2.

You might approach this by writing `$str cast as xs:integer`. However, as Chapter 9 explains, converting from `xs:string` to `xs:integer` parses the string according to the lexical rules for the `xs:integer` type, which doesn't allow a decimal point. Consequently, this would raise an error even for both values above.

You might next try `($str cast as xs:decimal) cast as xs:integer`. (Indeed, one member of the XQuery Working Group suggested this.) The first conversion (from string to decimal) successfully converts `"2.8"` into the decimal number `2.8` and `"2.0"` into `2.0`. However, the second conversion (from decimal to integer) then truncates the decimal digits, so that both `2.8` and `2.0` become `2.0`, without error, as shown in Listing 11.11.

Listing 11.11 Converting to integer is more subtle than you might think

```
"2.8" cast as xs:integer => error
"2.0" cast as xs:integer => error
("2.0" cast as xs:decimal) cast as xs:integer => 2.0
("2.8" cast as xs:decimal) cast as xs:integer => 2.0
```

One way to achieve the desired effect is to first cast to decimal, save the result, and then cast that to integer. If the final value equals the saved value, then no truncation occurred, so the original value was integral; otherwise, it raises an error. This solution is shown in Listing 11.12 and exploits numeric type promotion (described in Chapter 2).

Listing 11.12 One way to perform this integer conversion

```
declare function toInt($str as xs:string) as xs:integer {
  let $dec := $str cast as xs:decimal
  let $int := $dec cast as xs:integer
  return if ($dec = $int) then $int else error("Not an integer")
};

toInt("2.0") => 2
toInt("2.8") => error (: Not an integer :)
```

11.2.9 What's in a Name?

Many people mistakenly go through life believing that names accurately describe the things named. Don't commit the same error!

For example, `xs:integer` and `xs:int` aren't the same type. The former is arbitrary precision (even if your XQuery implementation uses limited 32-bit or 64-bit precision to represent it). The latter is always 32-bit only.

As another example, document order doesn't apply just to nodes within the same document. All nodes, even those from other documents or constructed fragments in the query, are ordered relative to one another. The ordering is implementation-dependent, but doesn't change during the execution of the query.

Don't believe things that tell you they don't exist. Untyped atomic values do have a type in XQuery, namely `xs:untypedAtomic`. The value `NaN` (not a number) is a numeric value—for example, the expression `(0E0 div 0) instanceof xs:double` returns true.

Conversely, just because something doesn't speak up doesn't mean it isn't there. I wish I had a dollar for every time I've misspelled a name in a path, and ended up with the empty sequence (because no nodes matched my typographical error).

11.2.10 FLWOR Doesn't Move the Current Context

In an XPath query, each step changes the current context item. However, FLWOR expressions don't change the current context item. This is both a blessing and a curse, as it allows you to express meanings not expressible in XPath, but can lead to confusion.

For example, in Listing 11.13, the dot . (the current context item) is first bound to the `Customer` element(s), and then bound to the `Detail` element(s). Each step moves the context along.

Listing 11.13 Paths alter the current context

```
Customer[@Region = "WA"]/Order[2]/Detail[./@Quantity = 10]
```

At first glance, Listing 11.14 may appear to do the same thing, but look again!

Listing 11.14 FLWOR expressions don't change the context

```
for $i in Customer
where ./@Region = "WA"
return
  for $j in Order
```

```
where position() = 2
return
  for $k in Detail
  where ./@Quantity = 10
  return $k
```

The current context item isn't changed by each FLWOR, so both . expressions in Listing 11.14 are bound to whatever the current context item was coming into this expression (not first `Customer` and then `Detail`). Similarly, `position()` and `last()` are unaffected by the FLWOR expressions. Even worse, the three relative paths `Customer`, `Order`, and `Detail` aren't relative to one another as they were in Listing 11.13. Instead, all three paths are relative to the current context item. This query produces a cross-product of three sets instead of the desired step-by-step navigation.

Listing 11.15 shows a corrected version of this FLWOR expression, using the variables bound by each FLWOR to manually start from the desired context. This corrected version has the same effect as the path shown in Listing 11.13.

Listing 11.15 A corrected version of Listing 11.14

```
for $i in Customer
where $i/@Region = "WA"
return
  for $j at $pos in $i/Order
  where $pos = 2
  return
    for $k in $j/Detail
    where $k/@Quantity = 10
    return $k
```

11.2.11 Nested FLWOR Is Different

As explained in Chapter 6, nesting FLWOR expressions produces a very different effect than combining them into a single FLWOR. The difference doesn't always show up immediately, which can lead to confusion when you later change the query slightly or try a more complex test case and obtain wildly different results.

Compare Listing 11.16 and Listing 11.17.

Listing 11.16 Nested FLWOR

```
for $i in (1, 2, 3)
return
  for $j in (4, 5, 6)
  return $i + $j
=>
(5, 6, 7, 6, 7, 8, 7, 8, 9)
```

Listing 11.17 Flattened FLWOR

```
for $i in (1, 2, 3)
for $j in (4, 5, 6)
return $i + $j
=>
(5, 6, 7, 6, 7, 8, 7, 8, 9)
```

Table 11.1 The tuple space corresponding to Listing 11.16

$i	return	
1	**$j** / 4, 5, 6	**return** / 5, 6, 7
2	**$j** / 4, 5, 6	**return** / 6, 7, 8
3	**$j** / 4, 5, 6	**return** / 7, 8, 9

Table 11.2 The tuple space corresponding to Listing 11.17

$i	$j	return
1	4	5
1	5	6
1	6	7
2	4	6
2	5	7
2	6	8
3	4	7
3	5	8
3	6	9

In this simple example, both sequences happen to produce the same end result, only because the sequence of integers doesn't reveal the structure. However, their intermediate tuple spaces are very different, as shown in Table 11.1 and Table 11.2.

To see the difference more clearly, just add a `where` or `order by` clause, or give the `return` clause structure (like XML elements).

For example, suppose we change the return clause from `$x + $y` to the more complex expression `<q>{$x + $y}</q>`. Then for Listing 11.16 we get the result `<q>5 6 7</q><q>6 7 8</q><q>7 8 9</q>` while for Listing 11.17 we get the result `<q>5 6 7 6 7 8 7 8 9</q>`. The nested FLWOR expression shows up as nested results; the flattened FLWOR expression produces flattened results.

11.3 Confusion over Syntax

Even without hidden meanings, it can be difficult to get the syntax correct. Although the XQuery syntax isn't very complicated compared to, say, C++, nevertheless there are many issues about which you should be aware.

11.3.1 Punctuation Is Tricky

So-called smart quotes " (U+201C) and " (U+201D) and smart apostrophes ' (U+2018) and ' (U+2019) are valid XML characters, but aren't treated as quotes or apostrophes by any of the XML standards, including XPath, XQuery, and XML itself. Be careful when copying and pasting from other applications that you correctly use the ordinary versions of the double-quote " (U+0022) and apostrophe ' (U+0027) characters, otherwise you may encounter strange syntax errors.

The hyphen - (U+002D) is a valid name character in addition to being an operator. Consequently, `x[y-2]` selects x elements where there exists a child element named `y-2`. Adding spaces completely changes the meaning: The XPath `x[y - 2]` selects x elements whose `position()` is equal to the numeric expression y minus 2. However, the hyphen may not begin a name, so `-y` always means negative y.

XQuery allows any number of unary plus and/or minus signs in front of an expression, as shown in Listing 11.18.

Listing 11.18 Any number of leading pluses and minuses are allowed

```
--+---+--------+++++----+-----42
```

11.3.2 The `<foo/><foo/>` Problem

Strange but true: The XQuery grammar allows you to write `<x><foo/><foo/></x>`, an element containing two sibling elements, and `(<foo/>,<foo/>)`, a sequence containing two unrelated elements, but doesn't allow `<foo/><foo/>` (a syntax error). Note also that the first two are very different (see Section 11.2.6).

11.3.3 XML Numbers Aren't XQuery Numbers

The definition of `Digits` in the XQuery 1.0 grammar (see Appendix E) doesn't match the definition of `Digit` in the XML grammar (at `http://www.w3.org/TR/REC-xml#NT-Digit`). Consequently, international digits are precluded from appearing as numbers in XQuery, although they are allowed in names and string literals.

Moreover, XQuery is clear that converting a string containing digit characters other than 0–9 results in an error. To work with international digits, you'll have to use user-defined functions (or possibly vendor extensions) to convert from these string representations to actual number values.

11.3.4 Wacky Paths

When it comes to paths, the XPath 1.0 grammar is unusual and the XQuery/XPath 2.0 grammar is even more so.

XPath 1.0 grammar disallowed predicates on the abbreviated steps . (self) and .. (parent), so that, for example, ..[1] results in an error even though the equivalent `parent::node()[1]` is allowed. Also, XPath 1.0 disallowed the union operator in steps, so that a/b | a/c was allowed but a/(b|c) was not.

In XQuery 1.0, both of these cases are now allowed. The expressions ..[1] and a/(b|c) are valid paths. However, so are many other new forms, such as (/)//(/), which selects the root of the input document, and x/root() (which does the same). As long as each step evaluates to a nodeset, the path is allowed.

Both XPath and XQuery allow some combinations of axes and node kind tests that are impossible, such as `attribute::comment()` and `parent::text()`. These expressions are syntactically valid even though they have no useful meaning.

Beware that 1/x doesn't perform division (for that you need 1 div x), but it also isn't a compile-time error! XQuery (and XPath 1.0) compiles this as a path expression, and then it's a run-time error because 1 isn't a sequence of nodes.

11.4 Conclusion

In this chapter we explored a few of the dark alleys of XQuery. Although some of the examples may seem bizarre, I've seen users struggle with every one of the issues listed here at one point or another. Hopefully, when you next encounter one of these situations, you'll remember this chapter and think, "Aha! I know what caused that to happen," and you'll know how to solve it, instead of being surprised.

CHAPTER 12

XQuery Serialization

12.1 Introduction

When working with XQuery, two different serialization issues arise, and in this chapter we contend with both of them.

The first is how to serialize the results of an XQuery as XML. This is difficult because the XQuery Data Model is larger than XML itself; for example, an XQuery can result in two documents, or a list of attributes and numbers, none of which are directly serializable as XML. This is known as *XQuery Serialization*.

The second issue is how to represent the query itself using XML. Representing query expressions as XML allows them to be manipulated using XQuery itself. This XML syntax is known as *XQueryX*.

At the time of this writing, neither of these serialization formats has solidified. XQuery serialization is a relatively new addition to the draft specification and is still undergoing significant changes at the time of this writing. In contrast, XQueryX has been a part of XQuery almost from the start, but hasn't been updated in more than two years.

It's not surprising, then, that most implementations lack support for one or both of these serialization formats. Check the documentation accompanying your XQuery implementation to be sure.

12.2 XQuery Serialization

Data Model serialization faces three main obstacles. First, some values simply may not be directly representable in the target format. For example, XML cannot contain arbitrary characters. Serialization formats usually deal with this complication by encoding the data into some other form that is representable.

Second, some serialized information may not round-trip. That is, deserializing the serialized form may result in a different data model instance than was serialized. In some cases, this information loss may be deemed acceptable.

And finally, the serialization format must reserve certain names for its own use, which could then collide with user names. A well-designed serialization format anticipates this problem and works around it.

In the realm of XML and text, additional complications arise, such as the character encoding to use, whether to perform whitespace or Unicode normalization, and various other text-formatting rules.

In the following sections, you will see how XQuery Serialization handles each of these obstacles.

12.2.1 Sequences of Values

XQuery serializes sequences of values using the same format as XML Schema: space-separated strings. For example, the sequence (1, 2.5, "x") is serialized by converting each atomic value to a string, adding spaces between consecutive atomic values, and then concatenating together the result, to produce "1 2.5 x".

There are two potential problems with this serialization choice. One is that now some values are ambiguous. For example, a sequence containing a single string value "x y" will be deserialized as a sequence containing two string values ("x","y") when the type is xs:string*. XQuery Serialization (like XML Schema) doesn't provide a way to work around this difficulty. The other is that the conversion to string uses the canonical representation of the value, which may differ slightly from how the user originally specified it. For example, you may have written 1e0 but the serialized result is 1.0E0. However, this difference is already considered insignificant by XQuery, so its effects should be minimal on your applications.

12.2.2 The Root

XQuery Serialization doesn't allow a data model instance that contains a single attribute, xs:QName value, or namespace node to be serialized (nor sequences of these). These items require some context, such as an enclosing element, to be serialized. Consequently, the results of the XQuery attribute a {"b"} cannot be serialized, but the results of <x>{attribute a {"b"}}</x> can be serialized.

If the root of the data model consists of a single value (which the previous section would have converted to xs:string), then the value is replaced by a text node containing that value. In this way, the serialized form is always a sequence of zero or more nodes. When serializing, each document node is omitted from the results; its children are used instead.

At this point, the result is a valid XML fragment, that is, a sequence of zero or more nodes, each of which is an element, comment, processing instruction, or text node.

12.2.3 Serialization Parameters

In addition to the rules described above, implementations may allow you to control certain other aspects of the serialization process, such as whether to use CDATA sections or whether to indent the output. These serialization parameters vary from one implementation to the next.

12.3 XQueryX

One of the requirements the W3C set for XQuery was that it must provide an XML syntax for queries. The commonly cited reason for this requirement is to allow queries to operate on queries (for example, this might enable you to write an XQuery interpreter using XQuery).

XQueryX obviously resembles XSLT in both form and function. In fact, people today use XSLT to generate or transform other XSLT transforms. However, XSLT is limited by the fact that embedded XPath queries are string values, and consequently difficult to manipulate. The idea behind XQueryX is to address this problem by defining a standard XML serialization of every XQuery expression, even paths.

At the time of this writing, the standard has not yet defined this serialization. However, it will likely end up being an XML serialization of the XQuery parse tree. Although it is too soon to provide concrete details about XQueryX, Listing 12.1 provides an idea of what it may eventually look like. This example shows a possible representation of the query a/b[2].

Listing 12.1 XQueryX may look like something like this

```
<query xmlns="urn:hypothetical-xqueryx">
  <path>
    <step axis="child">
      <name>a</name>
      <step axis="child">
        <name>b</name>
        <predicate>
```

```
            <integer>2</integer>
          </predicate>
        </step>
      </step>
    </path>
  </query>
```

12.4 Conclusion

In this chapter we explored how XQuery serializes its data model in XML. This serialization is complicated by the fact that the XQuery Data Model is so much more expressive than XML itself. Not all implementations support this serialization, in part because it's still being defined.

We also examined how XQuery may define serializing a query in XML (XQueryX). XQueryX defines essentially a parse tree for XQuery, in a standard way to allow interoperability across implementations. Not all implementations support XQueryX either, for the same reason.

CHAPTER 13

Query Optimization

13.1 Introduction

One of the key ideas behind XQuery was to create a language with a solid formal basis, like SQL has the relational calculus, and to encourage query optimization. In this chapter we explore what the XQuery standard says about optimization, and the effects query optimization have on your query—actually, more what effects your queries have on the optimizations that can be performed.

Every XQuery implementation optimizes its queries differently. Some don't perform any optimization at all, while others optimize queries so much you wouldn't even recognize them anymore. Here we focus on what optimizations can be performed, not necessarily what optimizations are performed by your particular implementation.

13.2 Common Query Optimizations

Let's begin by taking a look at three evaluation strategies commonly employed by XQuery implementations to achieve optimal performance.

13.2.1 Lazy Evaluation

The best way for a program to go quickly is to not compute anything at all—an empty loop sure is fast! Seriously though, not evaluating expressions whose values will never be used is one of the chief optimization techniques available to an XQuery processor.

Lazy evaluation applies to almost every XQuery expression. For example, dead code elimination involves not compiling functions that are never used. Variables are typically not evaluated until used. Operators such as `and` and `or` are short-circuited, meaning that if one operand is enough to determine the whole expression, then the other can be skipped. Function parameters that aren't used by the function needn't be evaluated.

13.2.2 Early Evaluation

Although it may seem contradictory, many expressions also benefit from being evaluated only once, and as early as possible. You are probably already familiar with many of the terms used to describe these kinds of optimizations.

For example, instead of computing the same expression several times, it's better to use a variable and compute it only once (common subexpression elimination). Predicates and `where` clauses are commonly reordered so that they can filter sequences as early as possible, reducing unnecessary later computations (loop-invariant code-motion). Constant-folding is applied, so that expressions that can be evaluated at compile-time are, instead of calculating them at run-time.

13.2.3 Streaming and Database Evaluation

A third evaluation strategy, often used along with the other two, involves reducing the working set. Instead of keeping all the XML data used by a query in memory, buffer as little as possible (streaming execution) and/or offload some data to disk for part of or all of the computation (database execution).

Simple path expressions like `doc("a.xml")/x/y[2]/z` don't need to load the entire document in-memory; instead, the XML can be processed using a streaming API. Expressions like `x[@id = 1]` can avoid looping through all elements to test the predicate for each one by instead storing and looking up the matching elements in a hash table or equivalent (i.e., indexing). As that example demonstrates, sometimes it's better to trade a little space for time. Other times, it's better to trade a little time for space. Query optimization is a difficult and fuzzy problem, with no single "correct" answer.

13.3 Barriers to Optimization

As you write queries, you should understand that some expressions hinder the kinds of optimizations just described, while others help them. In this section we focus on expressions that prevent optimization and ways to avoid or mitigate those expressions. We briefly consider examples of four well-known barriers to XML query optimization: node identity, sequence order, error preservation, and side effects.

13.3.1 Node Identity

Every XML node has a unique identity and some XQuery operators—such as union and node order comparisons—depend on it. However, node identity means that two of the most common optimization techniques, variable substitution and common subexpression elimination, don't work without serious analysis by the implementation.

To understand why, consider a simple query like the one in Listing 13.1. This query constructs exactly one node, which is then bound to a variable. The node comparison operator is returns true, because of course this node is the same as itself.

Listing 13.1 A query that thwarts variable substitution

```
let    $a := <a/>
return $a is $a
```

However, an implementation cannot eliminate the variable $a by replacing it with its value. If it did that, the result would be `<a/> is <a/>`, which constructs two different nodes, and then the is operator would return false.

This is just a simple example; this problem appears anywhere an expression results in a node or sequence of nodes. Potentially a lot of data-flow analysis is required to determine when a variable bound to a node can be substituted and when it cannot, or conversely, when an expression can be replaced by a variable (common subexpression elimination).

You can assist these optimizations by assigning variables to nodes only when you depend on node identity or when the computation is expensive. For example, if you just want the typed value of a node, extract that typed value when you assign the variable, instead of assigning the variable to the node and extracting its later when you use it. This way, the type conversion is cached along with the value. Listing 13.2 illustrates the difference.

Listing 13.2 Atomic values are cheaper than nodes

```
let $a := <x>42</x>       (: potentially expensive :)
let $b := data(<x>31</x>) (: potentially cheaper :)
return data($a) + $b
```

13.3.2 Sequence Order

Most databases work with tables whose rows are unordered. One of the reasons is that when you don't have to preserve ordering, many optimizations are possible. When you do have to preserve ordering, sorting the final results may completely wipe out the gains brought by the optimization in the first place.

In XML and XQuery, order matters. Nodes have an ordering (document order), and sequences are also ordered. Every path you write implicitly sorts its results by document order. Most implementations know that a path that involves only simple child steps is already in document order and does not need to be sorted. However, the moment that you use an operator such as union or // in the path, the sequence can end up out of order.

For example, in most implementations, the simple path //x/y requires a sort at the end because it's possible that the XML is shaped like Listing 13.3. The reason is that most implementations loop through the nodes of each step in order. In this case, the //x step selects the x nodes in order, but then selecting their y children finds the second y first. Of course, every implementation is different, but this gives you some idea of the impact of sorting on even simple path expressions.

Listing 13.3 Most implementations of //x/y reach the y elements out of order

```
<x>
  <x>
    <y id="1"/>
  </x>
  <y id="2"/>
</x>
```

As another example, consider two predicates applied to a sequence. The order in which the predicates are applied matters when position is used. For example, in the query (1, 2, 3, 4)[. > 2][2], the first predicate reduces the sequence to (3, 4), and then the second predicate selects the second of these (4). If the predicates are applied in the other order, then the result is the empty sequence (). Using position prevents the implementation from executing the predicates in just any order it wishes. One thing you can do to avoid these barriers to optimization is to refrain from using position unless necessary.

Some implementations also make use of the built-in unordered() function. This function doesn't change any values; it just tells an implementation that order is unimportant. For example, if you write unordered(//x/y), then an implementation doesn't need to maintain any particular ordering to the result. You've indicated that even if the nodes are out of order, that's okay.

13.3.3 Error Preservation

Consider the query `doc("a.xml")[doc("b.xml")]`, which says "select a.xml, but only if `b.xml` exists." Now, must this query load and parse a.xml entirely before testing whether b.xml exists, or can it test b.xml first and then load a.xml?

As another example, consider the query `$set["x" cast as xs:integer]`. If `$set` is empty, must the predicate (which results in an error) still be evaluated? Or may an implementation resolve the predicate at compile-time, finding the error before the query is even executed?

In general, XQuery has chosen a permissive set of rules for query evaluation. Generally speaking, most errors that are reported at compile-time can be reported at run-time instead, or vice versa. In equally broad terms, expressions that might result in an error can usually be skipped if the implementation doesn't need to evaluate them.

There are a few exceptions to this rule. One is that an implementation that chooses to perform static typing must report certain errors at compile-time, while an implementation that chooses dynamic typing must not report certain errors at compile-time.

The most important exceptions to these general policies occur with the conditional expression (`if/then/else`). XQuery requires that the condition always be evaluated, and that the corresponding branch be evaluated (and only that branch). Expressions like predicates and `where` clauses don't have these guarantees. When it's important to your application that errors be preserved (and not be optimized out), use conditionals.

13.3.4 Side Effects

Some XQuery expressions have side effects. For example, the expression `<a>{$nodes}</a>` has the side effect that all the nodes are copied. Even if you then navigate into this expression, like `(<a>{$nodes}</a>)/node()`, you don't get back the original node sequence, but instead get a copy of it. As you saw in Section 13.3.1, node identity matters, and one of the side effects of constructors is that they lose node identity by deep-copying their contents.

Some implementations also support external functions, and then of course all bets are off. If the external function depends on having side effects (for example, a random number generator or a counter that is incremented), then implementations must take that into account during query optimization. Consequently, most implementations that support external functions often do not heavily optimize queries and vice versa.

13.4 Formal Semantics

The XQuery Formal Semantics, one of the documents that makes up the XQuery standard, exists to help address these issues. The idea behind the Formal Semantics is to provide an algebraic framework for describing queries precisely, and then using this framework to prove which optimizations are valid and which are not.

It does this by taking a theoretical approach to XQuery. The XQuery Formal Semantics begins by stating some axioms and then establishing basic theorems that determine how expressions can be reduced into simpler (or faster) expressions. This is done using techniques from logic theory, including methods of type inferencing and formal reduction. Consequently, the Formal Semantics is of value only to XQuery implementers and researchers.

However, even the Formal Semantics is incomplete in its treatment of the issues facing XML query. Node identity, for example, isn't represented by the Formal Semantics, and issues such as streaming query and expressions with side effects aren't addressed at all.

13.5 Conclusion

In this chapter we considered some of the optimizations that implementations can perform, expressions that perform barriers to those optimizations, and how you can avoid these barriers. We also very briefly touched on the XQuery Formal Semantics, a document that attempts to establish a formal basis for the XQuery language.

13.6 Further Reading

If you're interested in the Formal Semantics, read *XQuery from the Experts: A Guide to the W3C XML Query Language*, which contains explanatory essays from the Formal Semantics editors. The Formal Semantics document itself can be found online at `http://www.w3.org/TR/xquery-semantics/`.

XML query optimization more generally is still a burgeoning field. Although many papers are published each year on this topic and related subjects such as graph rewrites, there doesn't yet exist one unified reference for the subject.

CHAPTER 14

Beyond the Standard

14.1 Introduction

This chapter discusses features that didn't make it into XQuery 1.0 but may appear in future versions. I begin by enumerating features that are likely (in my informed opinion) to change between now and the final XQuery 1.0 standard. Next, I describe how all the XQuery standards documents interrelate with one another and the rest of XML. I then speculate about some of the features that may appear in XQuery 1.1 or 2.0, and highlight two of these features: updating XML data and full-text search. Finally, this chapter ends with some of the performance benchmarks that are already beginning to spring up around XQuery.

14.2 Potential Changes

There's an old adage that people who love sausage, respect the law, and work with standards shouldn't watch any of them being made. XQuery has changed a lot since the Working Group committee published its first document in February 2001, from minor syntax changes, such as the keywords becoming lowercase instead of uppercase and the `sort` operator being replaced by an `order by` clause in the FLWOR expression (which originally was FLWR), to major semantics changes, such as the ever-evolving type system and navigation operators.

At the time of this writing, XQuery has reached the Last Call stage, the first point at which it has been deemed stable enough to solicit widespread public feedback. Several hundred issues have been raised publicly by vendors and other W3C standards groups, and will be addressed before XQuery becomes a final Recommendation. Many of these issues are minor and will not affect you in any major way, or will not lead to any change at all in the standard (except possibly the wording of it). However, some of the suggested changes would have a major impact on the queries you write. Only time will tell what these changes will be, but here are some of the more likely candidates.

14.2.1 Namespaces

The built-in namespaces and collation are all versioned at the time of this writing, for example, `http://www.w3.org/2003/11/xpath-functions`. The year and month in the URL correspond to the latest public draft. These will definitely change in the final XQuery standard, but their eventual values are unknown at this time.

14.2.2 Modules and Prolog

Modules are a relatively new feature in XQuery, and many issues are still being hashed out. Their interaction with the prolog, and the desire to design XQuery to allow for future changes, has led to many recent changes to both in the latest drafts. I expect both to continue to fluctuate between now and the final version. For example, recent drafts introduced semicolons after every prolog statement, changed the keywords used, and changed how global definitions in modules interact with each other and the main query.

14.2.3 Additional Types

There has been considerable pushback against the introduction of types not in XML Schema 1.0, namely `xdt:dayTimeDuration`, `xdt:yearMonthDuration`, `xdt:untypedAtomic`, and `xdt:anyAtomicType`.

The duration subtypes were introduced by the committee because the `xs:duration` type isn't totally ordered and presents barriers to using date/time arithmetic. These two new types and some twenty built-in functions for working with them were introduced to overcome these difficulties. It has been proposed that instead these types and their attending functions could be replaced by a couple of simple functions that convert `xs:duration` to and from a numeric type, like `xs:decimal`, which is then totally ordered and can be manipulated using all the usual arithmetic operators. Users would then have to do a little more work to operate on durations (but date/time programming always requires custom logic). Although the committee may revisit this issue, for now they have decided to keep the duration subtypes. Whether all the functions for working with them will also be kept remains to be seen.

The other two types are more difficult to remove. XML Schema 1.0 has two base types, `xs:anyType` and `xs:anySimpleType`. The former includes all schema types (even element and attribute node structures), and the latter includes all atomic types (even union and list types like `xs:IDREFS`). XQuery needs a base type that covers atomic types only, but excludes list and union types—hence `xdt:anyAtomicType`.

The `xdt:untypedAtomic` type exists to distinguish typed data from untyped data. Expressions that involve `xdt:untypedAtomic` values are defined to use essentially XPath 1.0 rules, while operators on typed values (or a mixture of typed and untyped) use new rules that make sense for XQuery and XML Schema. I expect that the type conversions of language expressions that use this type will undergo additional changes before XQuery is finalized. (They've changed in every draft so far!) However, it's unlikely that this type will be cut or otherwise significantly altered.

14.2.4 Simplify, Simplify

Many people believe that software starts out simple and becomes complex over time. In my experience, the exact opposite happens: Anyone can create a complex design, but considerable conscious effort and time are required to simplify one. In any case, the committee is actively simplifying parts of XQuery. I can safely predict that XQuery is a little more complex today than it will be when it is finalized.

Some complexity shows up as redundancy. For example, `concat()` is redundant with `string-join()`, and `cast as` is redundant with type constructors. However, neither of these is likely to be cut.

Some complexity shows up as "missing" functionality. For example, there is no `group by` operator and no `apply()` function (that would apply an operation to every member sequence), so users must write lengthier queries to accomplish the same tasks. At this point, the committee is unlikely to add any major new functionality to XQuery.

Some complexity shows up as irregularities. For example, some type conversions treat the `xs:integer` type (which is derived from `xs:decimal`) different from other derived types. Some prolog statements use an equal sign while others don't. Some string functions take an optional collation argument, and some don't. Although the committee continuees to smooth out the rough spots, some irregularities will inevitably remain in the final draft, if for no other reason than XQuery has been designed by many different people with different styles and goals.

Some complexity shows up as unnecessary case analysis (something the late Edsger Dijkstra loathed). The type conversion rules are an example of this; figuring out what happens in a query like the one in Listing 14.1 (or even whether it's legal at all) is too challenging in the current XQuery draft. I think the definitions of the type conversion rules will be greatly simplified for implementers, but probably with minimal changes to the final result seen by users.

Listing 14.1 Tricky type conversions

```
declare function foo($n as xs:decimal) as xs:integer* {
  $n
};
1 + foo(2 + 3.0) + foo(4)
```

14.2.5 Built-in Functions

There is a general sense that the built-in function library is too large. Eliminating the duration subtypes would also eliminate about 20% of the existing library, and other functions might be eliminated or added or changed in function signature.

14.3 Standards Roadmap

Belying its central nature, XQuery is connected to almost every other W3C XML standard. It also consists of several documents itself. This section provides a rough overview of how they all interconnect. You may also find the diagram at `http://kensall.com/big-picture/` enlightening (or at least entertaining).

14.3.1 Today

XQuery 1.0 is defined by more than ten different documents, spanning many thousands of pages. (See the Bibliography for complete references.) XQuery was set in motion by the *XML Query Requirements* document and the *XML Query Use Cases* document. The former describes the committee's objectives in creating XQuery, and the latter provides concrete examples that should be supported by XQuery. Together these two documents provide the framework within which XQuery was created.

The main document that ties them all together is *XQuery 1.0: An XML Query Language*. This document describes the aspects of the language that concern most users. This core language document is supported by several other documents that provide a formal theoretical basis for XQuery. Some of these documents are also shared with the XPath 2.0 and XSLT 2.0 standards.

For example, the *XQuery 1.0 and XPath 2.0 Functions and Operators* defines a vast library of built-in functions (as well as pseudo-functions that define operator behavior) shared between XQuery 1.0 and XPath 2.0.

As another example, the *XQuery 1.0 and XPath 2.0 Data Model* document defines the formal data model for XQuery. It is intricately connected with four older XML specifications: the *XML 1.0 Recommendation*, the *Namespaces in XML Recommendation*, the *XML Information Set (Infoset) Recommendation*, and the *XML Schema 1.0 Recommendation*.

XQuery and XPath also share the *XQuery 1.0 and XPath 2.0 Formal Semantics* document, which lays out a set of algebraic formalisms that govern the behavior of queries. This document is really only of interest to implementers and academics; end users don't need to know anything about it.

Additional XQuery specifications include the XQueryX document and the XQuery Serialization document. These two documents define an XML serialization format for XQuery queries and data models, respectively.

The XPath 1.0 and XSLT 1.0 Recommendations define query languages for XML that have some similarities to XQuery; XQuery draws on the past experiences of these, but is otherwise independent of them. The XPath 2.0 and XSLT 2.0 standards pick up where the previous versions left off. They are separate standards from XQuery, but are designed to share the common core described above.

14.3.2 Tomorrow

Beyond XQuery 1.0, there are many other standards in the pipeline, such as XML 1.1 and XML Schema 1.1, which address issues users have had with the first versions of those standards, as well as the possibility of someday an XQuery 1.1 or XQuery 2.0. XQuery 1.0 itself is tied to XML 1.0 and XML Schema 1.0, so future versions of those standards can only affect future versions of XQuery.

From an XQuery perspective, the main effect of XML 1.1 would be to allow many more characters in XML names and text, a change that could easily be accommodated by a future version of XQuery. The impact of XML Schema 1.1 on XQuery is mostly to address type system design issues that XQuery uncovered in XML Schema 1.0.

14.4 XQuery 1.1

There may never be another version of XQuery, but if there is, we can speculate as to some of the features it may add.

One feature that many people expected to appear in XQuery 1.0 is the ability to modify XML using the query language. Several proposals have been floated, but none made it into this first version of the language. I have more to say about this topic in Section 14.5.

Another feature that is near-and-dear to the hearts of many of the XQuery creators is support for full-text operations, including fuzzy-search capabilities. I say a little about this interesting topic in Section 14.6.

In XQuery 1.0, user-defined functions cannot overload one another or the built-in functions. It's possible that a future version might allow for more sophisticated function overloading, and of course extend the function library with even more built-in functions.

Another feature that received some discussion is the ability to create user-defined types directly in the query, without having to import an XML Schema. And finally, as users gain experience with XQuery 1.0, it's inevitable that certain features will be wished for, while some existing features turn out to be useless. Real-world experience will inevitably shape future versions of XQuery.

14.5 Data Manipulation

The ability to change, delete, or insert an existing XML instance using a query language goes by the name Data Manipulation Language (DML). The idea behind DML is to add keywords such as `update`, `delete`, and `insert` to the language, performing these operations instead of (or in addition to) constructing results.

DML is a tricky problem for several reasons, leading the committee to exclude it from the first version of XQuery. Some of these problems (such as view update and the "Halloween" problem) are already well known in relational database systems, but have not yet been completely solved for the XML domain. Other problems, such as node identity and consistency between parents and children, are peculiar to XML.

To give you an idea what form DML might take, the following three sections list proposals that have been made to add DML to XQuery.

14.5.1 XQuery DML

One possibility is to just take the query language as is, and add to it some keywords like `update`, `delete`, and `insert`. This is the most likely form that a future XQuery DML will take. These additional keywords would be usable at the top level, and probably also in place of the `return` clause in FLWOR. They might also be used as the branches of if/then/else statements, allowing for conditional data modification, and perhaps even in user-defined functions.

A few examples of what XQuery DML might look like are shown in Listing 14.2.

Listing 14.2 Potential XQuery DML instructions

```
insert <Employee/> into doc("team.xml")

delete doc("team.xml")//Employee[@years < 20]

update doc("team.xml")//Employee[@id="E0"]/Expertise
       with <Expertise>XQuery</Expertise>

for $i in doc("team.xml")//Employee
delete $i/Expertise

if ($final) then delete $tmp else insert <x/> into $tmp
```

There isn't any public documentation on XQuery DML at this time, nor any information as to whether it may include data definition features such as index management.

14.5.2 SiXDML

SiXDML is a proposal by Dare Obasanjo for a simple XML data definition and manipulation language. It actually predates XQuery, and has since been reformulated to include XQuery syntax. It does far more than simple insert/update/delete, including index and collection management.

SiXDML uses collections to persist XML documents. Collections can be indexed, deleted, modified, and constrained (using schemas) through the SiXDML syntax. Several projects have already implemented SiXDML, including Xindice. Listing 14.3 provides a few examples of SiXDML.

Listing 14.3 Sample SiXDML instructions

```
CREATE COLLECTION employees

INSERT doc("team.xml") NAMED team.xml INTO COLLECTION employees

CREATE INDEX val-index OF TYPE VALUE INDEX
       WITH KEY="@id", ELEMENT="//Employee" ON COLLECTION employees
```

14.5.3 XUpdate

XUpdate is a data manipulation language with an XML syntax, vaguely like XSLT. XUpdate defines operators for inserting, updating, removing, and renaming XML nodes. Like SiXDML, XUpdate has already been implemented by several projects, including X-Hive.

Listing 14.4 Sample XUpdate instructions

```
<xupdate:modifications version="1.0"
                xmlns:xupdate="http://www.xmldb.org/xupdate">
  <xupdate:insert-after select="//Employee[1]">
    <xupdate:element name="Phone"/>
  </xupdate:insert-after>
</xupdate:modifications>
```

14.6 Full-Text Search

XQuery 1.0 is focused on exact queries over mostly structured data. In many XML applications, however, data is less well-structured and/or user queries are more vague.

Documents such as this book, although containing some structure (chapters, sections, paragraphs, and sentences) are mostly unstructured. Or consider searching the Web for information, when you're not exactly sure what it is you seek. For such cases, full-text search provides ways to perform "fuzzy" searches and work with data that has large, unstructured text components.

Full-text search thus involves two main components: A "word breaker" or tokenizer that imposes structure (words, punctuation, etc.) on otherwise unstructured text, and a "score" or ranking that, instead of matching exact results, produces a number representing how closely the results correspond to the query. Full-text also usually includes "fuzzy" string matching (such as patterns that cover regional spelling differences, synonyms, homonyms, or even phonetic expressions) and word proximity.

The combination of full-text and structured query is especially powerful. Imagine searching, for example, for all sections in this book that contain the word "path" near "expression" and that occur in odd-numbered chapters. Imagine searching the Internet for all Web pages that contain a word similar to "abracadabra" and a table with exactly three columns. Imagine searching the Library of Congress for all bills on global warming authored by a particular senator.

It's not clear at this time how full-text might be incorporated into XQuery, although most likely it will be done using functions such as `score()`,`contains()`, or `proximity()`. See the Bibliography for additional references, including a very detailed full-text use cases document.

14.7 Performance Benchmarks

Although XQuery is a brand-new language, already many people have been hard at work creating performance benchmarks for it. These benchmarks tend to combine the kinds of processing found in existing XSLT benchmarks (like XSLTMark) with the kinds of processing found in existing SQL benchmarks (like TPC), producing a class of benchmarks that are uniquely XQuery.

The XMark suite was one of the first XQuery benchmarks; it can be found at `http://www.xml-benchmark.org`. XMark includes a program for generating large documents, and a collection of 20 queries that test various XQuery features from simple path navigation to complex grouping. Notably, this benchmark also tests type conversion overhead (a common source of performance problems in real-world XML applications).

Two other very interesting XQuery benchmarks are the Michigan Benchmark and XOO7, both of which are focused on XQuery in a database setting. The Michigan Benchmark is a kind of mini-TPC for XML. It tests 45 XML operations, mostly path queries but also a few joins and even 7 update cases (including bulkloading XML into a database). The XOO7 benchmark ports the OO7 benchmark for OODBMSs to XML. It contains 23 XQuery queries containing mostly variations on single-level FLWOR expressions.

14.8 Conclusion

In this chapter, we considered a few topics that aren't found in XQuery 1.0 but may appear in future versions, including data definition and manipulation and full-text search. We also briefly touched on performance benchmarks for XQuery, and on changes that may occur between the time of this writing and the finalization of the XQuery 1.0 standard.

14.9 Further Reading

For more information on these topics, consult the references listed in the Bibliography. This book's Web site also lists errata and updates.

The (fascinating) collected works of Edsger W. Dijkstra can be found at `http://www.cs.utexas.edu/users/EWD/`, possibly the oldest "Web log" in existence.

PART IV

Reference

Data Model and Type System Reference

A.1 Introduction

This appendix lists features of the XQuery Data Model and type system, sorted alphabetically and cross-referenced for convenience. See Chapter 2 for an introduction to these topics. This appendix also summarizes the sequence type syntax used by XQuery expressions such as function definitions, `typeswitch`, and `cast as`. Most of these operators are described in Chapter 9. Section A.5 covers all of the built-in atomic types, including value ranges and lexical forms.

A.2 Overview

The XQuery Data Model consists of sequences of *items* (including the empty sequence). Items are *nodes* or *atomic values*. XQuery defines 7 *node kinds* and 50 *atomic types*.

XQuery provides two different ways to refer to types: *single type* and *sequence type*. The single type syntax is used only in `cast as` and `castable as` expressions. The sequence type syntax is used in all other expressions: `typeswitch`, `instance of`, `treat as`, function definitions, and variable types.

A sequence type consists of either the `empty()` type test (which matches only the empty sequence) or else a single type together with an optional occurrence indicator. A single type is a subset of sequence type, consisting of a type test with either no occurrence indicator or else the question mark (`?`). The occurrence modifiers are listed in Table A.1.

Table A.1 Occurrence indicators in sequence types

Occurrence indicator	Meaning
	Exactly one
?	Zero or one
*	Zero or more
+	One or more

The item type can be an atomic type name (any QName), or a node kind type test. It can also be the special type test `item()`, which matches any item, or the type test `node()`, which matches any node.

XQuery defines one type test for each node kind: `attribute()`, `comment()`, `document-node()`, `element()`, `processing-instruction()`, and `text()`. Without arguments, these node kind tests match any node of the corresponding kind. Additionally, the `attribute()`, `element()`, and `processing-instruction()` node kind tests accept optional arguments. Table A.2 lists all of these. See Chapter 9 for additional examples.

Table A.2 Type names used in simple types and sequence types

Type name	Meaning
A qualified name	Atomic type with that name.
`item()`	Any item.
`node()`	Any node kind.
`xdt:anyAtomicType`	Any atomic type.
`xdt:untypedAtomic`	Untyped atomic data.
`attribute()`	Any attribute node.
`attribute(@ nodename)`	Any attribute node with the given name. The name may be a qualified name or the wildcard ° (matching any name).

Table A.2 cont.

Type name	Meaning
attribute(@ *nodename*, *typename*)	Any attribute node with the given name and type. The node and type names may be qualified names or the wildcard ° (matching any name or any type, respectively).
attribute(*context* @ *QName*)	Any attribute node matching the type specified by schema context path and type name.
comment()	Any comment node.
document-node()	Any document node.
document-node (*elementtest*)	Any document node whose content matches the given element node test.
element()	Any element node.
element(*nametest*)	Any element node with the given name. The name may be a qualified name or the wildcard ° (matching any name).
element(*nodename*, *typename*)	Any element node with the given name and type. The node and type names may be qualified names or the wildcard ° (matching any name or any type, respectively).
element(*nodename*, *typename* nillable)	Any element node with the given name and type that is nillable. The name and type test may be qualified names or the wildcard °.
element(*context QName*)	Any element node matching the type specified by schema context path and type name.
namespace()	Any namespace node.
processing-instruction()	Any processing instruction node.
processing-instruction (*string*)	Any processing instruction node with the given target, as in <?target content?>.
text()	Any text node.

A.3 Node Kinds

XQuery supports all seven XML node kinds and uses the XML syntax to construct them; for some node kinds, XQuery also provides an alternate syntax. Table A.3 summarizes both constructor styles. See Chapter 7 for additional examples and construction rules.

Every node belongs to a tree (possibly containing only that node). If the root node of the tree is an element, then the tree is a *fragment*; otherwise, the root node is a document node, and the tree is a *document*. Every node has a unique *node identity*, and all nodes are ordered relative to one another (*document order*). Nodes in the same tree are ordered in left-depth-first order; nodes from different trees may have any order, but the order doesn't change within the execution of a query.

Table A.4 lists the built-in node properties. For some node kinds, the property value is always the empty list. For some properties, the value is always a constant (such as node kind). Otherwise, the sequence type of the property is listed.

Table A.3 Constructors for each node kind

Node kind	Constructor(s)

attribute	`attribute` *name* `{ ` *content-expr* ` }`
	`attribute { ` *name-expr* ` } { ` *content-expr* ` }`
	name`="`*value*`"` (in element constructor only)

comment	`comment { ` *content-expr* ` }` `<!-- ` *content* ` -->`
document	`document { ` *content-expr* ` }`

element	`element` *name* `{ ` *content-expr* ` }`
	`element { ` *name-expr* ` } { ` *content-expr* ` }`
	`<`*name* *attributes* `/>`
	`<`*name* *attributes*`>`*content*`</`*name*`>`

namespace	`namespace` *prefix* `{ ` *uri-expr* ` }` `xmlns="`*uri*`"` (in element constructor only) `xmlns:`*prefix*`="`*uri*`"` (in element constructor only)
processing instruction	`processing-instruction { ` *target-expr* ` }` `{ ` *content-expr* ` } <?`*target* *content*`?>`
text	`text { ` *content-expr* ` }`

Table A.4 Node properties by node kind

	Attribute	Comment	Document	Element	Namespace	Processing Instruction	Text
attributes	()	()	()	attribute*	()	()	()
base-uri	xs:anyURI?	xs:anyURI?	xs:anyURI?	xs:anyURI?	xs:anyURI?	xs:anyURI?	xs:anyURI?
children	()	()	node()	node()	()	()	()
namespaces	()	()	()	namespace()*	()	()	()
nilled	()	()	()	xs:boolean	()	()	()
node-kind	"attribute"	"comment"	"document"	"element"	"namespace"	"processing-instruction"	"text"
node-name	xs:QName	()	()	xs:QName	xs:QName?	xs:QName	()
parent	element()?	(element() | document-node())?	()	(element() | document-node())?	element()?	(element() | document-node())?	(element() | document-node())?
string-value	xs:string	xs:string	xs:string	xs:string	xs:string	xs:string	xs:string
typed-value	xdt:anyAtomicType?	()	()	xdt:anyAtomicType?	()	()	xdt:anyAtomicType?
unique-id	()	()	()	xs:ID?	()	()	()

Table A.5 Expressions that access node properties

	Expression	See also
attributes	`attribute::*` `@*`	Chapter 3, Appendix B
base-uri	`fn:base-uri()`	Appendix C
children	`child::node()` `node()`	Chapter 3, Appendix B
namespaces	`fn:get-in-scope-namespaces()`	Appendix C
nilled	`instance of element(*, nilled)` `self::*[@xsi:nil="true"]`	Chapters 2 and 9
node-kind	`typeswitch` node kind tests	Chapters 2 and 9
node-name	`fn:node-name()` `fn:name()`	Appendix C
parent	`parent::*` `..`	Chapter 3
string-value	`fn:string()`	Chapter 9, Appendix C
typed-value	`fn:data()`	Chapter 9, Appendix C
unique-id	`fn:unique-id()`	Appendix C

The XQuery Data Model is an abstraction and not all of its properties are directly accessible in XQuery. For example, node identity and node order aren't directly accessible as values. Expressions that access values in the data model are summarized in Table A.5. See Chapter 2 for more information.

A.4 Atomic Types

Figure A.1 shows the entire XQuery atomic type hierarchy, and Table A.6 lists the meaning of every type. Arrows indicate inheritance (also known as *deri-*

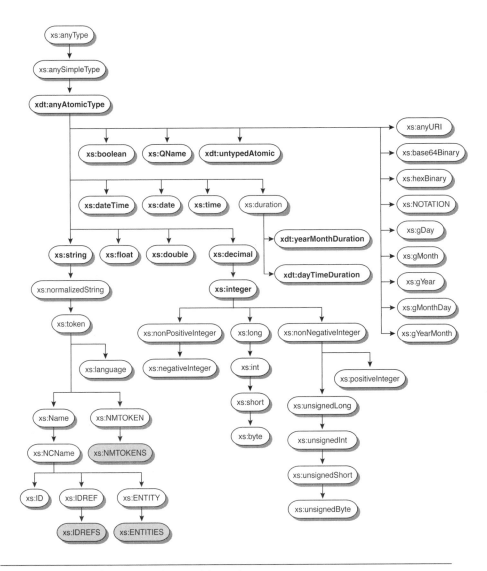

Figure A.1 The XQuery atomic type hierarchy

vation). Type names in bold are the "types you need to know" from Chapter 2. Grey boxes indicate built-in types that cannot be constructed (because they derive by list). All other types derive by restriction, and can be cast to and constructed.

Table A.6 The numeric types and their ranges

Type	Meaning	Range
xs:float	Single-precision floating-point	$m*2^E$ $-2^{24} < m < 2^{24}$ $-149 <= E <= 104$
xs:double	Double-precision floating-point	$m*2^E$ $-2^{53} < m < 2^{53}$ $-1075 <= E <= 970$
xs:decimal	Arbitrary-precision fixed-point (base 10)	Implementation-defined
xs:integer	Arbitrary-precision integer	Implementation-defined
xs:positiveInteger	Arbitrary-precision positive integer	> 0
xs:nonNegative Integer	Arbitrary-precision non-negative integer	>= 0
xs:negativeInteger	Arbitrary-precision negative integer	< 0
xs:nonPositiveInteger	Arbitrary-precision non-positive integer	<= 0
xs:byte	1-byte signed integer	-128 to 127 (-2^7 to 2^7-1)
xs:short	2-byte signed integer	-32768 to 32767 (-2^{15} to $2^{15}-1$)
xs:int	4-byte signed integer	-2147483648 to 2147483647 (-2^{31} to $2^{31}-1$)
xs:long	8-byte signed integer	-9223372036854775808 to 9223372036854775807 (-2^{63} to $2^{63}-1$)
xs:unsignedByte	1-byte unsigned integer	0 to 255 (0 to 2^8-1)
xs:unsignedShort	2-byte unsigned integer	0 to 65535 (0 to $2^{16}-1$)
xs:unsignedInt	4-byte unsigned integer	0 to 4294967295 (0 to $2^{32}-1$)
xs:unsignedLong	8-byte unsigned integer	0 to 18446744073709551615 (0 to $2^{64}-1$)

The prefix `xs` is bound to the namespace `http://www.w3.org/2001/XMLSchema` and the prefix `xdt` is bound to the namespace `http://www.w3.org/2003/11/xpath-datatypes`.

A.5 Primitive Type Conversions

This section summarizes all of the XQuery type conversions used by the `cast as` expression when converting to atomic types. Each table shows the conversions used from the row type (*source type*) to the column type (*target type*). The letters used in Tables A.7, A.9, and A.11 correspond to the rules listed in Tables A.8, A. 10, and A.12, respectively. A blank entry means the value is unchanged by the conversion (only its type changes).

All other type conversions not mentioned below or shown in Tables A.9 – A.12 result in errors. Some implementations detect these as compile-time (static) errors, and others as run-time (dynamic) errors.

Converting to the three types `xs:anySimpleType` or `xdt:untypedAtomic` is the same as converting to `xs:string`, except that list types cannot be converted to `xdt:untypedAtomic`.

Except for `xs:NOTATION`, every type can be converted to one of these three types without error, by taking its canonical representation. These three types can also be converted to any other type except `xs:NOTATION` (possibly resulting in an error), by attempting to parse according to other type's lexical format. See the individual entries for each type in Section A.5 for canonical and lexical representations.

The two binary types, `xs:base64Binary` and `xs:hexBinary`, can be converted to `xs:boolean`; see their descriptions in Section A.5 for details.

Table A.7 XQuery numeric type conversion chart

from\to	xs:bool	xs:float	xs:double	xs:integer	xs:decimal
xs:bool		A	A	A	A
xs:float	B		C	F	G
xs:double	B	D		F	G
xs:integer	B	E	C		
xs:decimal	B	E	C	F	

Table A.8 XQuery numeric type conversion rules

Rule	Meaning
A	True converts to the number 1, false converts to the number 0 in the target type.
B	Positive or negative zero and NaN convert to false; all others convert to true.
C	The string representation of the number is parsed as `xs:double`.
D	The string representation is parsed as `xs:float` (possibly losing precision). If the value exceeds the maximum or minimum float value, then the result is `+INF` or `-INF`, respectively. If underflow occurs, the result is 0.
E	The string representation is parsed as `xs:float` (possibly losing precision).
F	The fractional part, if any, is discarded, and the remaining value converted to `xs:integer`. If the value is too large or too small to be represented, or if the value is infinite or NaN, then an error is raised.
G	The number is converted to the closest decimal value that the implementation can represent (arbitrarily chosen when there is a tie). If the number is infinite or NaN, or if it is too large or too small to be represented, then an error is raised.

Table A.9 XQuery duration type conversion chart

from\to	xs: duration	xdt: dayTimeDuration	xdt: yearMonthDuration
xs:duration		A	B
xdt:dayTimeDuration			X
xdt:yearMonthDuration		X	

Table A.10 XQuery duration type conversion rules

Rule	Meaning
A	Only the year and month parts of the duration are kept.
B	Only the day and time parts of the duration are kept.
X	No conversion possible (error).

Table A.11 XQuery calendar type conversion chart

from\to	xs:dateTime	xs:date	xs:time	xs:gYear	xs:gYearMonth	xs:gMonth	xs:gDay	xs:gMonthDay
xs:dateTime		C	D	E	F	G	H	I
xs:date	A		X	E	F	G	H	I
xs:time	B	X		X	X	X	X	X

Table A.12 XQuery calendar type conversion rules

Rule	Meaning
A	The xs:dateTime has time 00:00:00, remaining parts from the xs:date.
B	The xs:dateTime has date equal to fn:current-date().
C	Only the date and time zone parts of the original xs:dateTime value.
D	Only the time and time zone parts of the original xs:dateTime value.
E	Only the year and time zone parts of the original value.
F	Only the year, month, and time zone parts of the original value.
G	Only the month and time zone parts of the original value.
H	Only the day and time zone parts of the original value.
I	Only the month, day, and time zone parts of the original value.
X	No conversion possible (error).

Of course, every type can be converted to itself or any of its supertypes without changing value. Types can also be converted to derived types, provided that they satisfy the additional restrictions of the derived type (otherwise an error is raised).

A.6 Built-in Atomic Types

In this section there is a one-line description of each concrete type followed by its type constructor, its lexical format, and its canonical form (when it differs from the lexical one). The lexical form is a regular expression describing the formats that are accepted when converting from string to this type. The canonical form describes the format used when converting to string. Except for the xs:NOTATION type, every type has a lexical and canonical form. These forms are described using the XQuery regular expression syntax (see Appendix D).

The three types xdt:anyAtomicType, xs:anySimpleType, and xs:anyType are abstract and so are not listed here. No atomic value has exactly one of these types, although every atomic type is derived from one of them. See Chapter 2 for details.

---

xs:anyURI

A Uniform Resource Identifier (URI) Reference.

```
xs:anyURI(xdt:anyAtomicType) as xs:anyURI
```

Lexical form:
```
[a-zA-Z][a-zA-Z0-9\+\-\.]*:([[#x20-#xFF]-[#x7F<>"'|\^\{\}\\]])*
```

The xs:anyURI type represents a Uniform Resource Identifier (URI) Reference, as defined by RFC 2396 and RFC 2732 (see the Bibliography for complete references). In XQuery, the xs:anyURI type is used to name collations, collections, and documents.

Listing A.1 xs:anyURI

```
xs:anyURI('http://www.awprofessional.com/')
xs:anyURI('ftp://ftp.w3.org/')
xs:anyURI('urn:relative/path')
```

An xs:anyURI value can be constructed from any string value that contains only ASCII characters, except for the following excluded characters: the special punctuation characters <>"{}|\^` and control characters (U+0000 through U+001F and U+007F). Whitespace (U+0020) is allowed but recommended to be escaped as %20. In addition, the punctuation characters ;/?:@&=+$, are reserved, so it is recommended to escape them also.

The sequence `%HH` where `H` is a hexadecimal digit is used to encode the character `U+00HH`. Disallowed characters (including non-ASCII characters) must be first converted to UTF-8, then hex-encoded as necessary to be represented as `xs:anyURI` values.

Note that `xs:anyURI` is a distinct type from `xs:string`, and isn't a subtype of it. A cast or constructor function must be used to convert one to the other.

Unfortunately, URI values are notoriously difficult to work with; for example, on some systems file system paths are case-sensitive while on others they are not. In general, it isn't possible to determine whether two URI values point to the same resource or not. Consequently, implementations are given some latitude in how they handle URI values. For example, some implementations may disallow `xs:anyURI("foo")` but allow `xs:anyURI("urn:foo")`, while others may allow both.

For more information, see RFC 2396 and RFC 2732 (complete references are provided in the Bibliography).

See also: `fn:base-uri()`, `fn:collection()`, `fn:default-collation()`, `fn:doc()`, `fn:escape-uri()`, and `fn:resolve-uri()` in Appendix C.

xs:base64Binary

A base64-encoded binary value.

```
xs:base64Binary(xdt:anyAtomicType) as xs:base64Binary
```

Lexical form:
```
S?([A-Za-z0-9+/]S?){4}*
([A-Za-z0-9+/]S?[AQgw]S?=S?=S?|
([A-Za-z0-9+/]S?){2}[AEIMQUYcgkosw048]S?=S?))?
```
where `S` denotes any XML whitespace character.

Canonical form:
```
([A-Za-z0-9+/]{76}#xA)*([A-Za-z0-9+/]{4}){0,18}
(([A-Za-z0-9+/]{4})|
([A-Za-z0-9+/]{2}[AEIMQUYcgkosw048]=)|
([A-Za-z0-9+/] [AQgw]==))?
```

The `xs:base64Binary` type represents base64-encoded binary data, as defined by RFC 2045. It consists of a sequence of ASCII characters `A-Z`, `a-z`, `0-9`, the punctuation characters `+/` and possibly one or two trailing `=` characters for padding; all other characters are ignored. Base64-encoding is a popular format for embedding arbitrary binary data in XML (among other things).

Each character represents 6 bits of data (most significant bit first); four consecutive characters thus encode 3 bytes of binary data. When the original input data has a length not divisible by three, trailing = symbols are used to pad the base64 encoding of the data. Trailing bits are zero-padded as necessary.

Listing A.2 `xs:base64Binary`

```
xs:base64Binary("ABBA")     (: encodes the three bytes 0, 16, 64 :)
xs:base64Binary("+XQuerY=") (: encodes 249, 116, 46, 122, 182 :)
```

XQuery doesn't provide any functions for working with base64- or hex-encoded binary data, but Chapter 10 includes a few user-defined functions that do so.

See also: `xs:hexBinary` and Chapter 10.

xs:boolean

A boolean value.

```
xs:boolean(xdt:anyAtomicType) as xs:boolean
```

Lexical form:
```
(true)|(false)|1|0
```

Canonical form:
```
(true)|(false)
```

The `xs:boolean` type represents a single boolean value (true or false).

In addition to the numeric and string type conversions summarized in Table A.7, values of type `xs:hexBinary` and `xs:base64Binary` can also be converted to `xs:boolean`. They convert to true if their string value is `"1"`, false if their string value is `"0"`, and otherwise result in an error.

Listing A.3 `xs:boolean`

```
xs:boolean("true")    => true
xs:boolean("1")       => true
xs:boolean(0)         => false
xs:boolean(0.0)       => error
xs:boolean(42)        => error
xs:boolean("ja")      => error
xs:boolean("")        => error
```

Casting to xs:boolean or using the xs:boolean() constructor differs from using the fn:boolean() function. Casting to xs:boolean converts "0" and "false" to false, "1" and "true" to true, and all other string values result in an error. In contrast, the built-in boolean() function returns true for all non-empty strings and false for the empty string. (The boolean() function can also be applied to non-singleton and non-atomic values, such as the empty sequence or nodes, while xs:boolean() cannot.)

See also: fn:boolean() in Appendix C.

xs:byte

A signed byte value (an integer in the range -128 to 127, inclusive).

```
xs:byte(xdt:anyAtomicType) as xs:byte
```

Lexical format:
```
[\+\-]?[0-9]+
```

Canonical format:
```
-?[1-9][0-9]*
```

The xs:byte type represents a signed, single-byte integer, which can range in value from -128 to 127. It is a derived type.

Because all XQuery arithmetic using xs:byte values takes place using its supertype, xs:integer, this type is useful only for validation and for constraining function parameters. Some implementations may also optimize values with this type to occupy less space, or may optimize the performance of certain query expressions to exploit the properties of this type.

Listing A.4 xs:byte

```
xs:byte("0")       => 0
xs:byte("127")     => 127
xs:byte("128")     => error (: out of range :)
xs:byte("-1")      => -1
xs:byte("2.5")     => error (: invalid format :)
xs:byte(2.5)       => 2
```

See also: xs:int, xs:integer, xs:long, xs:short, and xs:unsignedByte.

xs:date

A date value.

```
xs:date(xdt:anyAtomicType) as xs:date
```

Lexical format:
```
-?[1-9]*[0-9]{4}-[0-9]{2}-[0-9]{2}(Z|([\+\-][0-9]{2}:[0-9]{2}))?
```

Canonical format:
```
[1-9]*[0-9]{4}-[0-9]{2}-[0-9]{2}Z?
```
(also sometimes written pictorially as CCYY-MM-DDZ)

The xs:date type represents a single point on the calendar. It consists of the same year, month, day, and time zone parts as the xs:dateTime type (but it isn't derived from xs:dateTime).

Listing A.5 xs:date

```
xs:date("2004-08-24")       (: September 8, 2004 :)
xs:date("0001-01-01")       (: January 1, year 1 :)
xs:date("-0001-01-01")      (: January 1, year -1 :)
xs:date("2004-08-24Z")      (: September 8, 2004 in UTC :)
xs:date("2004-08-24-08:00") (: same date in PST :)
```

See also: xs:dateTime.

xs:dateTime

A date/time value.

```
xs:dateTime(xdt:anyAtomicType) as xs:dateTime
```

Lexical format:
```
-?[1-9]*[0-9]{4}-[0-9]{2}-[0-9]{2}
T[0-9]{2}:[0-9]{2}:[0-9]{2}(\.[0-9]*)?(Z|([\+\-][0-9]{2}:[0-9]{2}))?
```

Canonical format:
```
-?[1-9]*[0-9]{4}-[0-9]{2}-[0-9]{2}
T[0-9]{2}:[0-9]{2}:[0-9]{2}(\.[0-9]*)?Z?
```
(also sometimes written pictorially as CCYY-MM-DDThh:mm:ss.sssZ)

The `xs:dateTime` type represents a single point in time, and consists of seven parts: year, month, day, hour, minute, second, and time zone. The first five of these are integer values; the second part is a decimal value, and the time zone is either the empty sequence or else an hour and minute value (both integers). All of these must satisfy certain constraints, described next.

Often the first half (year, month, and day) is called the date part; the second half (hour, minute, and second) is called the time part. This is further encouraged by the `T` character that separates the two halves.

The year part always contains at least four digits (padded with leading zeros if necessary), but doesn't contain leading zeros beyond the fourth digit. It can be any integer value other than `0000`, including negative integers. Most implementations support only a limited range of year values, but conformant implementations are required to support at least four digits.

The month part always contains exactly two digits, and must be an integer between 01 and 12.

The day part always contains exactly two digits, and must be an integer valid for the given month and year. For month 2, it must be between 01 and 28 except in leap years when it may also be 29. For months 4, 6, 9, and 11, it must be between 01 and 30 inclusive. And in all remaining months, it must be between 01 and 31 inclusive.

The hour part must be a two-digit integer between 00 and 23 inclusive. The minute part must be a two-digit integer between 00 and 59, inclusive. The second part is a decimal value with exactly two digits before the decimal point. The decimal point and fractional digits are optional. Most implementations support only a limited number of digits after the decimal point (nanosecond precision is common). This decimal value is allowed to be greater than or equal to 60 only for leap seconds.

The time zone part is optional; when not specified, it is the empty sequence. It can also be specified using `z` (meaning UTC) or a positive or negative number of hours and minutes subject to the same constraints as above (meaning that offset from UTC).

Listing A.6 `xs:dateTime`

```
xs:dateTime("2004-09-08T00:00:00")         (: September 8, 2004 :)
xs:dateTime("2004-01-04T03:05:06")         (: Jan 4, 2004, 3:05:06 am :)
xs:dateTime("2004-09-08T00:00:00Z")        (: September 8, 2004 in UTC :)
xs:dateTime("2004-09-08T00:00:00-08:00")   (: same date in PST :)
```

See also: `xs:date` and `xs:dateTime`, and `fn:get-year-from-dateTime()`, `fn:implicit-timezone()`, and related functions in Appendix C.

xdt:dayTimeDuration

A duration value with day and time parts.

`xdt:dayTimeDuration(xdt:anyAtomicType) as xdt:dayTimeDuration`

Lexical format:
`-?P([0-9]+D)?T([0-9]+H)?([0-9]+M)?([0-9]+(\.[0-9]*)?S)?`

This type has been introduced by XQuery to allow durations to be compared. As its name suggests, it represents the day and time parts only from a duration. Its lexical and canonical forms are the same as those for `xs:duration`, including only the day and time parts.

See also: `xs:duration` and `xdt:yearMonthDuration`, and `fn:get-days-from-dayTimeDuration()`, `fn:get-hours-from-dayTimeDuration()`, `fn:get-minutes-from-dayTimeDuration()`, `fn:get-seconds-from-dayTimeDuration()`, and `fn:subtract-dateTimes-yielding-dayTimeDuration()` in Appendix C.

xs:decimal

A fixed-point decimal value.

`xs:decimal(xdt:anyAtomicType) as xs:decimal`

Lexical format:
`[\+\-]?(([0-9]+(\.[0-9]*)?)|(\.[0-9]+))`

Canonical format:
`-?[0-9]+\.[0-9]+`

The `xs:decimal` represents an arbitrary-precision fixed-point decimal number; in other words, all numbers of the form $m*10^{-n}$ where m is any `xs:integer` value and n is any non-negative integer. This type is commonly used in financial and scientific applications, where a fixed number of decimal digits are required, or when rounding is unacceptable.

In practice, most implementations limit the precision of this type by representing it using 64 or 128 bits (often a pair of integers, one for the value and one for the exponent).

In XQuery, decimal is the default type for all number literals that contain a decimal point. To use a floating-point number, use E notation after the number.

The decimal point and fractional digits are optional when casting from string (lexical format). When writing as a literal, the decimal point is required (although either the digits before or after the decimal point may be omitted). When casting to string (canonical format), the decimal point is required and digits must appear on either side of it.

Listing A.7 xs:decimal

```
1.0               => 1.0   (: decimal :)
1                 => 1     (: integer :)
xs:decimal("1")   => 1.0   (: decimal :)
1.0E0             => 1.0E0 (: double :)
1.0 div 0.0       => error (: division by zero :)
```

See also: xs:double, xs:float, and xs:integer.

xs:double

A double-precision floating-point number.

xs:double(xdt:anyAtomicType) as xs:double

Lexical format:
```
[\+\-]?(([0-9]+(\.[0-9]*)?)|(\.[0-9]+))((E|e)[\+\-]?[0-9]+)?
|[\+\-]?[iI][nN][fF]|[nN][aA][nN]
```

Canonical format:
```
-?[0-9]+\.[0-9]+E-?[0-9]+|INF|-INF|NaN
```

The xs:double type represents a double-precision (8-byte) floating-point value. Doubles are used to approximate real numbers, including the special values positive and negative infinity, positive and negative zero, and NaN (not a number). Except for these special values, every double value is a number $m*2^E$, where m is the mantissa, an integer between -2^{53} and 2^{53} exclusive, and E is the exponent, an integer between -1075 and 970, inclusive. The range of xs:double is thus considerably larger than that of xs:float.

The lexical format for `xs:double` is the same as that for `xs:float`: It consists of a decimal optionally followed by an exponent sign (E or e) and an integer. In other words, the double format consists of an optional sign (+ or -), any number of digits (possibly containing a decimal point), and an optional exponent consisting of an exponent sign (E or e), an optional sign (+ or -), and one or more digits. It is parsed into the closest possible double representation, using what is known as Clinger's algorithm.

If the string isn't in this format, then it is uppercased and if equal to +INF or INF results in positive infinity; -INF results in negative infinity, and NaN results in not-a-number. All other strings result in an error when converted to `xs:double`.

The canonical format for `xs:double` omits the + sign, always uses E for the exponent, always contains a decimal point with at least one digit before and at least one digit after the decimal point, and (except for these digits) omits leading and trailing zeros. Double values are converted to string using exactly as many but no more digits required to round-trip the value. The special values positive infinity, negative infinity, and not-a-number are converted to the strings "INF", "-INF", and "NaN", respectively. Implementations may omit the minus sign when converting negative zero to string.

Values of type `xs:double` can be written using the type constructor syntax, or using a double literal, which is a number followed by an exponent. (Numbers without exponents are `xs:decimal` values.)

Listing A.8 `xs:double`

```
xs:double("1")       => 1.0E0
xs:double("1.0")     => 1.0E0
xs:double("010.00")  => 1.0E1
xs:double("1E1")     => 1.0E1
xs:double("0.1")     => 1.0E-1
xs:double("INF")     => INF
xs:double("+iNf")    => INF
xs:double("NAN")     => NaN
1.0E0                => 1.0E0
1E-1                 => 1.0E-1
1E0 div 0E0          => INF
0E0 div 0E0          => NaN
```

See also: `xs:decimal`, `xs:float`, and `xs:integer`.

xs:duration

A duration value.

```
xs:duration(xdt:anyAtomicType) as xs:duration
```

Lexical format:
```
-?P([0-9]+Y)?([0-9]+M)?([0-9]+D)?
T([0-9]+H)?([0-9]+M)?([0-9]+(\.[0-9]*)S)?
```

The `xs:duration` type represents an interval of dates and/or times. Every `xs:duration` value has six parts: year, month, day, hour, minute, and second. As with the `xs:dateTime` type, the first five of these are integers, and the second part is a decimal value. The entire duration can be negative.

Each duration is constructed from a string that contains any or all of these parts, in the order given. When a part is omitted, it has the value `0`. When a time part (hour, minute, or second) is included, then the `T` is required; when no time part is present, then the `T` must not appear.

Listing A.9 `xs:duration`

```
xs:duration("P")          (: 0 length duration :)
xs:duration("P1Y")        (: 1 year :)
xs:duration("P1M")        (: 1 month :)
xs:duration("P1D")        (: 1 day :)
xs:duration("PT1H")       (: 1 hour :)
xs:duration("PT1M")       (: 1 minute :)
xs:duration("PT1S")       (: 1 second :)
xs:duration("P2Y3MT5.6S") (: 2 years, 3 months, 5.6 seconds :)
xs:duration("-P2MT3M")    (: negative 2 months, 3 minutes :)
```

See also: `xs:dateTime`, `xdt:dayTimeDuration`, and `xdt:yearMonthDuration`.

xs:ENTITIES

A list of XML ENTITY values.

The `xs:ENTITIES` type doesn't have a constructor because it derives by list from `xs:ENTITY`. In XQuery, a list of `xs:ENTITY` values has type `xs:ENTITY*`. Consequently, this type is useful only for validation.

See also: `xs:ENTITY`.

xs:ENTITY

An XML ENTITY.

```
xs:ENTITY(xdt:anyAtomicType) as xs:ENTITY
```

Lexical format:
```
\i\c*
```

The `xs:ENTITY` type is used to represent a reference to an XML unparsed entity, in association with the `xs:NOTATION` type. In XQuery, this type behaves the same way as `xs:NCName`. It is unlikely you will ever need the `xs:ENTITY` type.

See also: `xs:ENTITIES` and `xs:NCName`.

xs:float

A single-precision floating-point value.

```
xs:float(xdt:anyAtomicType) as xs:string?
```

Lexical format:
```
[\+\-]?(([0-9]+(\.[0-9]*)?)|(\.[0-9]+))((E|e)[\+\-]?[0-9]+)?
```

Canonical format:
```
-?[0-9]+\.[0-9]+E-?[0-9]+
```

The `xs:float` type represents a single-precision (4-byte) floating-point value. Floats are used to approximate real numbers, including the special values positive and negative infinity, positive and negative zero, and `NaN` (not a number). Except for these special values, every float value is a number $m*2^E$, where m is the mantissa, an integer between -2^{24} and 2^{24} exclusive, and E is the exponent, an integer between -149 and 104, inclusive.

The lexical format for `xs:float` is the same as that for `xs:double`: It consists of a decimal optionally followed by an exponent sign (`E` or `e`) and an integer. In other words, the float format consists of an optional sign (+ or -), any number of digits (possibly containing a decimal point), and an optional exponent consisting of an exponent sign (`E` or `e`), an optional sign (+ or -), and one or more digits. It is parsed into the closest possible float representation, using what is known as Clinger's algorithm.

If the string isn't in this format, then it is uppercased and if equal to `+INF` or `INF` results in positive infinity; `-INF` results in negative infinity, and `NaN` results in not-a-number. All other strings result in an error when converted to `xs:float`.

The canonical format for float omits the + sign, always uses E for the exponent, always contains a decimal point with at least one digit before and at least one digit after the decimal point, and (except for these digits) omits leading and trailing zeros. Float values are converted to string using exactly as many but no more digits required to round-trip the value. The special values positive infinity, negative infinity, and not-a-number are converted to the strings "INF", "-INF", and "NaN", respectively. Implementations may omit the minus sign when converting negative zero to string.

Although xs:float is a common type, it doesn't have a literal expression in XQuery. In other words, xs:float values must always be constructed using the type constructor syntax or a cast.

Listing A.10 xs:float

```
xs:float("1")        => 1.0E0
xs:float("1.0")      => 1.0E0
xs:float("010.00")   => 1.0E1
xs:float("1E1")      => 1.0E1
xs:float("0.1")      => 1.0E-1
xs:float("INF")      => INF
xs:float("+iNf")     => INF
xs:float("NAN")      => NaN
1E0 div 0E0          => INF
0E0 div 0E0          => NaN
```

See also: xs:decimal, xs:double, and xs:integer.

xs:gDay

A day in the Gregorian calendar.

```
xs:gDay(xdt:anyAtomicType) as xs:gDay
```

Lexical format:
```
--[0-9]{2}(Z|([\+\-][0-9]{2}:[0-9]{2}))?
```

The xs:gDay type represents a recurring day in the Gregorian calendar. It is written using two leading hyphens followed by two digits, and an optional time zone.

Unlike the date/time types (xs:date, xs:time, and xs:dateTime), the Gregorian types are relative. For example, xs:gDay("--30") means the thirtieth day of each month.

See also: xs:gMonth, xs:gMonthDay, xs:gYear, and xs:gYearMonth.

xs:gMonth

A month in the Gregorian calendar.

```
xs:gMonth(xdt:anyAtomicType) as xs:gMonth
```

Lexical format:
```
-[0-9]{2}-(Z|([\+\-][0-9]{2}:[0-9]{2}))?
```

The xs:gMonth type represents a recurring month in the Gregorian calendar. It is written using a hyphen followed by two digits and another hyphen, and an optional time zone.

Unlike the date/time types (xs:date, xs:time, and xs:dateTime), the Gregorian types are relative. For example, xs:gMonth("-02-") means the second month of each year.

See also: xs:gDay, xs:gMonthDay, xs:gYear, and xs:gYearMonth.

xs:gMonthDay

A month and day in the Gregorian calendar.

```
xs:gMonthDay(xdt:anyAtomicType) as xs:gMonthDay
```

Lexical format:
```
-[0-9]{2}-[0-9]{2}(Z|([\+\-][0-9]{2}:[0-9]{2}))?
```

The xs:gMonthDay type represents a recurring day of a month in the Gregorian calendar. It is written using a hyphen followed by two digits (the month, another hyphen and another two digits (the day), and an optional time zone.

Unlike the date/time types (xs:date, xs:time, and xs:dateTime), the Gregorian types are relative. For example, xs:gMonthDay("-02-14") means the fourteenth day of the second month of each year.

See also: xs:gDay, xs:gMonth, xs:gYear, and xs:gYearMonth.

xs:gYear

A year in the Gregorian calendar.

```
xs:gYear(xdt:anyAtomicType) as xs:gYear
```

Lexical format:
```
[0-9]{4}--(Z|([\+\-][0-9]{2}:[0-9]{2}))?
```

The `xs:gYear` type represents a single year in the Gregorian calendar. It is written using four digits followed by two hyphens and an optional time zone.

Unlike the date/time types (`xs:date`, `xs:time`, and `xs:dateTime`), the Gregorian types are relative. For example, `xs:gYear("2004--")` means the entire year 2004.

See also: `xs:gDay`, `xs:gMonth`, `xs:gMonthDay`, and `xs:gYearMonth`.

xs:gYearMonth

A month and year in the Gregorian calendar.

```
xs:gYearMonth(xdt:anyAtomicType) as xs:gYearMonth
```

Lexical format:
```
[0-9]{4}-[0-9]{2}-(Z|([\+\-][0-9]{2}:[0-9]{2}))?
```

The `xs:gYearMonth` type represents the entire month of a particular year in the Gregorian calendar. It is written using four digits (the year) followed by a hyphen, followed by two digits (the month), another hyphen, and an optional time zone.

Unlike the date/time types (`xs:date`, `xs:time`, and `xs:dateTime`), the Gregorian types are relative. For example, `xs:gYearMonth("2004-05")` means the fifth month of the year 2004.

See also: `xs:gDay`, `xs:gMonth`, `xs:gMonthDay`, and `xs:gYear`.

xs:hexBinary

A hex-encoded binary value.

```
xs:hexBinary(xdt:anyAtomicType) as xs:hexBinary
```

Lexical format:
```
[A-Fa-f0-9]{2}+
```

Canonical format:
```
[A-F0-9]{2}+
```

The `xs:hexBinary` type represents hex-encoded binary data. It consists of a sequence of pairs of hexadecimal digits `A-F`, `a-f`, `0-9`; all other characters are errors. Hex-encoding is a popular format for embedding arbitrary binary data in XML (among other things). Each pair of hexadecimal characters encodes a single byte of data (the byte with that hexadecimal value).

Listing A.11 `xs:hexBinary`

```
xs:hexBinary("ABBA")      (: encodes the two bytes 171, 186 :)
xs:hexBinary("012345")    (: encodes the bytes 1, 35, 69 :)
```

XQuery doesn't provide any functions for working with base64- or hex-encoded binary data; however, Chapter 10 includes a few examples of user-defined functions that do so.

See also: `xs:base64Binary` and Chapter 10.

xs:ID

An XML ID value.

```
xs:ID(xdt:anyAtomicType) as xs:ID
```

Lexical format:
```
\i\c*
```

The `xs:ID` type represents an XML ID value (an attribute or element value that uniquely identifies an element). This derived type satisfies the same lexical constraints as the `xs:NCName` type.

See also: `xs:NCName`, and `fn:id()` in Appendix C.

xs:IDREF

An XML IDREF value.

```
xs:IDREF(xdt:anyAtomicType) as xs:IDREF
```

Lexical format:
```
\i\c*
```

The `xs:IDREF` type represents a reference to an `xs:ID` value.
See also: `xs:ID` and `fn:idref()` in Appendix C.

xs:IDREFS

A list of XML IDREF values.

The `xs:IDREFS` type doesn't have a constructor because it derives by list from `xs:IDREF`. In XQuery, a list of `xs:IDREF` values has type `xs:IDREF*`. Consequently, this type is useful only for validation.

See also: `xs:IDREF`.

xs:int

A signed, 4-byte integer value (an integer in the range -2^{31} to $2^{31} - 1$, inclusive).

```
xs:int(xdt:anyAtomicType) as xs:int
```

Lexical format:
```
[\+\-]?[0-9]+
```

Canonical format:
```
-?[1-9][0-9]*
```

The `xs:int` type represents a signed, 4-byte integer, which can range in value from `-2147483648` to `2147483647`. It is a derived type.

Because all XQuery arithmetic using `xs:int` values takes place using its supertype, `xs:integer`, this type is primarily useful only for validation purposes and for placing constraints on function parameters. Some implementations may also optimize values with this type to occupy less space, or may optimize the performance of certain query expressions to exploit the properties of this type.

Listing A.12 `xs:int`

```
xs:int("0")           => 0
xs:int("2147483647")  => 2147483647
xs:int("2147483648")  => error (: out of range :)
xs:int("-1")          => -1
xs:int("2.5")         => error (: invalid format :)
xs:int(2.5)           => 2
```

See also: `xs:byte`, `xs:integer`, `xs:long`, `xs:short`, and `xs:unsignedInt`.

xs:integer

A signed integer value.

```
xs:integer(xdt:anyAtomicType) as xs:integer
```

Lexical format:
```
[\+\-]?[0-9]+
```

Canonical format:
```
-?[1-9][0-9]*
```

The xs:integer type represents a signed, arbitrary-precision integer. However, some implementations may choose to implement this type using a limited-precision type, such as 4- or 8-bytes. In that case, it behaves more like xs:int or xs:long, respectively.

Because the xs:integer type is so important in XQuery, its type constructor can be omitted. Any sequence of digits without a decimal point represents an xs:integer literal with that value.

This type is derived from xs:decimal, although in many cases it behaves more like a primitive type. For example, the type conversion rules for xs:integer are slightly different from those for other types derived from xs:decimal.

When converting from string, all signed integers allow an optional sign (+ or -) followed by one or more decimal digits. When converting to string, the + sign is always omitted, as are any leading zeros. Other numeric types can be converted to xs:integer, as described in Table A.7; values with digits after the decimal point have their fraction digits removed (truncation).

Listing A.13 xs:integer

```
xs:integer("0")    => 0
xs:integer("-1")   => -1
0                  => 0
-1                 => -1

(: on some implementations, this will error or overflow :)
xs:integer("18446744073709551617") => 18446744073709551617
```

See also: xs:byte, xs:decimal, xs:int, xs:long, xs:nonNegativeInteger, xs:nonPositiveInteger, and xs:short.

xs:language

An XML language.

```
xs:language(xdt:anyAtomicType) as xs:language
```

Lexical format:
```
[a-zA-Z]{2}[\-_][a-zA-Z]{2}
```

The xs:language type represents a value of the xml:lang attribute of XML. It specifies a language identifier as defined by RFC 1766, using two-letter country and language codes such as en-US (for U.S. English) and en_GB

(Great Britain English). The separator may be either a hyphen or an underscore (RFC 1766 allows both), although some implementations may support only one or the other.

This derived type generally behaves like its supertype xs:string. Its only real use is to validate that a string is a valid language identifier.

Listing A.14 xs:language

```
xs:language("en-US")
```

See also: xs:string and fn:lang() in Appendix C.

xs:long

A signed, 8-byte integer value (an integer in the range -2^{63} to $2^{63} - 1$, inclusive).

```
xs:long(xdt:anyAtomicType) as xs:long
```

Lexical format:
```
[\+\-]?[0-9]+
```

Canonical format:
```
-?[1-9][0-9]*
```

The xs:long type represents a signed, 8-byte integer, which can range in value from -9223372036854775808 to 9223372036854775807. It is a derived type.

Because all XQuery arithmetic using xs:long values takes place using its supertype, xs:integer, this type is primarily useful only for validation purposes and for placing constraints on function parameters. Some implementations may also optimize values with this type to occupy less space, or may optimize the performance of certain query expressions to exploit the properties of this type.

Listing A.15 xs:long

```
xs:long("0")                        => 0
xs:long("9223372036854775807")      => 9223372036854775808
xs:long("9223372036854775808")      => error (: out of range :)
xs:long("-1")                       => -1
xs:long("2.5")                      => error (: invalid format :)
xs:long(2.5)                        => 2
```

Implementations that represent `xs:integer` using a signed, 4-byte integer instead of using arbitrary-precision arithmetic have problems with this type, because it's a subtype of `xs:integer` but covers a larger range than `xs:integer` can represent.

See also: `xs:byte`, `xs:int`, `xs:integer`, `xs:short`, and `xs:unsignedLong`.

xs:Name

An XML name (Name) value.

```
xs:Name(xdt:anyAtomicType) as xs:Name
```

Lexical format:
```
(\i\c*:)\i\c*
```

The `xs:Name` type represents a valid XML name (including possibly the colon character). It consists of an optional prefix and colon separator, and a required local-name part. (Contrast this with the `xs:QName` type, which consists of the namespace and local-name parts, or the `xs:NCName` type, which represents unprefixed names).

See also: `xs:NCName` and `xs:QName`.

xs:NCName

An XML nonqualified name (NCName) value.

```
xs:NCName(xdt:anyAtomicType) as xs:NCName
```

Lexical format:
```
\i\c*
```

The `xs:NCName` type is derived from and similar to `xs:Name`, except that it cannot contain any colons (NCName stands for "Non-Colonized Name"). An XML prefix is an `xs:NCName`, and an XML local-name is an `xs:NCName`.

Values of this type must start with a letter, underscore (_), and then contain any number of subsequent letters, digits, hyphens (-), periods (.), underscores (_), and certain special Unicode characters (combining characters and extenders).

See also: `xs:Name` and `xs:QName`.

xs:negativeInteger

A negative integer value (non-zero and non-positive).

```
xs:negativeInteger(xdt:anyAtomicType) as xs:negativeInteger
```

Lexical format:
```
-[0-9]+
```

Canonical format:
```
-[1-9][0-9]*
```

The `xs:negativeInteger` type represents an arbitrary-precision integer with a negative value. It is a derived type.

Because all XQuery arithmetic using `xs:negativeInteger` values takes place using its supertype, `xs:integer`, this type is primarily useful only for validation purposes and for placing constraints on function parameters. Some implementations may also optimize the performance of certain query expressions to exploit the properties of this type.

See also: `xs:integer` and `xs:positiveInteger`.

xs:NMTOKEN

An XML NMTOKEN value.

```
xs:NMTOKEN(xdt:anyAtomicType) as xs:NMTOKEN
```

Lexical format:
```
(\c:)+
```

The `xs:NMTOKEN` type is similar to `xs:Name`, except that its first character can be any name character (not just name start characters). It is rarely used in XQuery.

See also: `xs:Name`.

xs:NMTOKENS

A list of XML NMTOKEN values.

The `xs:NMTOKENS` type doesn't have a constructor because it derives by list from `xs:NMTOKEN`. In XQuery, a list of `xs:NMTOKEN` values has type `xs:NMTOKEN*`. Consequently, this type is useful only for validation.

See also: `xs:NMTOKEN`.

xs:nonNegativeInteger

A non-negative integer value (that is, zero or positive).

```
xs:nonNegativeInteger(xdt:anyAtomicType) as xs:nonNegativeInteger
```

Lexical format:
```
\+?[0-9]+
```

Canonical format:
```
\+?[1-9][0-9]*
```

The xs:nonNegativeInteger type represents an arbitrary-precision integer with non-negative value. It is a derived type.

Because all XQuery arithmetic using xs:nonNegativeInteger values takes place using its supertype, xs:integer, this type is primarily useful only for validation purposes and for placing constraints on function parameters. Some implementations may also optimize the performance of certain query expressions to exploit the properties of this type.

See also: xs:integer, xs:nonPositiveInteger, and xs:positiveInteger.

xs:nonPositiveInteger

A non-positive integer value (that is, zero or negative).

```
xs:nonPositiveInteger(xdt:anyAtomicType) as xs:nonPositiveInteger
```

Lexical format:
```
-?[0-9]+
```

Canonical format:
```
-?[1-9][0-9]*
```

The xs:nonPositiveInteger type represents an arbitrary-precision integer with non-positive value. It is a derived type.

Because all XQuery arithmetic using xs:nonPositiveInteger values takes place using its supertype, xs:integer, this type is primarily useful only for validation purposes and for placing constraints on function parameters. Some implementations may also optimize the performance of certain query expressions to exploit the properties of this type.

See also: xs:integer, xs:negativeInteger, and xs:nonNegativeInteger.

xs:normalizedString

A whitespace-normalized string.

```
xs:anyURI(xdt:anyAtomicType) as xs:anyURI
```

Lexical format:
```
[^\t\r\n]*
```

The `xs:normalizedString` type represents strings that contains no tab (U+0009), new line (U+000A), or carriage return (U+000D) characters. It is a derived type that behaves like its supertype `xs:string` except for validation purposes.

See also: `xs:string`.

xs:NOTATION

An XML NOTATION.

```
xs:NOTATION(xdt:anyAtomicType) as xs:NOTATION
```

The `xs:NOTATION` type is a special type from XML 1.0 that is used to name an externally defined entity format or to describe the application targeted by processing instructions.

Note that `xs:NOTATION` is a distinct type from `xs:string`, and isn't a subtype of it. Although XQuery defines a constructor for it, the constructor will always result in an error because no other type can be cast to `xs:NOTATION`.

In XML, the `xs:NOTATION` type is sometimes used to represent enumeration values. However, XML Schema requires that `xs:NOTATION` not be used directly (only derived types of it), and also recommends that `xs:NOTATION` only be used to type attribute nodes, not elements.

XQuery doesn't have any expressions that use the `xs:NOTATION` type other than equality comparison (`eq`, `=`, `ne`, and `!=`), which performs a code point comparison on the underlying string values without respect to collation.

xs:positiveInteger

A positive integer value.

```
xs:positiveInteger(xdt:anyAtomicType) as xs:positiveInteger
```

Lexical format:
```
\+?[0-9]+
```

Canonical format:
```
[1-9][0-9]*
```

The `xs:positiveInteger` type represents an arbitrary-precision integer with a positive value. It is a derived type.

Because all XQuery arithmetic using `xs:positiveInteger` values takes place using its supertype, `xs:integer`, this type is primarily useful only for validation purposes and for placing constraints on function parameters. Some implementations may also optimize the performance of certain query expressions to exploit the properties of this type.

See also: `xs:integer` and `xs:negativeInteger`.

xs:QName

An XML qualified name (QName) value.

```
xs:QName(xdt:anyAtomicType) as xs:QName
```

Lexical format:
```
(\i\c*:)\i\c*
```

The `xs:QName` type represents an XML qualified name (that is, a local name and a possibly empty namespace URI). It is written exactly like an `xs:Name`, but the namespace prefix isn't part of the value; it is used only to look up the namespace uri part of the QName.

The `xs:QName` type is special in that it cannot be constructed using the usual type constructor syntax, but instead it has its own special constructor functions, `fn:expanded-QName()` and `fn:resolve-QName()`, that take either the namespace and local name parts or else a prefixed name string and a namespace context (respectively), and return the corresponding `xs:QName` value.

As with the calendar types, XQuery provides functions for accessing the individual parts of an `xs:QName` value: `get-local-name-from-QName()` and `get-namespace-from-QName()`. Each of these takes an `xs:QName` value and returns the corresponding part as an `xs:string`.

Listing A.16 QName accessors

```
get-local-name-from-QName(expanded-QName("", "x"))
=> "x"

get-namespace-uri-from-QName(expanded-QName("urn:foo", "x"))
=> "urn:foo"
```

See also: `xs:Name`, and `fn:expanded-QName()`, `fn:get-local-name-from-QName()`, `fn:get-namespace-uri-from-QName()`, and `fn:resolve-QName()` in Appendix C.

xs:short

A signed, 2-byte integer value (an integer in the range -2^{15} to $2^{15}-1$, inclusive).

```
xs:short(xdt:anyAtomicType) as xs:short
```

Lexical format:
```
[\+\-]?[0-9]+
```

Canonical format:
```
-?[1-9][0-9]*
```

The `xs:short` type represents a signed, 2-byte integer, which can range in value from `-32768` to `32767`. It is a derived type.

Because all XQuery arithmetic using `xs:short` values takes place using its supertype, `xs:integer`, this type is primarily useful only for validation purposes and for placing constraints on function parameters. Some implementations may also optimize values with this type to occupy less space, or may optimize the performance of certain query expressions to exploit the properties of this type.

Listing A.17 `xs:short`

```
xs:short("0")      => 0
xs:short("32767")  => 32767
xs:short("32768")  => error (: out of range :)
xs:short("-1")     => -1
xs:short("2.5")    => error (: invalid format :)
xs:short(2.5)      => 2
```

See also: `xs:byte`, `xs:int`, `xs:integer`, `xs:long`, and `xs:unsignedShort`.

xs:string

A string value.

```
xs:string(xdt:anyAtomicType) as xs:string
```

Lexical format:
```
.*
```

The `xs:string` type represents any string value. XQuery strings are sequences of Unicode code point values, without respect to any particular encoding or character representation. XQuery strings can theoretically be of any length, although in practice most implementations limit string values to some maximum size (often determined by available memory).

See also: `fn:codepoints-to-string()` and `fn:string-to-codepoints()` in Appendix C, and Chapter 8.

xs:time

A time value.

```
xs:time(xdt:anyAtomicType) as xs:time
```

Lexical format:
```
[0-9]{2}:[0-9]{2}:[0-9]{2}(\.[0-9]*)?(Z|([\+\-][0-9]{2}:[0-9]{2}))?
```

Canonical format:
```
[0-9]{2}:[0-9]{2}:[0-9]{2}(\.[0-9]*)?Z?
```
(also sometimes written pictorially as *hh:mm:ss.sssZ*)

The `xs:time` type represents a single point on the calendar. It consists of the same hour, minute, second, and time zone parts as the `xs:dateTime` type (but it isn't derived from `xs:dateTime`).

Listing A.18 `xs:time`

```
xs:time("08:05:01")       (: 8 hours, 5 minutes, 1 second :)
xs:time("23:59:59.99")    (: 23 hours, 59 minutes, 59.99 seconds :)
xs:time("08:05:01Z")      (: 8 hours, 5 minutes, 1 second in UTC :)
xs:time("08:05:01-08:00") (: same time in PST :)
```

See also: `xs:dateTime`.

xs:token

A token value (a string without spaces).

```
xs:token(xdt:anyAtomicType) as xs:token
```

Lexical format:
```
^$|[^\t\r\n ]|[^\t\r\n ]([^\t\r\n ]|( [^\t\r\n ]))*[^\t\r\n ]
```

The `xs:token` type is a normalized string that doesn't contain any leading or trailing space characters or any sequence of adjacent spaces. The `normalize-space()` and `tokenize()` functions can be used to convert any string value into a valid `xs:token` or to split an `xs:token` value into separate values not containing spaces.

This type can be used in XQuery type conversions to normalize space characters and can also be useful for constraining function parameters.

See also: `xs:normalizedString`, and `fn:normalize-space()` and `fn:tokenize` in Appendix C.

xs:unsignedByte

An unsigned byte value (an integer in the range 0 to 255, inclusive).

```
xs:unsignedByte(xdt:anyAtomicType) as xs:unsignedByte
```

Lexical form:
```
[0-9]+
```

Canonical form:
```
[1-9][0-9]*
```

The `xs:unsignedByte` type represents an unsigned, single-byte integer that can range in value from `0` to `255`. It is a derived type.

Because all XQuery arithmetic using `xs:unsignedByte` values takes place using its supertype, `xs:integer`, this type is primarily useful only for validation purposes and for placing constraints on function parameters. Some implementations may also optimize values with this type to occupy less space than `xs:integer`, or may optimize the performance of certain query expressions to exploit the properties of this type.

Listing A.19 `xs:unsignedByte`

```
xs:unsignedByte("0")   => 0
xs:unsignedByte("255") => 255
xs:unsignedByte("256") => error (: out of range :)
xs:unsignedByte("-1")  => error (: invalid format :)
xs:unsignedByte("2.5") => error (: invalid format :)
xs:unsignedByte(2.5)   => 2
```

See also: `xs:byte`, `xs:nonNegativeInteger`, `xs:unsignedInt`, `xs:unsignedLong`, and `xs:unsignedShort`.

xs:unsignedInt

An unsigned int value (an integer in the range 0 to 2^{32} - 1, inclusive).

```
xs:unsignedInt(xdt:anyAtomicType) as xs:unsignedInt
```

Lexical form:
```
[0-9]+
```

Canonical form:
```
[1-9][0-9]*
```

The `xs:unsignedInt` type represents an unsigned, 4-byte integer, which can range in value from `0` to `4294967295`. It is a derived type.

Because all XQuery arithmetic using `xs:unsignedInt` values takes place using its supertype, `xs:integer`, this type is primarily useful only for validation purposes and for placing constraints on function parameters. Some implementations may also optimize values with this type to occupy less space than `xs:integer`, or may optimize the performance of certain query expressions to exploit the properties of this type.

Listing A.20 `xs:unsignedInt`

```
xs:unsignedInt("0")          => 0
xs:unsignedInt("4294967295") => 4294967295
xs:unsignedInt("4294967296") => error (: out of range :)
xs:unsignedInt("-1")         => error (: invalid format :)
xs:unsignedInt("2.5")        => error (: invalid format :)
xs:unsignedInt(2.5)          => 2
```

Implementations that represent `xs:integer` using a signed, 4-byte integer instead of using arbitrary-precision arithmetic have problems with this type, because it's a subtype of `xs:integer` yet in that case covers a larger range.

See also: `xs:int`, `xs:nonNegativeInteger`, `xs:unsignedByte`, `xs:unsigned-Long`, and `xs:unsignedShort`.

xs:unsignedLong

An unsigned long value (an integer in the range 0 to 2^{64} - 1, inclusive).

```
xs:unsignedLong(xdt:anyAtomicType) as xs:unsignedLong
```

Lexical form:
```
[0-9]+
```

Canonical form:
```
[1-9][0-9]*
```

The `xs:unsignedLong` type represents an unsigned, 8-byte integer that can range in value from `0` to `18446744073709551615`. It is a derived type.

Because all XQuery arithmetic using `xs:unsignedLong` values takes place using its supertype, `xs:integer`, this type is primarily useful only for validation purposes and for placing constraints on function parameters. Some implementations may also optimize values with this type to occupy less space than `xs:integer`, or may optimize the performance of certain query expressions to exploit the properties of this type.

Listing A.21 `xs:unsignedLong`

```
xs:unsignedLong("0")                    => 0
xs:unsignedLong("18446744073709551615") => 18446744073709551615
xs:unsignedLong("18446744073709551616") => error (: out of range :)
xs:unsignedLong("-1")                   => error (: invalid format :)
xs:unsignedLong("2.5")                  => error (: invalid format :)
xs:unsignedLong(2.5)                    => 2
```

Implementations that represent `xs:integer` using a signed, 4-byte integer or a signed, 8-byte integer instead of using arbitrary-precision arithmetic have problems with this type, because it's a subtype of `xs:integer` yet in that case covers a larger range than `xs:integer` can represent.

See also: `xs:long`, `xs:nonNegativeInteger`, `xs:unsignedByte`, `xs:unsignedInt`, and `xs:unsignedShort`.

xs:unsignedShort

An unsigned short value (an integer in the range 0 to 2^{16} - 1, inclusive).

```
xs:unsignedShort(xdt:anyAtomicType) as xs:unsignedShort
```

Lexical form:
```
[0-9]+
```

Canonical form:
```
[1-9][0-9]*
```

The `xs:unsignedShort` type represents an unsigned, 2-byte integer that can range in value from 0 to 65535. It is a derived type.

Because all XQuery arithmetic using `xs:unsignedShort` values takes place using its supertype, `xs:integer`, this type is primarily useful only for validation purposes and for placing constraints on function parameters. Some implementations may also optimize values with this type to occupy less space than `xs:integer`, or may optimize the performance of certain query expressions to exploit the properties of this type.

Listing A.22 `xs:unsignedShort`

```
xs:unsignedShort("0")     => 0
xs:unsignedShort("65535") => 65535
xs:unsignedShort("65536") => error (: out of range :)
xs:unsignedShort("-1")    => error (: invalid format :)
xs:unsignedShort("2.5")   => error (: invalid format :)
xs:unsignedShort(2.5)     => 2
```

See also: `xs:nonNegativeInteger`, `xs:short`, `xs:unsignedByte`, `xs:unsignedInt`, and `xs:unsignedLong`.

xdt:untypedAtomic

An "untyped" value (from XML without an associated schema).
`xdt:untypedAtomic(xdt:anyAtomicType) as xdt:untypedAtomic`

Lexical form:
`.*`

The `xdt:untypedAtomic` type is a pseudo-type given to all untyped XML data (XML data without a schema), including XML attributes constructed in an XQuery when there isn't any schema type for that attribute in scope. Consequently, despite the name, untyped data actually is typed.

In practice, untyped values behave like weakly-typed `xs:string` values. For type conversion purposes, `xdt:untypedAtomic` behaves exactly like `xs:string`; however, for other operators, it often behaves more like XPath 1.0 than XQuery 1.0. For example, adding two `xs:string` values is a type error in XQuery. Adding two `xdt:untypedAtomic` values first converts both values to `xs:double`, and then performs the addition on those numeric values, just like in XPath 1.0.

See also: `xdt:anyAtomicType`, `xs:anySimpleType`, and `xs:string`, and Chapter 2.

---

xdt:yearMonthDuration

A duration with year and month parts only.

`xdt:yearMonthDuration(xdt:anyAtomicType) as xdt:yearMonthDuration`

Lexical format:
`-?P([0-9]+D)?T([0-9]+H)?([0-9]+M)?([0-9]+(\.[0-9]*)S)?`

This type has been introduced by XQuery to allow durations to be compared. As its name suggests, it represents the year and month parts only from a duration. It has the expected lexical and canonical forms (the subset of the forms for `xs:duration` that includes only the year and month parts).

See also: `xdt:dayTimeDuration` and `xs:duration`, and `fn:get-months-from-yearMonthDuration()`, `fn:get-years-from-yearMonthDuration()`, and `fn:subtract-dateTimes-yielding-yearMonthDuration()` in Appendix C.

Expression Reference

B.1 Introduction

This appendix describes all of the built-in XQuery keywords and operators, listed alphabetically (symbols first) for convenient reference. When a symbol occurs only in the context of others, for example, `by` occurs only in `order by`, then its entry may be omitted.

Each expression description begins with the syntax for the expression, followed by an explanation of its behavior, including optional parts and exceptional cases. In the syntax description, user-supplied parts of the expression appear in italics, and use the sequence type syntax described in Appendix A. In some expression syntaxes, additional descriptive words may be used as expression "types," including `stringliteral`, `sequencetype`, and `characters`, with the obvious meanings.

Each expression is cross-referenced to related expressions and other parts of the book.

!= (inequality sign)

General comparison operator tests whether there exist unequal values in two sequences.

`item* != item*`

The inequality operator `!=` first atomizes its operands, turning them into sequences of atomic values. It then tests whether there exists an atomic value in the first sequence, and independently whether there exists an atomic value in the second sequence, such that the two compare unequal with the operator `ne`.

Listing B.1 inequality (!=) examples

```
'a' != 'b'                    => true
                              (: depends on the default collation :)


(1, 2, 3) != 4                => true
(1, 2, 3) != (1, 2, 4)        => true
(1, 2, 3) != ()               => false
xdt:untypedAtomic("2") != 2   => false
<a/> != <b/>                  => false
```

As shown in Listing B.1, the != operator has some surprising effects: not($a = $b) has a different effect from $a != $b; and != applied to elements can return false even when the elements have different names and attributes (see Chapter 11 for additional examples and explanation).

When comparing pairs of atomic values, if either one has the dynamic type xdt:untypedAtomic, then it is first promoted to some other type using a rule that is slightly different from that of the ne operator itself (which always promotes xdt:untypedAtomic to xs:string). Instead, != always promotes untyped values to xs:double if the other value is numeric, xs:string if the other value is also xdt:untypedAtomic, and otherwise to the same type as the other operand.

In this way, the simple expression $a != $b is equivalent to the more complex expression in Listing B.2, where promote-general() is a user-defined function for general comparisons that performs the promotion rules just described (see Appendix A).

Listing B.2 An expression equivalent to $a != $b

```
some $i in fn:data($a), $j in fn:data($b)
satisfies promote-general($i, $j) ne promote-general($j, $i)

declare function promote-general($expr, $type) {
    typeswitch ($expr)
      case xdt:untypedAtomic return
        typeswitch($type)
          case xs:decimal        return cast as xs:double($expr)
          case xs:double         return cast as xs:double($expr)
          case xs:float          return cast as xs:double($expr)
          case xdt:untypedAtomic return cast as xs:string($expr)
```

```
        default                  return same-type($expr, $type)
    default return $expr
};
```

See also: Chapter 5; `ne` and `=` (equality) in this appendix; `fn:compare()` and `fn:deep-equal()` in Appendix C; the section "Atomization" in Chapter 2; and Chapter 11.

" (quotation mark, U+0022)

Character used around string values and attribute content.

`"characters"`

The quote character is used around string literals and attribute content (in directly constructed attributes). Don't confuse the quotation mark (Unicode code point `U+0022`) with the so-called "smart-quote" characters used by some word processors (`U+201C` and `U+201D`).

In quoted strings, the quote character (`"`) and ampersand (`&`) are special: the quote character because it denotes the end of the string, and the ampersand because it is used for entity references (named, hexadecimal, and decimal). If the string needs to contain the quote character, then either double it up (`""`) or use one of the three entity references: `&quot;`, `&#x22;`, or `&#34;`. Similarly, the ampersand can be escaped using one of the three entity references: `&amp;`, `&#x26;`, or `&#38;`.

All other characters (including new line characters, if the quoted string spans multiple lines) are part of the string value.

Listing B.3 Quotation mark (`"`) examples

```
"abcde"
"apostrophe (') needs no escape here, but quote ("") and ampersand (&amp;)
do"
<x y="z" />
```

See also: Chapter 1, and `'` (apostrophe), `""` (quote escape sequence), `&quot;` (quote entity reference), `&#x` (hexadecimal character reference), `&#` (decimal character reference), and `&amp;` (ampersand entity reference) in this appendix.

"" (quote escape sequence)

Quote escape sequence used inside quote-delimited expressions.

```
" "
```

In a quoted string or attribute value, the quote character must be escaped or entitized to be used as a character in the string. The quote character can be escaped by doubling it (`" "`).

Listing B.4 Quote escape sequence (`" "`) examples

```
"apostrophe (') needs no escape here, but quote ("") does"
```

See also: Chapter 1, and `"` (quotation mark) and `&quot;` (quote entity reference) in this appendix.

$ (variable)

Character used in front of a qualified name to denote a variable with that name.

```
$QName
```

Variables in XQuery always begin with the dollar sign followed by a qualified name. If the name is prefixed, then the namespace of the variable is the in-scope namespace corresponding to that prefix (an error is raised if the prefix is not in scope). If the name is unprefixed, then the variable has no namespace part.

Variables can be introduced by the following expressions: FLWOR, quantification (`some` and `every`), `typeswitch`, and `declare variable`. Additionally, variables may be introduced into scope by `import module` (if the module contains global variable declarations) or through an implementation's API. Also, in the definition of a user-defined function, all the parameters passed to the function are assigned to variables that are in scope for the body of the function.

Once a variable is in scope, it cannot be redefined. Consequently, variable definitions are fixed and don't change (although in some cases, such as FLWOR and quantification, the variable may take on different values during the expression's evaluation).

Listing B.5 Variable examples

```
$yourVariable
$my:variable
```

See also: Chapter 1; the section "Query Prolog" in Chapter 5; and `declare function`, `declare variable`, `every`, `FLWOR`, `import module`, `some`, and `type-switch` in this appendix.

&# (decimal character reference)

Decimal character reference.

`&#N;`

In strings and XML content, the decimal character reference can be used to represent any particular Unicode character. The character reference consists of the characters `&#` followed by one or more decimal digits (any of `0-9`), and finally a semicolon (`;`). The integer value provided specifies the Unicode code point value represented by the reference.

The main reason to use character references is to conveniently represent characters that are difficult to type, or to distinguish them from other characters when the difference is not normally visible (for example, the nonbreaking space character ` `).

The character represented by the character reference must still be a valid XML character; character references don't allow you to embed arbitrary binary data in XML (a common misconception). For that, you'll need to use a binary encoded type, such as `xs:hexBinary` or `xs:base64Binary` (see Appendix A).

Listing B.6 Decimal character reference examples

```
"&#72;&#105;&#33;"
```

See also: Chapter 7; `&#x` (hexadecimal character reference), `&amp;`, `&apos;`, `&gt;`, `&lt;`, and `&quot;` in this appendix; and `fn:codepoints-to-string()` in Appendix C.

&#x (hexadecimal character reference)

Hexadecimal character reference.

`&#xH;`

In strings and XML content, hexadecimal character references can be used to represent any particular character. The character reference consists of the characters `&#` followed by one or more hexadecimal characters (any of `0-9`, `a-f`, or A-F), and finally a semicolon (;). The hexadecimal number provided specifies the Unicode code point value that is represented by the character reference.

The main reason to use character references is to conveniently represent characters that are difficult to type or to distinguish them from other characters when the difference is not normally visible (for example, the nonbreaking space character).

The character represented by the character reference must still be a valid XML character; character references don't allow you to embed arbitrary binary data in XML (a common misconception). For that, you'll need to use a binary encoded type, such as xs:hexBinary or xs:base64Binary (see Appendix A).

Listing B.7 Hexadecimal character reference examples

```
"&#x6c;&#x33;&#x033;&#x74;&#x003F;"
```

See also: Chapter 7; &# (decimal character reference), &, ', >, <, and " in this appendix; and fn:codepoints-to-string() in Appendix C.

& (ampersand entity reference)

One of the five built-in named character entity references (ampersand).

```
&amp;
```

The entity reference & is used in string literals and XML constructors to denote the ampersand character (&).

Listing B.8 & examples

```
"&amp;"
<x>&amp;</x>
```

See also: Chapter 7, and &# (decimal character reference), &#x (hexadecimal character reference), ', >, <, and " in this appendix.

' (apostrophe entity reference)

One of the five built-in named character entity references (apostrophe).

```
&apos;
```

The entity reference `&apos;` is used in string literals and XML constructors to denote the apostrophe character (').

Listing B.9 `&apos;` examples

```
"&apos;"
<x>&apos;</x>
```

See also: Chapter 7, and ' (apostrophe), '' (apostrophe escape), `&#` (decimal character reference), `&#x` (hexadecimal character reference), `&amp;`, `&gt;`, `&lt;`, and `&quot;` in this appendix.

`&gt;` (greater-than sign entity reference)

One of the five built-in named character entity references (greater-than sign).

```
&gt;
```

The entity reference `&gt;` is used in string literals and XML constructors to denote the greater-than sign (>).

Listing B.10 `&gt;` examples

```
"&gt;"
<x>&gt;</x>
```

See also: Chapter 7, and > (greater-than sign), `&#` (decimal character reference), `&#x` (hexadecimal character reference), `&amp;`, `&apos;`, `&lt;`, and `&quot;` in this appendix.

`&lt;` (less-than sign entity reference)

One of the five built-in named character entity references (less-than sign).

```
&lt;
```

The entity reference `&lt;` is used in string literals and XML constructors to denote the less-than sign (<).

Listing B.11 `&lt;` examples

```
"&lt;"
<x>&lt;</x>
```

See also: Chapter 7, and < (less-than sign), `&#` (decimal character reference), `&#x` (hexadecimal character reference), `&amp;`, `&apos;`, `&gt;`, and `&quot;` in this appendix.

`&quot;` (quote entity reference)

One of the five built-in named character entity references (quote).

`&quot;`

The entity reference `&quot;` is used in string literals and XML constructors to denote the quotation mark (").

Listing B.12 `&quot;` examples

```
"&quot;"
<x>&quot;</x>
```

See also: Chapter 7, and " (quotation mark), "" (quote escape), `&#` (decimal character reference), `&#x` (hexadecimal character reference), `&amp;`, `&apos;`, `&gt;`, and `&lt;` in this appendix.

' (apostrophe, U+0027)

Character used around string values and attribute content.

`'characters'`

The apostrophe character is used around string literals and attribute content (in directly constructed attributes). Do not confuse the apostrophe (Unicode code point U+0027) with the so-called "smart quote" characters used by some word processors (U+2018 and U+2019).

In apostrophed strings, the apostrophe character (') and ampersand (&) are special: the apostrophe character because it denotes the end of the string, and the ampersand because it is used for entity references (named, hexadecimal, and decimal). If the string needs to contain the apostrophe character, then either double it up ('') or use one of the three entity references: ', ', or '. Similarly, the ampersand can be escaped using one of the three entity references: &, &, or &.

All other characters (including new line characters, if the string spans multiple lines) are part of the string value.

Listing B.13 Apostrophe (') examples

```
'abcde'
'quote (") needs no escape here, but apostrophe ('') and ampersand (&amp;)
do'
<x y='z' />
```

See also: Chapter 1, and " (quotation mark), '' (apostrophe escape sequence), and ' (apostrophe entity reference) in this appendix.

'' (apostrophe escape sequence)

Apostrophe escape sequence used inside apostrophe-delimited expressions.

''

Inside an apostrophe-delimited string or attribute value, the apostrophe character must be doubled-up to be used as a character in the string.

Listing B.14 Apostrophe escape sequence ('') examples

```
'quote (") needs no escape here, but apostrophe ('') does'
```

See also: Chapter 1, and ' (apostrophe) and ' (apostrophe entity reference) in this appendix.

((left parenthesis, U+0028)

Start of a parenthesized expression, always paired with a matching).

(*expr*)

Parentheses are used in XQuery for several purposes. The empty parentheses () denote the empty sequence. Parentheses can be used as grouping operators to express the order in which expressions should be evaluated.

Parentheses are required by some expressions, such as `if` and `typeswitch`. Parentheses are also used in function definitions and invocations as a wrapper around the function arguments. And finally, parentheses are used in some node kind tests and sequence types, like `node()` and `item()`, which look like functions but are not.

Listing B.15 Parentheses examples

```
()
(1 + 2) * (3 + 4)
if ($done) then () else repeat()
subsequence( (1,2,3), 2 )
```

See also: Chapter 1; `declare function`, `if`, `typeswitch`, and `validate` in this appendix; and the section "Operator Precedence" in Appendix E.

(: (XQuery comment)

XQuery comments appear in between `(:` and `:)`.

```
(:characters:)
```

XQuery comments may appear anywhere that ignorable whitespace may appear, and also within element content (i.e., everywhere except inside literals, entity references, wildcards, and direct XML constructors other than elements). The entire comment is removed from the query during processing, and so contributes nothing to the query.

Comments are useful both for documentation purposes and for temporarily commenting out parts of your code during development. Comments may contain any character sequence except `:)` (which terminates the comment). Comments may also be nested to any depth.

XQuery comments should not be confused with XML comments, which are a kind of XML node.

Listing B.16 XQuery comment examples

```
(: code is read by people; use comments wisely :)
((:this is an empty sequence (: containing nested comments :):))
<x a="(:not a comment:)">(:a comment:)<!--(:not a comment:)--></x>
```

See also: Chapter 1, and `(::` (pragma/extension) and `<!--` (XML comment constructor) in this appendix.

(:: (pragma/extension)

Extension mechanisms for XQuery implementations.

```
(:: pragma QName characters ::)
(:: extension QName characters ::)
```

Pragmas are ignorable instructions to an XQuery implementation. If the implementation doesn't support the pragma, then it must ignore the pragma (except for parsing it). If the implementation does support the pragma, then the pragma will have whatever meaning the implementation has assigned to it. In contrast, if an implementation doesn't support an extension used by the query, then it must raise an error.

The distinction allows porting queries to other implementations; features the query requires should be extensions, while features that are optional should be pragmas. Pragmas are typically used for debugging and tracing, while extensions are typically used for function libraries and extended operators (such as DML and full-text search).

Listing B.17 Examples of `pragma` and `extension`

```
(::pragma once::)
(:: pragma warn-level 4 ::)
(:: extension full-text ::)
```

See also: Chapter 5 and Chapter 14.

) (right parenthesis,))

End sequence of a parenthesized expression.
See the entry for `(` (left parenthesis) in this appendix.

* (asterisk, U+002A)

Indicate the cardinality of a sequence type (zero or more).

singletype*

The asterisk character (*) has several uses in XQuery (see also wildcard and multiplication). One use is in type names. When a type name is followed by an asterisk, it represents a sequence of zero or more values of the given type.

Listing B.18 * (asterisk) examples

```
declare function example($x as xs:integer*) { 2*3 };
```

See also: Chapter 2, Appendix A, and * (wildcard), * (multiplication), ? (question mark), and + (plus sign) in this appendix.

* (wildcard)

Wildcard name test.

```
*
NCName:*
*:NCName
```

In paths (and element and attribute type tests), the wildcard (*) can be used as a name test. There are three variations of the wildcard: * matches any name, NCName:* matches names with any local part and the namespace corresponding to the given prefix, and *:NCName matches names with the given local part in any namespace.

When used in a path, the wildcard name test matches element nodes in all axes except the attribute axis, where it matches attribute nodes.

Listing B.19 Wildcard examples

```
//*
x:*/*:y
```

See also: Chapter 3 and node() in Appendix A.

* (multiplication)

Multiply two expressions.

```
expr * expr
```

When used as a binary operator, the asterisk multiplies two expressions. Like all arithmetic operators, it first atomizes both operands. If either sequence of atomic values is empty, then it returns the empty sequence. If either sequence contains more than one value, then it raises an error.

Otherwise, if either operand is type `xdt:untypedAtomic`, it is converted to `xs:double`. If both operands are numeric, then they are promoted to a common type (see Appendix A). No other type conversions are performed; the two operands must support multiplication or an error is raised.

Listing B.20 Multiplication examples

```
1 * 1                        => 1
1 * xdt:untypedAtomic("2")   => 2.0E0
1 * "2"                      => error
xs:dayTimeDuration("P3D") * 3 => xs:dayTimeDuration("P9D")
```

Multiplication is symmetrical. In the list below, the types may appear in either order. The pairs of types that support multiplication are:

- Both numeric types (`xs:decimal`, `xs:double`, and `xs:float`, and subtypes of these)
- `xs:decimal` and `xdt:yearMonthDuration` (resulting in `xdt:yearMonthDuration`)
- `xs:decimal` and `xdt:dayTimeDuration` (resulting in `xdt:dayTimeDuration`)

See also: Chapter 5; + (addition), - (subtraction), `div`, `idiv`, `mod`, * (asterisk), and * (wildcard) in this appendix; and the section "Atomization" in Chapter 2.

+ (plus sign, U+002B)

Indicate the cardinality of a sequence type (one or more).

singletype+

The plus sign (+) has several uses in XQuery (see also unary plus and addition). One use is in type names. When a type name is followed by a plus sign, it represents a sequence of one or more values of the given type.

Listing B.21 + (plus sign) examples

```
declare function example($x as xs:integer+) { 2+3 };
```

See also: Chapter 5; Appendix A; + (unary plus), + (addition), e notation, * (asterisk), and ? (question mark) in this appendix; and fn:one-or-more() in Appendix C.

+ (unary plus)

Unary plus operator.

+ *expr*

When used as a unary operator, the plus sign has the following effects: First, it atomizes its operand, turning it into a sequence of atomic values. If the sequence is empty, then it results in the empty sequence. Otherwise, if the sequence has length greater than one, an error is raised.

If the value has dynamic type xdt:untypedAtomic, it is converted to xs:double. Otherwise, if the value is not numeric (i.e., not xs:decimal, xs:double, xs:float, or a subtype of these), then an error is raised.

Listing B.22 Unary plus examples

```
+1                      => 1
+xdt:untypedAtomic("2") => 2.0E0
+"2"                    => error (: operand is not numeric :)
+current-time()         => error (: operand is not numeric :)
```

Unary plus can be a convenient way to force the static type of an expression to be numeric without writing treat as. Otherwise, it has no real purpose except symmetry with the unary minus operator (-).

See also: Chapter 5; - (unary minus), + (plus sign), and + (addition) in this appendix; and the section "Atomization" in Chapter 2.

+ (addition)

Add two expressions.

expr + *expr*

When used as a binary operator, the plus sign adds two expressions. Like all arithmetic operators, it first atomizes both operands. If either sequence of atomic values is empty, then it returns the empty sequence. If either sequence contains more than one value, then it raises an error.

Otherwise, if either operand is type `xdt:untypedAtomic`, it is converted to `xs:double`. If both operands are numeric, then they are promoted to a common type (see Appendix A). No other type conversions are performed; the two operands must support addition or an error is raised.

Listing B.23 Addition examples

```
1+1                     => 2
1+xdt:untypedAtomic("2") => 3.0E0
1+"2"                   => error (: operand is not numeric :)

xs:date("2004-05-13") + xs:dayTimeDuration("P17D")
=> xs:date("2004-05-30")
```

Addition is symmetrical. In the list below, the types may appear in either order. The pairs of types that support addition are:

- Both numeric types (`xs:decimal`, `xs:double`, and `xs:float`, and subtypes of these)
- `xs:date` and `xdt:yearMonthDuration` (resulting in `xs:date`)
- `xs:date` and `xdt:dayTimeDuration` (resulting in `xs:date`)
- `xs:dateTime` and `xdt:yearMonthDuration` (resulting in `xs:dateTime`)
- `xs:dateTime` and `xdt:dayTimeDuration` (resulting in `xs:dateTime`)
- `xs:time` and `xdt:dayTimeDuration` (resulting in `xs:time`)
- `xdt:yearMonthDuration` and `xdt:yearMonthDuration` (resulting in `xdt:yearMonthDuration`)
- `xdt:dayTimeDuration` and `xdt:dayTimeDuration` (resulting in `xdt:dayTimeDuration`)

Note that in XQuery, + does not perform string concatenation as it does in many other languages. For that purpose, use either the `fn:concat()` or `fn:string-join()` function.

See also: Chapter 5; - (subtraction), * (multiplication), div, idiv, mod, + (plus sign), and + (unary plus) in this appendix; and the section "Atomization" in Chapter 2.

, (comma, U+002C)

The comma operator separates items in a sequence or other expression.

expr , expr

XQuery uses the comma (,) symbol in two ways. One use is as a separator between items in a sequence. Because comma has the lowest precedence among all XQuery operators, you may need to enclose the sequence in parentheses.

Also, certain expressions, such as FLWOR, quantification (some, every), function invocation, and function definitions use commas to separate variable declarations and parameters. When used in this way, the items aren't actually in a sequence.

Listing B.24 Comma examples

```
1, 2, 4                  (: used to separate items in a sequence :)
concat("a", "b")         (: used to separate parameters :)
subsequence((1, 2), 3)   (: used in both ways :)
```

See also: Chapter 1 and the section "Operator Precedence" in Appendix E.

- (hyphen, U+002D)

The hyphen (-) is used in E-notation and in names (it is a valid name character). Additionally, it is used as both a binary subtraction operator and unary minus operator.

The hyphen (U+002D) shouldn't be confused with similar characters used by some word processors, such as the en-dash (U+2013), em-dash (U+2014), or soft hyphen (U+00AD).

See the entries for - (unary minus), - (subtraction), and E-notation in this appendix.

- (unary minus)

Unary minus operator.

- expr

When used as an unary operator, the minus sign has the following effects: First, it atomizes its operand, turning it into a sequence of atomic values. If the sequence is empty, then it results in the empty sequence. Otherwise, if the sequence has length greater than one, an error is raised.

If the value has dynamic type `xdt:untypedAtomic`, it is converted to `xs:double`. Otherwise, if the value isn't numeric (i.e., not `xs:decimal`, `xs:double`, `xs:float`, or a subtype of these), then an error is raised.

Finally, it negates the value.

Listing B.25 Unary minus examples

```
-1                      => -1
-xdt:untypedAtomic("2") => -2.0E0
-"2"                    => error (: operand is not numeric :)
-current-time()         => error (: operand is not numeric :)
```

See also: Chapter 5; + (unary plus), - (hyphen), and - (subtraction) in this appendix; and the section "Atomization" in Chapter 2.

- (subtraction)

Subtract two expressions.

expr - expr

When used as a binary operator, the minus sign subtracts two expressions. Like all arithmetic operators, it first atomizes both operands. If either sequence of atomic values is empty, then it returns the empty sequence. If either sequence contains more than one value, then it raises an error.

Otherwise, if either operand is type `xdt:untypedAtomic`, it is converted to `xs:double`. If both operands are numeric, then they are promoted to a common type (see Appendix A). No other type conversions are performed; the two operands must support subtraction or an error is raised.

Listing B.26 Subtraction examples

```
1-1                     => 0
1-xdt:untypedAtomic("2") => -1.0E0
1-"2"                    => error (: operand is not numeric :)

xs:date("2004-05-30") - xs:dayTimeDuration("P17D")
=> xs:date("2004-05-13")
```

Subtraction is asymmetrical. In the list below, the operand types must occur in order. The pairs of types that support subtraction are:

- Both numeric types (`xs:decimal`, `xs:double`, `xs:float`, and subtypes of these)
- `xs:date` and `xs:date` (resulting in `xdt:dayTimeDuration`)
- `xs:date` and `xdt:yearMonthDuration` (resulting in `xs:date`)
- `xs:date` and `xdt:dayTimeDuration` (resulting in `xs:date`)
- `xs:dateTime` and `xs:dateTime` (resulting in `xdt:dayTimeDuration`)
- `xs:dateTime` and `xdt:yearMonthDuration` (resulting in `xs:dateTime`)
- `xs:dateTime` and `xdt:dayTimeDuration` (resulting in `xs:dateTime`)
- `xs:time` and `xs:time` (resulting in `xdt:dayTimeDuration`)
- `xs:time` and `xdt:dayTimeDuration` (resulting in `xs:time`)

To subtract two `xs:dateTime` values and get an `xdt:yearMonthDuration`, use the built-in function `fn:subtract-dateTimes-yielding-yearMonthDuration()`.

See also: Chapter 5; + (addition), * (multiplication), `div`, `idiv`, `mod`, - (hyphen), and - (unary minus) in this appendix; the section "Atomization" in Chapter 2; and `fn:subtract-dateTimes-yielding-dayTimeDuration()` and `fn:subtract-dateTimes-yielding-yearMonthDuration()` in Appendix C.

—> (XML comment constructor)

End sequence of an XML comment.

See the entry for `<!--` (XML comment constructor) in this appendix.

. (current context item, U+002E)

The current context item.

.

In XPath 1.0, the dot operator (.) selected the current context node. In XQuery, its behavior is similar, except that the current context item can be an atomic value or the empty sequence (when the context sequence is empty).

The current context item is perhaps most useful in predicates, where it can be used to compare the value of the current node or pass it to a function. Be aware that the predicate `[.]` will filter by position when the current context item is numeric.

Listing B.27 Current context item (.) examples

```
a[. = "x"]
a[contains(., "x")]
(1, "x", 4)[.]
```

See also: Chapter 3 and .. (navigation operator) in this appendix.

.. (parent navigation)

Navigate to the parent node.

```
..
```

As in XPath 1.0, the .. operator is just an abbreviation for `parent:
:node()`. It navigates to the parent of the current context node. If the current context item isn't a node, then it raises an error.

Note that the path `x/y/..` is not equivalent to the path `x` (a common misconception). Instead, the path is equivalent to the path `x[y]`, because it selects `x` only when it has at least one `y` child element.

Listing B.28 Parent navigation (..) examples

```
a[.. = "x"]
node()[.. and not(../..)]    (: matches only nodes at the top :)
```

See also: Chapter 3, and . (current context item) and `parent` (axis) in this appendix.

/ (slash, U+002F)

Navigation operator separating steps in a path, or navigating to the root.

```
step / step
/ step
/
```

The slash operator (`/`) by itself or at the start of a path navigates to the root node of the fragment to which the current context node belongs, exactly like a call to the built-in `fn:root()` function. If the current context item is not a node, it raises an error. So, the path `/` is equivalent to `fn:root(.)`, while the path `/step` is equivalent to `fn:root(.)/step`. Otherwise, the `/` operator has no real meaning except to separate steps in a path.

Listing B.29 Slash (/) examples

```
/
/top
/comment()
a/b/c
a[@b = "x"]/c/@d
```

See also: Chapter 3 and `fn:root()` in Appendix C.

// (navigation operator)

Navigation operator separating steps in a path.

```
step // step
// step
```

The double slash (`//`) operator is similar to the slash (`/`) operator in that it can begin a path or separate steps in a path. However, `//` is actually an abbreviation for `/descendant-or-self::node()/`, so, for example, `a//b` means `a/descendant-or-self::node()/b`. Unlike `/`, `//` must always have a step expression following it.

The path `a//b` is equivalent to `a/descendant-or-self::node()/b`, which is equivalent to `a/descendant::b`.

Listing B.30 `descendant-or-self` (`//`) examples

```
//x      (: this selects every x element in document order :)
x//y     (: this selects every y element descendant of x :)
```

Although `//` is easy to write, it's also easy to misuse. In some implementations, `//a` is much slower than directly seeking to the `a` element (when you know the path in advance). On other implementations, the converse is true. (In still other implementations, both queries perform equally well when schema information is provided.) The path `a//b` is almost always slower than directly seeking to the `b` element (when you know the path in advance).

Also, `//` has some surprises, such as the difference between `//x[1]` and `(//x)[1]`. See Chapter 11 for additional examples and discussion.

Listing B.31 `//x[1]` versus `(//x)[1]`

```
//x[1]    (: this selects the first x child element of each node :)
(//x)[1]  (: this selects the first x element overall :)
```

See also: Chapter 3; `/` (slash), `descendant`, and `descendant-or-self` in this appendix; and Chapter 11.

`/>` (XML element constructor)

End sequence of a self-closing XML element constructor.
See the entry for `<` (XML element constructor) in this appendix.

`:` (colon, U+003A)

XQuery uses the colon character for several purposes: to separate the local and namespace parts in a qualified name, to separate a navigation axis from the node test, and in comments, pragmas, and extensions.
See the entries for `::` (axis separator), `(:` and `:)` (XQuery comment), and `(::` and `::)` (pragma/extension) in this appendix, and `xs:NCName` and `xs:QName` in Appendix A.

`:)` (XQuery comment)

End sequence of an XQuery comment.
See the entry for `(:` (XQuery comment) in this appendix.

`::` (axis separator)

Separates the axis and node test in a navigation step.

```
axis::nodetest
```

The axis separator isn't really an operator. It exists to syntactically separate the axis name from the node test (which may also be a name). Whitespace is allowed between the separator and the axis and/or node test.

Listing B.32 Axis separator (`::`) examples

```
child::w/descendant::x:y / attribute :: z
```

See also: Chapter 3, and `attribute` (axis), `child`, `descendant`, `descendant-or-self`, `parent`, and `self` in this appendix.

`::)` (pragma or extension)

End sequence of a pragma or extension.
See the entry for `(::` (pragma/extension) in this appendix.

`:=` (assignment)

The assignment operator (`:=`) is used only with the `let` keyword.
See the entry for FLWOR in this appendix.

`<` (less-than sign, U+003C)

General comparison operator tests whether there exist values with one less than the other.

item* < item*

The less-than operator, `<`, first atomizes its operands, turning them into sequences of atomic values. It then tests whether there exists an atomic value in the first sequence, and independently whether there exists an atomic value in the second sequence, such that the first compares less than the second using the value comparison operator `lt`.

Because `<` is also used for other purposes (including element constructors), it is parsed differently depending on the character following it. For example, `<a><<b/>` is a parse error because `<<` parses as the node comparison operator, while `<a/>< <b/>` (with a space between the two `<` characters) parses as expected.

Listing B.33 Less-than (`<`) examples

```
'a' < 'b'                  => true
                           (: depends on the default collation :)
(1, 2, 3) < 4              => true
(1, 2, 3) < (1, 2, 4)      => true
(1, 2, 3) < ()             => false
xdt:untypedAtomic("2") < 2 => false
<a/> < <b/>                => false
```

As shown in Listing B.1, the < operator has some surprising effects, especially with the empty sequence (see Chapter 11 for additional surprises and explanations).

When comparing pairs of atomic values, if either one has the dynamic type `xdt:untypedAtomic`, then it is first promoted to some other type using a rule that is slightly different from that of the `lt` operator itself (which always promotes `xdt:untypedAtomic` to `xs:string`). Instead, < always promotes untyped values to `xs:double` if the other value is numeric, to `xs:string` if the other value is also `xdt:untypedAtomic`, and otherwise to the same type as the other operand.

In this way, the simple expression `$a < $b` is equivalent to the more complex expression in Listing B.2, where `promote-general()` is a hypothetical user-defined function that performs the general comparison promotion rules just described.

Listing B.34 An expression equivalent to `$a < $b`

```
some $i in fn:data($a), $j in fn:data($b)
satisfies promote-general($i, $j) lt promote-general($j, $i)
```

See also: Chapter 5; `lt` and `<=` (less than or equal to) in this appendix; `fn:compare()` and `fn:deep-equal()` in Appendix C; the section "Atomization" in Chapter 2; and Chapter 11.

< (XML element constructor)

Construct an XML element.

```
<qname attributes/>
<qname attributes>content</qname>
```

XQuery uses almost the same syntax for constructing XML elements as XML does, with one exception: the curly brace characters, { and }, have special meaning for XQuery. They indicate that an XQuery compiler should parse the enclosed expression as an XQuery expression instead of as character content for the XML node. To use these characters as content, double them up.

In XQuery, the XML element syntax is called *direct element constructor* to distinguish it from the computed element constructor syntax that uses the `element` keyword. The computed syntax is capable of computing not only the element content, but also its name. The direct constructor syntax is equivalent to the computed syntax with a constant name.

Space characters in constructed XML elements may be stripped or preserved, depending on the `xmlspace` policy.

Listing B.35 Direct XML element constructor examples

```
<x y="1">z</x>           => <x y="1">z</x>
<x y="1+1">1+1</x>       => <x y="1+1">1+1</x>
<x y="{1+1}">{1+1}</x>   => <x y="2">2</x>
```

See also: Chapter 7, and { (left curly brace), {{ (left curly brace escape sequence), }} (right curly brace escape sequence), `declare xmlspace`, and `element` (constructor) in this appendix.

<!— (XML comment constructor)

Construct an XML comment node.

```
<!--chars-->
```

XQuery uses the same syntax for constructing XML comments as XML does. Unfortunately, XQuery doesn't provide any way to construct a comment node with computed content.

XML comments shouldn't be confused with XQuery comments. XML comments construct nodes; XQuery comments are ignored by the compiler.

Listing B.36 Direct XML comment constructor examples

```
<!---->
<!-- this is an XML comment -->
```

See also: Chapter 7, and < (XML element constructor), <? (XML processing instruction constructor), <![CDATA[(CDATA section constructor), and (: (XQuery comment) in this appendix.

<![CDATA[(CDATA section constructor)

Construct an XML CDATA section.

```
<![CDATA[chars]]>
```

XQuery uses the same syntax for constructing XML CDATA sections as XML does. Unfortunately, XQuery doesn't provide any way to construct a CDATA section with computed content.

XML CDATA sections exist only to allow you to avoid using lots of entity and character references. They cannot contain characters that are invalid for XML, and they cannot contain the sequence]]> because that is used to signify the end of a CDATA section. One way to overcome the second limitation is to use two CDATA sections: `<![CDATA[]]]]><![CDATA[>]]>`.

Listing B.37 Direct XML CDATA constructor example

```
<x><![CDATA[Special characters like &, <, and > do not require escaping in
CDATA sections]]></x>
```

See also: Chapter 7 and `text` (constructor) in this appendix.

`</` (XML element constructor)

Start of the closing tag of an XML element constructor.

See the entry for < (XML element constructor) in this appendix.

`<<` (before)

Test whether one node appears before another in document order.

expr `<<` *expr*

The node comparison operator << ("before") takes two arguments, which must be either singleton nodes or the empty sequence. If either operand is empty, then << returns the empty sequence. Otherwise, it returns true if the first node appears before the second in document order, and false otherwise.

Listing B.38 Before (<<) example

```
doc("foo.xml") << doc("foo.xml")  => false
```

See also: Chapter 5 and >> (after) in this appendix.

<= (less than or equal to)

General comparison operator tests whether two values exist with one at most the other.

```
item* <= item*
```

The less-than-equals operator, `<=`, first atomizes its operands, turning them into sequences of atomic values. It then tests whether there exists an atomic value in the first sequence, and independently whether there exists an atomic value in the second sequence, such that the first compares less than or equal to the second using the value comparison operator `le`.

Listing B.39 Less-than-equals (`<=`) examples

```
'a' <= 'b'                => true
                          (: depends on the default collation :)

(1, 2, 3) <= 4            => true
(1, 2, 3) <= (1, 2, 4)    => true
(1, 2, 3) <= ()           => false
xdt:untypedAtomic("2") <= 2 => true
<a/> <= <b/>              => false
```

As shown in Listing B.1, the `<=` operator has some surprising effects, especially with the empty sequence (see Chapter 11 for additional surprises and explanations).

When comparing pairs of atomic values, if either one has the dynamic type `xdt:untypedAtomic`, then it is first promoted to some other type using a rule that is slightly different from that of the `le` operator itself (which always promotes `xdt:untypedAtomic` to `xs:string`). Instead, `<=` always promotes untyped values to `xs:double` if the other value is numeric, to `xs:string` if the other value is also `xdt:untypedAtomic`, and otherwise to the same type as the other operand.

In this way, the simple expression `$a <= $b` is equivalent to the more complex expression in Listing B.2, where `promote-general()` is a user-defined function for general comparisons that performs the promotion rules just described (see Appendix A).

Listing B.40 An expression equivalent to `$a <= $b`

```
some $i in fn:data($a), $j in fn:data($b)
satisfies promote-general($i, $j) le promote-general($j, $i)
```

See also: Chapter 5; `le` and `<` (less-than) in this appendix; `fn:compare()` and `fn:deep-equal()` in Appendix C; the section "Atomization" in Chapter 2; and Chapter 11.

`<?` (XML processing instruction constructor)

Construct an XML processing instruction node.

```
<?chars?>
```

XQuery uses the same syntax for constructing XML processing instructions as XML does. Unfortunately, XQuery doesn't provide any way to construct a processing instruction node with computed content.

Listing B.41 Direct XML processing instruction constructor examples

```
<? example ?>
<?process this?>
```

See also: Chapter 7, and `<` (XML element constructor) and `<!--` (XML comment constructor) in this appendix.

`=` (equals sign, U+003D)

General comparison operator tests whether two values exist that are equal to each other.

```
item* = item*
```

The equality operator `=` first atomizes its operands, turning them into sequences of atomic values. It then tests whether there exists an atomic value in the first sequence, and independently whether there exists an atomic value in the second sequence, such that the first compares equal to the second using the value comparison operator `eq`.

Listing B.42 Equals (=) examples

```
'a' = 'b'                   => false
                            (: depends on the default collation :)

(1, 2, 3) = 4               => false
(1, 2, 3) = (1, 2, 4)       => true
(1, 2, 3) = ()              => false
xdt:untypedAtomic("2") = 2  => true
<a/> = <b/>                 => false
```

As shown in Listing B.1, the = operator has some surprising effects, especially with the empty sequence (see Chapter 11 for additional surprises and explanations).

When comparing pairs of atomic values, if either one has the dynamic type xdt:untypedAtomic, then it is first promoted to some other type using a rule that is slightly different from that of the eq operator itself (which always promotes xdt:untypedAtomic to xs:string). Instead, = always promotes untyped values to xs:double if the other value is numeric, to xs:string if the other value is also xdt:untypedAtomic, and otherwise to the same type as the other operand.

In this way, the simple expression $a = $b is equivalent to the more complex expression in Listing B.2, where promote-general() is a user-defined function for general comparisons that performs the promotion rules just described (see Appendix A).

Listing B.43 An expression equivalent to $a = $b

```
some $i in fn:data($a), $j in fn:data($b)
satisfies promote-general($i, $j) eq promote-general($j, $i)
```

See also: Chapter 5; eq and != (inequality) in this appendix; fn:compare() and fn:deep-equal() in Appendix C; the section "Atomization" in Chapter 2; and Chapter 11.

= (equality symbol)

In addition to its use as an operator, the equality symbol (=) appears in many XQuery prolog expressions, and is also used to separate attribute names and values in direct XML constructors.

See the entries for `declare default collation`, `declare default element namespace`, `declare default function namespace`, `declare namespace`, `declare xmlspace`, `import module`, `import schema`, and `<` (element constructor) in this appendix.

> (greater-than sign, U+003E)

General comparison operator tests whether two values exist with one greater than the other.

```
item* > item*
```

The greater-than operator, `>`, first atomizes its operands, turning them into sequences of atomic values. It then tests whether there exists an atomic value in the first sequence, and independently whether there exists an atomic value in the second sequence, such that the first compares greater than the second using the value comparison operator `gt`.

Listing B.44 Greater-than (>) examples

```
'a' > 'b'                 => false
                          (: depends on the default collation :)

(1, 2, 3) > 4             => false
(1, 2, 3) > (1, 2, 4)     => true
(1, 2, 3) > ()            => false
xdt:untypedAtomic("2") > 2 => false
<a/> > <b/>               => false
```

As shown in Listing B.1, the `>` operator has some surprising effects, especially with the empty sequence (see Chapter 11 for additional surprises and explanations).

When comparing pairs of atomic values, if either one has the dynamic type `xdt:untypedAtomic`, then it is first promoted to some other type using a rule that is slightly different from that of the `gt` operator itself (which always promotes `xdt:untypedAtomic` to `xs:string`). Instead, `>` always promotes untyped values to `xs:double` if the other value is numeric, to `xs:string` if the other value is also `xdt:untypedAtomic`, and otherwise to the same type as the other operand.

In this way, the simple expression `$a > $b` is equivalent to the more complex expression in Listing B.2, where `promote-general()` is a hypothetical user-defined function that performs the general comparison promotion rules just described.

Listing B.45 An expression equivalent to `$a > $b`

```
some $i in fn:data($a), $j in fn:data($b)
satisfies promote-general($i, $j) gt promote-general($j, $i)
```

See also: Chapter 5; `gt` and `>=` (greater-than or equal to) in this appendix; `fn:compare()` and `fn:deep-equal()` in Appendix C; the section "Atomization" in Chapter 2; and Chapter 11.

>> (after)

Test whether one node appears after another in document order.

node? >> node?

The node comparison operator `>>` ("after") takes two arguments, which must be either singleton nodes or the empty sequence. If either operand is empty, then `>>` returns the empty sequence. Otherwise, it returns true if the first node appears after the second in document order, and false otherwise.

Listing B.46 After (>>) example

```
doc("foo.xml") >> doc("foo.xml")  => false
```

See also: Chapter 5, `<<` (before) in this appendix, and Chapter 2.

>= (greater than or equal to)

General comparison operator tests whether two values exist with one less than the other.

item >= item**

The greater-than-equals operator, `>=`, first atomizes its operands, turning them into sequences of atomic values. It then tests whether there exists an atomic value in the first sequence, and independently whether there exists an atomic value in the second sequence, such that the first compares greater than or equal to the second using the value comparison operator `ge`.

Listing B.47 Greater-than-equals (>=) examples

```
'a' >= 'b'                    => false
                              (: depends on the default collation :)

(1, 2, 3) >= 4                => false
(1, 2, 3) >= (1, 2, 4)        => true
(1, 2, 3) >= ()               => false
xdt:untypedAtomic("2") >= 2   => true
<a/> >= <b/>                  => false
```

As shown in Listing B.1, the >= operator has some surprising effects, especially with the empty sequence (see Chapter 11 for additional surprises and explanations).

When comparing pairs of atomic values, if either one has the dynamic type xdt:untypedAtomic, then it is first promoted to some other type using a rule that is slightly different from that of the ge operator itself (which always promotes xdt:untypedAtomic to xs:string). Instead, >= always promotes untyped values to xs:double if the other value is numeric, to xs:string if the other value is also xdt:untypedAtomic, and otherwise to the same type as the other operand.

In this way, the simple expression $a >= $b is equivalent to the more complex expression in Listing B.2, where promote-general() is a user-defined function for general comparisons that performs the promotion rules just described (see Appendix A).

Listing B.48 An expression equivalent to $a >= $b

```
some $i in fn:data($a), $j in fn:data($b)
satisfies promote-general($i, $j) ge promote-general($j, $i)
```

See also: Chapter 5; ge and > (greater-than sign) in this appendix; fn:compare() and fn:deep-equal() in Appendix C; the section "Atomization" in Chapter 2; and Chapter 11.

? (question mark, U+003F)

Indicate the cardinality of a sequence type (zero or one).

singletype?

When a type name is followed by a question mark, it represents a sequence of zero or one values of the given type.

Note that in a function, a parameter that occurs zero or one times must still occur; it isn't an optional parameter. For example, the function in Listing B.49 must still be passed two parameters, even if they are both empty.

The question mark also appears in XML processing instruction constructors, for example, `<?pi?>`.

Listing B.49 ? (question mark) examples

```
declare function example($x as xs:integer?) external;
$y cast as xs:string?
```

See also: Chapter 2; `*` (asterisk), `+` (plus sign), and `<?` and `?>` (XML processing instruction constructors) in this appendix; and `fn:zero-or-one()` in Appendix C.

?> (XML processing instruction constructor)

End sequence of an XML processing instruction.

See the entry for `<?` (XML processing instruction constructor) in this appendix.

@ (at sign, U+0040)

Abbreviation for the attribute axis.

@nodetest

The @ symbol is most commonly used as a convenient abbreviation for the attribute axis. It also appears in front of names in the `attribute()` type test, to emphasize that it matches attributes.

Listing B.50 Attribute navigation examples

```
a[@b = 1]/@c
```

See also: Chapter 3, `attribute` (axis) in this appendix, and `attribute()` type test in Appendix A.

[(left square bracket, U+005B)

Filter a step with a predicate expression.

```
step [ expr ]
```

XQuery, like XPath, uses square brackets to enclose predicate expressions. The predicate is a postfix operator, applied after an expression (the sequence to be filtered) and containing an expression (the predicate expression).

The predicate expression is evaluated for each item in the sequence to be filtered, using that item as the current context item (and deriving the rest of the focus from it, including the context position). If the predicate evaluates to true, then the item is kept in the result; otherwise, it is omitted.

If the predicate evaluates to a numeric value, then it is true if the context position is equal to that number. Otherwise, the predicate is converted to boolean exactly like the `fn:boolean()` function.

Listing B.51 Predicate examples

```
("a", "b", "c")[2]      => "b"
("a", "b", "c")[2.5]    => ()
("a", "b", "c")[false()] => ()
("a", "b", "c")[true()]  => ("a", "b", "c")

x[y]    (: selects x if it has a child element y :)
x[@y=1] (: selects x if it has an attribute y equal to 1 :)
```

When the entire predicate is the current context item and the sequence to be filtered contains atomic values, "surprising" results can occur, as shown in Listing B.52. Numbers are compared to the context position, and all other values are converted to boolean.

Listing B.52 More predicate examples

```
(1, 5, 3, 4, 2)[.]      => (1, 3, 4)
("a", "", "b")[.]       => ("a", "b")
(true(), false(), 3)[.] => (true(), 3)
```

See also: Chapter 3, and . (current context item) in this appendix.

] (right square bracket, U+005D)

End sequence of a predicate.

See the entry for [(left square bracket) in this appendix.

]]> (CDATA section constructor)

End sequence of a CDATA section.

See the entry for <![CDATA[(CDATA section constructor) in this appendix.

{ (left curly brace, U+007B)

Used by some expressions to distinguish a subexpression from the rest of the query.

```
{ expr }
```

Curly braces are used in the following expressions: `declare variable`, `declare function`, and `validate`, and the computed node constructors (`attribute`, `document`, `element`, and `text`).

The most important use of curly braces is inside element and attribute content to denote that the enclosed expression should be evaluated as an XQuery expression, instead of just treated as ordinary characters. To use a curly brace as an ordinary character in element or attribute content, double it up (or use a character escape).

Listing B.53 Curly brace examples

```
<x y="{1 div 2}">{ 1 + 1 }</x> => <x y="0.5">2</x>
<x y="{{">}}</x>                => <x y="{">}</x>
```

See also: Chapter 7; {{ (left curly brace escape sequence), }} (right curly brace escape sequence), < (XML element constructor), `attribute` (constructor), `declare function`, `declare variable`, `document` (constructor), `element` (constructor), `text` (constructor), and `validate` in this appendix.

{{ (left curly brace escape sequence)

Escape sequence for the character { in element content.

```
{{
```

In direct element constructors, the curly brace characters are used to enclose XQuery expressions. Consequently, if the element needs to contain a curly brace character itself, it must be escaped. There's no named entity reference for the curly braces, and it's difficult to remember their decimal or hexadecimal character references, so XQuery allows these characters to be escaped by doubling them.

Listing B.54 Left curly brace escape sequence examples

```
<x>{{</x>          => <x>{</x>
<x>{1}{{{2}</x>    => <x>1{2</x>
```

See also: Chapter 7, and }} (right curly brace escape sequence), { (left curly brace), and < (XML element constructor) in this appendix.

| (vertical bar, U+007C)

Another form of the `union` operator.

See the entry for `union` in this appendix.

} (right curly brace, U+007D)

See the entry for { (left curly brace) in this appendix.

}} (right curly brace escape sequence)

Escape sequence for the character } in element content.

```
}}
```

In direct element constructors, the curly brace characters are used to enclose XQuery expressions. Consequently, if the element needs to contain a curly brace character itself, it must be escaped. There's no named entity reference for the curly braces, and it's difficult to remember their decimal or hexadecimal character references, so XQuery allows these characters to be escaped by doubling them.

Listing B.55 Right curly brace escape sequence examples

```
<x>}}</x>          => <x>}</x>
<x>{1}}}{2}</x>    => <x>1}2</x>
```

See also: Chapter 7, and `{{` (left curly brace escape sequence), `}` (right curly brace), and `<` (XML element constructor) in this appendix.

ancestor

Navigation axis that selects ancestor nodes.

`ancestor::nodetest`

The `ancestor` axis matches all ancestors of the current context node. The node test can be used to filter the ancestors further, for example, matching only those with a particular name or node kind.

XQuery implementations aren't required to support the `ancestor` axis; Chapter 10 provides a workaround.

Listing B.56 `ancestor` axis examples

```
count(ancestor::*)
x[ancestor::y]/ancestor::z
```

See also: Chapter 3, Chapter 10, and `ancestor-or-self` and `parent` in this appendix.

ancestor-or-self

Navigation axis that selects ancestor nodes and the current node itself.

`ancestor-or-self::nodetest`

The `ancestor-or-self` axis matches all ancestors of the current context node, as well as the node itself. XQuery implementations aren't required to support the `ancestor-or-self` axis; Chapter 10 provides a workaround.

Listing B.57 `ancestor-or-self` axis examples

```
ancestor-or-self::foo/bar
count(ancestor-or-self::*)
```

See also: Chapter 3, Chapter 10, and `ancestor` and `parent` in this appendix.

and

Logical binary operator tests whether both values are true.

expr and *expr*

The `and` operator first converts both of its operands to boolean using the `fn:boolean()` function (also known as the Effective Boolean Value). If either operand is true, then `and` returns true, otherwise it returns false.

Listing B.58 and examples

```
true() and false()        => false
"" and 0.0                => false
"x" and 1.0               => true
() and (true(), true())   => false
```

The order in which the `and` operator evaluates its arguments is implementation-dependent, and implementations are also allowed (and encouraged) to "short-circuit" this operator (evaluating only one of its operands if that is enough to determine the overall result). Consequently, expressions like `error() and false()` and `false() and error()` may raise an error or may return false, depending on the implementation.

See also: Chapter 5, and `fn:boolean()` and `fn:not()` in Appendix C.

as

The keyword `as` appears wherever variables can be introduced, and also in the three type expressions `cast as`, `treat as`, and `castable as`.

See the entries for `cast as`, `castable as`, `declare function`, `declare variable`, `every`, FLWOR, `some`, `treat as`, and `typeswitch` in this appendix.

ascending

Sort in increasing order (the default).
See the entry for FLWOR.

at

Introduce a positional variable.
See the entry for FLWOR.

attribute (axis)

Navigation axis that selects attribute nodes.

```
attribute::nodetest
```

The `attribute` axis matches all attributes of the current context node. The node test can be used to filter the attributes further, for example, matching only those with a particular name.

It's common practice to use @ as an abbreviation instead of writing `attribute`. When using the abbreviation, no axis separator is required.

Listing B.59 `attribute` axis examples

```
count(attribute::*)
x[attribute::y = 1 or attribute::z]
x[@y = 1 or @z]
```

See also: Chapter 3, and @ (at sign), `child`, `descendant`, `descendant-or-self`, `parent`, and `self` in this appendix.

attribute (constructor)

Attribute constructor with computed name and content.

```
attribute name { expr }
attribute { expr } { expr }
```

The computed attribute constructor takes two arguments, the name and the content. The name expression can be an ordinary name, or an expression (enclosed in curly braces) that computes the name. Attributes with constant names can be constructed using the ordinary XML syntax, so the computed name case is the more interesting of the two.

When the name is computed, the name expression must result in either an `xs:QName` value or else an `xs:string` value which is then parsed into a QName using the in scope namespaces. If the name cannot be parsed or isn't a QName, then an error is raised. Otherwise, the resulting QName value is the name of the attribute.

The content expression is first atomized, and then each item in the (possibly empty) sequence of atomic values is converted to string and then concatenated together with spaces separating them. In other words, `attribute name { $x }` is equivalent to `attribute name { string-join(" ", data($x)) }`.

The type of the constructed attribute is `xdt:untypedAtomic`, regardless of the type of its content expression, and the attribute isn't validated (unless it is used in an expression such as element construction or `validate`).

Listing B.60 Computed `attribute` constructor examples

```
<x>{ attribute foo { () } }</x>          => <x foo="" />
<x>{ attribute { "ab" } { "c", "d", 3 } => <x ab="c d 3" />
```

See also: Chapter 7; `document` (constructor), `element` (constructor), and `text` (constructor) in this appendix; and the section "Atomization" in Chapter 2.

case

See the entry for `typeswitch` in this appendix.

cast as

Convert an expression to a given type.

expr cast as *singletype*

The `cast as` operator takes two arguments: an expression and a single type (the target type).

It first atomizes the expression. If the result contains more than one atomic value, then an error is raised. If the atomized sequence is empty, then the cast succeeds (and results in the empty sequence) only if the single type is followed by the `?` occurrence indicator. Otherwise, `cast as` attempts to convert this single value to the target type, and either succeeds (resulting in a value with that type) or else raises an error using one of the following three rules:

1. If the expression type is equal to or derived from the target type, then `cast as` returns the value unchanged but with the target type.
2. Otherwise, if the target type is a derived type and the expression type is (or is derived from) `xs:string` or `xdt:untypedAtomic`, or if the target type derives from the expression type (down-cast), then the conversion process first works lexically, converting the value to a space-normalized

string and then validating that string according to the rules of the target type. Then, the lexical string is converted into a value of that type.

3. Otherwise, the expression is first up-cast (if necessary) to its primitive supertype, using rule 1 above. Then it is converted to the primitive supertype of the target type according to the primitive conversion chart described in Appendix A. Then, it is down-cast (if necessary) to the target type, using rule 2 above.

These conversion steps can result in an error. For example, converting `"2.0"` into an `xs:integer` will fail because the decimal point isn't allowed in the lexical format for `xs:integer`. Converting `"2004-02-30"` into `xs:date` will fail because although the string satisfies the lexical constraints for `xs:date`, it isn't a valid `xs:date` value (the second month never has 30 days).

Listing B.61 `cast as` examples

```
xs:string("2.0") cast as xs:decimal => 2.0
xs:string("2.0") cast as xs:integer => error
xs:string("2") cast as xs:decimal   => 2.0
xs:string("2") cast as xs:integer   => 2
```

See also: Chapter 9; `castable as`, `treat as`, and `validate` in this appendix; Chapter 11; and section A.4 in Appendix A.

castable as

Test whether an expression can be cast to a given type.

expr castable as *singletype*

The `castable as` operator takes two arguments, an expression and a single type. It returns true if the expression can be cast into that type (by the `cast as` operator), otherwise it returns false.

This operator is mainly used to avoid conversion errors by first testing whether an expression can be converted.

Listing B.62 `castable as` examples

```
1.0 castable as xs:integer => true
1.5 castable as xs:integer => false
```

See also: Chapter 9, `cast as` in this appendix, and Chapter 2.

child

Navigation axis that selects child nodes.

```
child::nodetest
```

The `child` axis matches all children (element, text, comment, and process-ing-instruction nodes) of the current context node. The node test can be used to filter the children further, for example, matching only those with a particular name or node kind.

It's common practice to omit the child axis, because it is the default axis. When using the abbreviation, no axis separator is required.

Listing B.63 `child` axis examples

```
count(child::*)
count(child::comment())
x[child::y]/child::z
x[y]/z
```

See also: Chapter 3, and `/` (slash), `attribute`, `descendant`, `descendant-or-self`, `parent`, and `self` in this appendix.

collation

Specify a collation to use for string comparisons.

See the entries for `default collation` and FLWOR in this appendix, and Chapter 8.

comment (constructor)

Comment constructor with computed content.

```
comment { expr }
```

The computed `comment` constructor takes one argument, which becomes the content of the comment node. The content is first atomized. If the resulting sequence is empty, then the content is the empty string. Otherwise, each atomic value is cast to `xs:string`, concatenated together with a space character in between each consecutive pair, and the final result becomes the content of the constructed comment node.

Listing B.64 Computed `comment` constructor examples

```
comment { "foo" } => <!--foo-->
comment { (1, 2) } => <!--1 2-->
```

See also: Chapter 7, and `attribute` (constructor), `document` (constructor), `element` (constructor), `namespace` (constructor), `pi` (constructor), and `text` (constructor) in this appendix.

context

Specify the schema validation context.

See the entry for `validate` in this appendix.

declare base-uri

Set the base-uri (prolog only).

```
declare base-uri stringliteral;
```

The base URI declaration sets the base-uri value of the static context, which is used by functions such as `base-uri()` and `doc()`.

See also: Chapter 5, and `base-uri()` in Appendix C.

declare default collation

The default collation declaration (prolog only).

```
declare default collation stringliteral;
```

The query prolog may contain a default collation declaration, which specifies the default collation to be used in the query (for comparing strings). The value must be a string literal naming a collation supported by the implementation, or else an error is raised. At most one default collation declaration may be used.

When no default collation declaration is used, the default collation is implementation-defined. Many implementations will use the Unicode code point collation as their default; its URI is `http://www.w3.org/2003/11/`

`xpath-functions/collation/codepoint`. The Unicode code point collation is the only collation implementations are required to support.

Listing B.65 Default collation declaration example

```
declare default collation "http://www.unicode.org/lang/en-us";
```

See also: Chapter 8, and `fn:default-collation()` in Appendix C.

declare default element namespace

The default element namespace declaration (prolog only).

```
declare default element namespace stringliteral;
```

The query prolog may contain a default element namespace declaration, which specifies the default namespace to be used for all element names (including constructors and paths) and type names (in `cast as` and other expressions).

At most one default element namespace declaration may appear in the prolog. Element constructors may override the default namespace using `xmlns`.

Listing B.66 Default element namespace declaration examples

```
declare default element namespace "http://www.w3c.org";
<x>
  <y xmlns="http://www.w3c.org" />
</x>
```

Unlike ordinary namespace declarations, the namespace string may be the empty string (which is also the default value), in which case the default element namespace is no namespace at all. Otherwise, the namespace must be a valid namespace URI.

See also: Chapter 5, and `declare default function namespace` and `declare namespace` in this appendix.

declare default function namespace

The default function namespace declaration (prolog only).

```
declare default function namespace stringliteral;
```

The query prolog may contain a default function namespace declaration, which specifies the default namespace to be used for all function names (function invocations and definitions) in the module. At most one default function namespace declaration may be used in the prolog.

Listing B.67 Default function namespace declaration example

```
declare default function namespace "http://www.w3c.org";
foo("xyz")
```

Unlike ordinary namespace declarations, the namespace string may be the empty string, in which case the default function namespace is no namespace at all. Otherwise, the namespace must be a valid namespace URI.

If a default function namespace declaration isn't provided, then in the main module the default namespace is the same one that is bound to the built-in `fn` prefix (`http://www.w3.org/2003/11/xpath-functions`). In library modules, the default is the target namespace of the module.

The default function namespace must not cause two functions to have the same (unprefixed) name and number of arguments, or else an error is raised (duplicate function declaration).

See also: Chapter 5, and `declare default element namespace`, `declare namespace`, and `module` in this appendix.

declare function

Describe a user-defined function.

```
declare function qname ( params ) { expr };
declare function qname ( params ) as sequencetype { expr };
declare function qname ( params ) external;
declare function qname ( params ) as sequencetype external;
```

where `params` consists of zero or more untyped parameters.
```
$varname
```
or typed parameters
```
$varname as sequencetype
```
that are separated by commas.

Function definitions are specified after the query prolog but before the query body, using the `declare function` keyword.

Functions are defined by name. If the name doesn't have a prefix, then it isn't in a namespace; otherwise, it is in the namespace corresponding to that prefix. User-defined functions may not be overloaded (i.e., only one definition per name), may not override built-in functions, and always take a fixed number of arguments. In contrast, many built-in functions are overloaded (e.g., `compare()`) and one (`concat()`) takes a variable number of arguments.

User-defined functions declare zero or more parameters, which are then in scope for the entire function body. Untyped parameters have the most generic type (`item*`). All parameters must have different names.

User-defined functions have a return type. If omitted, then the return type of the function is the most generic type (`item*`). The function body must match (according to sequence type matching) its declared type or an error is raised.

Listing B.68 User-defined functions are powerful

```
(: Compute $b raised to the $exp power :)
declare function pow($b as xs:integer,
                     $exp as xs:integer) as xs:integer {
  if ($exp > 1)
    then $b * pow($b, $exp - 1)
  else if ($expr = 1)
    then $b
  else
    1
};
```

To allow interoperability with other languages, XQuery allows you to declare externally defined functions by using the `external` keyword instead of a function body. It's up to implementations whether and how to handle externally defined functions (including translating XQuery types into other languages' types and vice versa).

See also: Chapter 4, and `declare variable` in this appendix.

declare namespace

Introduce a namespace declaration (prolog only).

```
declare namespace NCName = stringliteral;
```

Table B.1 Predefined namespaces

Prefix	Namespace
fn	http://www.w3.org/2003/11/xpath-functions
xdt	http://www.w3.org/2003/11/xpath-datatypes
xml	http://www.w3.org/XML/1998/namespace
xs	http://www.w3.org/2001/XMLSchema
xsi	http://www.w3.org/2001/XMLSchema-instance

The namespace declaration introduces a namespace prefix into scope, binding it to the given namespace URI. The string literal must be a valid, non-empty URI. Every namespace declaration in the prolog must use a different prefix, although elements may override prefix bindings using `xmlns` or the namespace constructor.

The namespace URI must not be the empty string. To define the default namespace, use `declare default element namespace` or `declare default function namespace`, depending on the desired effect.

Listing B.69 Namespace declaration example

```
declare namespace p = "http://www.w3c.org";
<p:x>
  <p:y xmlns:p="http://www.aw.com" />
</p:x>
```

XQuery predefines the five namespaces listed in Table B.1. The first two of these are tied to the current version of the XQuery drafts in progress; the other three are final. All of these except for the `xml` prefix may be redefined using `declare namespace`.

See also: Chapter 5, `declare default element namespace` and `declare default function namespace` in this appendix, and `fn:get-inscope-name-space-prefixes()` in Appendix C.

declare validation

The validation declaration (prolog only).

```
declare validation mode;
```

The validation declaration specifies the default validation mode to be used with the `validate` operator and element constructors. The mode must be one of `lax`, `skip`, or `strict`. If no validation declaration is used, then the default validation mode is `lax`.

Listing B.70 Validation examples

```
declare validation lax;
declare validation skip;
declare validation strict;
```

See also: Chapter 9, and `validate` and < (XML element constructor) in this appendix.

declare variable

Declare a global variable or external parameter (prolog only).

```
declare variable $varName { expr };
declare variable $varName as sequenceType { expr };
declare variable $varName external;
declare variable $varName as sequenceType external;
```

Global variable declarations introduce a variable name into global scope. Optionally, the variable declaration may be typed. Then the variable is either assigned a value, or else declared to be an external parameter whose value is provided at runtime. These are called global variables and global (external) parameters, respectively. The name "variable" is somewhat misleading, because the value doesn't vary.

If the type is omitted for a global variable, then its static type is the static type of its value. This type must be compatible with the type of the expression used for the variable value. If the type is omitted for a global parameter, then its static type is `xs:anyType`.

How external parameter values are supplied to the query depends entirely on the implementation, but an error is raised if a value isn't supplied or its type is incompatible with the static type.

Listing B.71 Variable declaration examples

```
declare variable $meaningOfLife as xs:integer { 42 };
declare variable $my:zero { 0 };
declare variable $unknown external;
declare variable $userID as xs:string external;
```

See also: Chapter 5, and `declare function` and `$` (variable) in this appendix.

declare xmlspace

The xmlspace declaration (prolog only).

```
declare xmlspace mode;
```

The xmlspace declaration specifies how boundary whitespace characters in XML element and attribute constructors are handled. The mode must be either `preserve` or `strip` (`strip` is the default), meaning preserve or remove boundary whitespace, respectively.

Listing B.72 xmlspace declaration examples

```
declare xmlspace strip;
declare xmlspace preserve;
```

See also: Chapter 7 and `<` (element constructor) in this appendix.

default

The `default` keyword is used in several expressions, including the default collation, element namespace, and function namespace declarations in the prolog, schema imports, and the `typeswitch` operator.

See the entries for `declare default collation`, `declare default element namespace`, `declare default function namespace`, `import schema`, and `typeswitch` in this appendix.

descendant

Navigation axis that selects descendant nodes.

```
descendant::nodetest
```

The `descendant` axis matches all descendants (element, text, comment, and processing-instruction nodes) of the current context node. The node test can be used to filter the descendants further (for example, matching only those with a particular name or node kind).

Note that the `descendant` axis excludes the current node itself; to include the current node, use the `descendant-or-self` axis. The `descendant` axis itself doesn't have an abbreviation, although often the `//` abbreviation ends up having that meaning; for example, `a//b` is equivalent to `a/descendant::b` (but only because its actual expansion, `a/descendant-or-self::node()/b`, happens to reduce to that).

Listing B.73 `descendant` axis examples

```
count(descendant::*)
count(descendant::comment())
x[descendant::y]/descendant::z
```

The `descendant` axis can have surprising results when it matches nodes contained in other matched nodes. In this case, both the containing node (including all its content) and the contained node are selected. The contained node will thus appear more than once in the output (once in the selection, and once in each other selected node that contains it).

Listing B.74 `descendant` can select nodes contained in other selected nodes

```
(<a><b id="1"><b id="2"/></b></a>)/descendant::b
=>
<b id="1"><b id="2"/></b><b id="2"/>
```

See also: Chapter 3, and `//` (navigation operator), `attribute`, `child`, `descendant-or-self`, `parent`, and `self` in this appendix.

descendant-or-self

Navigation axis that selects descendant nodes (and the current node itself).

```
descendant-or-self::nodetest
```

The `descendant-or-self` axis matches all descendants (element, text, comment, and processing-instruction nodes) of the current context node, and also the node itself. The node test can be used to filter this selection further, for example, matching only those with a particular name or node kind. Note that the `descendant-or-self` axis includes the current node itself; to exclude it, use the `descendant` axis.

The `descendant-or-self` axis itself can be abbreviated using `//`, which actually stands for `/descendant-or-self::node()/`. Because this abbreviation involves multiple steps, predicates applied to the step after it may not have the meaning you expect. For example, `//x` selects every x element in the current document. However, `//x[1]` doesn't select the first x element in the current document. Instead, `//x[1]` expands to `/descendant-or-self::node()/x[1]`, which first matches every node in the current document (including the document node itself) and then for each one selects the first child element named x. Depending on the document, this can result in a single x element or many. To select the first x element in the entire document, you would need to use `(//x)[1]`.

Listing B.75 `descendant-or-self` axis examples

```
count(//*)
count(//comment())
x[.//y]//z
x[descendant-or-self::node()/y]/descendant-or-self::node()/z
```

Like the `descendant` axis, the `descendant-or-self` axis can have surprising results when it matches nodes contained in other matched nodes. In this case, both the containing node (including all its content) and the contained node are selected. The contained node will thus appear more than once in the serialized output (once in the selection, and once in each other selected node that contains it). For example, the query in Listing B.76 selects the outer b element with `id="1"` followed by the inner b element with `id="2"`. The inner element also appears a second time in the output, as the child of the outer element.

Listing B.76 `descendant-or-self` can seem to select duplicate nodes

```
(<a><b id="1"><b id="2"/></b></a>)//b
=>
<b id="1"><b id="2"/></b><b id="2"/>
```

See also: Chapter 3; // (navigation operator); `attribute`, `child`, `descendant`, `parent`, and `self` in this appendix; and Chapter 11.

descending

Sort in decreasing order.
See the entry for FLWOR in this appendix.

div

Divide two expressions.

expr `div` *expr*

In XQuery, like XPath 1.0, division is expressed using the `div` keyword, not slash (/). Slash is used for paths.

Like all arithmetic operators, `div` first atomizes both operands. If either sequence of atomic values is empty, then it returns the empty sequence. If either sequence contains more than one value, then it raises an error. Otherwise, if either operand is type `xdt:untypedAtomic`, it is converted to `xs:double`. If both operands are numeric, then they are promoted to a common type (see Appendix A). No other type conversions are performed; the two operands must support division or an error is raised.

On numeric types, the result of division is always `xs:double`. To perform integer division, either use the `idiv` operator or else one of the rounding functions (`floor()`, `ceiling()`, `round()`, and `round-to-even()`).

Note that when using floating-point types, division by zero doesn't result in an error. Instead, it results in a special double value (positive infinity, negative infinity, or not-a-number).

Listing B.77 Division examples

```
1 div 2                      => 0.5
1E0 div 2                    => 5E-1
1 div 0                      => error (: division by zero :)
1E0 div 0                    => INF
1 div xdt:untypedAtomic("2") => 5E-1
1 div "2"                    => error (: operand is not numeric :)
```

Division is asymmetrical. In the list below, the operand types must occur in the order given (left to right). The pairs of types that support division are:

- Both numeric types (`xs:decimal`, `xs:double`, and `xs:float`, and subtypes of these). When both operands are `xs:integer`, `div` returns `xs:decimal`.
- `xdt:yearMonthDuration` and `xs:decimal` (resulting in `xdt:yearMonthDuration`).
- `xdt:dayTimeDuration` and `xs:decimal` (resulting in `xdt:dayTimeDuration`).

All others raise an error.

See also: Chapter 5; `idiv`, `mod`, * (multiplication), - (subtraction), + (addition), and / (slash) in this appendix; and the section "Atomization" in Chapter 2.

document (constructor)

Construct a document node with computed content.

```
document { expr }
```

XQuery provides only one way to construct a document node in the query: The `document` constructor, which takes a single argument, the content of the document node.

Each item in the content sequence is processed as follows:

- Element, processing-instruction, text, and comment nodes are deep-copied. Element nodes copied in this way are typed as `xs:anyType`, and attribute nodes copied in this way are typed as `xs:anySimpleType`, even if the originals had more specific types.
- Sequences of atomic values are converted into text nodes as if by the text constructor (the values are converted to string and separated by spaces).
- All other items (i.e., document and attribute nodes) result in an error.

The resulting sequence of items (possibly empty) is the content of the constructed document node. The document constructor does not enforce XML well-formedness rules (such as that the document must contain exactly one element node), although some implementations may enforce them anyway (during serialization, or before).

Listing B.78 Computed `document` constructor examples

```
document { () }
document { <root>{ doc("foo.xml") } </root> }
```

The `document` constructor is most useful in situations where you want to change the schema types of nodes, or when you want to create an entire XML document (as if by the `doc()` function). Use the `validate` operator to apply more specific types to the constructed document.

See also: Chapter 7, and `attribute` (constructor), `element` (constructor), `text` (constructor), and `validate` in this appendix.

---

e

Exponential notation in double-precision floating-point literals.

See the entry for E notation in this appendix.

E notation

Exponential notation in double-precision floating-point literals.

```
decimalEinteger
decimalE+integer
decimalE-integer
```

XQuery uses "scientific E-notation" to indicate that a number is a double-precision floating-point number (instead of an integer or decimal).

`E` notation can be written using either a lowercase or uppercase E followed by an exponent (which can be positive or negative; if no sign is provided, then the exponent is positive). The result is the number in front of the E times ten raised to the exponent power. For example, `1.0e2` is 100, while `1.0E-2` is one one-hundredth (.01).

Listing B.79 E notation examples

```
1.0e2
1.0e+2
1.0E+2
2.34e+0
56E-2
```

See also: Chapter 1, and `xs:double` in Appendix A.

element (constructor)

Element constructor with computed name and content.

```
element name { expr }
element { expr } { expr }
```

The computed `element` constructor takes two arguments: the name and the content. The name expression can be an ordinary name, or an expression (enclosed in curly braces) that computes the name. Elements with constant names can be constructed using the ordinary XML syntax (`<name>{con-tent}</name>`), so the computed name case is the one that more commonly uses the computed `element` constructor.

When the name is computed, the name expression must result in either an `xs:QName` value or else an `xs:string` value, which is then parsed into a QName using the in-scope namespaces. If the name cannot be parsed or isn't a QName, then an error is raised. Otherwise, the resulting QName value is the name of the element.

Each item in the (possibly empty) content expression is handled as follows:

- Nodes are deep-copied. Element nodes copied in this way are typed as `xs:anyType`, and attribute nodes copied in this way are typed as `xs:anySimpleType`, even if the originals had more specific types.
- Sequences of atomic values are converted into text nodes as if by the text constructor (the values are converted to string and separated by spaces).
- Document nodes aren't allowed in the content (resulting in an error).
- Attribute nodes aren't allowed after any other node kinds. Attributes at the start of the content sequence become attributes of the constructed element, and an error is raised if any two of them have the same name.

The resulting sequence of items (possibly empty) is the content of the constructed element node.

Unlike the computed `document` constructor, the computed `element` constructor implicitly validates its content (and therefore also enforces XML well-formedness rules), using the current validation mode and validation context. When the element name is constant, it is added to the validation context; otherwise, the validation context is set to `global`. If there aren't any types in scope, then the constructed element type is `xs:anyType`.

Listing B.80 Computed `element` constructor examples

```
element foo { () }                       => <foo/>
element { concat("a", "b") } { "c", "d", 3 } => <ab>c d 3</ab>
```

See also: Chapter 7, and `attribute` (constructor), `comment` (constructor), `declare validation`, `document` (constructor), `namespace` (constructor), `pi` (constructor), and `text` (constructor) in this appendix.

else

False branch of a conditional statement.
  See the entry for `if` in this appendix.

empty greatest

Treat the empty sequence as having the greatest order when sorting.
  See the entry for FLWOR in this appendix.

empty least

Treat the empty sequence as having the lowest order when sorting.
  See the entry for FLWOR in this appendix.

eq

Value comparison operator tests whether the first operand is equal to the second.

expr eq *expr*

The `eq` operator takes two operands, which can be arbitrary expressions. It first atomizes both operands; an error is raised if the atomized operands aren't single atomic values. If either atomized operand is type `xdt:untypedAtomic`, then it is cast to `xs:string`.

Then `eq` returns true if the first operand is equal to the second. If the two operands aren't comparable types, then an error is raised. See Chapter 5 for details.

Listing B.81 eq examples

```
2 eq 1.0                 => false
2 eq 2.0                 => true
"10" eq 2                => error
"10" eq "2"              => false (: depends on default collation :)
```

See also: Chapter 5; the section "Atomization" in Chapter 2; and = (equals sign), ne, is, gt, ge, lt, and le in this appendix.

every

Test whether every item in a sequence satisfies a condition.

```
every $var in expr satisfies expr
every $var in expr, $var2 in expr2, ... satisfies expr
```

The every operator performs universal quantification; that is, it tests whether every item satisfies a condition. It takes one or more variable clauses separated by commas. Each of these introduces a variable into scope for the remainder of the every expression, and causes that variable to range over some sequence. The condition expression is specified after the keyword satisfies at the end of the expression. The result is true if every variable assignment causes the condition expression to evaluate to true.

Listing B.82 every examples

```
every $i in (1, 2, 3) satisfies $i >= 4                   => false
every $i in (1, 2, 3) satisfies $i < 4                    => true
every $i in (1, 2), $j in (3, 4) satisfies $i * $j = 10   => false
every $i in (1, 2), $j in (3, 4) satisfies $i * $j = 8    => false
```

The every operator can be expressed less conveniently using exists() and FLWOR. For example, every $var1 in $expr1, $var2 in $expr2, ... satisfies $condition is equivalent to the double-negated expression not(exists(for $var1 in $expr1, $var2 in $expr2, ... where not($condition) return 1)).

See also: Chapter 6, and FLOWR and some in this appendix.

except

Compute the set difference of two node sequences.

node* except *node**

The `except` operator takes two operands, which must be node sequences (possibly empty). It returns all the nodes that are in the first sequence but not in the second (using node identity to determine equality), and sorts the resulting node sequence by document order.

Listing B.83 except example

```
let $a := <a/>, $b := <b/>, $c := <c/>
return ($a, $b) except ($b, $c)
=>
  $a
```

Unlike the set intersection and union operators, the set difference operator is asymmetric. The symmetric set difference (all the nodes that are in one of the two sets but not in both) can be computed using either of the two expressions in Listing B.84.

Listing B.84 Two ways to compute the symmetric difference of two node sets $a and $b

```
($a except $b) union ($b except $a)
($a union $b) except ($a intersect $b)
```

See also: Chapter 5, and `intersect` and `union` in this appendix.

extension

An instruction to the implementation that must be supported.
See the entry for `(::` (pragma/extension) in this appendix.

external

Specify that a function or variable is defined externally to the XQuery.
See the entries for `declare function` and `declare variable` in this appendix.

FLWOR

Construct and filter a tuple space with variables, and return a result (possibly ordered).

```
for $var1 in $expr1 at $pos1, $var2 in $expr2, ...
let $v1 := $e1, $v2:= $e2, ...
where condition
stable? order by sortkey1 modifier1, sortkey2 modifier2, ...
return expr
```

where each modifier has any or all of the following parts (in order):

```
(ascending | descending)?
(empty (greatest | least))?
(collation stringliteral)?
```

The FLWOR ("flower") expression is the most complex, but also the most important, expression in XQuery. It is the only way to construct a sequence sorted in any order other than document order. It is also the most convenient way to introduce variables into scope or to join a sequence with others (or itself).

FLWOR uses one or more `for` and `let` clauses (in any order), an optional `where` clause, an optional `order by` clause, and a `return` clause. FLWOR gets its name from the first letters of these clauses (`for`, `let`, `where`, `order by`, `return`).

The `for` and `let` clauses construct what is known as a *tuple space*, which can be visualized as a matrix of columns and rows. Each variable introduced by a `for` or `let` is a column in the matrix. The `where` clause filters that tuple space, the `order by` clause sorts it, and then the `return` clause returns an item for each row remaining in the tuple space. The overall result is this filtered, sorted sequence of items.

for

Each `for` clause introduces one or more variables into scope, each iterating over sequences of zero or more items. The tuple space gets one row for each item in the cross-product of all the `for` clauses; consequently, if any of the `for` clauses iterate over an empty sequence, then the tuple space is empty. If there aren't any `for` clauses, then the tuple space consists of a single row.

Listing B.85 `for` clauses iterate over sequences

```
for $i in (1, 2), $j in (3, 4, 5)
for $k in (6, 7)
return ($i, $j, $k)
=>
(1, 3, 6, 1, 3, 7, 1, 4, 6, 1, 4, 7, 1, 5, 6, 1, 5, 7,
 2, 3, 6, 2, 3, 7, 2, 4, 6, 2, 4, 7, 2, 5, 6, 2, 5, 7)
```

Each `for` variable may optionally introduce an additional position variable using the keyword `at`. Each position variable tracks the position of the `for` variable as it iterates through the sequence, as shown in Listing B.86.

Listing B.86 Position variables track position for each `for` clause independently

```
for $i in ("a", "b", "c") at $pos
return ($i, $pos)
=>
("a", 1, "b", 2, "c", 3)
```

let

Each `let` clause introduces one or more variables into scope, binding them to values. Unlike the `for` clauses, the `let` clauses don't contribute to the rows of the tuple space.

Listing B.87 `let` assigns variables to values instead of iterating over them

```
let $i := ("x", "y", "z")
return count($i)
=>
3

for $i in ("x", "y", "z")
return count($i)
=>
(1, 1, 1)
```

The `let` clause is most commonly used when an expression is used several times. However, note that variables preserve node identity, and so they aren't quite the same as writing the expression twice.

Listing B.88 Variables preserve identity

```
let $x := <x/>    (: constructs one node :)
return $x is $x
=>
true

<x/> is <x/>    (: constructs two nodes :)
=>
false
```

Variables introduced using `for` and `let` clauses are in scope for all remaining expressions, including later `for` and `let` clauses, as shown in Listing B.89.

Listing B.89 Variables are in scope for the rest of the FLWOR, even other `for`/`let` clauses

```
for $i in (1, 2, 3) at $p
let $j := $i * $p
for $k in ($i, $j)
return $k
=>
(1, 1, 2, 4, 3, 9)
```

where

The `where` clause specifies a condition expression, which is converted to a boolean value using the Effective Boolean Value rule (see Chapter 2). If no `where` clause is given, then the condition is always true. The condition is evaluated once for each row in the tuple space, before the `order by` clause is applied, and only those rows for which the condition is true are kept.

Listing B.90 The `where` clause filters the tuple space

```
for $i in ("a", "b", "c", "d") at $p
where $p > 2
return $i
=>
("c", "d")
```

In this way, the `where` clause is very similar to a predicate applied to a path. The `where` clause is especially useful for joining two or more sequences according to some conditions, as shown in Listing B.91.

Listing B.91 FLWOR is commonly used to join sequences

```
for $i in ("a", "b", "c", "d") at $pos
for $j in (6, 3, 1, 2)
where $pos = $j
return $i
=>
"c", "a", "b"
```

order by

The `order by` clause sorts the rows of the filtered tuple space (after the `where` clause is applied). It takes a list of one or more sort keys, and uses these to sort the expression.

Listing B.92 `order by` sorts the filtered tuple space

```
for $i in ("a", "b", "c", "d") at $p
where $p > 2
order by $p descending  (: sorting occurs after filtering :)
return $i
=>
("d", "c")
```

Additionally, each sort key may specify modifiers that control how it affects the sort order. These modifiers may specify a direction (`ascending` or `descending`; `ascending` is the default), a collation to use for sorting strings (`collation "name"`; the default collation is used if no other is specified), and whether empty sequences should sort first or last (`empty least` or `empty greatest`; the default is implementation-defined). The entire `order by` clause can also require the ordering to be `stable` (the default is implementation-defined). Complete explanations of these modifiers are given in Chapter 6.

return

Finally, the `return` clause constructs a result for each row in the filtered, sorted tuple space. If the `return` clause itself is a sequence, then the sequences are all combined in order and then flattened to produce a single sequence result.

Listing B.93 The `return` clause constructs a result for each row in the tuple space

```
for $i in ("a", "b", "c", "d")
for $j in (4, 1, 3, 2, 4)
where $i = $j
return <x y="{$i}"/>
=>
<x y="d"/>
<x y="a"/>
<x y="c"/>
<x y="b"/>
<x y="d"/>
```

See also: Chapter 6; `every`, `some`, and `$` (variable) in this appendix; and the section "Effective Boolean Value" in Chapter 2.

following

Navigation axis that selects nodes after the current context in document order.

```
following::nodetest
```

The `following` axis matches all nodes that are in the same document as the current context node and come after it in document order. The node test can be used to filter these nodes further, for example, matching only those with a particular name or node kind. XQuery implementations aren't required to support the `following` axis.

Listing B.94 `following` axis examples

```
count(following::*)
x[following::y]/following::z
```

See also: Chapter 3, and `following-sibling`, `preceding`, `preceding-sib-ling`, `>>` (after), and `<<` (before) in this appendix.

following-sibling

Navigation axis that selects all siblings after the current node in document order.

```
following-sibling::nodetest
```

The `following-sibling` axis matches all siblings of the current context node that come after it in document order. XQuery implementations aren't required to support the `following-sibling` axis.

Listing B.95 `following-sibling` axis examples

```
following-sibling::foo/bar
count(following-sibling::*)
```

See also: Chapter 3, and `following`, `preceding`, `preceding-sibling`, `>>` (after), and `<<` (before) in this appendix.

for

Introduce a variable.
See the entry for FLWOR in this appendix.

ge

Value comparison operator tests whether one value is greater than or equal to another.

```
expr ge expr
```

The `ge` operator takes two operands, which can be arbitrary expressions. It first atomizes both operands; an error is raised if the atomized operands aren't single atomic values. If either atomized operand is type `xdt:untypedAtomic`, then it is cast to `xs:string`.

Then, `ge` returns true if the first operand is greater than or equal to the second. If the two operands aren't comparable types, then an error is raised. See Chapter 5 for details.

Listing B.96 ge examples

```
2 ge 1.0              => true
2 ge 2.0              => true
"10" ge 2             => error
"10" ge "2"           => false (: depends on default collation :)
```

See also: Chapter 5; the section "Atomization" in Chapter 2; and >= (greater than or equal to), gt, lt, le, eq, and ne in this appendix.

global

Specify a schema context.

See the entry for validate in this appendix.

gt

Value comparison operator tests whether one value is greater than another.

expr gt *expr*

The gt operator takes two operands, which can be arbitrary expressions. It first atomizes both operands; an error is raised if the atomized operands aren't single atomic values. If either atomized operand is type xdt:untypedAtomic, then it is cast to xs:string.

Then gt returns true if the first operand is greater than the second. If the two operands aren't comparable types, then an error is raised. See Chapter 5 for details.

Listing B.97 gt examples

```
2 gt 1.0              => true
2 gt 2.0              => false
"10" gt 2             => error
"10" gt "2"           => false (: depends on default collation :)
```

See also: Chapter 5; the section "Atomization" in Chapter 2; and > (greater-than sign), ge, lt, le, eq, and ne in this appendix.

idiv

Divide two integers.

expr idiv *expr*

The idiv operator performs integer division on two integer values. Like all arithmetic operators, idiv first atomizes both operands. If either sequence of atomic values is empty, then it returns the empty sequence. If either sequence contains more than one value, then it raises an error.

Otherwise, if either operand is type xdt:untypedAtomic, it is converted to xs:integer. No other type conversions are performed; the two operands must both be xs:integer (or a subtype of it) or else an error is raised.

Listing B.98 Integer division examples

```
1 idiv 2                      => 0
1E0 idiv 2                    => error (: operand not integer :)
1 idiv 0                      => error (: division by zero :)
1 idiv xdt:untypedAtomic("2") => 0
1 idiv "2"                    => error (: operand not integer :)
```

See also: Chapter 5; div, mod, * (multiplication), - (subtraction), + (addition), and / (slash) in this appendix; the section "Atomization" in Chapter 2; and fn:round() in Appendix C.

if

Choose an expression based on a condition.

if (*expr*) then *expr* else *expr*

The if operator takes a conditional expression (in parentheses) and two branch expressions. If the condition is true, then the first branch (then) is the result; if the condition is false, then the second branch (else) is the result.

The condition can be any expression at all; if converts it to a boolean value by applying the Effective Boolean Value rule.

Listing B.99 `if` examples

```
if (true()) then "1" else 1.0          => "1"
if (1 < 2 and 2 < 3) then "x" else "y" => "x"
```

Conditionals can be chained together one after another, as shown in Listing B.100, but a final `else` branch is always required.

Listing B.100 Conditionals can be chained together

```
if ($x) then 1
else if ($y) then 2
else if ($z) then 3
else 0
```

See also: Chapter 5; the section "Effective Boolean Value" in Chapter 2; and FLWOR, `typeswitch`, and `[` (left square bracket) in this appendix.

import module

Import a module (prolog only).

```
import module target;
import module target at locationHint;
import module namespace NCName = target;
import module namespace NCName = target at locationHint;
```

A module import includes all the functions and variables defined in another module (the *target module*) into the current one (the *source module*). All other definitions, such as namespace declarations, are not imported. Modules may import any number of other modules.

Each module import names the target namespace of the target module; the namespace must be a string literal. Optionally, a module import may assign a namespace prefix to this namespace (with the same effect as `declare namespace`) and/or may provide a location hint to the implementation. The location hint must be a string literal.

Each module has its own independent static context. If any of the imported functions or variables already exists in the source module, an error is raised. When the target module is imported, none of the modules that it has imported are imported with it. (For example, if module X imports module Y, and module

Y imports module Z, then module X has not imported module Z without a separate `import module` statement.)

Moreover, all of the "public" types—that is, the return type and parameter types of functions, and the types of global variables—that are used by the target module must be already available in the source module. For example, if X imports module Y, and Y has a function that uses type T as its return type or a parameter type, or has a global variable of type T, then T must be already defined in X.

Listing B.101 `import module` examples

```
import module "urn:foo";
import module x = "urn:bar";
```

See also: The section "Query Prolog" in Chapter 5, the section "Modules" in Chapter 4, and `module` in this appendix.

import schema

Import the types from a schema (prolog only).

```
import schema uri;
import schema uri at string;
import schema namespace prefix = uri;
import schema namespace prefix = uri at string;
import schema default element namespace uri;
import schema default element namespace uri at string;
```

The `import schema` prolog instruction has several different forms. The most basic one takes a string argument that specifies the target namespace of the schema; the implementation must know how to locate the given schema. Optionally, you may also specify the schema location (which may be ignored by the implementation). The effect is to load those schema types into the given target namespace.

The most common use of `import schema` is to accomplish two tasks at once: declare a namespace prefix and import the schema for that namespace. This is done by writing `import schema prefix = namespace` (and again optionally specifying a schema location, which may be ignored by the implementation). To use the namespace as the default element namespace, use the keywords `default element namespace` instead of a prefix. These different forms are illustrated in Listing B.102.

Listing B.102 `import schema` examples

```
import schema "urn:foo";
import schema "urn:foo" at "http://www.w3c.org/foo.xsd";
import schema x = "urn:foo" at "http://www.w3c.org/foo.xsd";
import schema default element namespace "urn:foo";
```

See also: The section "Query Prolog" in Chapter 5, the section "Validation" in Chapter 9, and `validate` in this appendix.

in

Used in variable definitions.

See the entries for `every`, FLWOR, and `some` in this appendix.

instance of

Test whether an expression matches a given type.

expr `instance of` *sequencetype*

The `instance of` operator takes an expression and a sequence type, and performs sequence type matching. If the value matches the type, then `instance of` returns true, otherwise it returns false.

Listing B.103 `instance of` examples

```
<x/> instance of element()        => true
<x/> instance of xs:integer       => false
(1, 2, 3) instance of xs:integer* => true
() instance of xs:integer*        => true
() instance of xs:integer+        => false
```

See also: Chapter 9; `castable as`, `treat as`, and `typeswitch` in this appendix; and the section "Sequence Type Matching" in Chapter 2.

intersect

Compute the set intersection of two node sequences.

node* `intersect` *node**

The `intersect` operator takes two operands, which must be node sequences (possibly empty). It returns all the nodes that are in both sequences (using node identity to determine equality), and returns the resulting node sequence sorted in document order.

Listing B.104 `intersect` examples

```
let $a := <a/>, $b := <b/>, $c := <c/>
return ($a, $b) intersect ($b, $c)
=>
  $b
```

See also: Chapter 5, and `except` and `union` in this appendix.

is

Test whether two nodes are the same (by identity).

node? is *node?*

The node comparison operator `is` takes two operands, each of which must be either a single node or the empty sequence or else a type error is raised. If either operand is empty, then `is` returns the empty sequence. Otherwise, `is` returns true if the two nodes are the same (by identity) and otherwise false.

Listing B.105 `is` examples

```
() is ()                        => ()
doc("foo.xml") is doc("foo.xml") => true
<x/> is <x/>                    => false
let $x := <x/> return $x is $x  => true
```

See also: Chapter 5 and `fn:deep-equal()` in Appendix C.

lax

A validation mode.

See the entries for `declare validation` and `validate` in this appendix.

le

Value comparison operator tests whether one value is less than or equal to another.

expr le *expr*

The le operator takes two operands, which can be arbitrary expressions. It first atomizes both operands; an error is raised if the atomized operands aren't single atomic values. If either atomized operand is type xdt:untypedAtomic, then it is cast to xs:string.

Then le returns true if the first operand is less than or equal to the second. If the two operands aren't comparable types, then an error is raised. See Chapter 5 for details.

Listing B.106 le examples

```
2 le 1.0             => false
2 le 2.0             => true
"10" le 2            => error
"10" le "2"          => true (: depends on default collation :)
```

See also: Chapter 5; the section "Atomization" in Chapter 2; and <= (less than or equal to), ge, gt, lt, eq, and ne in this appendix.

let

Introduce a variable.

See the entry for FLWOR in this appendix.

lt

Value comparison operator tests whether the first operand is less than the second.

expr lt *expr*

The lt operator takes two operands, which can be arbitrary expressions. It first atomizes both operands; an error is raised if the atomized operands aren't single atomic values. If either atomized operand is type xdt:untypedAtomic, then it is cast to xs:string.

Then, `lt` returns true if the first operand is less than the second. If the two operands aren't comparable types, then an error is raised. See Chapter 5 for details.

Listing B.107 `lt` examples

```
2 lt 1.0              => false
2 lt 2.0              => false
"10" lt 2             => error
"10" lt "2"           => true (: depends on default collation :)
```

See also: Chapter 5; the section "Atomization" in Chapter 2; and < (less than sign), `ge`, `gt`, `le`, `eq`, and `ne` in this appendix.

mod

Compute the modulo of one number with another.

expr mod *expr*

The `mod` operator performs modulo arithmetic on two numbers. Like all arithmetic operators, `mod` first atomizes both operands. If either sequence of atomic values is empty, then it returns the empty sequence. If either sequence contains more than one value, then it raises an error.

Otherwise, `mod` performs truncating division and returns the remainder. The sign of the result is the same as the sign of the left expression.

Formally, the expression `lhs mod rhs` returns the value x such that `(lhs tdiv rhs)*rhs + x` equals `lhs` and the absolute value of x is less than the absolute value of `rhs`, where `tdiv` means truncating division (truncating the result to an integer value). If either operand is `NaN`, or if the left expression is infinite or the right expression is zero, then the result is `NaN`. Otherwise, if the right expression is infinite then the result is the left expression is unchanged.

Listing B.108 `mod` examples

```
4 mod 3                         => 1
4 mod 3.0                       => 1.0
4E0 mod 3                       => 1E0
4E0 mod 0                       => NaN
4 mod xdt:untypedAtomic("3")    => 1E0
4 mod "3"                       => error (: operand not numeric :)
```

See also: Chapter 5; `div`, `idiv`, `*` (multiplication) , `+` (addition) , and `-` (subtraction) in this appendix; and the section "Atomization" in Chapter 2.

module

Declare this query to be a library module (prolog only).

```
module namespace prefix = "targetNamespace";
```

The module declaration indicates that a query is a library module (instead of the main module). Library modules aren't evaluated directly, but may define functions and variables for other modules to use. The module declaration is mutually exclusive with the query body; a query can have one but not the other.

The module declaration requires a prefix and namespace (which must be a string literal). This is the target namespace of the module, and also its default function namespace. All variables and functions defined in the module must belong to this namespace, or else an error is raised.

Library modules may import other library modules using `import module`.

Listing B.109 `module` example

```
module namespace foo = "urn:bar";
```

See also: The section "Query Prolog" in Chapter 5, the section "Modules" in Chapter 4, and `import module` in this appendix.

namespace (constructor)

Namespace constructor with computed content.

```
namespace prefix { expr }
```

The computed namespace constructor takes a prefix (which cannot be computed) and an enclosed expression, which is computed to produce the namespace uri. It constructs a namespace node binding the prefix to that namespace.

The content expression is processed the same as with the computed comment constructor: First, it is first atomized. If the resulting sequence is empty, then the content is the empty string. Otherwise, each atomic value is cast to `xs:string`, concatenated together with a space character in between each consecutive pair, and the final result becomes the namespace value.

Computed namespace nodes can be used only in `element` constructors (computed or direct).

Listing B.110 Computed namespace constructor example

```
namespace foo { "urn:bar" }  => xmlns:foo="urn:bar"
```

See also: Chapter 7, and `attribute` (constructor), `comment` (constructor), `document` (constructor), `element` (constructor), `pi` (constructor), and `text` (constructor) in this appendix.

namespace

See the entries for `declare default element namespace`, `declare default function namespace`, `declare namespace`, `import module`, `import schema`, and `namespace` (constructor) in this appendix.

ne

Value comparison operator tests whether one value is not equal to another.

```
expr ne expr
```

The `ne` operator takes two operands, which can be arbitrary expressions. It first atomizes both operands; an error is raised if the atomized operands aren't single atomic values. If either atomized operand is type `xdt:untypedAtomic`, then it is cast to `xs:string`.

Then `ne` returns true if the first operand is not equal to the second. If the two operands aren't comparable types, then an error is raised. See Chapter 5 for details.

Listing B.111 ne examples

```
2 ne 1.0            => true
2 ne 2.0            => false
"10" ne 2           => error
"10" ne "2"         => true (: depends on default collation :)
```

See also: Chapter 5, the section "Atomization" in Chapter 2, and `!=` (inequality sign), `eq`, `ge`, `gt`, `le`, and `lt` in this appendix.

nillable

Specify that element content can be empty (xs:nillable="true").
See the entry for element() in Appendix A.

or

Logical operator tests whether either value is true.

expr or *expr*

The or operator first converts both of its operands to boolean using the
fn:boolean() function (Effective Boolean Value). If either operand is true,
then or returns true, otherwise it returns false.

Listing B.112 or examples

```
true() or false()        => true
"" or 0.0                => false
"x" or 1.0               => true
() or (false(), false()) => true
```

The order in which the or operator evaluates its arguments is implementation-dependent, and implementations are also allowed (and encouraged) to
"short-circuit" this operator (evaluating only one of its operands if that is
enough to determine the overall result). Consequently, expressions like
error() or true() and true() or error() may raise an error or may return
true, depending on the implementation.

See also: Chapter 5, and in this appendix, and fn:boolean() and fn:not()
in Appendix C.

order by

Sort a sequence.
See the entry for FLWOR in this appendix.

parent

Navigation axis that selects parent nodes.

parent::*nodetest*

The `parent` axis selects the parent node of the current context node (if it has a parent; the root document or element node does not, in which case the parent axis is empty). The node test can be used to filter the parent further, for example, matching only those with a particular name or node kind.

It's common practice to abbreviate the `parent` axis with two periods (`..`), like file systems use to navigate to the parent directory. The abbreviation expands to `parent::node()`.

Listing B.113 `parent` axis examples

```
count(parent::node())
x/parent::node()
x/..
```

See also: Chapter 3, and `..` (parent navigation), `.` (dot), `attribute`, `child`, `descendant`, `descendant-or-self`, and `self` in this appendix.

Listing B.114 Computed processing instruction constructor examples

```
processing-instruction { "foo" }           => <? foo?>
processing-instruction { "foo" } { "bar" } => <?foo bar?>
```

See also: Chapter 7, and `attribute` (constructor), `comment` (constructor), `document` (constructor), `element` (constructor), `namespace` (constructor), and `text` (constructor) in this appendix.

pragma

An instruction to the implementation that may be ignored.
See the entry for `(::` (pragma/extension) in this appendix.

preceding

Navigation axis that selects nodes before the current context in document order.

```
preceding::nodetest
```

The `preceding` axis matches all nodes in the same document as the current context node and comes before it in document order. The node test can be used to filter these nodes further, for example, matching only those with a particular name or node kind. XQuery implementations aren't required to support the `preceding` axis.

Listing B.115 `preceding` axis examples

```
count(preceding::*)
x[preceding::y]/preceding::z
```

See also: Chapter 3, and `following`, `following-sibling`, `preceding-sibling`, >> (after), and << (before) in this appendix.

preceding-sibling

Navigation axis that selects all siblings before the current node in document order.

```
preceding-sibling::nodetest
```

The `preceding-sibling` axis matches all siblings of the current context node that come before it in document order. XQuery implementations aren't required to support the `preceding-sibling` axis.

Listing B.116 `preceding-sibling` axis examples

```
preceding-sibling::foo/bar
count(preceding-sibling::*)
```

See also: Chapter 3, and `following`, `following-sibling`, `preceding`, >> (after), and << (before) in this appendix.

preserve

An XML space mode.
See the entry for `declare xmlspace` in this appendix.

pi (constructor)

Processing instruction constructor with computed content.

```
processing-instruction { expr }
processing-instruction { expr } { expr }
```

The computed processing instruction constructor takes one or two enclosed expressions, and uses them to construct a processing instruction node. If two expressions are given, then the first one is used to compute the processing instruction target. The other expression is the string content of the processing instruction.

The name expression, if any, must either return a qualified name (`xs:QName`) or a string that can be converted to `xs:QName`.

The content expression is processed the same as with the computed comment constructor: First, the value is first atomized. If the resulting sequence is empty, then the content is the empty string. Otherwise, each atomic value is cast to `xs:string`, concatenated together with a space character in between each consecutive pair, to produce the final content result.

return

Specify the result of certain complex expressions.

See the entries for FLWOR and `typeswitch` in this appendix.

satisfies

The condition clause in a quantification.

See the entries for `every` and `some` in this appendix.

self

Navigation axis that selects at most the current node.

```
self::nodetest
```

The `self` axis selects the current context node. The node test can be used to filter the context node, for example, matching only those with a particular name or node kind.

It's common practice to abbreviate the `self` axis with one period (`.`), like file systems use to navigate to the current directory. In XPath 1.0, this abbreviation expands to `self::node()`; however, in XQuery, `.` selects the current context item (which may or may not be a node).

At first glance, the `self` axis may appear useless, but actually it is very helpful in predicates, where it can be used to navigate relative to the current context node, or access its value. It is also sometimes useful for testing the node kind or the name of the current context node.

Listing B.117 `self` axis examples

```
x[.//y] (: .//y is a relative path, starting from the current node :)
x[//y]  (: //y is an absolute path, starting from the root :)
x[data(.) = 1]
self::comment()
```

See also: Chapter 3, and . (current context item), `attribute`, `child`, `descendant`, `descendant-or-self`, and `parent` in this appendix.

skip

A validation mode.

See the entries for `declare validation` and `validate` in this appendix.

some

Test whether some item in a sequence satisfies a condition.

```
some $var in expr satisfies expr
some $var in expr, $var2 in expr2, ... satisfies expr
```

The `some` operator performs existential quantification; that is, it tests whether there exists an item satisfying a condition. It takes one or more variable clauses separated by commas. Each of these introduces a variable into scope for the remainder of the `some` expression, and causes that variable to range over some sequence. The condition expression is specified after the keyword `satisfies` at the end of the expression. The existence test checks whether there exists an assignment to all the variables such that the condition is true.

Listing B.118 `some` examples

```
some $i in (1, 2, 3) satisfies $i >= 4                => false
some $i in (1, 2, 3) satisfies $i < 4                 => true
some $i in (1, 2), $j in (3, 4) satisfies $i * $j = 10 => false
some $i in (1, 2), $j in (3, 4) satisfies $i * $j = 8  => true
```

The `some` operator can be expressed less conveniently using `exists()` and FLWOR. For example, `some $var1 in $expr1, $var2 in $expr2, ... satisfies $condition` is equivalent to the expression `exists(for $var1 in $expr1, $var2 in $expr2, ... where $condition return 1)`.

See also: Chapter 6, and FLWOR and `every` in this appendix.

stable

Specify that equal items should not have their relative ordering changed during sorting.

See the entry for FLWOR in this appendix.

strict

A validation mode.
See the entries for `declare validation` and `validate` in this appendix.

strip

An XML space mode.
See the entry for `declare xmlspace` in this appendix.

text (constructor)

Text constructor with computed content.

```
text { expr? }
```

The `text` constructor takes an optional argument, which is the content of the text node. It first atomizes the content. If the sequence is empty (or if the argument is omitted), then no text node is constructed and the result is the empty sequence. Otherwise, each atomic value is converted to string as if by using the `cast as` operator, and concatenated together by inserting spaces in between them. The resulting string value (which may be empty) is the content of the computed text node.

In other words, the expression `text { $X }` is equivalent to the much lengthier expression in Listing B.119

Listing B.119 An expression equivalent to `text { $X }`

```
if (empty($X)) then ()
else text { string-join(" ", for $i in data($X) return string($i) }
```

The `text` constructor is most useful in situations where you want absolute control over how XML is constructed, such as mixed-content elements. The `text` constructor can also be used to construct text nodes without an enclosing element.

Listing B.120 Computed `text` constructor examples

```
text { }                        => ()
text { () }                     => ()
text { 1, 2, 3 }                => text { "1 2 3" }
<x>{ <y/>, text { "zzz" } }</x> => <x><y/>zzz</x>
```

See also: Chapter 7, and `attribute` (constructor), `document` (constructor), and `element` (constructor) in this appendix.

then

The true branch of a conditional.

See the entry for `if` in this appendix.

to

Compute a range of integer values.

expr `to` *expr*

The range operator `to` takes two arguments, each of which is converted to `xs:integer` using function conversion rules (raising a conversion error if necessary).

The range operator then constructs the sequence of integers between the two arguments, inclusive. If the first argument is less than the second, then the sequence is increasing. If the first argument is greater than the second, then the sequence is empty. If the first argument is equal to the second, then the sequence contains only the one integer value.

Listing B.121 `to` examples

```
1 to 3 => (1, 2, 3)
3 to 1 => ()
3 to 3 => 3
xdt:untypedAtomic("-1") to xs:long(2) => (-1, 0, 1, 2)
```

See also: Chapter 5, and the section "Function Conversion Rules" in Chapter 4.

treat as

Change the type of an expression without changing its value.

expr `treat as` *sequencetype*

The `treat as` operator takes two arguments: an expression and a sequence type. If the expression value is an instance of the given type, then `treat as` returns the value unchanged; otherwise, an error is raised.

In other words, `treat as` is just a way to ensure that an expression has the correct static type. Unlike the `cast as` operator, `treat as` doesn't change the value or its type. In some languages, this is known as `down-casting`.

Listing B.122 `treat as` examples

```
2 treat as xs:decimal    => 2
2.0 treat as xs:integer => error

2 cast as xs:decimal     => 2.0
2.0 cast as xs:integer   => 2
```

See also: Chapter 9, `cast as` and `instance of` in this appendix, and the section "Sequence Type Matching" in Chapter 2.

type()

Specify schema context for validation.

See the entry for `validate` in this appendix.

typeswitch

Choose a value based on the type of an expression.

```
typeswitch (expr) caseClause+ defaultClause
```

where each `caseClause` is one of the two forms:

```
    case sequencetype return expr
case $var as sequencetype return expr
```

and the `defaultClause` is one of the two forms:

```
    defaultClause return expr
defaultClause $var return expr
```

The `typeswitch` operator takes an expression and then chooses the first case that matches its type (or the default branch if there isn't a match). The sequence type matching process is described in Appendix A.

Each case (including the default one) may optionally introduce a variable, which is bound to the original expression but more strongly typed using the type named in the case (in the default case, the variable's static type is the same as that of the original expression). The variable is in scope for the clause of that case only; multiple cases may use the same variable name.

Note that `typeswitch` requires at least one case and exactly one default branch. Also, don't forget that the comma operator has lower precedence than `typeswitch`, so the default case return clause must use parentheses to return a sequence of expressions.

Listing B.123 `typeswitch` examples

```
typeswitch (<hello/>)
  case $a as attribute return concat("a:", local-name($a))
  case $e as element return concat("e:", local-name($e))
  default return "x"
=>
"e:hello"

for $i in (1, <x/>, "2")
return typeswitch ($i)
        case xs:integer return "integer"
        case xs:decimal return "decimal"
        case xs:string  return "string"
        case node()     return "node"
        default         return error("unknown type")
=>
("integer", "node", "string")
```

The `typeswitch` operator is useful whenever you need to perform different actions for different item kinds, node kinds, or atomic types. For example, you can write a function that computes the built-in XQuery type name of an expression (see Listing B.124). The first matching case is used, so the order of the case clauses matters. In general, when using `typeswitch`, list subtypes first.

Listing B.124 A user-defined function for computing sequence type names

```
declare function sequence-type-of($expr) as xs:string {
    if (count($expr) > 1) then concat(single-type-of($expr), "+")
    else single-type-of($expr)
};

declare function single-type-of($expr) as xs:string {
    typeswitch ($expr)
        case empty()                    return "empty()"
```

```
    case element()*              return "element()"
    case attribute()*            return "attribute()"
    case text()*                 return "text()"
    case comment()*              return "comment()"
    case document-node()*        return "document-node()"
    case processing-instruction()* return "processing-instruction()"
    case node()*                 return "node()"
    case xdt:untypedAtomic*      return "xdt:untypedAtomic"
    case xs:unsignedByte*        return "xs:unsignedByte"
    case xs:unsignedShort*       return "xs:unsignedShort"
    case xs:unsignedInt*         return "xs:unsignedInt"
    case xs:unsignedLong*        return "xs:unsignedLong"
    case xs:positiveInteger*     return "xs:positiveInteger"
    case xs:nonNegativeInteger*  return "xs:nonNegativeInteger"
    case xs:byte*                return "xs:byte"
    case xs:short*               return "xs:short"
    case xs:int*                 return "xs:int"
    case xs:long*                return "xs:long"
    case xs:negativeInteger*     return "xs:negativeInteger"
    case xs:nonPositiveInteger*  return "xs:nonPositiveInteger"
    case xs:integer*             return "xs:integer"
    case xs:decimal*             return "xs:decimal"
    case xs:ENTITY*              return "xs:ENTITY"
    case xs:IDREF*               return "xs:IDREF"
    case xs:ID*                  return "xs:ID"
    case xs:NCName*              return "xs:NCName"
    case xs:Name*                return "xs:Name"
    case xs:NMTOKEN*             return "xs:NMTOKEN"
    case xs:language*            return "xs:language"
    case xs:token*               return "xs:token"
    case xs:normalizedString*    return "xs:normalizedString"
    case xs:string*              return "xs:string"
    case xdt:dayTimeDuration*    return "xdt:dayTimeDuration"
    case xdt:yearMonthDuration*  return "xdt:yearMonthDuration"
    case xs:duration*            return "xs:duration"
    case xs:NOTATION*            return "xs:NOTATION"
    case xs:QName*               return "xs:QName"
    case xs:anyURI*              return "xs:anyURI"
    case xs:double*              return "xs:double"
    case xs:float*              return "xs:float"
    case xs:hexBinary*           return "xs:hexBinary"
    case xs:base64Binary*        return "xs:base64Binary"
```

```
          case xs:boolean*              return "xs:boolean"
          case xs:date*                 return "xs:date"
          case xs:time*                 return "xs:time"
          case xs:dateTime*             return "xs:dateTime"
          case xs:gMonth*               return "xs:gMonth"
          case xs:gDay*                 return "xs:gDay"
          case xs:gMonthDay*            return "xs:gMonthDay"
          case xs:gYear*                return "xs:gYear"
          case xs:gYearMonth*           return "xs:gYearMonth"
          case xdt:anyAtomicType*       return "xdt:anyAtomicType"
          case xs:anySimpleType*        return "xs:anySimpleType"
          case xs:anyType*              return "xs:anyType"
          default                       return "item()"
    };
```

See also: Chapter 9; Appendix A; `fn:data()` in Appendix C, and `cast as`, `if`, `instance of`, and `validate` in this appendix.

union

Compute the set union of two node sequences.

node* union *node**

The `union` operator takes two operands, both of which must be node sequences (possibly empty). It combines both sequences, removes duplicate nodes (by node identity), and sorts the result in document order. The `union` operator can also be written as | (the vertical bar).

Listing B.125 union examples

```
let $a := <a/>, $b := <b/>, $c := <c/>
return ($a, $b) union ($b, $c)
=>
  ($a, $b, $c)


() | () => ()
```

See also: Chapter 5, and `except` and `intersect` in this appendix.

validate

Perform XML Schema validation on an expression.

```
validate mode context { node }
```

The `validate` operator specifies an optional schema mode, which must be either `lax`, `skip`, or `strict`. If the mode is omitted, then the default validation mode is used. (The default validation mode can be set using the `declare validation` declaration in the schema prolog.) The mode used becomes the default validation mode for all nested expressions.

The `validate` operator also specifies an optional schema context, which must be one of the following expressions: `global`, `type(qname)`, or a simple path starting with either a `qname` or `type(qname)` and followed by one or more `/qname` steps. If the context is omitted, then it defaults to `global`. The context used becomes the default validation context for all nested expressions.

The `validate` operator takes one operand, which is the expression to be validated (enclosed in curly braces). The expression must evaluate to exactly one document or element node.

The result of the `validate` expression is either the result of converting the operand into an XML Infoset, validating that infoset, and converting the validated result back into the XQuery Data Model, or else a type error (if the operand cannot be converted into a well-formed XML Infoset, or if a validation error occurs).

Listing B.126 validate examples

```
validate { <x>12</x> }
validate strict { <x>12</x> }
validate strict type(y)/z { <x>12</x> }
```

See also: Chapter 9; `cast as`, `declare validation`, and `typeswitch` in this appendix; and Appendix A.

version

See the entry for `xquery version` in this appendix.

where

Filter a sequence by a condition.

See the entry for FLWOR in this appendix.

xquery version

Version declaration (prolog only).

```
xquery version stringliteral;
```

The version declaration, if used, must appear before all the rest of the prolog. It takes one string argument, which is the version string. If omitted, the version defaults to the string value "1.0". An XQuery compiler must raise an error if the version string isn't supported by it.

The purpose of the version declaration is to provide a mechanism for compatibility with potential future versions of XQuery.

Listing B.127 xquery version example

```
xquery version "1.0";
```

Function Reference

C.1 Introduction

This appendix describes all of the built-in XQuery functions, listed alphabetically for convenient reference. Each function description begins with a one-line summary of the function's purpose followed by its function signature(s). Next comes an explanation of the arguments and their default values (if any), exceptional and error cases, and finally the function's normal behavior with examples. Each function is also cross-referenced to related functions.

The type syntax used in the function signature is the sequence type syntax described in Chapter 2 and Appendix A, with the same meaning. For example, `xs:string?` means zero or one string values.

All XQuery built-in functions belong to the default function namespace, `http://www.w3.org/2003/11/xpath-functions`, which is associated with the built-in namespace prefix `fn`. For example, the `true()` function can also be written `fn:true()`. For brevity, I omitted these prefixes everywhere except section headers.

In addition to the functions listed here, XQuery also defines constructor functions for the built-in types. See Chapter 2 and Appendix A for information.

fn:abs

Compute the absolute value of a number.

```
abs(numeric?) as numeric?
```

The return value has the same type as the argument.

If the argument is the empty sequence, then `abs()` returns the empty sequence. Otherwise, `abs()` returns the absolute value of the argument. (Negative values are negated, non-negative values are returned unchanged.)

Listing C.1 abs examples

```
abs(2)        => 2
abs(-2)       => 2
abs(-1.5)     => 1.5
abs(-1 div 0) => INF
```

See also: Chapter 5.

fn:adjust-date-to-timezone

Construct a date with a particular time zone value.

```
adjust-date-to-timezone(xs:date?) as xs:date?
adjust-date-to-timezone(xs:date?, xdt:dayTimeDuration?) as xs:date?
```

The first parameter is the date to be adjusted. The optional second parameter is the time zone to use; when omitted, the implicit time zone is used.

If the first argument is the empty sequence, then the empty sequence is returned. An error is raised if the time zone is less than -PT14H00M or greater than PT14H00M.

Otherwise, this function returns a date value with its time zone replaced by the provided time zone. If the provided time zone is the empty sequence, then the date is returned without a time zone (removing the time zone from the original date, if it had one).

Listing C.2 adjust-date-to-timezone example

```
adjust-date-to-timezone(xs:date('2004-05-13'),
                        xdt:dayTimeDuration('PT6H00M'))
```

See also: adjust-dateTime-to-timezone(), adjust-time-to-timezone(), and implicit-timezone().

fn:adjust-dateTime-to-timezone

Construct an xs:dateTime value with a particular time zone.

```
adjust-dateTime-to-timezone(xs:dateTime?) as xs:dateTime?
adjust-dateTime-to-timezone(xs:dateTime?, xdt:dayTimeDuration?)
                                        as xs:dateTime?
```

The first argument is the `xs:dateTime` value to be adjusted. The optional second argument is the time zone to use; when omitted, the implicit time zone is used.

If the first argument is the empty sequence, then the empty sequence is returned. An error is raised if the time zone is less than `-PT14H00M` or greater than `PT14H00M`.

Otherwise, this function returns a dateTime value with its time zone replaced by the provided time zone. If the provided time zone is the empty sequence, then the dateTime is returned without a time zone (removing the time zone from the original dateTime, if it had one).

Listing C.3 `adjust-dateTime-to-timezone` example

```
adjust-dateTime-to-timezone(xs:dateTime('2004-05-13T09:55:00'),
                    xdt:dayTimeDuration('PT6H00M'))
```

See also: `adjust-date-to-timezone()`, `adjust-time-to-timezone()`, and `implicit-timezone()`.

fn:adjust-time-to-timezone

Construct a time with a particular time zone value.

```
adjust-time-to-timezone(xs:time?) as xs:time?
adjust-time-to-timezone(xs:time?, xdt:dayTimeDuration?) as xs:time?
```

The `adjust-time-to-timezone` function can be used to construct a time with a particular time zone value.

The first argument is the time to be adjusted. The optional second argument is the time zone to use; when omitted, the implicit time zone is used.

If the first argument is the empty sequence, then the empty sequence is returned. An error is raised if the time zone is less than `-PT14H00M` or greater than `PT14H00M`.

Otherwise, this function returns a time value with its time zone replaced by the provided time zone. If the provided time zone is the empty sequence, then the time is returned without a time zone (removing the time zone from the original time, if it had one).

Listing C.4 `adjust-time-to-timezone` example

```
adjust-time-to-timezone(xs:time('09:55:00'),
                        xdt:dayTimeDuration('PT6H00M'))
```

See also: `adjust-date-to-timezone()`, `adjust-dateTime-to-time-zone()`, and `implicit-timezone()`.

fn:avg

Compute the average value of a sequence.

```
avg(xdt:anyAtomicType*) as xdt:anyAtomicType?
```

The argument is the sequence of values to be averaged.

If the sequence is empty, then the empty sequence is returned. Untyped items are converted to `xs:double`. If all items in the sequence cannot be promoted to a common type, or don't have types that can be summed and divided by an integer, then an error occurs.

Otherwise, all items in the sequence are promoted to a common type, summed, and divided by the number of items in the sequence to produce the average result. If any value in the sequence is NaN, then the result is NaN.

Listing C.5 `avg` examples

```
avg((1.0, 2, 3.0E0)) => 2.0E0
avg(())              => ()
avg(0)               => 0
avg(1, 3)            => 2
```

See also: `count()`, `max()`, `min()`, and `sum()`.

fn:base-uri

Select the base-uri property of a node or the static context.

```
base-uri(node) as xs:string?
base-uri() as xs:string?
```

The optional first argument specifies the node to use. When omitted, the base-uri is selected from the static context.

If the node doesn't have a base-uri, or its base-uri is empty, then the base-uri of its parent (if it has one) is returned. If it doesn't have a parent, then the empty sequence is returned. Only document, element, and processing-instruction nodes may have a non-empty base-uri.

Listing C.6 `base-uri` examples

```
base-uri()
base-uri(doc('input.xml'))
```

See also: `declare base-uri` in Appendix B.

fn:boolean

Convert a value to a boolean value using Effective Boolean Value rules.

```
boolean(item*) as xs:boolean
```

The argument specifies an arbitrary sequence to be converted to `xs:boolean`. The argument is converted to boolean as follows: If the expression is the empty sequence, the empty string, zero (in any numeric type), or the special number NaN (floating-point types only), then it is converted to false. Otherwise, it is converted to true.

This conversion was used by XPath 1.0, and in the context of XQuery is usually called the Effective Boolean Value. It is implicitly applied in many contexts, including path predicates; the `boolean()` function provides a way to apply the conversion explicitly.

Listing C.7 `boolean` examples

```
boolean('')                  => false()
boolean('false')             => true()
cast as xs:boolean('')       => error
cast as xs:boolean('false')  => false
```

The `boolean()` function differs from `cast as xs:boolean` in its handling of strings and non-singleton sequences, both of which are converted to true if they are non-empty. In contrast, `cast as xs:boolean` inspects the value of the string (treating `"true"` and `"1"` as true, `"false"` and `"0"` as false, and all other values as errors) and errors on non-singleton sequences.

See also: `number()` and `string()`, and `cast as` in Appendix B.

fn:ceiling

Compute the least integer greater than this number (round to positive infinity).

```
ceiling(numeric?) as numeric?
```

The argument specifies the value to be rounded. The return value has the same type as the argument.

If the argument is the empty sequence, then `ceiling()` returns the empty sequence. If the argument type is `xs:float` or `xs:double` and is one of the special values positive zero, negative zero, positive infinity, negative infinity, or `NaN`, then it is returned unchanged.

Otherwise, `ceiling()` returns the least integer greater than the argument. (Negative values that round up to zero result in negative zero.) This process is also commonly known as "round toward positive infinity."

Listing C.8 `ceiling` examples

```
ceiling(2)        =>  2
ceiling(1.5)      =>  2.0
ceiling(1.2)      =>  2.0
ceiling(-1.5)     => -1.0
ceiling(1 div 0) =>  INF
See also: floor(), round(), and round-half-to-even().
```

fn:codepoints-to-string

Return the string consisting of a sequence of integer Unicode code points.

```
codepoints-to-string(xs:integer*) as xs:string
```

The argument specifies a sequence of integer Unicode code points.

If an integer in the sequence doesn't correspond to a legal XML character (the `Char` production from the XML 1.0 standard), then an error is raised. If the sequence is empty, then `codepoints-to-string()` returns the empty string. Otherwise, `codepoints-to-string()` returns the string that results from concatenating the Unicode characters corresponding to these code points.

Listing C.9 `codepoints-to-string` examples

```
codepoints-to-string((72,101,108,108,111)) => "Hello"
codepoints-to-string(())                    => ""
```

See also: `string-to-codepoints()`.

fn:collection

Access a named collection of nodes.

```
collection(xs:string) as node*
```

The first argument specifies the collection name. An error occurs if it cannot be converted to `xs:anyURI`. Otherwise, if it is a relative URI, then it is first resolved into an absolute URI using the base URI property of the static context (as returned by `base-uri()`).

If there isn't a collection corresponding to this URI, then an error is raised. Otherwise, `collection()` returns the node sequence corresponding to the named collection. Like the `doc()` function, the same node (by identity) is returned every time this function is invoked with the same argument.

Listing C.10 `collection` examples

```
collection("items")
collection("http://www.w3.org/TR/XQuery")
```

See also: `base-uri()`, `doc()`, and `input()`.

fn:compare

Compare two strings for equality.

```
compare(xs:string?, xs:string?) as xs:integer?
compare(xs:string?, xs:string?, xs:string) as xs:integer?
```

The first two arguments are the strings to be compared. The optional third argument specifies a collation to use for the comparison; if omitted, the default collation of the static context is used.

If either argument is the empty sequence, then `compare()` returns the empty sequence. Otherwise, it returns -1, 0, or 1 if the first string is less than, equal to, or greater than the second string (respectively).

One way to remember the return value of compare() is to think of its correspondence with the general comparison operators. For every general comparison operator op, the expression $L op $R has the same result as compare(L, R) op 0. For example, $L <= $R is the same as compare($L, $R) <= 0.

Listing C.11 compare examples

```
compare("abc", () )            => ()
compare( (), "abc" )           => ()
compare("abc", "abc")          =>  0 (equal)
compare("abc", "xyz")          => -1 (less-than)
compare("xyz", "abc")          =>  1 (greater-than)
compare("Hello, world", "Hello") =>  1
```

See also: The section "Collations" in Chapter 8.

fn:concat

Concatenate zero or more strings into a single string value.

```
concat() as xs:string
concat(xs:string?) as xs:string
concat(xs:string?, xs:string?, ...) as xs:string
```

The concat() function is special among all the XQuery functions in that it accepts a variable number of arguments (zero or more). Each argument must be a singleton string or the empty sequence (which is treated like the empty string).

The concat() function returns the string concatenation of all its arguments. When called without any arguments, it returns the empty string.

Listing C.12 concat examples

```
concat()                => ""
concat(())              => ""
concat("a", "b", "", "c") => "abc"
concat("x", 2)          => error (: 2 is not a string :)
concat(("a", "b", "c"))  => error (: argument contains more than one item
:)
```

To concatenate sequences containing more than one string (for example, FLWOR statements returning strings), or to insert spaces, commas, or other characters in between strings, use the `string-join()` function.

See also: `string-join()`.

---

fn:contains

Test whether a string contains a substring.

```
contains(xs:string?, xs:string?) as xs:boolean
contains(xs:string?, xs:string?, xs:string) as xs:boolean
```

The first argument specifies the string to search, and the second argument specifies the substring to seek. The optional third argument specifies the collation to use; it defaults to the Unicode code point collation.

If the second argument is the empty sequence or the empty string, then `contains()` returns true. Otherwise, if the first argument is the empty sequence or the empty string, it returns false.

Otherwise, `contains()` returns true if the string contains the substring, and returns false otherwise. The collation is used to perform substring comparisons.

Listing C.13 `contains` examples

```
contains('hello', () )  => true
contains('hello', 'll') => true
contains('hello', 'x')  => false
contains('hello', '')   => true
contains('', 'll')      => false
```

See also: `matches()` and `substring()`.

---

fn:count

Compute the length of a sequence.

```
count(item*) as xs:integer
```

The first argument specifies the sequence to be counted.

The `count()` function returns the number of items in the sequence.

Listing C.14 `count` examples

```
count(())      => 0
count("xyz")   => 1
count((1, "a")) => 2
```

See also: `last()` and `string-length()`.

fn:current-date

Access the current date from the static context.

```
current-date() as date
```

Selects the date part of the current dateTime of the static context. Within a query, every invocation of this function returns the same value. The value of the current dateTime is implementation-dependent.

Listing C.15 `current-date` example

```
current-date() => "2004-02-06"
```

See also: `current-dateTime()`, `current-time()`, and `implicit-timezone()`.

fn:current-dateTime

Access the current dateTime from the static context.

```
current-dateTime() as dateTime
```

Selects the current dateTime of the static context. Within a query, every invocation of this function returns the same value. The value of the current dateTime is implementation-dependent.

Listing C.16 `current-dateTime` example

```
current-dateTime() => "2004-02-06T12:00:00"
```

See also: `current-date()`, `current-time()`, and `implicit-timezone()`.

fn:current-time

Access the current time from the static context.

```
current-time() as time
```

Select the time part of the current dateTime of the static context. Within a query, every invocation of this function returns the same value. The value of the current dateTime is implementation-dependent.

Listing C.17 `current-time` example

```
current-time() => "12:00:00"
```

See also: `current-date()`, `current-dateTime()`, and `implicit-timezone()`.

fn:data

Atomize a sequence of items, returning their typed values.

```
data(item*) as xdt:anyAtomicType*
```

The argument specifies the sequence of items to be atomized. For each item in the sequence, if it's an atomic value then it's returned unchanged; if it's a node, then it's replaced by its typed value. The `data()` function then returns the resulting sequence.

If the typed value of a node is a list type (for example, `xs:IDREFS`) or the empty sequence, then the returned sequence may have a different length than the original.

Listing C.18 `data` examples

```
data(<x xsi:type="xs:integer">{1}</x>) => 1
data("a", 2.5, <x>hello</x>)           => ("a", 2.5, "hello")
```

See also: The section "Atomization" in Chapter 2.

fn:deep-equal

Test two item sequences for deep equality.

```
deep-equal(item*, item*) as xs:boolean
deep-equal(item*, item*, string) as xs:boolean
```

The first two arguments specify the sequences to be compared. The optional third argument specifies a collation to use for string comparisons; if omitted, the default collation is used.

If both sequences are empty, then deep-equal() returns true. If the lengths of the two sequences differ, then deep-equal() returns false.

Otherwise, deep-equal() iterates through the two sequences together and compares the members at the same positions. If each such pair of members compare equal (using the eq operator for values, or deep equality for nodes as explained below), then deep-equal() returns true, otherwise it returns false.

Listing C.19 deep-equal examples

```
deep-equal((), ())                          => true
deep-equal((1,2), (1,2))                     => true
deep-equal((1,2,3), (1,2))                   => false
deep-equal(<x/>, <x/>)                       => true
deep-equal(<x a="1"><y>2</y></x>,
           <x a="1"><y>2</y></x>)            => true
deep-equal(<x a="1"><y>2</y></x>,
           <x a="3"><y>4</y></x>)            => false
```

Deep equality of nodes is determined using a recursive definition—two nodes are deep-equal when all of the following conditions hold:

- They have the same node kind.
- They either both lack names, or else have the same expanded QName.
- If they are text, comment, processing-instruction, or namespace nodes, then they have equal string values (using the collation for comparison).
- If they are element nodes, then neither node has an attribute that isn't deep-equal to an attribute on the other.
- If they are attribute, element, or document nodes, then either:
- Neither has element content, both have simple content, and their typed content compares equal using deep-equal() with the supplied collation.
- Both have element content, and all their child nodes are pairwise in order of appearance, ignoring comment and processing-instruction nodes, and compare equal using deep-equal() with the supplied collation.

This process can also be written as a recursive XQuery function (in which node-kind() is a hypothetical function that returns the node kind of a node as a string value).

Listing C.20 A user-defined `deep-equal` function equivalent to the built-in one

```
declare function my:deep-equal($seq0 as item*, $seq1 as item*,
                              $collation as xs:string) {
count($seq0) eq count($seq1)
and
empty (
  for $i in $seq0 at $pos
  let $j := $seq1[$pos]
  let $inode := $i instance of node()
  let $jnode := $j instance of node()
  where
    if ($inode and $jnode)
    then (
      (: both nodes, perform complex test :)
      let $ii := treat as node() ($i)
      let $jj := treat as node() ($j)
      return
          node-kind($ii) ne node-kind($jj)
        or node-name($ii) != node-name($jj)
        or if (node-kind($ii)=("element", "attribute", "document"))
          then not(
            count($ii/@*) eq count($jj/@*) and (
              every $attr in $ii/@* satisfies
                (some $attr2 in $jj/@* satisfies
                 my:deep-equal(data($attr), data($attr2), $collation))
            ) and (
                my:deep-equal(($ii/(*|text()), data($ii)),
                              ($jj/(*|text()), data($jj)),
                              $collation)
            )
          )
          else compare(string($ii), string($jj), $collation) ne 0
    )
    else if ($inode or $jnode)
    then true()     (: different item kinds, so always fail :)
    else $i ne $j   (: both atomic values, just use ne :)
  return $i
)
};
```

See also: `eq` in Appendix B.

fn:default-collation

Access the default collation of the static context.

```
default-collation() as xs:anyURI?
```

Selects the default collation from the static context, or the empty sequence if no default collation is defined.

Listing C.21 `default-collation` example

```
default-collation() =>
"http://www.w3.org/2003/11/xpath-functions/collation/codepoint"
```

See also: `declare default collation` in Appendix B, and the section "Collations" in Chapter 8.

fn:distinct-values

Eliminate duplicates (by value) from a sequence of values.

```
distinct-values(xdt:anyAtomicType*) as xdt:anyAtomicType*
distinct-values(xdt:anyAtomicType*, xs:string) as xdt:anyAtomicType*
```

The first argument specifies a sequence of atomic values. The optional second argument specifies the collation to use for string comparisons; if omitted, the default collation is used.

If the second argument isn't a valid URI or doesn't specify a valid collation, then an error is raised. If the first argument is empty, then the empty sequence is returned.

Otherwise, `distinct-values()` returns the sequence of values with duplicates (by value equality) removed. All members of the sequence must be the same type (or subtypes of it), and equality must be defined for that type. NaN is considered equal to itself, and positive zero is considered equal to negative zero. Types with an empty time zone component are adjusted to the implicit time zone before comparison.

The order of the result and in some cases the values themselves are implementation-defined, and may vary even when given the same arguments as input.

Listing C.22 `distinct-values` examples

```
distinct-values((1,2,3,2,2))
=> (1,2,3) (: in any order :)

distinct-values(("example", "example"),
"http://www.w3.org/2003/11/xpath-functions/collation/codepoint")
=> "a"

distinct-values((1, 1.0))
=> 1 or 1.0 (: implementation-defined :)
```

fn:doc

Load an XML document.

```
doc(xs:string?) as document-node()?
```

The first argument specifies a document location. If it is the empty sequence, then the empty sequence is returned.

Otherwise, it is converted to `xs:anyURI`; if it cannot be converted, then an error is raised. If it is a relative URI, then it is first resolved to an absolute URI using the base URI property of the static context.

The behavior of the `doc()` function is essentially implementation-defined, although XQuery guarantees that within a particular query, every invocation of `doc()` with the same value results in the same node (by identity). Implementations may choose to return the same node (by identity) under other circumstances, such as if they determine that two different URI values refer to the same underlying document.

Implementations may also choose how to handle cases such as if the document doesn't exist, exists but isn't well-formed, or exists and is well-formed but is invalid according to its schema. In such cases, implementations may choose to raise an error, return the empty sequence, return another document, or provide some other implementation-defined fallback.

Implementations may also statically type the result of this function if the location is known to it at compile-time.

Listing C.23 `doc` examples

```
doc(())
doc("input.xml")
doc("http://www.w3.org/TR/xquery/XQuery.xml")
```

See also: `base-uri()`, `collection()`, and `input()`.

fn:document-uri

Access the document-uri property of a node.

```
document-uri(node) as xs:string?
```

The argument specifies the node to use. This function selects the `document-uri` property of the node if it has one and it is an absolute URI, otherwise `document-uri()` returns the empty sequence.

Listing C.24 `document-uri` example

```
document-uri(doc("input.xml"))
```

See also: `resolve-uri()` and Appendix A.

fn:empty

Test whether a sequence is empty.

```
empty(item*) as xs:boolean
```

The first argument specifies the sequence to be tested. The `empty()` function returns true if the sequence is empty, and returns false otherwise.

Listing C.25 `empty` examples

```
empty(()) => true
empty(1)  => false
```

See also: `exists()`.

fn:ends-with

Test whether a string ends with a substring.

```
ends-with(xs:string?, xs:string?) as xs:boolean
ends-with(xs:string?, xs:string?, xs:string) as xs:boolean
```

The first argument specifies the string to be searched; the second argument specifies the substring to seek. The optional third argument specifies the collation to use for comparisons; it defaults to the Unicode code point collation.

If the second argument is the empty sequence or the empty string, then `ends-with()` returns true. Otherwise, if the first argument is the empty sequence or the empty string, then `ends-with()` returns false.

Otherwise, `ends-with()` returns true if the string ends with the substring, and false otherwise. This function is redundant with the more powerful `matches()` function, but is retained for compatibility with XPath 1.0 and convenience.

Listing C.26 `ends-with` examples

```
ends-with("Hello, world", ())       => true
ends-with("Hello, world", "Hello")  => false
ends-with("Hello, world", "world")  => true
ends-with("Hello, world", "")       => true
ends-with("", "world")              => false
```

See also: `contains()`, `matches()`, and `starts-with()`.

fn:error

Cause an error to terminate processing.

```
error() as none
error(item?) as none
```

The optional argument has implementation-defined meaning, although usually it is used as a message to the user. The `error()` function terminates execution of the XQuery at the point where it is invoked. This function can be used to create user-defined error conditions.

Listing C.27 `error` examples

```
error("Internal error, abort, abort!")
error(err:message142)
error(<log time="{current-time()}" msg="query failed"/>)
```

See also: `trace()`.

fn:escape-uri

Perform URI-escaping on a string.

```
escape-uri(string, xs:boolean) as xs:string
```

The first argument specifies the URI to be escaped. The second argument specifies whether to escape reserved characters.

The `escape-uri()` function escapes URI characters according to the URI standards (RFC 2396 and RFC 2732). Each special character in the string will be replaced by a URI escape sequence `%NN` where `NN` is the hexadecimal value of the character (returned using uppercase hexadecimal characters). Characters already escaped in this form are unchanged. The string argument isn't required to be a valid URI.

If the second argument is true, then all characters are escaped *except* lowercase and uppercase ASCII letters, the digits 0 to 9, and the punctuation characters hyphen (-), underscore (_), period (.), exclamation mark (!), tilde (~), asterisk (*), apostrophe (`'`), and parentheses (`(` and `)`). The percent sign (`%`) is escaped only if it isn't followed by two hexadecimal digits. This mode is useful when encoding most of the URI, including the domain and path.

If the second argument is false, then in addition to the exceptions listed above, the following characters are also exempted from escaping: semicolon (`;`), slash (`/`), question mark (`?`), colon (`:`), at sign (`@`), ampersand (`&`), equals (`=`), plus (`+`), dollar sign (`$`), comma (`,`), number sign (`#`), and square brackets (`[` and `]`). This mode is useful when encoding the part of a URI containing parameters.

Listing C.28 `escape-uri` examples

```
escape-uri("%20abcABC123+*$%", true())  => "%20abcABC123%2B*%24%25"
escape-uri("%20abcABC123+*$%", false()) => "%20abcABC123+*$%25"
```

fn:exactly-one

Error if the sequence isn't a singleton.

```
exactly-one(item*) as item
```

Returns the sequence unchanged if it has length exactly one, otherwise it raises an error.

Listing C.29 `exactly-one` examples

```
exactly-one(())     => error
exactly-one(1)      => (1)
exactly-one((1,2))  => error
```

Many functions and operators in XQuery require singletons. One way to ensure that a sequence has the required length is to use the `exactly-one()` function.

Listing C.30 Using `exactly-one` to pass static typing

```
collection(base-uri(exactly-one(..))
```

See also: `one-or-more()` and `zero-or-one()`.

fn:exists

Test whether a sequence exists (i.e., is non-empty).

```
exists(item*) as xs:boolean
```

The first argument specifies the sequence to be tested. The `exists()` function returns true if the sequence is non-empty, and false otherwise.

Listing C.31 `exists` examples

```
exists(()) => false
exists(1)  => true
```

See also: `empty()`.

fn:expanded-QName

Construct a QName from its local-name and namespace-uri parts.

```
expanded-QName(xs:string, xs:string) as xs:QName
```

The first argument specifies the namespace URI, and the second argument specifies the local name. If the namespace is the empty string, then it doesn't represent a namespace. If the local name isn't a valid `xs:NCName`, then an error is raised.

The `expanded-QName()` function returns an `xs:QName` value with the given namespace and local name parts.

Listing C.32 `expanded-QName` example

```
expanded-QName("http://www.awprofessional.com/", "example")
```

See also: `resolve-QName()`, and `xs:QName` in Appendix A.

fn:false

The boolean literal for false.

```
false() as xs:boolean
```

Returns the boolean constant false.

XQuery defines the false constant using a function mainly for backwards compatibility with XPath 1.0 and to eliminate the need for reserved keywords.

Listing C.33 `false` example

```
false()   => false
```

See also: `true()`.

fn:floor

Compute the greatest integer less than this number (round to negative infinity).

```
floor(numeric?) as numeric?
```

The argument specifies the value to be rounded. The return value has the same type as the argument.

If the argument is the empty sequence, then `floor()` returns the empty sequence. If the argument type is `xs:float` or `xs:double` and is one of the special values positive zero, negative zero, positive infinity, negative infinity, or `NaN`, then it is returned unchanged. Otherwise, `floor()` returns the greatest integer less than the argument. This process is also commonly known as "round toward negative infinity."

Listing C.34 `floor` examples

```
floor(2)       =>  2
floor(1.5)     =>  1.0
floor(1.2)     =>  1.0
floor(-1.5)    =>  -2.0
floor(1 div 0) =>  INF
```

See also: `ceiling()`, `round()`, and `round-half-to-even()`.

fn:get-day-from-date

Select the day part of a date value.

```
get-day-from-date(xs:date?) as xs:integer?
```

The argument specifies the date value. If the argument is the empty sequence, then the function returns the empty sequence. Otherwise, it returns the integer day part of the date.

Listing C.35 `get-day-from-date` examples

```
get-day-from-date(xs:date("2004-09-08")) => 8
get-day-from-date(())                     => ()
```

See also: `get-month-from-date()`, `get-timezone-from-date()`, and `get-year-from-date()`.

fn:get-day-from-dateTime

Select the day part of an xs:dateTime value.

```
get-day-from-dateTime(xs:dateTime?) as xs:integer?
```

The argument specifies the `xs:dateTime` value. If the argument is the empty sequence, then the function returns the empty sequence. Otherwise, it returns the integer day part of the `xs:dateTime` value.

Listing C.36 `get-day-from-dateTime` examples

```
get-day-from-dateTime(xs:dateTime("2004-09-08T04:30:00")) => 8
get-day-from-dateTime(())                                 => ()
```

See also: `get-hours-from-dateTime()`, `get-minutes-from-dateTime()`, `get-month-from-dateTime()`, `get-seconds-from-dateTime()`, `get-timezone-from-dateTime()`, and `get-year-from-dateTime()`.

fn:get-days-from-dayTimeDuration

Select the days part of a dayTimeDuration value.

```
get-days-from-dayTimeDuration(xdt:dayTimeDuration?) as xs:integer?
```

The argument specifies the duration value. If the argument is the empty sequence, then the function returns the empty sequence. Otherwise, it returns the integer number of days in the duration.

Listing C.37 `get-days-from-dayTimeDuration` examples

```
get-days-from-dayTimeDuration(xdt:dayTimeDuration("P5D")) => 5
get-days-from-dayTimeDuration(())                          => ()
```

See also: `get-hours-from-dayTimeDuration()`, `get-minutes-from-dayTimeDuration()`, and `get-seconds-from-dayTimeDuration()`.

fn:get-hours-from-dateTime

Select the hours part of an xs:dateTime value.

```
get-hours-from-dateTime(xs:dateTime?) as xs:integer?
```

The argument specifies the `xs:dateTime` value. If the argument is the empty sequence, then the function returns the empty sequence. Otherwise, it returns the integer hours part of the `xs:dateTime` value.

Listing C.38 `get-hours-from-dateTime` examples

```
get-hours-from-dateTime(xs:dateTime("2004-05-13T08:41:00")) => 8
get-hours-from-dateTime(())                                 => ()
```

See also: `get-day-from-dateTime()`, `get-minutes-from-dateTime()`, `get-month-from-dateTime()`, `get-seconds-from-dateTime()`, `get-timezone-from-dateTime()`, and `get-year-from-dateTime()`.

fn:get-hours-from-dayTimeDuration

Select the hours part of an xdt:dayTimeDuration value.

```
get-hours-from-dayTimeDuration(xdt:dayTimeDuration?) as xs:integer?
```

The argument specifies the duration value. If the argument is the empty sequence, then the function returns the empty sequence. Otherwise, it returns the integer number of hours in the duration.

Listing C.39 `get-hours-from-dayTimeDuration` examples

```
get-hours-from-dayTimeDuration(xdt:dayTimeDuration("PT5H")) => 5
get-hours-from-dayTimeDuration(())                          => ()
```

See also: `get-days-from-dayTimeDuration()`, `get-minutes-from-dayTimeDuration()`, and `get-seconds-from-dayTimeDuration()`.

fn:get-hours-from-time

Select the hours part of a time value.

```
get-hours-from-time(xs:time?) as xs:integer?
```

The argument specifies the time value. If the argument is the empty sequence, then the function returns the empty sequence. Otherwise, it returns the integer hours part of the time.

Listing C.40 `get-hours-from-time` examples

```
get-hours-from-time(xs:time("08:41:03.1")) => 8
get-hours-from-time(())                     => ()
```

See also: `get-minutes-from-time()`, `get-seconds-from-time()`, and `get-timezone-from-time()`.

fn:get-in-scope-prefixes

Access the namespaces in scope for an element.

```
get-in-scope-prefixes(element) as xs:string*
```

The argument specifies the element to use for the namespace scope. The `get-in-scope-prefixes()` function returns a list of all the namespace prefixes in scope on that element. If there is a default namespace in scope, it is returned as the empty string.

Listing C.41 `get-in-scope-prefixes` example

```
get-in-scope(<x/>) => ("xs", "fn", "xdt", "xsi", "xml")
```

Note that elements constructed in an XQuery automatically have several namespace definitions in scope, as the example in Listing C.41 demonstrates.

See also: `get-namespace-uri-for-prefix()`, and `declare namespace` in Appendix B.

fn:get-local-name-from-QName

Select the local-name part of a QName value.

```
get-local-name-from-QName(xs:QName?) as xs:string?
```

The first argument specifies the QName value to use. If the argument is the empty sequence, then the empty sequence is returned. Otherwise, `get-local-name-from-QName()` returns the local part of the QName value.

Listing C.42 `get-local-name-from-QName` examples

```
get-local-name-from-QName(())                        => ()
get-local-name-from-QName(node-name(<x/>))           => "x"
get-local-name-from-QName(node-name(<x xmlns="y"/>)) => "x"
```

See also: `get-namespace-uri-from-QName()`, and `xs:QName` in Appendix A.

fn:get-minutes-from-dateTime

Select the minutes part of an xs:dateTime value.

```
get-minutes-from-dateTime(xs:dateTime?) as xs:integer?
```

The argument specifies the `xs:dateTime` value. If the argument is the empty sequence, then the function returns the empty sequence. Otherwise, it returns the integer minutes part of the `xs:dateTime` value.

Listing C.43 `get-minutes-from-dateTime` examples

```
get-minutes-from-dateTime(xs:dateTime("2003-09-08T08:41:00")) => 41
get-minutes-from-dateTime(())                                 => ()
```

See also: `get-day-from-dateTime()`, `get-hours-from-dateTime()`, `get-month-from-dateTime()`, `get-seconds-from-dateTime()`, `get-timezone-from-dateTime()`, and `get-year-from-dateTime()`.

fn:get-minutes-from-dayTimeDuration

Select the minutes part of a dayTimeDuration value.

```
get-minutes-from-dayTimeDuration(xdt:dayTimeDuration?) as xs:integer?
```

The argument specifies the duration value. If the argument is the empty sequence, then the function returns the empty sequence. Otherwise, it returns the integer number of minutes in the duration.

Listing C.44 `get-minutes-from-dayTimeDuration` examples

```
get-minutes-from-dayTimeDuration(xdt:dayTimeDuration("PT5M")) => 5
get-minutes-from-dayTimeDuration(())                          => ()
```

See also: `get-days-from-dayTimeDuration()`, `get-hours-from-dayTimeDuration()`, and `get-seconds-from-dayTimeDuration()`.

fn:get-minutes-from-time

Select the minutes part of a time value.

```
get-minutes-from-time(xs:time?) as xs:integer?
```

The argument specifies the time value. If the argument is the empty sequence, then the function returns the empty sequence. Otherwise, it returns the integer minutes part of the time.

Listing C.45 `get-minutes-from-time` examples

```
get-minutes-from-time(xs:time("08:55:03.1")) => 55
get-minutes-from-time(())                     => ()
```

See also: `get-hours-from-time()`, `get-seconds-from-time()`, and `get-timezone-from-time()`.

fn:get-month-from-date

Select the months part of a date value.

```
get-month-from-date(xs:date?) as xs:integer?
```

The argument specifies the date value. If the argument is the empty sequence, then the function returns the empty sequence. Otherwise, it returns the integer month part of the date.

Listing C.46 `get-month-from-date` examples

```
get-month-from-date(xs:date("2004-09-08")) => 9
get-month-from-date(())                     => ()
```

See also: `get-day-from-date()`, `get-timezone-from-date()`, and `get-year-from-date()`.

fn:get-month-from-dateTime

Select the months part of an xs:dateTime value.

```
get-month-from-dateTime(xs:dateTime?) as xs:integer?
```

The argument specifies the `xs:dateTime` value. If the argument is the empty sequence, then the function returns the empty sequence. Otherwise, it returns the integer month part of the `xs:dateTime` value.

Listing C.47 `get-month-from-dateTime` examples

```
get-month-from-dateTime(xs:dateTime("2004-09-08T08:41:00")) => 9
get-month-from-dateTime(())                                 => ()
```

See also: `get-day-from-dateTime()`, `get-hours-from-dateTime()`, `get-minutes-from-dateTime()`, `get-seconds-from-dateTime()`, `get-timezone-from-dateTime()`, and `get-year-from-dateTime()`.

fn:get-months-from-yearMonthDuration

Select the months part of a yearMonthDuration value.

```
get-months-from-yearMonthDuration(xdt:yearMonthDuration?) as xs:integer?
```

The argument specifies the duration value. If the argument is the empty sequence, then the function returns the empty sequence. Otherwise, it returns the integer number of months in the duration.

Listing C.48 `get-months-from-yearMonthDuration` examples

```
get-months-from-yearMonthDuration(xdt:yearMonthDuration("P5M"))=> 5
get-months-from-yearMonthDuration(())                           => ()
```

See also: `get-years-from-yearMonthDuration()`.

fn:get-namespace-uri-for-prefix

Look up a namespace prefix among the namespaces in scope for an element.

```
get-namespace-uri-for-prefix(element, xs:string) as xs:string?
```

The first argument specifies an element to use for the namespace scope. The second argument specifies the prefix to look up.

If the element has an in-scope namespace with that prefix, then `get-name-space-uri-for-prefix()` returns that namespace URI (the empty string prefix corresponds to the default namespace). Otherwise, it returns the empty sequence.

Listing C.49 `get-namespace-uri-for-prefix` examples

```
get-namespace-uri-for-prefix(<x xmlns="y"/>, "")    => "y"
get-namespace-uri-for-prefix(<x xmlns:p="y"/>, "p") => "y"
```

See also: `get-in-scope-prefixes()` and `get-namespace-uri-from-QName()`.

fn:get-namespace-uri-from-QName

Select the namespace-uri part of a QName value.

```
get-namespace-uri-from-QName(xs:QName?) as xs:string?
```

The first argument specifies the QName value to use. If the argument is the empty sequence, or if the QName doesn't have a namespace, then the empty sequence is returned. Otherwise, `get-namespace-uri-from-QName()` returns the namespace part of the QName value.

Listing C.50 `get-namespace-uri-from-QName` examples

```
get-namespace-uri-from-QName(())                        => ()
get-namespace-uri-from-QName(node-name(<x/>))           => ()
get-namespace-uri-from-QName(node-name(<x xmlns="y"/>)) => "y"
```

See also: `get-local-name-from-prefix()` and `get-local-name-from-QName()`.

fn:get-seconds-from-dateTime

Select the seconds part of a dateTime value.

```
get-seconds-from-dateTime(xs:dateTime?) as xs:decimal?
```

The argument specifies the dateTime value. If the argument is the empty sequence, then the function returns the empty sequence. Otherwise, it returns the decimal seconds part of the dateTime.

Listing C.51 `get-seconds-from-dateTime` examples

```
get-day-from-dateTime(xs:dateTime("2004-09-08T08:41:00")) => 0.0
get-day-from-dateTime(())                                 => ()
```

See also: `get-day-from-dateTime()`, `get-hours-from-dateTime()`, `get-minutes-from-dateTime()`, `get-month-from-dateTime()`, `get-timezone-from-dateTime()`, and `get-year-from-dateTime()`.

fn:get-seconds-from-dayTimeDuration

Select the seconds part of a dayTimeDuration value.

```
get-seconds-from-dayTimeDuration(xdt:dayTimeDuration?) as xs:decimal?
```

The argument specifies the duration value. If the argument is the empty sequence, then the function returns the empty sequence. Otherwise, it returns the decimal number of the seconds in the duration.

Listing C.52 `get-seconds-from-dayTimeDuration` examples

```
get-seconds-from-dayTimeDuration(xdt:dayTimeDuration("PT5S")) => 5.0
get-seconds-from-dayTimeDuration(())                          => ()
```

See also: `get-days-from-dayTimeDuration()`, `get-hours-from-yearMonthDuration()`, and `get-minutes-from-dayTimeDuration()`.

fn:get-seconds-from-time

Select the seconds part of a time value.

```
get-seconds-from-time(xs:time?) as xs:decimal?
```

The argument specifies the time value. If the argument is the empty sequence, then the function returns the empty sequence. Otherwise, it returns the decimal seconds part of the time.

Listing C.53 `get-seconds-from-time` examples

```
get-seconds-from-time(xs:time("08:55:03.1")) => 3.1
get-seconds-from-time(())                     => ()
```

See also: `get-hours-from-time()`, `get-minutes-from-time()`, and `get-timezone-from-time()`.

fn:get-timezone-from-date

Select the time zone part of a date value.

```
get-timezone-from-date(xs:date?) as xdt:dayTimeDuration?
```

The argument specifies the date value. If the argument is the empty sequence, then the function returns the empty sequence. Otherwise, it returns the time zone part of the date as an `xdt:dayTimeDuration` value.

Listing C.54 `get-timezone-from-date` examples

```
get-timezone-from-date(xs:date("2004-05-30"))
get-timezone-from-date(())                     => ()
```

See also: `get-day-from-date()`, `get-month-from-date()`, and `get-year-from-date()`.

fn:get-timezone-from-dateTime

Select the time zone part of a dateTime value.

```
get-timezone-from-dateTime(xs:dateTime?) as xdt:dayTimeDuration?
```

The argument specifies the dateTime value. If the argument is the empty sequence, then the function returns the empty sequence. Otherwise, it returns the time zone part of the dateTime as an `xdt:dayTimeDuration` value.

Listing C.55 `get-timezone-from-dateTime` examples

```
get-timezone-from-dateTime(xs:dateTime("2004-05-13T08:55:03.1"))
get-timezone-from-dateTime(())                                    => ()
```

See also: `get-day-from-dateTime()`, `get-hours-from-dateTime()`, `get-minutes-from-dateTime()`, `get-month-from-dateTime()`, `get-seconds-from-dateTime()`, and `get-year-from-dateTime()`.

fn:get-timezone-from-time

Select the time zone part of a time value.

```
get-timezone-from-time(xs:time?) as xdt:dayTimeDuration?
```

The argument specifies the time value. If the argument is the empty sequence, then the function returns the empty sequence. Otherwise, it returns the time zone part of the time as an `xdt:dayTimeDuration` value.

Listing C.56 `get-timezone-from-time` examples

```
get-timezone-from-time(xs:time("08:55:03.1"))
get-timezone-from-time(())                     => ()
```

See also: `get-hours-from-time()`, `get-minutes-from-time()`, and `get-seconds-from-time()`.

---
fn:get-year-from-date

Select the year part of a date value.

```
get-year-from-date(xs:date?) as xs:integer?
```

The argument specifies the date value. If the argument is the empty sequence, then the function returns the empty sequence. Otherwise, it returns the integer year part of the date.

Listing C.57 `get-year-from-date` examples

```
get-year-from-date(xs:date("2004-09-08")) => 2004
get-year-from-date(())                    => ()
```

See also: `get-day-from-date()`, `get-month-from-date()`, and `get-timezone-from-date()`.

---
fn:get-year-from-dateTime

Select the year part of a dateTime value.

```
get-year-from-dateTime(xs:dateTime?) as xs:integer?
```

The argument specifies the dateTime value. If the argument is the empty sequence, then the function returns the empty sequence. Otherwise, it returns the integer year part of the dateTime.

Listing C.58 `get-year-from-dateTime` examples

```
get-year-from-dateTime(xs:dateTime("2004-09-08T08:41:00")) => 2004
get-year-from-dateTime(())                                 => ()
```

See also: `get-day-from-dateTime()`, `get-hours-from-dateTime()`, `get-minutes-from-dateTime()`, `get-month-from-dateTime()`, `get-seconds-from-dateTime()`, and `get-timezone-from-dateTime()`.

---
fn:get-years-from-yearMonthDuration

Select the years part of a yearMonthDuration value.

```
get-years-from-yearMonthDuration(xdt:yearMonthDuration?) as xs:integer?
```

The argument specifies the duration value. If the argument is the empty sequence, then the function returns the empty sequence. Otherwise, it returns the integer number of years in the duration.

Listing C.59 `get-years-from-yearMonthDuration` examples

```
get-years-from-yearMonthDuration(xdt:yearMonthDuration("P5Y")) => 5
get-years-from-yearMonthDuration(())                            => ()
```

See also: `get-months-from-yearMonthDuration()`.

fn:id

Look up the element with this ID value.

```
id(xs:string*) as element*
```

The first argument specifies a sequence of string values to be looked up.

If there isn't a context node, then an error is raised. If the sequence is empty, then the result is the empty sequence. Otherwise, each string value in the sequence is parsed as a space-separated sequence of IDREF values. Values that cannot be cast to `xs:IDREF` are ignored. All of these IDREF values are looked up, and the sequence of corresponding elements are returned in document order without duplicates (by node identity). An element is matched if it is in the same document as the current context node and either it has an attribute of type `xs:ID` equal to one of the IDREF values or else the element itself is type `xs:ID` and its value is equal to one of the IDREF values.

The ID/IDREF string matching uses Unicode code points only, ignoring collation. Also, it is possible to match against a well-formed but schema-invalid document, in which case multiple elements could have the same ID or values could be declared as type `xs:ID` but invalid according to that type. In these cases, the first matching element is selected and invalid ID values are ignored.

Listing C.60 `id` examples

```
id("x y")               => look up elements with IDs x and y
id(("a", "b", "c d")    => look up elements with IDs a, b, c, and d.
id(())                  => ()
id("3")                 => () (: 3 is not a valid xs:IDREF :)
```

See also: `idref()`.

fn:idref

Look up the node with this IDREF value.

```
idref(xs:string*) as node*
```

The first argument specifies a sequence of string values to be looked up.

If there isn't a current context node, then an error is raised. If the sequence is empty, then the empty sequence is returned. Otherwise, as with the `id()` function, each string in the sequence is parsed as a space-separated list of ID values. Invalid ID values are ignored. For each ID value, `idref()` finds all `xs:IDREF` and `xs:IDREFS`-typed nodes in the same document as the current context node that refer to that ID value. String equality is determined by Unicode code points, irrespective of collation. The nodes are returned in document order without duplicates (by node identity).

Listing C.61 `idref` examples

```
idref("x") => all nodes in the current context document that refer to x
idref("3") => () (: 3 is not a valid xs:ID :)
idref(())  => ()
```

See also: `id()`.

fn:implicit-timezone

Access the default time zone from the static context.

```
implicit-timezone() as xdt:dayTimeDuration?
```

Select the time zone part of the current dateTime of the static context. Returns the empty sequence if the time zone is undefined.

Within a query, every invocation of this function returns the same value. The value of the current dateTime is implementation-dependent.

Listing C.62 `implicit-timezone` example

```
implicit-timezone()
```

See also: `current-date()`, `current-dateTime()`, and `current-time()`.

fn:index-of

Finds the position(s) where an item appears in a sequence.

```
index-of(xdt:anyAtomicType*, xdt:anyAtomicType) as xs:integer*
index-of(xdt:anyAtomicType*, xdt:anyAtomicType, xs:string) as xs:integer*
```

The first argument specifies a sequence of values, and the second argument specifies a value to search for in that sequence. The optional third argument specifies a collation to use for string comparisons; if omitted, the default collation is used.

If the collation is specified and isn't a valid URI or doesn't name a valid collation, then an error is raised. If the sequence is empty, then the empty sequence is returned.

Otherwise, `index-of()` finds all the positions in the sequence where the item occurs, and returns those positions in increasing order. (Remember, 1 is the first position.) If it doesn't occur in the sequence, then `index-of()` returns the empty sequence.

Listing C.63 `index-of` examples

```
index-of((1,2,3), 2)            => 2
index-of((), 'anything')        => ()
index-of(('a','b',1,2,'a'), 'a') => (1, 5)
```

fn:insert-before

Return the sequence with a subsequence inserted at a given position.

```
insert-before(item*, xs:integer, item*) as item*
```

The first argument specifies the original sequence, and the second argument specifies the insertion position. (Remember, the first item occurs at position 1.) The third argument specifies a sequence of items to be inserted.

If the first argument is the empty sequence, then the third argument is returned. If the third argument is the empty sequence, then the first argument is returned. If the position is less than 1, then `insert-before()` returns the sequence of items to be inserted followed by the original sequence. If the position is greater than the length of the original sequence, then `insert-before()` returns the original sequence followed by the sequence to be inserted.

Otherwise, `insert-before()` returns a new sequence formed from three parts: the subsequence of the original up to but not including the item at the specified position, the items to be inserted, and the remaining items from the original sequence.

In other words, the expression `insert-before($seq, $pos, $items)` is equivalent to the expression `(subsequence($seq, 1, $pos-1), $items, subsequence($seq, $pos))`.

Listing C.64 `insert-before` examples

```
insert-before((1,4), 2, (2,3)) => (1,2,3,4)
insert-before((1,4), 1, (2,3)) => (2,3,1,4)
insert-before((1,4), 3, (2,3)) => (1,4,2,3)
```

See also: `remove()` and `subsequence()`.

fn:lang

Tests the language of the current context node.

```
lang(xs:string) as xs:boolean
```

The argument specifies the language string. If there isn't a context item, or it isn't a node, then `lang()` returns false.

Otherwise, `lang()` returns true if the language of the current context node (that is, the value of the last `xml:lang` attribute in scope) is the same as, or a sublanguage of, the given string, ignoring case.

Listing C.65 `lang` examples

```
lang("en-gb")
lang("SP")
```

The `lang()` function is equivalent to the user-defined function in Listing C.66.

Listing C.66 A user-defined `lang()` function equivalent to the built-in one

```
declare function my:lang(string $s) as xs:boolean {
  let $u := lower-case($s)
  let $x := lower-case( string(
                        (ancestor-or-self::*/@xml:lang)[last()] ) )
  return $u = $x or $u = substring-before($x, "-")
};
```

See also: `xml:lang` in Appendix A.

fn:last

Access the length of the current context sequence.

```
last() as xs:integer?
```

Selects the length of the current context sequence. Returns the empty sequence when the context is empty.

Listing C.67 `last` example

```
(1,2,4)[last()]    => 4
```

See also: `count()` and `position()`.

fn:local-name

Access the local-name property of a node.

```
local-name() as xs:string
local-name(node?) as xs:string
```

The optional argument specifies the node to use; when omitted, it defaults to the current context node. If the current context item isn't a node, an error is raised.

The result is the local part of the node's name. If the node doesn't have a name, then `local-name()` returns the empty string.

Listing C.68 `local-name` examples

```
local-name(<x/>)                  => "x"
local-name(<x:y xmlns:x="hello"/>) => "y"
local-name(<!-- comment -->)       => ""
```

See also: `name()`, `namespace-uri()`, and `node-name()`.

fn:lower-case

Convert a string to lowercase.

```
lower-case(xs:string?) as xs:string?
```

The argument specifies the string to be converted to lowercase.

If the argument is the empty sequence, `lower-case()` returns the empty sequence. Otherwise, `lower-case()` returns the string with all characters translated into their lowercase forms. Characters without uppercase forms are unchanged.

Note that changing case can alter the length of the string.

Listing C.69 `lower-case` examples

```
lower-case("Hello, world") => "hello, world"
lower-case("")             => ""
lower-case(())             => ()
```

See also: `upper-case()`.

fn:matches

Test whether a string matches a regular expression.

```
matches(xs:string?, xs:string) as xs:boolean?
matches(xs:string?, xs:string, xs:string) as xs:boolean?
```

The first argument specifies the input string, and the second argument specifies a regular expression match pattern. The optional third argument specifies flags that modify how the match is performed; if omitted, it defaults to the empty string.

If the first argument is the empty sequence, then `matches()` returns the empty sequence. If the second argument isn't a valid match pattern, or if the third argument contains invalid flags, then `matches()` returns an error. Otherwise, `matches()` returns true if the string matches the regular expression and false if it does not.

Unless the match pattern uses anchors (^ or $), it can match anywhere in the string. See Appendix D for more information about the regular expression syntax and flags used by `matches()` and `replace()`.

Listing C.70 `matches` examples

```
matches("Hello, world", "hello")        => false
matches("Hello, world", "hello", "i")   => true
matches("Hello, world", "hello$", "i")  => false
matches("Hello, world", "\w, \w")       => true
```

See also: `replace()` and Appendix D.

fn:max

Compute the maximum value in a sequence.

```
max(xdt:anyAtomicType*) as xdt:anyAtomicType?
max(xdt:anyAtomicType*, string) as xdt:anyAtomicType?
```

The first argument specifies the sequence to use. The optional second argument specifies the collation to use for string comparisons; if omitted, the default collation is used.

If the sequence is empty, then the empty sequence is returned. If the sequence doesn't contain values all of the same type or types that can be promoted to a common type, then an error is raised. Only types that can be compared using `gt` are allowed.

If there are any NaN values in the sequence, then `max()` returns NaN. Otherwise, `max()` returns the greatest value in the sequence.

Listing C.71 `max` examples

```
max((1.0, 2, 3.0E0)) => 3.0E0
max(())              => ()
max(0)               => 0
max(1, 3)            => 3
```

See also: `min()`.

fn:min

Compute the minimum value in a sequence.

```
min(xdt:anyAtomicType*) as xdt:anyAtomicType?
min(xdt:anyAtomicType*, string) as xdt:anyAtomicType?
```

The first argument specifies the sequence to use. The optional second argument specifies the collation to use for string comparisons; if omitted, the default collation is used.

If the sequence is empty, then the empty sequence is returned. If the sequence doesn't contain values all of the same type or types that can be promoted to a common type, then an error is raised. Only types that can be compared using `gt` are allowed.

If there are any `NaN` values in the sequence, then `min()` returns `NaN`. Otherwise, `min()` returns the least value in the sequence.

Listing C.72 min examples

```
min((1.0, 2, 3.0E0))  => 1.0
min(())               => ()
min(0)                => 0
min(1, 3)             => 1
```

See also: `max()`.

fn:name

Access the name property of a node.

```
name() as xs:string
name(node?) as xs:string
```

The optional argument specifies the node to use; when omitted, it defaults to the current context node. If the current context item isn't a node, an error is raised.

The result is the name of the node as an `xs:string` value (that is, the prefix and local name parts). If the node doesn't have a name, then `name()` returns the empty string. The `name()` function is mainly retained for backwards compatibility with XPath 1.0.

The `name()` function differs slightly from the `node-name()` function, which returns the name as an `xs:QName` value (namespace and local name parts) and returns the empty sequence for nodes with no name.

Listing C.73 name examples

```
name(<x/>)                   => "x"
name(<x:y xmlns:x="hello"/>) => "x:y"
name(<!-- comment -->)       => ""
```

See also: `local-name()`, `namespace-uri()`, and `node-name()`

.fn:namespace-uri

Access the namespace-uri property of a node.

```
namespace-uri() as xs:string
namespace-uri(node?) as xs:string
```

The optional argument specifies the node to use; when omitted, it defaults to the current context node. If the current context item isn't a node, an error is raised.

The result is the namespace part of the node's name. If the node doesn't have a name, or if the name doesn't have a namespace, then `namespace-uri()` returns the empty string.

Listing C.74 namespace-uri examples

```
namespace-uri(<x/>)                   => ""
namespace-uri(<x:y xmlns:x="hello"/>) => "hello"
namespace-uri(<!-- comment -->)       => ""
```

See also: `local-name()`, `name()`, and `node-name()`.

fn:node-name

Access the name property of a node.

```
node-name(node) as xs:QName?
```

The argument specifies the node to use.

The result is the name of the node as an `xs:QName` value (that is, the namespace and local name parts, without a prefix). If the node doesn't have a name, then `node-name()` returns the empty sequence.

The `node-name()` function differs slightly from the `name()` function, which returns the name as a string value (prefix and local name parts) and returns the empty string for nodes with no name.

Listing C.75 `node-name` examples

```
node-name(<x/>)                       => xs:QName((), "x")
node-name(<x:y xmlns:x="hello"/>) => xs:QName("hello", "y")
node-name(<!-- comment -->)           => ()
```

See also: `local-name()`, `name()`, and `namespace-uri()`.

fn:normalize-space

Perform whitespace normalization on a string.

```
normalize-space() as xs:string?
normalize-space(xs:string?) as xs:string?
```

The optional first argument specifies the input string; if omitted, it defaults to the string value of the current context item (in other words, `string(.)`).

If the argument is the empty sequence, then the empty sequence is returned. Otherwise, `normalize-space()` performs XML whitespace normalization to the string value. This process strips leading and trailing whitespace characters (`&#x9;`, `&#xA;`, `&#xD;`, and `&#x20;`) and replaces consecutive sequences of more than one whitespace character by a single space character (`&#x20;`).

Listing C.76 `normalize-space` examples

```
normalize-space(" Hello,    world  ") => "Hello, world"
normalize-space(())                   => ()
```

See also: `normalize-unicode()`.

fn:normalize-unicode

Perform Unicode normalization on a string.

```
normalize-unicode(xs:string?) as xs:string?
normalize-unicode(xs:string?, xs:string) as xs:string?
```

The first argument specifies the input string. The optional second argument specifies the Unicode normalization rule to be applied; if omitted, it defaults to the string `"NFC"`.

If the first argument is the empty sequence, then the empty sequence is returned. The second argument has leading and trailing whitespace removed and is converted to uppercase. If the result is the empty string, then the input string is returned unchanged. If the resulting normalization rule isn't supported by the implementation, then an error is raised.

Otherwise, `normalize-unicode()` returns the string that results from performing the requested normalization. Implementations are required to support only the default normalization form (`"NFC"`), may support four others defined by the Unicode Standard and W3C character model (`"NFD"`, `"NFKC"`, `"NFKD"`, and `"W3C"`), and may support other normalization forms.

Listing C.77 `normalize-unicode` examples

```
normalize-unicode("&#x97;&#x769;")          => "&#x225;"
normalize-unicode("&#x97;&#x769;", "NFC") => "&#x225;"
normalize-unicode("&#x97;&#x769;", "")      => "&#x97;&#x769;"
```

See also: `codepoints-to-string()`, `normalize-space()`, and `string-to-codepoints()`.

fn:not

Compute the logical negation of an expression.

```
not(item*) as xs:boolean
```

The first argument is the expression to be negated. It is first converted to boolean as if by a call to the `boolean()` function. Then `not()` turns true into false and vice versa.

XQuery expresses this operator as a function mainly for backwards compatibility with XPath 1.0; the other logical operators are keywords.

Listing C.78 not examples

```
not(true())     => false
not(false())    => true
not(1)          => false
not(0)          => true
not(())         => true
```

See also: `boolean()`, and the entries `and` and `or` in Appendix B.

fn:number

Convert an expression to double using XPath rules.

```
number() as xs:double
number(item?) as xs:double
```

The optional argument specifies an item to be converted to `xs:double`; when omitted, it defaults to the current context item.

If the item is the empty sequence, then `NaN` is returned. If the item is atomic, or a node with an atomic type, then its value is converted to double exactly like `cast as xs:double`. Otherwise, the string value of the item is computed as if by a call to the `string()` function, and then that value is converted to double using the same rules as `cast as xs:double`.

Note, however, that if the conversion to double fails, then instead of raising an error like `cast as xs:double` would, `number()` instead returns `NaN`.

Listing C.79 number examples

```
number("1.0")   => 1.0E0
number(false()) => 0.0E0
number(())      => NaN
```

See also: `boolean()` and `string()`, and `cast as` in Appendix B.

fn:one-or-more

Error if a sequence is empty.

```
one-or-more(item*) as item+
```

The argument specifies the sequence to use. Returns the sequence unchanged if it has length of at least one, otherwise it raises an error.

Listing C.80 `one-or-more` examples

```
one-or-more(())     => error
one-or-more(1)      => (1)
one-or-more((1,2)) => (1,2)
```

See also: `exactly-one()` and `zero-or-one()`.

fn:position

Compute the position in the current context.

```
position() as xs:integer?
```

Selects the position of the current context item within its sequence. Returns the empty sequence when the context is empty.

Listing C.81 `position` examples

```
()[error(position())] => error invoked with empty sequence
(1,2,4)[position()]    => (1, 2)
```

See also: `count()`, FLWOR, and `last()` in Appendix B.

fn:remove

Return a sequence with one item removed.

```
remove(item*, xs:integer) as item*
```

The first argument specifies the sequence to use. The second argument specifies the position of the item to be removed.

If the sequence is empty, then the empty sequence is returned. If the position is less than 1 or greater than the length of the sequence, then the sequence is returned unchanged.

Otherwise, the `remove()` function returns all the items in the sequence not at that position.

Listing C.82 remove examples

```
remove(('a','b','c','d'), 1) => ('b', 'c', 'd')
remove(('a','b','c','d'), 3) => ('a', 'b', 'd')
remove(('a','b','c','d'), 0) => ('a', 'b', 'c', 'd')
remove((), 1)                => ()
```

See also: subsequence().

fn:replace

Perform string replacement using regular expressions.

```
replace(xs:string?, xs:string, xs:string) as xs:string?
replace(xs:string?, xs:string, xs:string, xs:string) as xs:string?
```

The first argument specifies the input string, the second argument specifies a regular expression match pattern, and the third argument specifies the replacement pattern. The optional fourth argument specifies flags that modify how the match is performed; if omitted, it defaults to the empty string.

If the first argument is the empty sequence, then replace() returns the empty sequence. If the second argument isn't a valid match pattern, the third argument isn't a valid replacement pattern, or the fourth argument contains invalid flags, then replace() returns an error. Otherwise, replace() returns the string that results from performing the requested regular expression match and replacement.

Unless the match pattern uses anchors (^ or $), it can match anywhere in the string. See Appendix D for more information about the regular expression syntax and flags used by matches() and replace().

Listing C.83 replace examples

```
replace("Hello, world", "hello", "Bye")        => "Hello, world"
replace("Hello, world", "hello", "Bye", "i")   => "Bye, world"
replace("Hello, world", "l.", "")              => "Heo, world"
replace("Hello, world", "(H)(.*)(w)", "$3$2$1") => "wello, Horld"
```

See also: matches(), translate(), and Appendix D.

fn:resolve-QName

Parse a string as a qualified name, using the provided namespace scope.

```
resolve-QName(xs:string, element) as xs:QName
```

The first argument specifies a string to be parsed as a qualified name. The second argument specifies an element whose in-scope namespaces are to be used when parsing the qualified name (to resolve its prefix or default namespace).

If the string isn't a valid QName, or has a prefix for which there isn't an in-scope namespace defined on the element, then an error is raised.

Otherwise, if the string has a prefix, then the corresponding namespace is used. If the string doesn't have a prefix and the element has a default namespace in scope, then that namespace is used. If the string doesn't have a prefix, then no namespace is used.

Listing C.84 `resolve-QName` examples

```
resolve-QName("hello", <x/>)            => xs:QName((), "hello")
resolve-QName("hello", <x xmlns="hi"/>)  => xs:QName("hi","hello")
resolve-QName("x:hello",<x/>)           => error
resolve-QName("x:hello",<x xmlns:x="hi"/>)=> xs:QName("hi","hello")
```

See also: `expanded-QName()` and `get-in-scope-prefixes()`.

fn:resolve-uri

Resolve a URI value into an absolute URI.

```
resolve-uri(xs:string?) as xs:string
resolve-uri(xs:string?, xs:anyURI) as xs:string
```

The first argument specifies an optional relative URI string. The optional second argument specifies an absolute URI; when omitted, it defaults to the base URI of the static context (if there isn't one, then an error is raised).

If the base URI isn't an absolute URI, then an error is raised. If the relative URI is already absolute, then it is returned unchanged. If the relative URI is the empty string, then the string value of the provided base URI is returned. Otherwise, the relative URI is resolved against the base URI to produce an absolute URI, and the string value of this URI is returned.

Listing C.85 `resolve-uri` examples

```
resolve-uri("", xs:anyURI("http://www.awprofessional.com"))
=> "http://www.awprofessional.com"
resolve-uri("http://www.awprofessional.com")
=> "http://www.awprofessional.com"
resolve-uri("cseng", xs:anyURI("http://www.awprofessional.com"))
=> "http://www.awprofessional.com/cseng"
```

See also: `base-uri()`.

fn:reverse

Reverse a sequence.

```
reverse (item*) as item*
```

The `reverse()` function takes a single argument that specifies a sequence of items, and returns a new sequence with those items in reverse order. If the argument is the empty sequence, then `reverse()` returns the empty sequence.

Listing C.86 `reverse` examples

```
reverse (())       => ()
reverse (1 to 3)   => (3,2,1)
```

See also FLWOR (order by).

fn:root

Navigate to the root node in the same tree.

```
root() as node
root(node) as node
```

The optional first argument specifies a node; it defaults to the current context node. If there isn't a current context node and an argument isn't provided, then an error is raised.

Otherwise, `root()` returns the root node in the same tree as the supplied context node. There is always exactly one such root node, and it is always an element or document node.

Listing C.87 `root` examples

```
root()
root(<x/>)
```

See also: / (slash) in Appendix B.

fn:round

Round a number to an integer (round to closest, round half up).

```
round(numeric?) as numeric?
```

The argument specifies the value to be rounded. The return value has the same type as the argument.

If the argument is the empty sequence, then `round()` returns the empty sequence. If the argument type is `xs:float` or `xs:double` and is one of the special values positive or negative zero, positive or negative infinity, or `NaN`, then it is returned unchanged.

Otherwise, `round()` returns the integer closest to the argument. (Negative values that round up to zero result in negative zero.) Ties are broken by rounding up. This process is also commonly known as "round to closest, round half up."

Listing C.88 `round` examples

```
round(2)        =>   2
round(1.5)      =>   2.0
round(1.2)      =>   1.0
round(-1.5)     =>  -1.0
round(1 div 0)  =>   INF
```

See also: `ceiling()`, `floor()`, and `round-half-to-even()`.

fn:round-half-to-even

Round a number to an integer (round to closest, round half to even).

```
round-half-to-even(numeric?) as numeric?
round-half-to-even(numeric?, xs:integer) as numeric?
```

The first argument specifies the value to be rounded. The return value has the same type as this argument. The optional second argument specifies a precision to be used when rounding; the default value is zero.

If the first argument is the empty sequence, then `round-half-to-even()` returns the empty sequence. If the argument type is `xs:float` or `xs:double` and is one of the special values positive or negative zero, positive or negative infinity, or `NaN`, then it is returned unchanged.

Otherwise, `round-half-to-even()` rounds to the integer closest to the argument. (Negative values that round up to zero result in negative zero.) Ties are broken by rounding to even integers. This process is also commonly known as "round to closest, round half to even" or "banker's rounding" (because it is commonly used by financial applications to evenly distribute rounding errors).

Listing C.89 `round-half-to-even` examples

```
round-half-to-even(2)       =>  2
round-half-to-even(1.5)     =>  2.0
round-half-to-even(1.2)     =>  1.0
round-half-to-even(-1.5)    => -2.0
round-half-to-even(1 div 0) =>  INF
```

Before rounding takes place, the value is first divided by ten to the power of the precision; after rounding takes place, the argument is multiplied by ten to the power of the precision. The overall effect is to control the digit position at which rounding occurs.

Listing C.90 `round-half-to-even` with precision examples

```
round-half-to-even(123.456, 0)  => 123
round-half-to-even(123.456, 1)  => 123.4
round-half-to-even(123.456, 2)  => 123.46
round-half-to-even(123.456, 3)  => 123.456
round-half-to-even(123.456, -1) => 120.0
round-half-to-even(123.456, -2) => 100.0
round-half-to-even(123.456, -3) => 0.0
```

See also: `ceiling()`, `floor()`, and `round()`.

fn:starts-with

Test whether a string starts with a substring.

```
starts-with(xs:string?, xs:string?) as xs:boolean
starts-with(xs:string?, xs:string?, xs:string) as xs:boolean
```

The first argument specifies the string to be searched and the second argument specifies the substring to seek. The optional third argument specifies the collation to use for comparisons; it defaults to the Unicode code point collation.

If the second argument is the empty sequence or the empty string, then `starts-with()` returns true. Otherwise, if the first argument is the empty sequence or the empty string, then `starts-with()` returns false.

Otherwise, `starts-with()` returns true if the first argument begins with the second argument and returns false otherwise. This function is redundant with the more powerful `matches()` function, but is retained for compatibility with XPath 1.0 and convenience.

Listing C.91 `starts-with` examples

```
starts-with("Hello, world", ())      => true
starts-with("Hello, world", "Hello") => true
starts-with("Hello, world", "world") => false
starts-with("Hello, world", "")      => true
starts-with("", "world")             => false
```

See also: `contains()`, `ends-with()`, and `matches()`.

fn:string

Convert an item to xs:string using XPath rules.

```
string() as xs:string
string(item?) as xs:string
```

The optional argument specifies an arbitrary item to be converted to `xs:string`; when omitted, it defaults to the current context item.

If the argument is the empty sequence, then the empty string is returned. If the argument is a node, then its string value is returned. If the argument is xs:anyURI, then the URI is converted to string without escaping special characters. Otherwise, string($expr) returns the same result as cast as xs:string ($expr).

The string() function is from XPath 1.0; XQuery has just extended it to cover its additional types. In the process, XQuery has also changed how the string() function converts values of type xs:double to string. In XPath 1.0, doubles didn't use scientific notation and the special values positive and negative infinity converted to the strings "Infinity" and "-Infinity", respectively. In XQuery, doubles do use scientific E-notation, and the infinities are converted to "INF" and "-INF", respectively (matching the string representation used by XML Schema).

Listing C.92 string examples

```
string(())                   => ""
string(true())               => "true"
string(1.0)                  => "1.0"
string(xs:double(1.0))       => "1.0E0"
string(1 div 0)              => INF
string(<x>a<y>b</y><x>)      => "ab"
string(xs:date("2004-09-08")) => "2004-09-08"
```

See also: boolean() and number(), Appendix A, and cast as in Appendix B.

fn:string-join

Concatenate a sequence of strings with a delimiter in between values.

```
string-join(xs:string*, xs:string) as xs:string
```

The first argument specifies the sequence of strings to join. The second argument specifies a delimiter to insert between strings.

If the first argument is the empty sequence, then the empty string is returned. If the second argument is the empty string, then the strings are concatenated together like with the concat() function. Otherwise, string-join() concatenates the strings together, inserting the delimiter between them (when there are two or more strings in the sequence).

Listing C.93 `string-join` examples

```
string-join(("a", "b", "c"), "")    => "abc"
string-join(("a", "b", "c"), " ")   => "a b c"
string-join(("a", "b", "c"), ", ")  => "a, b, c"
string-join((), "x")                => ""
string-join("a", "x")               => "a"
string-join(("a", "b", "c"))  => error (: requires two arguments :)
string-join("a", "b", "c")    => error (: requires two arguments :)
```

See also: `concat()`.

fn:string-length

Compute the length of a string.

```
string-length() as xs:integer
string-length(xs:string?) as xs:integer
```

The optional argument specifies the string expression to measure. If omitted, then `string-length()` is applied to the current context item, converting it to string as if by calling the `string()` function.

If the argument is the empty sequence, then `string-length()` returns zero. Otherwise, `string-length()` returns the integer length of the string. It is exactly the same as `count(string-to-codepoints($theString))`.

Listing C.94 `string-length` examples

```
string-length(())            => 0
string-length('')            => 0
string-length("Hello, world") => 12
string-length(1)             => error()
```

See also: `count()` and `string()`.

fn:string-to-codepoints

Return the sequence of integer Unicode code points that make up a string.

```
string-to-codepoints(xs:string) as xs:integer*
```

The argument specifies a string. If the argument is the empty string, then `string-to-codepoints()` returns the empty sequence. Otherwise, `string-to-codepoints()` returns the sequence of integer Unicode code points corresponding to the characters in the string.

Listing C.95 `string-to-codepoints` examples

```
string-to-codepoints("Hello") => (72, 101, 108, 108, 111)
string-to-codepoints("")      => ()
```

See also: `codepoints-to-string()`.

fn:subsequence

Compute the subsequence of a sequence.

```
subsequence(item*, xs:double) as item*
subsequence(item*, xs:double, xs:double) as item*
```

The first argument specifies the sequence to use and the second argument specifies a start position (remember, the first item is at position 1). The optional third argument specifies the length of the subsequence; when omitted, `subsequence()` returns all items from the start position to the end of the original sequence.

If the sequence is empty, then `subsequence()` returns the empty sequence. Otherwise, `subsequence()` first applies `round()` to the position and length arguments, and then returns the subsequence of items starting at the rounded position value and continuing for the rounded length. If the rounded starting position is less than 1, then the subsequence starts from the beginning of the sequence. If the rounded length plus the rounded starting position exceeds the length of the sequence, then the subsequence includes all items from the start position to the end of the sequence.

In this way, `subsequence($seq $start, $len)` is equivalent to the path `($seq)[round($start) <= position() and position() < round($start) + round($len)]` and, similarly, the expression `subsequence($sequence, $start)` is equivalent to the path `($sequence)[round($start) < position()]`.

Listing C.96 subsequence examples

```
subsequence((1,2,4), 2)      => (2, 4)
subsequence((1,2,4), 2, 1) => 2
subsequence((1,2,4), 0, 3) => (1, 2)
subsequence((1,2,4), -1)     => (1, 2, 4)
```

See also: remove().

fn:substring

Compute the substring of a string.

```
substring(xs:string?, xs:double) as xs:string
substring(xs:string?, xs:double, xs:double) as xs:string
```

The first argument specifies the original string, and the second argument specifies the index at which to begin the substring. The optional third argument specifies the length of the substring; when omitted, the substring continues to the end of the string. The second and third arguments are rounded to an integer as if by the round() function.

If the first argument is the empty sequence, then substring() returns the empty string. Otherwise, substring returns a (possibly empty) substring of the original string. If the start index is less than 1 after rounding, then the substring begins at the first character. Remember that XQuery uses 1-based indices, so the first character is position 1. If the length after rounding is greater than the number of remaining characters, then the substring continues to the end of the string.

As in XPath 1.0, substring() uses the Unicode code point collation to perform the substring comparison.

Listing C.97 substring examples

```
substring((), 1, 2)                => ""
substring("Hello, world", 8, 0)    => ""
substring("Hello, world", 8, 5)    => "world"
substring("Hello, world", 8)       => "world"
substring("Hello, world", 8, 100)  => "world"
substring("Hello, world", 7.5, 4.5) => "world"
substring("Hello, world", 7.4, 4.4) => " wor"
substring("Hello, world", -1)      => "Hello, world"
substring("Hello, world", 1)       => "Hello, world"
```

```
substring("Hello, world", 2)       => "ello, world"
substring("abc", -1 div 0)         => "abc"
substring("abc", -1 div 0, 3)      => ""
```

See also: `substring-after()` and `substring-before()`.

fn:substring-after

Return the portion of a string that occurs after a substring.

```
substring-after(xs:string?, xs:string?) as xs:string
substring-after(xs:string?, xs:string?, xs:string) as xs:string
```

The first argument specifies the original string and the second argument specifies the substring match pattern. The optional third argument specifies the collation to use for comparisons; it defaults to the Unicode code point collation.

If the first argument is the empty sequence or the empty string, then `substring-after()` returns the empty string. Otherwise, if the second argument is the empty sequence or the empty string, then `substring-after()` returns the first argument.

Otherwise, `substring-after()` searches from the beginning of the original string for the first occurrence of the substring match pattern (using the collation to perform comparisons). If no match is found, or the first match occurs at the end of the original string, then `substring-after()` returns the empty string. Otherwise, it returns the substring of the original string from the first character after the match to the end of the original string.

Listing C.98 `substring-after` examples

```
substring-after((), "x")              => ""
substring-after("x", ())              => "x"
substring-after("Hello, world", "")   => "Hello, world"
substring-after("Hello, world", " ")  => "world"
substring-after("Hello, world", "ll") => "o, world"
substring-after("Hello, world", "x")  => ""
```

See also: `substring()` and `substring-before()`, and `collation` in Appendix B.

fn:substring-before

Return the portion of a string that occurs before a substring.

```
substring-before(xs:string?, xs:string?) as xs:string?
substring-before(xs:string?, xs:string?, xs:string) as xs:string?
```

The first argument specifies the original string, and the second argument specifies the substring match pattern. The optional third argument specifies the collation to use for comparisons; it defaults to the Unicode code point collation.

If the first argument is the empty sequence or the empty string, then `substring-before()` returns the empty string. Otherwise, if the second argument is the empty sequence or the empty string, then `substring-before()` returns the first argument.

Otherwise, `substring-before()` searches from the beginning of the original string for the first occurrence of the substring match pattern (using the collation to perform comparisons). If no match is found, or the first match occurs at the beginning of the original string, then `substring-before()` returns the empty string. Otherwise, it returns the substring of the original string from the first character of the original string to the beginning of the match.

Listing C.99 `substring-before` examples

```
substring-before((), "x")             => ""
substring-before("x", ())             => "x"
substring-before("Hello, world", "")  => "Hello, world"
substring-before("Hello, world", " ") => "Hello,"
substring-before("Hello, world", "ll") => "He"
substring-before("Hello, world", "x") => ""
```

See also: `substring()` and `substring-after()`, and `collation` in Appendix B.

fn:subtract-dateTimes-yielding-dayTimeDuration

Subtract two xs:dateTime values and return the result as xdt:dayTimeDuration.

```
subtract-dateTimes-yielding-dayTimeDuration(xs:dateTime?, xs:dateTime?)
                                as xdt:dayTimeDuration?
```

The first argument specifies the initial `xs:dateTime` value; the second argument specifies the `xs:dateTime` value to subtract from the first argument. If either argument is the empty sequence, then the empty sequence is returned.

Both arguments are first normalized, including adjusting to the implicit time zone if necessary (see `adjust-dateTime-to-timezone()`). Then the second is subtracted from the first, producing some (possibly negative) number of seconds. From this value, the number of days, hours, minutes, and seconds are calculated and returned as an `xdt:dayTimeDuration`, and the remainder (years and months) is discarded.

Listing C.100 `subtract-dateTimes-yielding-dayTimeDuration` example

```
subtract-dateTimes-yielding-dayTimeDuration(
    xs:dateTime("2004-06-20T18:05:13.8"),
    xs:dateTime("2002-02-18T11:42:00")
) => xdt:dayTimeDuration("P2DT6H23M13.8S")
```

See also: `adjust-dateTime-to-timezone()` and `subtract-dateTimes-yielding-yearMonthDuration()`.

fn:subtract-dateTimes-yielding-yearMonthDuration

Subtract two xs:dateTime values and return the result as xdt:yearMonthDuration.

```
subtract-dateTimes-yielding-yearMonthDuration(xs:dateTime?,
                        xs:dateTime?) as xdt:yearMonthDuration?
```

The first argument specifies the initial `xs:dateTime` value; the second argument specifies the `xs:dateTime` value to subtract from the first argument. If either argument is the empty sequence, then the empty sequence is returned.

Both arguments are first normalized, including adjusting to the implicit time zone if necessary (see `adjust-dateTime-to-timezone()`). Then the second is subtracted from the first, producing some (possibly negative) number of seconds. From this value, the number of years and months are calculated and returned as an `xdt:yearMonthDuration`, and the remainder (days, hours, minutes, and seconds) is discarded.

Listing C.101 subtract-dateTimes-yielding-yearMonthDuration example

```
subtract-dateTimes-yielding-yearMonthDuration(
    xs:dateTime("2004-06-20T18:05:13.8"),
    xs:dateTime("2002-02-18T11:42:00")
) => xdt:yearMonthDuration("P2Y4M")
```

See also: adjust-dateTime-to-timezone() and subtract-dateTimes-yielding-dayTimeDuration().

fn:sum

Compute the sum of a sequence of values.

```
sum(xdt:anyAtomicType*) as xdt:anyAtomicType?
```

The argument is the sequence of values to be summed.

If the sequence is empty, then the double value 0.0E0 is returned. Any untyped items are promoted to xs:double. If all items in the sequence cannot be promoted to a common type, or don't have types that can be summed, then an error occurs.

Otherwise, all items in the sequence are promoted to a common type and added together to produce the result. If any value is NaN, then sum() returns NaN.

Listing C.102 sum examples

```
sum((1.0, 2, 3.0E0)) => 6.0E0
sum(())              => 0.0E0
sum(0)               => 0
sum(1, 3)            => 4
```

See also: avg(), count(), max(), and min().

fn:tokenize

Split a string into a sequence of tokens.

```
tokenize(xs:string?, xs:string) as xs:string*
tokenize(xs:string?, xs:string, xs:string) as xs:string*
```

The first argument specifies the input string, and the second argument specifies the delimiter that separates tokens. An optional third string can be used to specify flags that control how the tokenization is performed; if omitted, it defaults to the empty string.

If the first argument is the empty sequence, then the empty sequence is returned. If the third argument contains invalid flags, then an error is raised. Otherwise, `tokenize()` splits the string at every occurrence of the delimiter, resulting in a sequence of substrings (tokens), excluding the delimiter itself. Whenever the delimiter appears twice in a row or at the beginning or end of the input string, an empty string is used in the return sequence.

The same flags that are used to modify `matches()` and `replace()` are used by `tokenize()`. See Appendix D for details.

The `tokenize()` function is essentially the opposite of the `string-join()` function.

Listing C.103 `tokenize` examples

```
tokenize("Hello, world", ", ")     => ("Hello", "world")
tokenize("Hello, world", "l")      => ("He", "", "o, wor", "d")
tokenize("Hello, world", "h", "i") => ("", "ello, world")
```

Unfortunately, the pattern used by `tokenize()` isn't a regular expression. However, you can achieve a similar effect by first applying `replace()` to match the regular expression of interest and replace it with some pattern that doesn't otherwise occur in the string, and then applying `tokenize()` to the replaced string.

Listing C.104 `tokenize` can be combined with regular expressions

```
tokenize(replace("Hello, world", "l.", "X"), "X") => ("He", "o, wor", "")
```

See also: `matches()`, `replace()`, `string-join()`, and Appendix D.

fn:trace

Implementation-defined function for debugging.

```
trace(item*, xs:string) as item*
```

The first argument is the return value for this function, and may also be used by the implementation during tracing. The second argument is a trace message.

The effect of the `trace()` function is implementation-defined; the idea is to provide the ability to emit messages during execution without terminating the query (similar to the `<xsl:message>` instruction in XSLT), but implementations are free to do anything, including nothing. The return value of the trace function is its first argument.

Also note that implementations may reorder or eliminate instructions; for example, `trace(true(), "x")` and `trace(false(), "y")` might execute neither, one, or both trace methods, in any order, depending on how the query is optimized and executed.

Listing C.105 `trace` example

```
trace(("x", $x), "The value of {1} is {2}.")
```

See also: `error()`.

fn:translate

Translate some characters in a string into other characters.

```
translate(xs:string?, xs:string?, xs:string?) as xs:string?
```

The first argument is the original string. The second and third arguments specify the characters to be replaced.

If any argument is the empty sequence, then `translate()` returns the empty sequence. If the third argument is longer than the second argument, extra characters are ignored. Otherwise, `translate()` replaces in the original string all occurrences of characters in the second argument by the corresponding characters in the third argument. When there isn't a corresponding character in the third argument (because the second argument is longer), then the character is removed.

Listing C.106 `translate` examples

```
translate("Hello, world", "le", "pix")        => "Hippo, worpd"
translate("Hello, world", "elo w", "")         => "Herd"
translate("Hello", "abcdefghijklmnopqrstuvwxyz",
             "ABCDEFGHIJKLMNOPQRSTUVWXYZ") => "HELLO"
translate("Hello", (), "x")                    => ()
```

The `translate()` function is in XQuery primarily for backwards compatibility with XPath 1.0 (where it was used mainly as a poor-man's `upper-case()` and `lower-case()`).

See also: `lower-case()`, `replace()`, and `upper-case()`.

fn:true

The boolean literal representing truth.

```
true() as xs:boolean
```

Returns the boolean constant true.

XQuery defines the true constant using a function mainly for backwards compatibility with XPath 1.0 and to eliminate the need for reserved keywords.

Listing C.107 `true` example

```
true()    => true
```

See also: `false()`.

fn:unordered

Provide an optimization hint that the order of an expression is unimportant.

```
unordered(item*) as item*
```

The first argument specifies the sequence to use. The `unordered()` function then returns this sequence in any order (often in the same order as the original).

This function is really useful only as an optimization hint to the query processor that the expression order doesn't need to be maintained. For example, most path expressions implicitly sort by document order, but if this is unimportant to your application, then applying the `unordered()` function to such expressions may improve performance (depending on the implementation).

Listing C.108 `unordered` example

```
unordered(doc('orders.xml')//order)
```

See also: Chapter 13.

fn:upper-case

Convert a string to uppercase.

```
upper-case(xs:string?) as xs:string?
```

The argument specifies the string to be converted to uppercase.

If the argument is the empty sequence, `upper-case()` returns the empty sequence. Otherwise, `upper-case()` returns the string with all characters translated into their uppercase forms. Characters without uppercase forms are unchanged.

Note that changing case can alter the length of the string.

Listing C.109 `upper-case` examples

```
upper-case("Hello, world") => "HELLO, WORLD"
upper-case("")             => ""
upper-case(())             => ()
```

See also: `lower-case()`.

fn:zero-or-one

Error if a sequence contains more than one item.

```
zero-or-one(item*) as item?
```

The argument specifies the sequence to use. This function returns the sequence unchanged if it has length at most one, otherwise it raises an error.

Listing C.110 `zero-or-one` examples

```
zero-or-one(())    => ()
zero-or-one(1)     => (1)
zero-or-one((1,2)) => error
```

Many functions and operators in XQuery work only on sequences with a length of at most one. One way to ensure that a sequence has the required length is to use the `zero-or-one()` function, as shown in Listing C.111.

Listing C.111 Applying an operator to a sequence using `zero-or-one`

```
doc(zero-or-one(locations/@href))
```

A different way to achieve a similar effect is to iterate over the sequence with FLWOR and apply the operator to each member of the sequence individually, as shown in Listing C.112. Note that this can result in a sequence of more than one value; the choice of this approach versus `zero-or-one()` depends on the desired effect.

Listing C.112 Applying an operator to a sequence memberwise

```
for $i in locations/@href
return doc($i)
```

See also: `exactly-one()` and `one-or-more()`.

Regular Expressions

D.1 Introduction

This appendix provides an overview of the XQuery regular expression syntax, which is based on the syntax used by XML Schema. In theory, this is the syntax supported by all XQuery implementations, although in practice you may find that your implementation varies slightly from the description here. When in doubt, consult the documentation accompanying your implementation.

This appendix begins with an overview of the regular expression syntax used by the built-in `matches()` and `replace()` functions (see Appendix C). It then provides a grammar for this regular expression language (Listing D.6) and a table of the Unicode properties (Table D.3).

D.2 Overview

Regular expressions, also known as *regexps* or *regexes*, provide a simple but powerful language for performing sophisticated string matching and replacement. Regexps are often more efficient and easier to maintain than hand-written programs that accomplish the same tasks, but sometimes are overlooked because they are perceived as complex and difficult to use.

XQuery uses a regular expression syntax that is derived from the ones used by XML Schema 1.0 and Perl. In XQuery, regular expressions match according to Unicode code point values, so collation isn't used. Only two functions (`matches()` and `replace()`) use regular expressions, but they are powerful tools for text manipulation.

Each regular expression consists of one or more *branches* separated by vertical bars (`|`). Each branch corresponds to a choice of expressions to match; the regular expression matches a string if any of its branches match.

Each branch consists of zero or more *atoms*, each of which may have an optional *modifier*. Each atom matches a character; atoms can be many different expressions, but most commonly are ordinary characters or the wildcard character (.). (Don't confuse regular expression atoms with atomic values, or the regular expression wildcard character with the wildcard node test used in paths.)

Ordinary characters match only themselves; the wildcard character matches (almost) any character. We explore the other kinds of atoms later in this section. Note that whitespace is significant in regular expressions, so don't add extra space characters unless you mean to do so.

Listing D.1 Basic regular expressions

```
replace("xyz", "x", "a")          => "ayz"
replace("xyz", ".", "a")          => "aaa"
replace("xyz", "x|z", "a")        => "aya"
replace("xyz", "x |z", "a")       => "xya"
replace("x y z", "x |z", "a")     => "ay a"
```

The modifier immediately follows an atom and determines the number of times that atom must appear. It consists of a *quantifier* and an optional *reluctant quantifier*. The quantifiers and their meanings are listed in Table D.1. Listing D.2 demonstrates their use.

An error is raised if in the expression {n,m}, n is greater than m. If the modifier indicates the atom must appear exactly zero times, then it's equivalent to the empty string (in other words, as if the atom hadn't been listed in the regular expression at all).

Table D.1 Regular expression quantifiers

Modifier	Meaning
none	Atom must appear exactly once
?	Atom must appear zero or one times
*	Atom must appear zero or more times
+	Atom must appear one or more times
{n}	Atom must appear exactly n times
{n,}	Atom must appear at least n times
{n,m}	Atom must appear at least n and at most m times

Listing D.2 Using regular expression modifiers

```
matches("abc", "d?")         => true
replace("abc", "ad?", "x") => "xbc"
matches("abc", "d*")         => true
matches("abc", "d+")         => false
matches("xxx", "x{2}")       => false
matches("xxx", "x{3}")       => true
matches("xxx", "x{2,}")      => true
matches("xxx", "x{2,4}")     => true
matches("xxx", "x{4,5}")     => false
```

Because certain characters, such as parentheses, have special meaning in regular expressions, they cannot be expressed directly. These meta-characters require a backslash escape in front of them. Most backslash-escaped characters result in the character being escaped, for example, \. matches the period (.). The exceptions are the three escapes \t, \n, and \r, which match the tab, new line, and carriage return characters, respectively (U+0009, U+000A, and U+000D). Listing D.3 shows how to escape a meta-character.

Listing D.3 Meta-characters require escaping in regular expressions

```
replace("x(z", "(", "y")    => error (: invalid regexp :)
replace("x(z", "\(", "y")   => "xyz"
replace("x.y.z", ".", "-") => "-----"
replace("x.y.z", "\.", "-") => "x-y-z"
```

At this point, you already know enough about XQuery regular expressions to be productive with them. However, there are some additional features that may be worth learning.

The caret (^) and dollar sign ($) meta-characters may be used to represent the beginning and end of the string, respectively. These are especially useful for ensuring that the entire string matches the pattern.

The functions that use regular expressions take an optional additional parameter that can specify two flags, i and m. The i flag indicates that the regular expression matches should be carried out case-insensitively. The m flag indicates that the regular expression should match in "multi-line" mode. In multi-line mode, the wildcard character doesn't match the new line character,

Table D.2 Additional escapes

Escape sequence	Meaning	Equivalent to
\c	XML name characters.	n/a
\d	XML digit characters.	\p{Nd}
\i	XML initial name characters.	[_\p{L}]
\n	New line character (U+000A)	[#x000A]
\p{IsBlock}	Match characters within the named Unicode block, such as IsBasicLatin or IsKatakana. See the Unicode Database for a list of all block names.	n/a
\p{Property}	Match characters having the named Unicode property, such as Lu (upper-case) or Mn (non-spacing).	n/a
\r	Carriage return character (U+000D)	[#x000D]
\s	Any XML whitespace character.	[\n\r\t]
\t	Tab character (U+0009)	[#x0009]
\w	Word characters—all characters except punctuation, separator, and "other" characters.	[#x0000-#x10FFFF]-[\p{P}\p{Z}\p{C}]

and the ^ and $ meta-characters match the beginning or end of lines, in addition to the beginning or end of the string.

In addition to the character escapes described previously, XQuery (and XML Schema) support escapes that match entire classes of Unicode characters. These escapes can match characters according to certain properties (or the absence of those properties), or match characters that belong to certain predefined categories (or don't belong). Given some escape \x, the capitalized version \X has the negated meaning. For example, \s matches any whitespace character, while \S matches any non-whitespace character. Table D.2 summarizes these special escape sequences and Listing D.4 demonstrates their use.

Note that implementations are free to implement new blocks or properties as they become part of the Unicode Database. In my experience, many implementations don't support these Unicode property escapes (\p). Also, some implementations don't support subtracted subgroups like [A-Z]-[AEIOU].

Listing D.4 Character escapes in regular expressions

```
replace("Hello, world", "\s", "X") => "Hello,Xworld"
replace("Hello, world", "\S", "X") => "XXXXX, XXXXX"
replace("Hello, world", "\p{Lu}", "")  => "ello, world"
replace("Hello, world", "\p{P}\s", "") => "Helloworld"
```

D.3 Advanced Regexps

Parenthesized subexpressions are treated as groups. The matching part of the input string is called a *captured substring*, and can be referenced in the replacement using backslash followed by the number of the group (the first group is number 1). XQuery requires implementations to support references in replacements only; some implementations may also allow back references in the match pattern. Listing D.5 demonstrates the use of parenthesized groups.

Listing D.5 Using parentheses to capture substrings

```
replace("xylophone", "xylo(.*)", "tele$1") => "telephone"
replace("<x/><y/>", "<(.*)/>", "$1")       => "x/><y"
replace("<x/><y/>", "<(\w*)/>", "$1")      => "xy"
matches("abcabc", "(abc)$1")               => false
                        (: some implementations return true :)
```

Normally, regular expressions match greedily (matching the longest substring possible). Greedy matching can sometimes produce unexpected results; for example, in the second example in Listing D.5, the pattern <(.*)/> matches everything between the first < and the last /> as a single pattern, instead of matching each element separately. The third example works around this by using the more specific pattern <(\w*)/>, but another way is to use a reluctant qualifier, as shown in Listing D.6. The optional reluctant quantifier (?) indicates that instead the regular expression should match the shortest substring possible for the regular expression to still succeed. This "reluctance" makes a difference only when using the replace() function.

Listing D.6 Ordinary and reluctant quantifiers

```
replace("<x/><y/>", "<(.*)/>", "$1")   => "x/><y"
replace("<x/><y/>", "<(.*?)/>", "$1")  => "xy"
replace("xyzxyzxyz", "x(.*)z", "$1")   => "yzxyzxy"
replace("xyzxyzxyz", "x(.*?)z", "$1")  => "yyy"
```

D.4 Regexp Language

XQuery doesn't actually define a grammar for its regular expression syntax, but instead refers to the XML Schema 1.0 Recommendation. Surprisingly, that document also neglects to provide a formal definition, relying instead on prose description. I used that description together with the additional features introduced by XQuery to produce the grammar in Listing D.7.

In this grammar, `Char` is any XQuery character that isn't a meta-character (`MetaChar`) for the regular expression language, and `XmlChar` is any character that isn't a square bracket (`[` or `]`) or hyphen (`-`). The final production `Property` corresponds to the character properties listed in Table D.3, and the `Block` production corresponds to the names of character ranges in the Unicode Database.

Listing D.7 The regular expression language of XQuery

```
Regexp     := Branch ( '|' Branch)*
Branch     := (Atom Modifier?)*
Modifier   := Quantifier ('?')?
Quantifier := '?' | '*' | '+' | '{' Quantity '}'
Quantity   := QRange | QExact
QRange     := QExact ',' QExact?
QExact     := [0-9]+
Atom       := Char | Escape | Group | '(' Regexp ')'
MetaChar   := '^' | '$' | '.' | '\' | '?' | '*' | '+'
              | '(' | ')' | '[' | ']' | '{' | '}'
Group      := '[' (PosGroup | NegGroup | SubGroup) ']'
PosGroup   := (Range | Escape)+
NegGroup   := '^' PosGroup
SubGroup   := (PosGroup | NegGroup) '-' Group
Range      := XmlChar | CharOrEsc '-' CharOrEsc
```

```
CharOrEsc  := XmlChar | SingleEsc
Escape     := SingleEsc | MultiEsc | CatEsc | ComplEsc | WildEsc
WildEsc    := '.'
SingleEsc  := '\' (MetaChar | 'n' | 'r' | 't' | '-')
MultiEsc   := '\' EscSeq
EscSeq     := 's' | 'i' | 'c' | 'd' | 'w'
           | 'S' | 'I' | 'C' | 'D' | 'W'
CatEsc     := '\p{' CharProp '}'
ComplEsc   := '\P{' CharProp '}'
CharProp   := Property | Block
```

D.5 Character Properties

The table is reproduced from the XML Schema 1.0 Recommendation. The Unicode blocks accepted by the `\p{}` expression (such as `Katakana` and `BasicLatin`) are listed in the Unicode Database, and are omitted here for brevity.

Table D.3 Character properties for use with \p

Category	Property	Meaning
Letters	L	All letters
	Lu	Uppercase letters
	Ll	Lowercase letters
	Lt	Titlecase letters
	Lm	Modifier
	Lo	Other
Marks	M	All marks
	Mn	Non-spacing
	Mc	Spacing combining
	Me	Enclosing
Numbers	N	All numbers
	Nd	Decimal digit
	Nl	Letter
	No	Other

Table D.3 cont

Category	Property	Meaning
Punctuation	P	All punctuation
	Pc	Connector
	Pd	Dash
	Ps	Open
	Pe	Close
	Pi	Initial quote
	Pf	Final quote
	Po	Other
Separators	Z	All separators
	Zs	Space
	Zl	Line
	Zp	Paragraph
Symbols	S	All symbols
	Sm	Math
	Sc	Currency
	Sk	Modifier
	So	Other
Other	C	All others
	Cc	Control
	Cf	Format
	Co	Private use
	Cn	Not assigned

Grammar

E.1 Introduction

This appendix provides an EBNF grammar for the XQuery language. This grammar differs from the official one printed in the standard only in presentation (for example, some names have been changed and some productions cleaned up to make the grammar easier to read).

XQuery borrows two definitions from the XML 1.0 and XML Names specifications: `Char` and `NCName`. Because these definitions involve large character tables, I didn't include them here but instead refer you to the URLs in the grammar below.

The XQuery grammar requires that characters be recognized and parsed differently in certain contexts (i.e., a context-sensitive lexer). For example, within element or attribute content, characters are parsed differently than outside it. XQuery also requires that whitespace be handled differently in some contexts.

In general, XQuery requires three characters of lookahead to handle expressions like XML comments, XQuery pragmas, and CDATA sections. XQuery often requires one or two tokens of lookahead to disambiguate production choices.

E.2 The XQuery Grammar

Expressions on the left consist of the productions on the right of the `::=` symbol. Quoted strings and regular expression character ranges indicate literal text. The EBNF symbols `*`, `+`, `?`, `|`, and `()` are used with their usual meanings (zero or more, one or more, zero or one, choice, and group, respectively).

Listing E.1 The XQuery grammar

```
Module          ::= Version? (Main | Library)
Main            ::= Prolog QueryBody
Library         ::= ModuleDecl Prolog
ModuleDecl      ::= "module" namespace prefix "=" String ";"
Prolog          ::= ((BaseURIDecl
                    | CollationDecl
                    | DefaultNsDecl
                    | FunctionDecl
                    | ModuleImport
                    | NamespaceDecl
                    | SchemaImport
                    | ValidationDecl
                    | VarDecl
                    | XMLSpaceDecl) ";")*
Version         ::= "xquery" "version" String ";"
BaseURIDecl     ::= "declare" "base-uri" StringLiteral
CollationDecl   ::= "declare" "default" "collation" "=" String
DefaultNsDecl   ::= "declare" "default" ("element" | "function")
                    "namespace" "=" String
FunctionDecl    ::= "declare" "function" QName "(" ParamList? ")"
                    ("as" SequenceType)? (EnclosedExpr | "external")
ParamList       ::= Param ("," Param)*
Param           ::= Variable TypeDecl?
ModuleImport    ::= "import" "module" ("namespace" NCName "=")?
                    String ("at" String)?
NamespaceDecl   ::= "declare" "namespace" NCName "=" String
ValidationDecl  ::= "declare" "validation" ("lax" | "strict" | "skip")
VarDecl         ::= "declare" S "variable" Variable TypeDecl?
                    ((EnclosedExpr) | "external")
XMLSpaceDecl    ::= "declare" "xmlspace" "=" ("preserve" | "strip")
QueryBody       ::= Expr
Expr            ::= ExprSingle ("," ExprSingle)*
ExprSingle      ::= FLWOR
                    | Quantified
                    | Typeswitch
                    | Conditional
                    | Disjunction
FLWOR           ::= (For | Let)+ Where? OrderBy? Return
For             ::= "for" ForDecl ("," ForDecl)*
ForDecl         ::= Variable TypeDecl? PositionVar? "in" ExprSingle
```

```
PositionVar    ::= "at" Variable
Let            ::= "let" LetDecl ("," LetDecl)*
LetDecl        ::= Variable TypeDecl? ":=" ExprSingle
Where          ::= "where" Expr
OrderBy        ::= "stable"? "order" "by" OrderByList
OrderByList    ::= OrderSpec ("," OrderSpec)*
OrderSpec      ::= ExprSingle OrderModifier
OrderModifier  ::= ("ascending" | "descending")?
                   ("empty" ("greatest" | "least"))?
                   ("collation" String)?
Return         ::= "return" ExprSingle
Quantified     ::= ("some" | "every") QuantList "satisfies" ExprSingle
QuantList      ::= QuantDecl ("," QuantDecl)*
QuantDecl      ::= Variable TypeDecl? "in" ExprSingle
Typeswitch     ::= "typeswitch" "(" Expr ")" CaseClause+
                   "default" Variable? "return" ExprSingle
CaseClause     ::= "case" (Variable "as")? SequenceType
                   "return" ExprSingle
Conditional    ::= "if" "(" Expr ")" "then" Expr "else" ExprSingle
Disjunction    ::= Conjunction ( "or" Conjunction )*
Conjunction    ::= InstanceOf ( "and" InstanceOf )*
InstanceOf     ::= TreatAs ( "instance" "of" SequenceType )?
TreatAs        ::= CastableAs ( "treat" "as" SequenceType )?
CastableAs     ::= CastAs ( "castable" "as" SingleType )?
CastAs         ::= Comparison ( "cast" "as" SingleType )?
Comparison     ::= Range ( CompOp Range)?
CompOp         ::= ValueComp
                   | GeneralComp
                   | NodeComp
                   | OrderComp
ValueComp      ::= "eq" | "ne" | "lt" | "le" | "gt" | "ge"
GeneralComp    ::= "=" | "!=" | "<" | "<=" | ">" | ">="
NodeComp       ::= "is"
OrderComp      ::= "<<" | ">>"
Range          ::= Addition ( "to" Addition )?
Addition       ::= Multiplication ( ("+" | "-") Multiplication )*
Multiplication ::= Unary ( ("*" | "div" | "idiv" | "mod") Unary )*
Unary          ::= ("-" | "+")* Union
Union          ::= Set ( ("union" | "|") Set )*
Set            ::= Value ( ("intersect" | "except") Value )*
Value          ::= Validation | Path
```

```
Path            ::= ("/" RelativePath?)
                  | ("//" RelativePath)
                  | RelativePath
RelativePath    ::= StepExpr (("/" | "//") StepExpr)*
StepExpr        ::= AxisStep | FilterStep
AxisStep        ::= Step Predicate*
FilterStep      ::= PrimaryExpr Predicate*
Step            ::= Axis "::" NodeTest | AbbrStep
AbbrStep        ::= "." | ".." | "@" NameTest | NodeTest
Axis            ::= "ancestor"
                  | "ancestor-or-self"
                  | "attribute"
                  | "child"
                  | "descendant-or-self"
                  | "descendant"
                  | "following"
                  | "following-sibling"
                  | "parent"
                  | "preceding"
                  | "preceding-sibling"
                  | "self"
NodeTest        ::= KindTest | NameTest
NameTest        ::= QName | Wildcard
Wildcard        ::= (NCName ":")? "*"
                  | "*" ":" NCName
PrimaryExpr     ::= Literal | FunctionCall | Variable | "(" Expr? ")" | Ctor
Predicate       ::= "[" Expr "]"
Validation      ::= "validate" SchemaMode? SchemaContxt? EnclosedExpr
SchemaContxt    ::= "context" SchemaCtxtLoc | "global"
Ctor            ::= ElementCtor
                  | XmlComment
                  | XmlPI
                  | CdataSection
                  | CompDocCtor
                  | CompElemCtor
                  | CompAttrCtor
                  | CompTextCtor
                  | CompNsCtor
                  | CompCommentCtor
                  | CompPiCtor
Literal         ::= Number | String
Number          ::= Integer | Decimal | Double
```

```
FunctionCall   ::= QName "(" Expr? ")"
ElementCtor    ::= "<" QName AttrList
                   ("/>" | (">" ElemContent* "</" QName S? ">"))
XmlComment     ::= "<!—" Char* "—>"
XmlPI          ::= "<?" NCName Char* "?>"
CdataSection   ::= "<![CDATA[" Char* "]]>"
CompDocCtor    ::= "document" EnclosedExpr
CompElemCtor   ::= "element" (QName | EnclosedExpr) "{" Expr? "}"
CompAttrCtor   ::= "attribute" (QName | EnclosedExpr) "{" Expr? "}"
CompTextCtor   ::= "text" "{" Expr? "}"
CompNsCtor     ::= "namespace" NCName "{" Expr "}"
CompCommentCtor::= "comment" "{" Expr "}"
CompPiCtor     ::= "processing-information" ("{" Expr "}")? "{" Expr? "}"
ElemContent    ::= ElementChar
                   | Content
                   | ElementCtor
                   | CdataSection
                   | XmlComment
                   | XmlPI
AttrList       ::= (S (QName S? "=" S? AttrValue)?)*
AttrValue      ::= ('"' (EscapeQuot | AttrContent)* '"')
                   | ("'" (EscapeApos | AttrContent)* "'")
AttrContent    ::= QuoteAttrChar
                   | AposAttrChar
                   | Content
Content        ::= CharRef
                   | "{{"
                   | "}}"
                   | EnclosedExpr
                   | EntityRef
EnclosedExpr   ::= "{" Expr "}"
TypeDecl       ::= "as" SequenceType
SingleType     ::= AtomicType "?"?
SequenceType   ::= ItemType Occurrence?
                   | "empty" "(" ")"
ItemType       ::= AtomicType | KindTest | "item" "(" ")"
Occurrence     ::= "?" | "*" | "+"
AtomicType     ::= QName
KindTest       ::= DocumentTest
                   | ElementTest
                   | AttributeTest
                   | PITest
```

```
                          | CommentTest
                          | TextTest
                          | AnyKindTest
ElementTest      ::= "element" "(" (SchemaCtxtPath QName |
                            NodeName ("," TypeName "nillable"?)? )? ")"
AttributeTest    ::= "attribute" "(" (SchemaCtxtPath "@" QName |
                            "@" NodeName ("," TypeName)?)? ")"
NodeName         ::= QName | "*"
TypeName         ::= QName | "*"
PITest           ::= "processing-instruction" "(" String? ")"
DocumentTest     ::= "document-node" "(" ElementTest? ")"
CommentTest      ::= "comment" "(" ")"
TextTest         ::= "text" "(" ")"
AnyKindTest      ::= "node" "(" ")"
SchemaCtxtPath   ::= SchemaGlobCtxt "/" (SchemaCtxtStep "/")*
SchemaCtxtLoc    ::= (SchemaCtxtPath QName) | SchemaGlobType
SchemaImport     ::= "import" "schema" SchemaPrefix? String
                        ("at" String)?
SchemaPrefix     ::= ("namespace" NCName "=")
                      | ("default" "element" "namespace" "=")
SchemaMode       ::= "lax" | "strict" | "skip"
SchemaGlobType   ::= "type" "(" QName ")"
SchemaGlobCtxt   ::= QName | SchemaGlobType
SchemaCtxtStep   ::= QName
QName            ::= (NCName ':')? NCName
Variable         ::= "$" QName
Integer          ::= Digits
Decimal          ::= ("." Digits) | (Digits "." [0-9]*)
Double           ::= (("." Digits) | (Digits ("." [0-9]*)?))
                        ("e" | "E") ("+" | "-")? Digits
String           ::= ('"' (EntityRef | CharRef | EscQuot | [^"&])* '"')
                      | ("'" (EntityRef | CharRef | EscApos | [^'&])* "'")
EscQuot          ::= '"' '"'
EscApos          ::= "'" "'"
S                ::= (#x20 | #x9 | #xD | #xA)+
Comment          ::= "(:" (Char | Comment)* ":)"
Pragma           ::= "(::" "pragma" QName Char* "::)"
Extension        ::= "(::" "extension" QName Char* "::)"
EntityRef        ::= "&" ("lt" | "gt" | "amp" | "quot" | "apos") ";"
Digits           ::= [0-9]+
HexDigits        ::= ([0-9] | [a-f] | [A-F])+
```

```
CharRef        ::= "&#" (Digits | ("x" HexDigits)) ";"
ElementChar    ::= Char - [{}<&]
QuoteAttrChar  ::= Char - ["{}<&]
AposAttrChar   ::= Char - ['{}<&]
Char           ::= [http://www.w3.org/TR/REC-xml#NT-Char]
NCName         ::= [http://www.w3.org/TR/REC-xml-names/#NT-NCName]
```

E.3 Reserved Keywords

XQuery prohibits the following keywords from being used as un-prefixed user-defined function names (however, you may still use them as the prefix or local parts of a qualified name): `if`, `typeswitch`, `node`, `comment`, `text`, and `processing-instruction`.

Except for this special case, XQuery doesn't reserve any keywords. For example, it is perfectly legal to write an XQuery like the one in Listing E.2.

Listing E.2 XQuery doesn't reserve keywords

```
declare namespace namespace="namespace";
declare namespace as="as";
declare function function($function as as:as) returns item* {
  for $for in in
  return return
};
```

In this silly example, keywords like `namespace` and `as` are used as namespace prefixes, the `function` keyword is used as function and variable names, the `for` keyword is used as a variable name, and the `in` and `return` keywords are used as element names for path navigation.

Of course, you shouldn't write queries like this unless you're trying to win an Obfuscated XQuery contest (and then you should be prepared to beat queries like the ones in Listing E.3).

Listing E.3 Obfuscated XQuery samples

```
(/)//(/)

***

<x>{{{()>>()<<()}}}</x>

treat as text? (true or false)

to/be or not(to/be) is the(question)
```

E.4 Operator Precedence

As a consequence of the grammar, the XQuery operators satisfy the precedence listed in Table E.1. Operators are listed from highest to lowest precedence, with operators of the same precedence sharing the same row in the table.

Table E.1 XQuery operator precedence (highest to lowest)

Operators	Associativity
() constructors	left to right
[]	left to right
/ //	right to left
validate	left to right
intersect except	left to right
union |	left to right
+ - (unary)	right to left
* div idiv mod	left to right
+ - (binary)	left to right
to	left to right

Table E.1 cont.

Operators	Associativity
= != < <= << >> >= > eq ne lt le gt ge is	left to right
cast as	left to right
castable as	left to right
treat as	left to right
instance of	left to right
and	left to right
FLWOR some every typeswitch if or	left to right
,	left to right

Bibliography

Standards

Internet Engineering Task Force (IETF). RFC 3066. *Tags for the Identification of Languages*. January 2001. http://www.ietf.org/rfc/rfc3066.txt.

International Organization for Standardization (ISO). ISO 8601:2000. *Representations of Dates and Times*. 3 August 2000. http://www.iso.ch/.

The Unicode Consortium (http://www.unicode.org/):

The Unicode Standard, Version 4.0. Boston, MA: Addison-Wesley, 2003. http://www.unicode.org/versions/Unicode4.0.0/.

Unicode Standard Annex (UAX) #21. *Case Mappings*. 26 March 2001. http://www.unicode.org/unicode/reports/tr21/tr21-5.html.

Unicode Technical Standard (UTS) #10. *Unicode Collation Algorithm*. 16 July 2002. http://www.unicode.org/reports/tr10/tr10-11.html.

World Wide Web Consortium (http://www.w3.org/):

Document Object Model (DOM) Level 2 Core. W3C Recommendation, 13 November 2000. http://www.w3.org/TR/2000/REC-DOM-Level-2-Core-20001113/.

Extensible Markup Language (XML) 1.0. W3C Recommendation, 10 February 1998. http://www.w3.org/TR/1998/REC-xml-19980210.

Namespaces in XML. W3C Recommendation, 14 January, 1999. http://www.w3.org/TR/1999/REC-xml-names-19990114/.

XML Path Language (XPath) Version 1.0. W3C Recommendation, 16 November 1999. http://www.w3.org/TR/1999/REC-xpath-19991116.

XML Schema, Part 0: Primer. W3C Recommendation, 2 May 2001. http://www.w3.org/TR/2001/REC-xmlschema-0-20010502/.

XML Schema, Part 1: Structures. W3C Recommendation, 2 May 2001. http://www.w3.org/TR/2001/REC-xmlschema-1-20010502/.

XML Schema, Part 2: Data Types. W3C Recommendation, 2 May 2001. http://www.w3.org/TR/2001/REC-xmlschema-2-20010502/.

XSL Transformations (XSLT) 1.0. W3C Recommendation, 16 November 1999. http://www.w3.org/TR/1999/REC-xslt-19991116.

Working Drafts and Notes

Character Model for the World Wide Web 1.0. W3C Working Draft, 30 August 2003. http://www.w3.org/TR/2003/WD-charmod-20030822/.

Date and Time Formats. W3C Note, 15 September 1997. http://www.w3.org/TR/NOTE-datetime-19980827.

XML Path Language (XPath) Version 2.0. W3C Working Draft, 22 August, 2003. http://www.w3.org/TR/2003/WD-xpath20-20030822/.

XML Query 1.0 Requirements. W3C Working Draft, 27 June 2003. http://www.w3.org/TR/2003/WD-xquery-requirements-20030627/.

XML Query Use Cases. W3C Working Draft, 22 August 2003. http://www.w3.org/TR/2003/WD-xquery-use-cases-20030822/.

XQuery 1.0: A Query Language for XML. W3C Working Draft, 22 August 2003. http://www.w3.org/TR/2003/WD-xquery-20030822/.

XQuery 1.0 and XPath 2.0 Data Model. W3C Working Draft, 2 May 2003. http://www.w3.org/TR/2003/WD-xpath-datamodel-2003502/.

XQuery 1.0 and XPath 2.0 Functions and Operators. W3C Working Draft, 2 May 2003. http://www.w3.org/TR/2003/WD-xquery-operators-20030502/.

XQuery 1.0 Formal Semantics. W3C Working Draft, 22 August 2003. http://www.w3.org/TR/2003/WD-xquery-semantics-20030822/.

XQuery and XPath Full-Text Requirements. W3C Working Draft, 2 May 2003. http://www.w3.org/TR/2003/WD-xquery-full-text-require-ments-20030502/.

XQuery and XPath Full-Text Use Cases. W3C Working Draft, 14 February 2003. http://www.w3.org/TR/2003/WD-xmlquery-full-text-use-cases-20030214/.

XQueryX, Version 1.0. W3C Working Draft, 7 June 2001. http://www.w3.org/TR/2001/WD-xqueryx-20010607/.

XSL Transformations (XSLT) 2.0. W3C Working Draft, 2 May 2003. http://www.w3.org/TR/2003/WD-xslt20-20030502/.

Further Reading

Abiteboul, Serge, Dan Suciu, and Peter Buneman. *Data on the Web: From Relations to Semistructured Data and XML*. San Francisco: Morgan Kaufmann, 1999.

Apple Computer, Inc. "Sherlock Scripting Language Support," *Apple Developer Connection*. http://developer.apple.com/documentation/AppleApplications/Conceptual/Sherlock/Concepts/Languages.html.

Bourret, Ronald. "XML Papers." http://www.rpbourret.com/xml/.

Box, Don, Aaron Skonnard, and John Lam. *Essential XML: Beyond Markup*. Boston, MA: Addison-Wesley, 2000.

Bressan, Stéphane, and Mong Lee, et al. "The XOO7 Benchmark." *Lecture Notes in Computer Science*. New York: Springer-Verlag, 2002. http://www.comp.nus.edu.sg/~ebh/XOO7.html.

Chamberlin, Don, Jonathan Robie, and Daniela Florescu. *Quilt: An XML Query Language for Heterogeneous Data Sources*. http://www.almaden.ibm.com/cs/people/chamberlin/quilt_lncs.pdf.

Cover, Robin. *XML Cover Pages*. http://xml.coverpages.org/.

Date, C. J. *An Introduction to Database Systems, 8th ed*. Boston MA: Addison-Wesley, 2003.

Dijkstra, E.W. "In Pursuit of Simplicity: The Manuscripts of Edsger W. Dijkstra." http://www.cs.utexas.edu/users/EWD/.

Eisenberg, Andrew, and Jim Melton. "XQuery API for Java (XQJ)." Java Specification Request #225. http://www.jcp.org/en/jsr/detail?id=225.

Entacher, Karl. "A collection of selected pseudorandom number generators with linear structures." http://random.mat.sbg.ac.at/~charly/server/server.html.

Friedl, Jeffrey E. F. *Mastering Regular Expressions, 2nd Edition*. San Francisco: O'Reilly & Associates, 2002.

Goldberg, David. "What Every Computer Scientist Should Know About Floating Point Arithmetic." *ACM Computing Surveys*, 1991. http://citeseer.nj.nec.com/goldberg91what.html.

Harold, Elliotte Rusty. *Effective XML: 50 Specific Ways to Improve Your XML*. Boston, MA: Addison-Wesley, 2004.

Huth, Michael, and Mark Ryan. *Logic in Computer Science: Modelling and reasoning about systems.* New York: Cambridge University Press, 2000. `http://www.cis.ksu.edu/~huth/lics/`.

IBM Corporation. "General Decimal Arithmetic." `http://www2.hursley.ibm.com/decimal/decimal.html`.

Jenkins, Bob. "Bob Jenkins' Web Site." `http://burtleburtle.net/bob/index.html`.

Jennings, Roger. "Get Ready for XQuery." *XML & Web Services Magazine*, August, 2002. `http://www.fawcette.com/xmlmag/2002_08/online/xml_rjennings_08_12_02/`.

Katz, Howard et al. *XQuery from the Experts: A Guide to the W3C XML Query Language.* Boston, MA: Addison-Wesley, 2003.

Korpela, Jukka. "Characters and Encodings." `http://www.cs.tut.fi/~jkorpela/chars`.

Lenz, Evan. "XQuery: Reinventing the Wheel?" February 21, 2001. `http://www.xmlportfolio.com/xquery.html`.

Matsumoto, Makoto, and Takuji Nishimura, "Mersenne Twister: A 623-dimensionally equidistributed uniform pseudorandom number generator." *ACM Transactions on Modeling and Computer Simulation*, Vol. 8, No. 1 (January 1998), Pages 3-30.

Microsoft Corporation. "Culture Info Class." `http://msdn.microsoft.com/library/default.asp?url=/library/en-us/cpref/html/frlrfsystem-globalizationcultureinfoclasstopic.asp`

North, Ken. "The Center of the Universe." *Intelligent Enterprise*, CMP Media, May 31, 2003. `http://www.intelligententerprise.com/030531/609feat1_1.shtml`.

Obasanjo, Dare. *Simple XML Data Manipulation Language.* `http://www.sixdml.org`. Also published as "A Proposal for an XML Data Definition and Manipulation Language" in *Lecture Notes in Computer Science* #2590. New York: Springer-Verlag, 2003.

Ray, Erik, and Christopher Maden. *Learning XML, 2nd edition.* San Francisco: O'Reilly and Associates, 2003.

Ritchie, Dennis. "The Evolution of the Unix Time-sharing System." *Lecture Notes in Computer Science #7: Language Design and Programming Methodology.* New York: Springer-Verlag, 1980. `http://cm.bell-labs.com/cm/cs/who/dmr/hist.html`.

Runapongsa, Kanda, Jignesh Patel, et al. "The Michigan Benchmark: Towards XML Query Performance Diagnostics." *Proceedings of the 29th VLDB Conference*, 2003. `http://www.eecs.umich.edu/db/mbench/`.

Schmidt, Albrecht, Florian Waas, et al. "The XML Benchmark Project." *Technical Report INS-R0103*, CWI, Amsterdam, The Netherlands, 2001. `http://www.xml-benchmark.org`.

Skonnard, Aaron, and Martin Gudgin. *Essential XML Quick Reference: A Programmer's Reference to XML, XPath, XSLT, XML Schema, SOAP, and More*. Boston, MA: Addison-Wesley, 2001.

Walmsley, Priscilla. *Definitive XML Schema*. Upper Saddle River, NJ: Prentice-Hall, 2001.

Williams, Kevin, Michael Brundage, et al. *Professional XML Databases*. Birmingham, UK: Wrox Press, 2000.

XML:DB Working Group. "XUpdate—XML Update Language." `http://www.xmldb.org/xupdate/`.

Index

Symbols

Available from Addison-Wesley

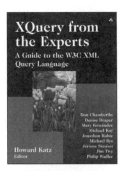
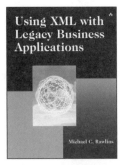

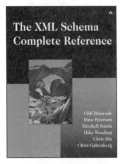
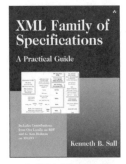
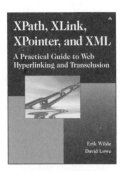
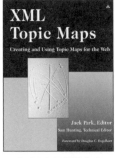

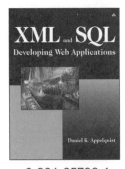

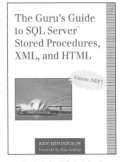
For more information, please visit www.awprofessional.com.

informIT

Register
Your Book

at www.awprofessional.com/register

You may be eligible to receive:
- Advance notice of forthcoming editions of the book
- Related book recommendations
- Chapter excerpts and supplements of forthcoming titles
- Information about special contests and promotions throughout the year
- Notices and reminders about author appearances, tradeshows, and online chats with special guests

Contact us

If you are interested in writing a book or reviewing manuscripts prior to publication, please write to us at:

Editorial Department
Addison-Wesley Professional
75 Arlington Street, Suite 300
Boston, MA 02116 USA
Email: AWPro@aw.com

Visit us on the Web: http://www.awprofessional.com